A Devil and Her Love Song

Story & Art by
Miyoshi Tomori

Volume 2

A Devil and Her Love Song

Volume 2
CONTENTS

The devil makes me LOVELY!!!

STORY THUS FAR

After being expelled from the prestigious St. Katria Girls' High School because of "an act of violence," Maria Kawai transfers to Totsuka High, a place that's unremarkable in every way. Maria's blunt, no-nonsense attitude keeps her new classmates at a distance—all but Yusuke Kanda and Shin Meguro. Yusuke tries to teach Maria the art of putting a "lovely spin" on everything in hopes that she'll fit in better, while Shin grudgingly finds himself taking her under his wing. Now Maria and Yusuke have come to visit their classmate Tomoyo Kohsaka, who has been absent from school for a week...

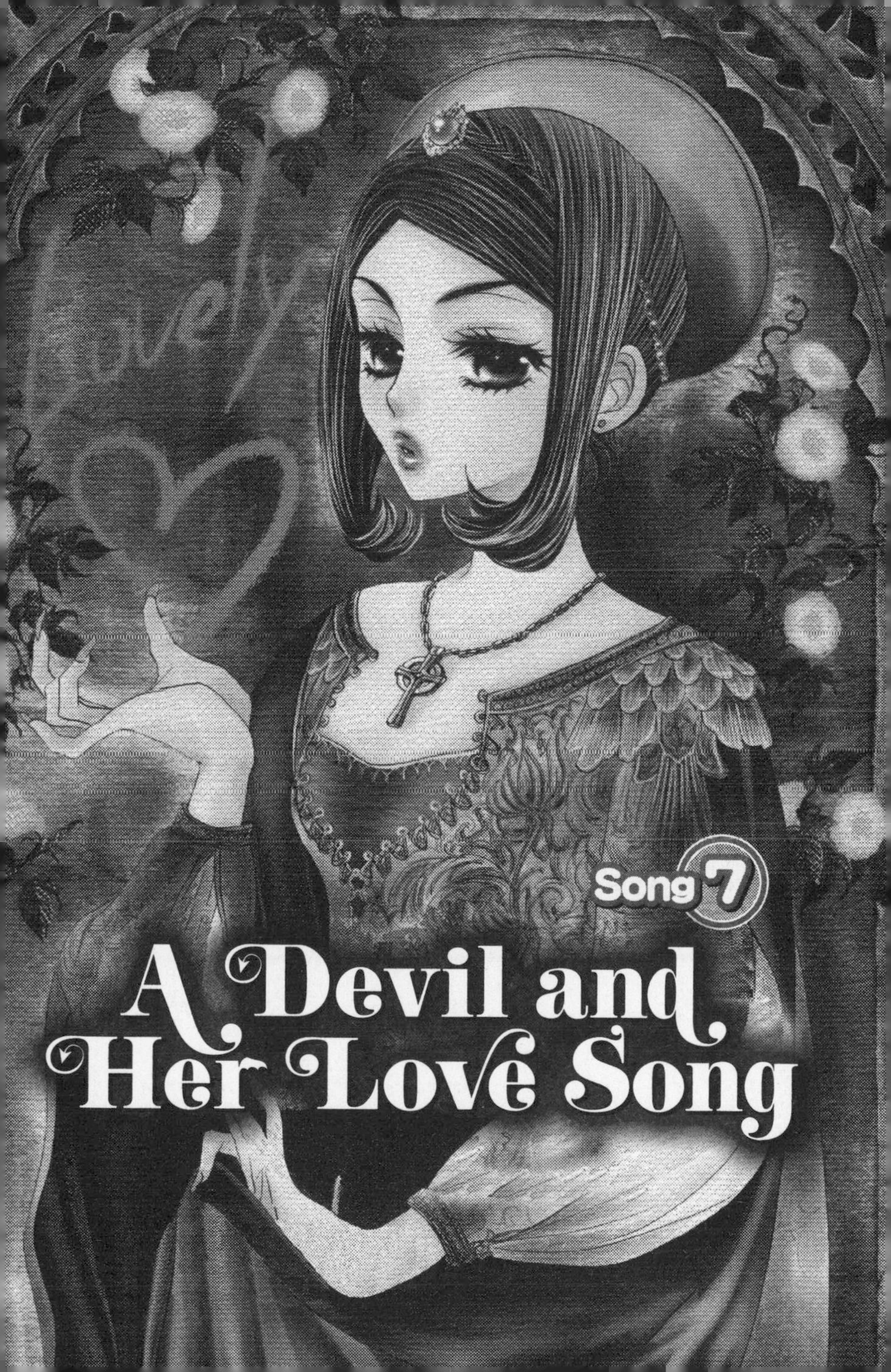
Song 7
A Devil and Her Love Song

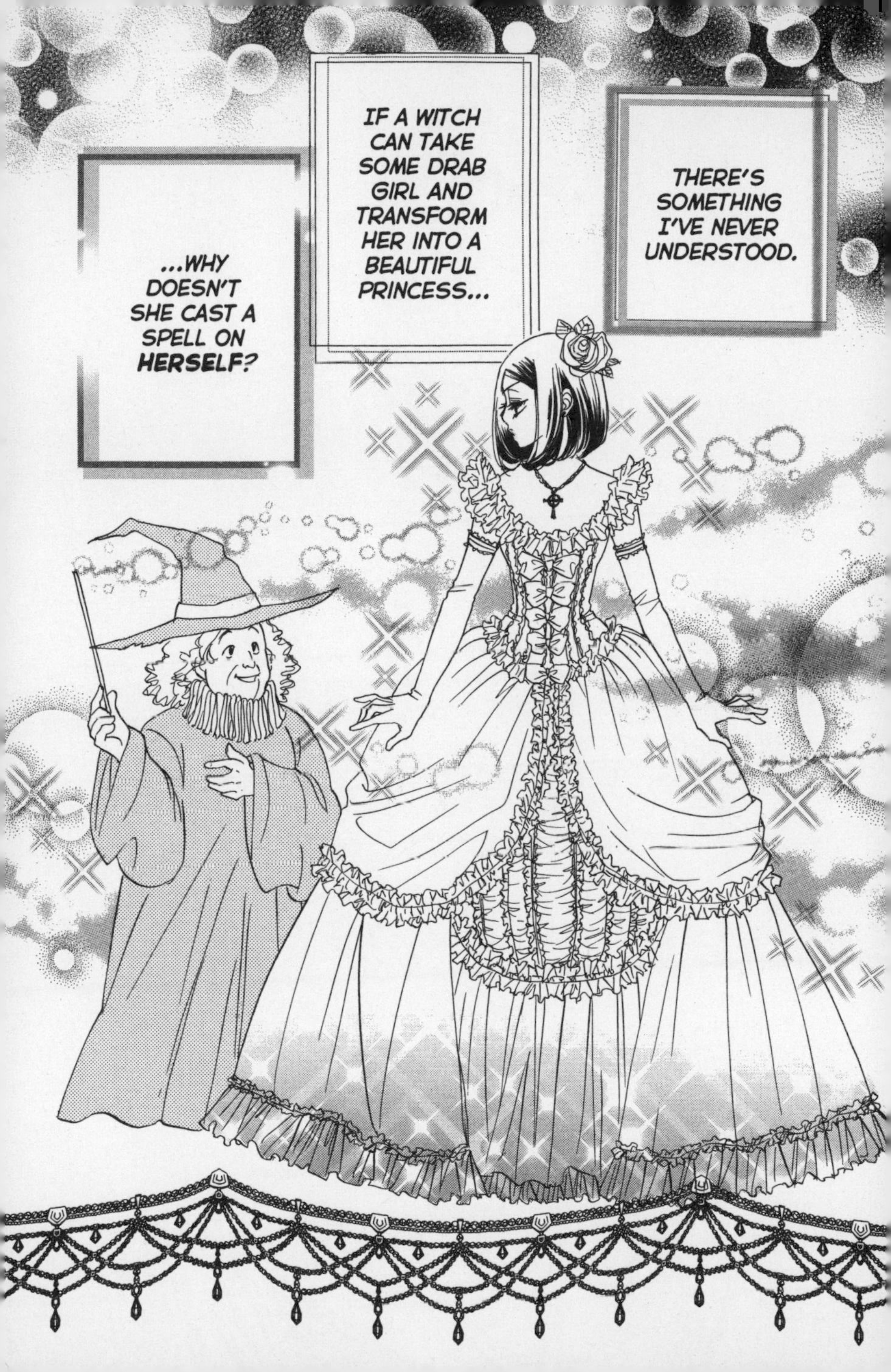
THERE'S SOMETHING I'VE NEVER UNDERSTOOD.
IF A WITCH CAN TAKE SOME DRAB GIRL AND TRANSFORM HER INTO A BEAUTIFUL PRINCESS...
...WHY DOESN'T SHE CAST A SPELL ON HERSELF?

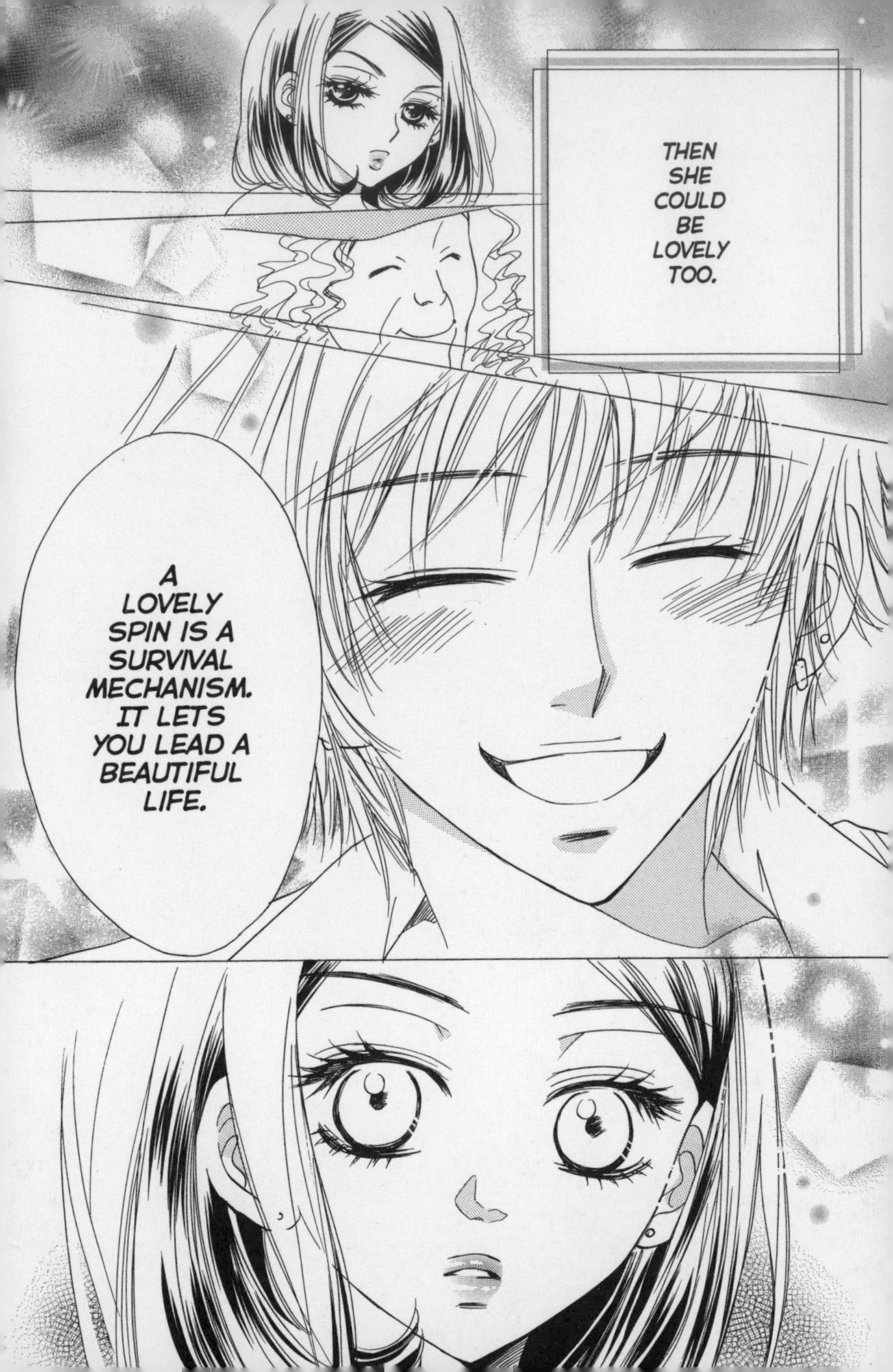
THEN SHE COULD BE LOVELY TOO.
A LOVELY SPIN IS A SURVIVAL MECHANISM. IT LETS YOU LEAD A BEAUTIFUL LIFE.

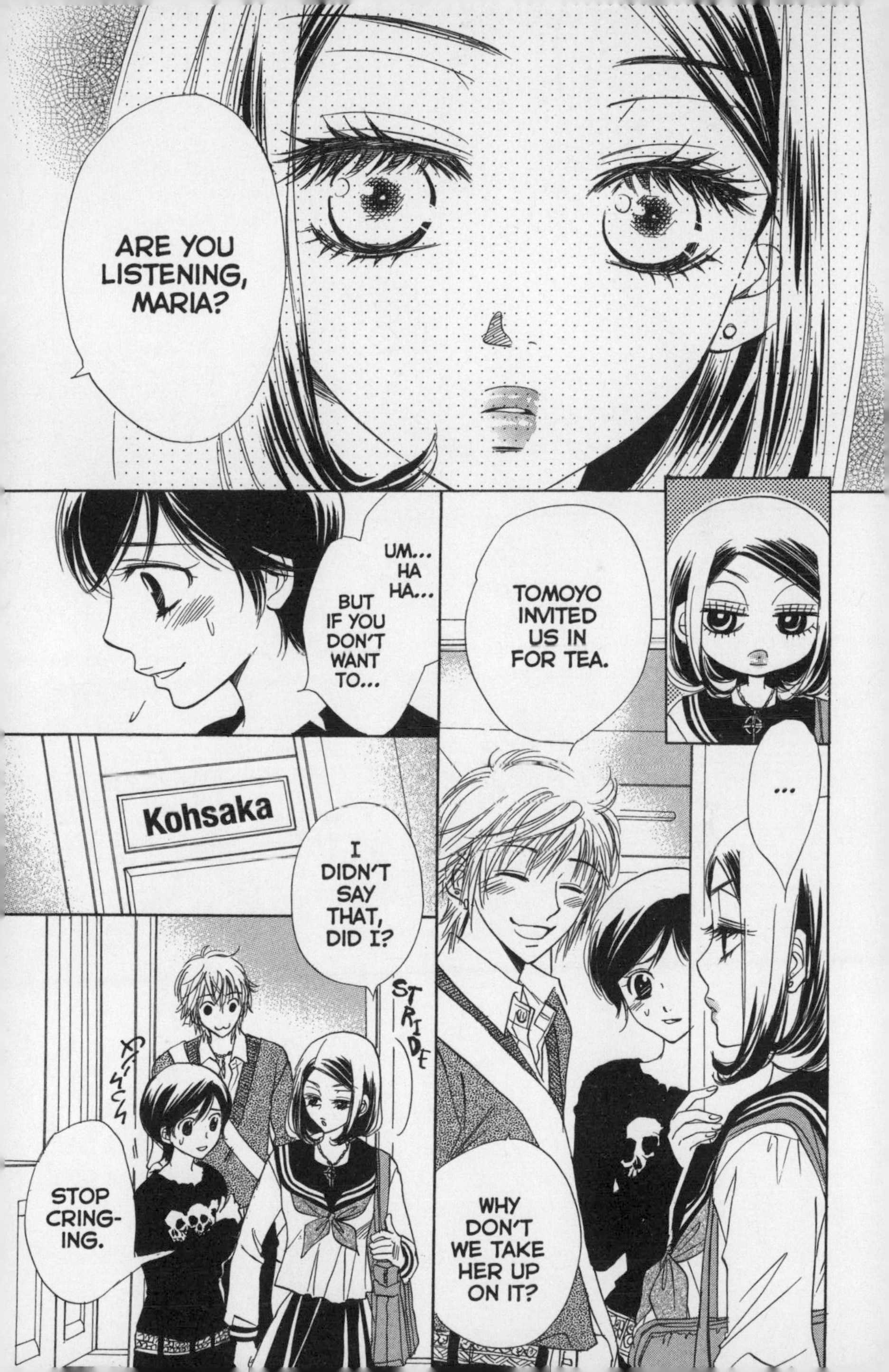
ARE YOU LISTENING, MARIA?
TOMOYO INVITED US IN FOR TEA.
UM... HA HA...
BUT IF YOU DON'T WANT TO...
...
WHY DON'T WE TAKE HER UP ON IT?
Kohsaka
I DIDN'T SAY THAT, DID I?
STRIDE
STOP CRING-ING.

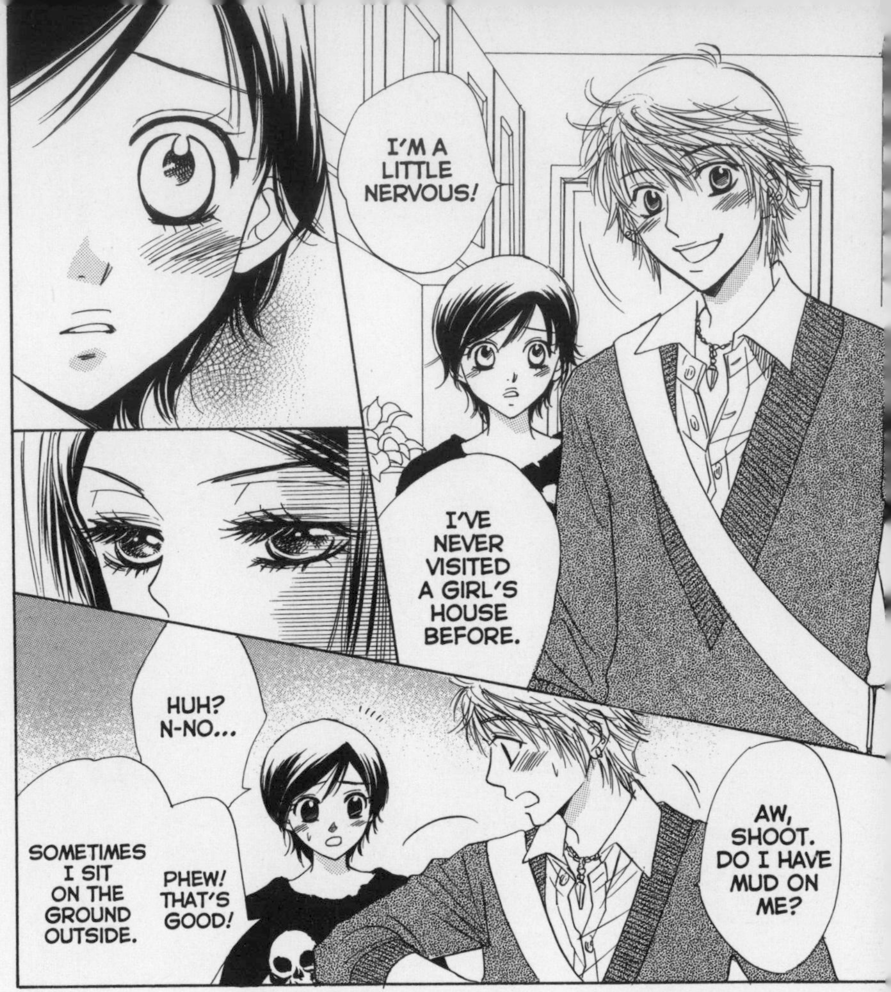
I'M A LITTLE NERVOUS!
I'VE NEVER VISITED A GIRL'S HOUSE BEFORE.
AW, SHOOT. DO I HAVE MUD ON ME?
HUH? N-NO...
PHEW! THAT'S GOOD!
SOMETIMES I SIT ON THE GROUND OUTSIDE.

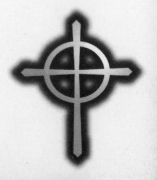

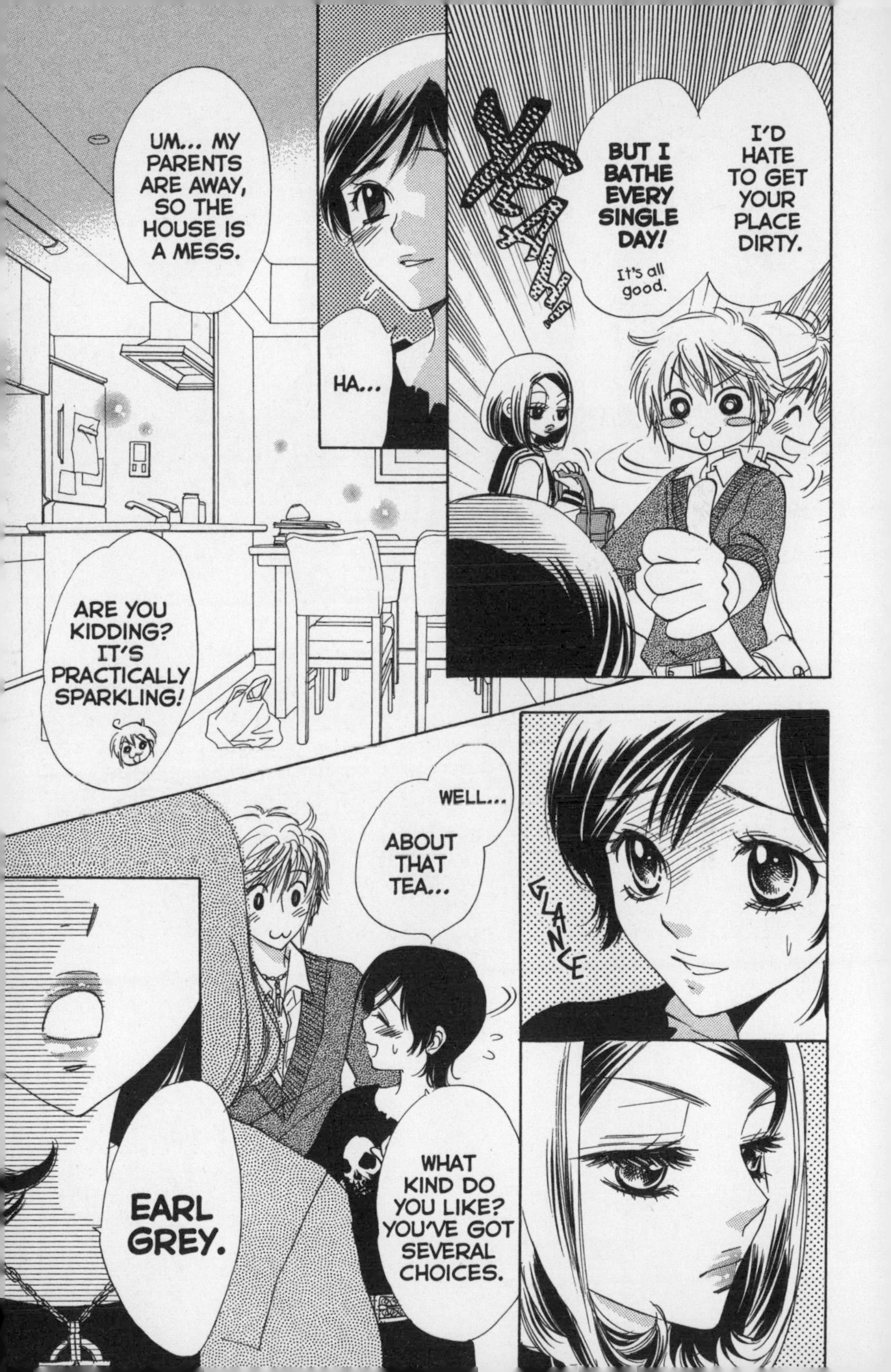
I'D HATE TO GET YOUR PLACE DIRTY.
BUT I BATHE EVERY SINGLE DAY!
YEAH
It's all good.
HA...
UM... MY PARENTS ARE AWAY, SO THE HOUSE IS A MESS.
ARE YOU KIDDING? IT'S PRACTICALLY SPARKLING!
GLANCE
WELL...
ABOUT THAT TEA...
WHAT KIND DO YOU LIKE? YOU'VE GOT SEVERAL CHOICES.
EARL GREY.

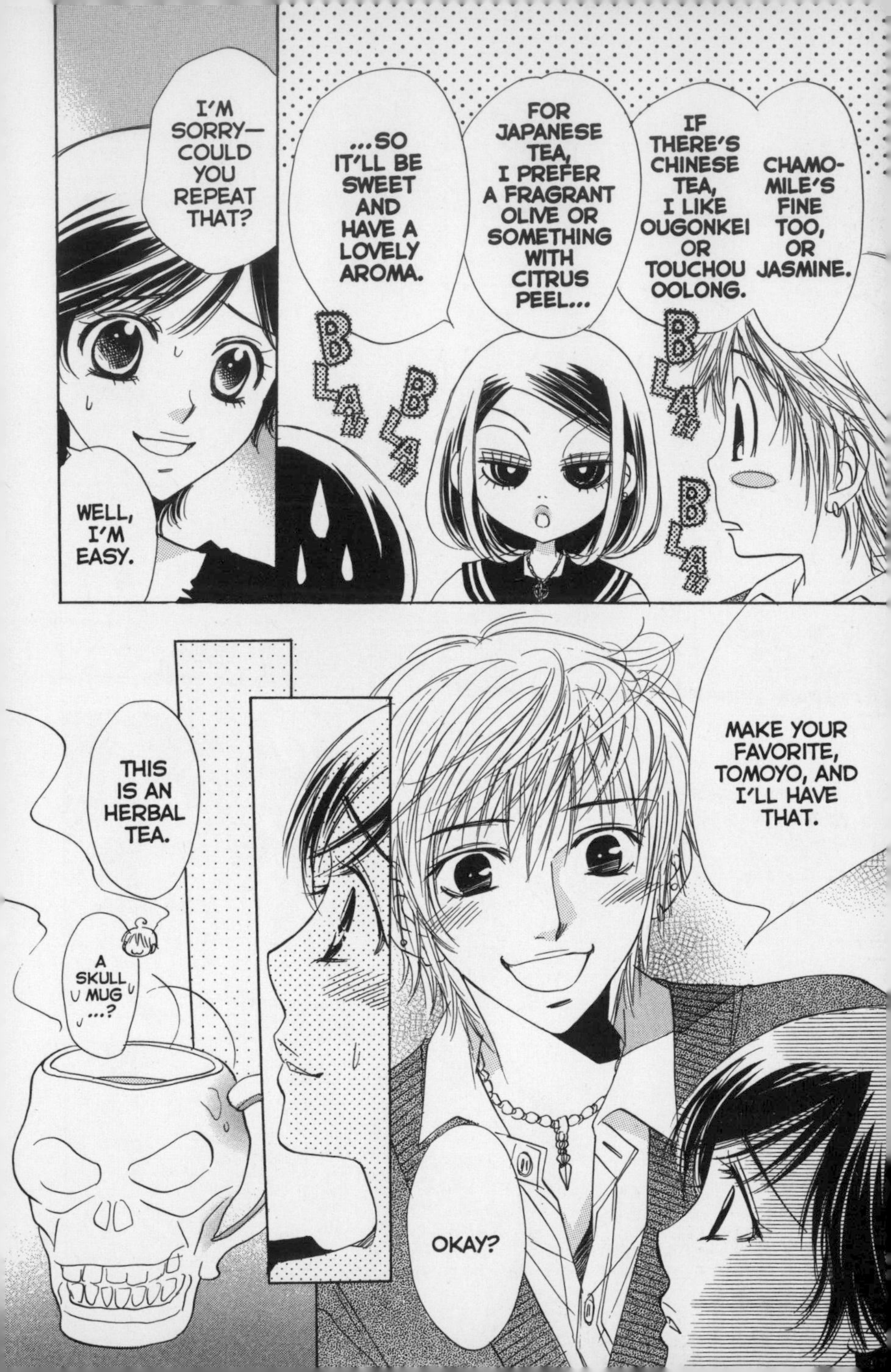
IF THERE'S CHINESE TEA, I LIKE OUGONKEI OR TOUCHOU OOLONG. CHAMOMILE'S FINE TOO, OR JASMINE.
FOR JAPANESE TEA, I PREFER A FRAGRANT OLIVE OR SOMETHING WITH CITRUS PEEL...
...SO IT'LL BE SWEET AND HAVE A LOVELY AROMA.
BLAH
BLAH
BLAH
BLAH
I'M SORRY—COULD YOU REPEAT THAT?
WELL, I'M EASY.
MAKE YOUR FAVORITE, TOMOYO, AND I'LL HAVE THAT.
OKAY?
THIS IS AN HERBAL TEA.
A SKULL MUG...?

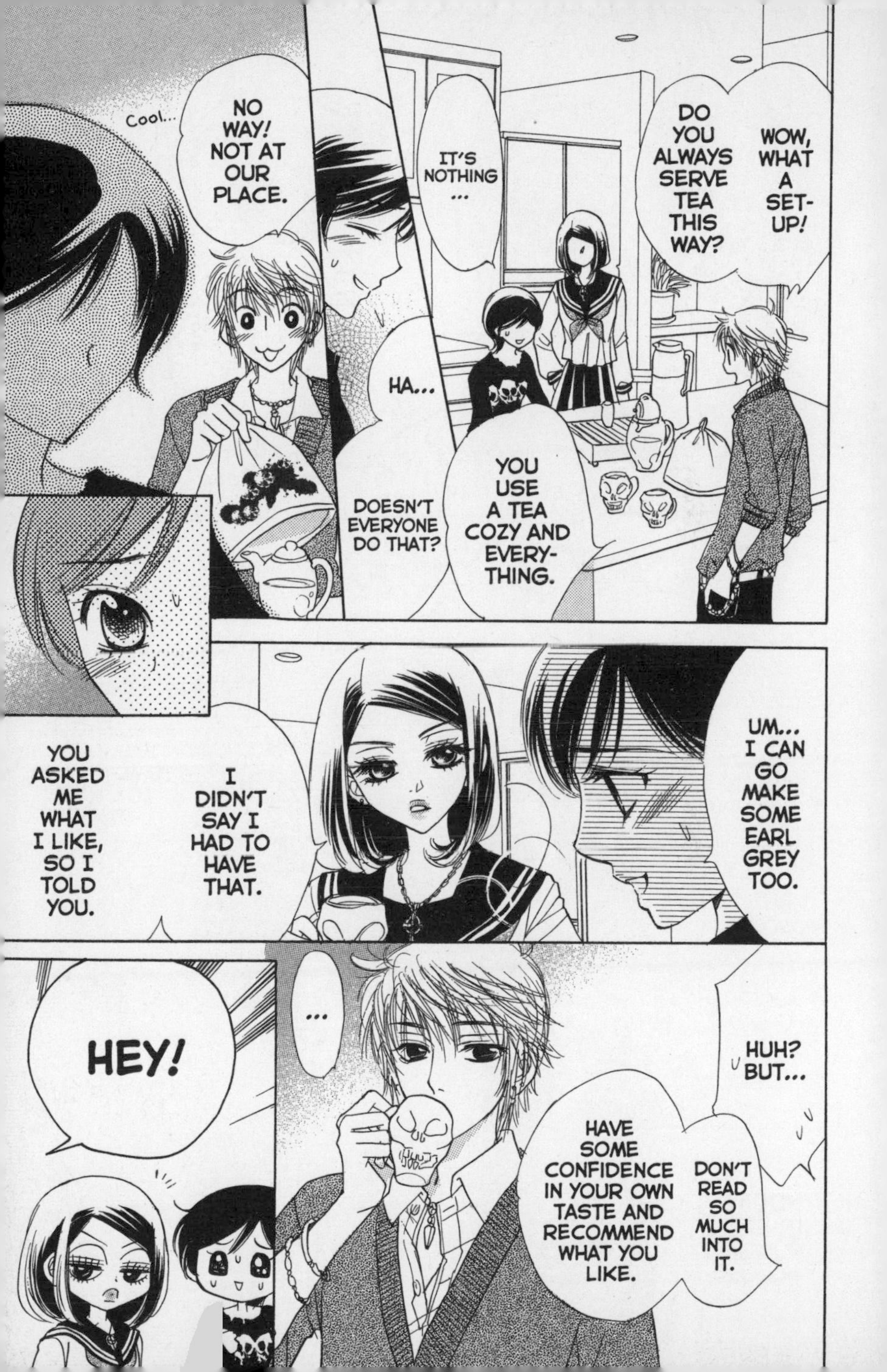
WOW, WHAT A SET-UP!
DO YOU ALWAYS SERVE TEA THIS WAY?
IT'S NOTHING...
YOU USE A TEA COZY AND EVERYTHING.
HA...
DOESN'T EVERYONE DO THAT?
NO WAY! NOT AT OUR PLACE.
Cool...
UM... I CAN GO MAKE SOME EARL GREY TOO.
I DIDN'T SAY I HAD TO HAVE THAT.
YOU ASKED ME WHAT I LIKE, SO I TOLD YOU.
HUH? BUT...
DON'T READ SO MUCH INTO IT.
HAVE SOME CONFIDENCE IN YOUR OWN TASTE AND RECOMMEND WHAT YOU LIKE.
...
HEY!

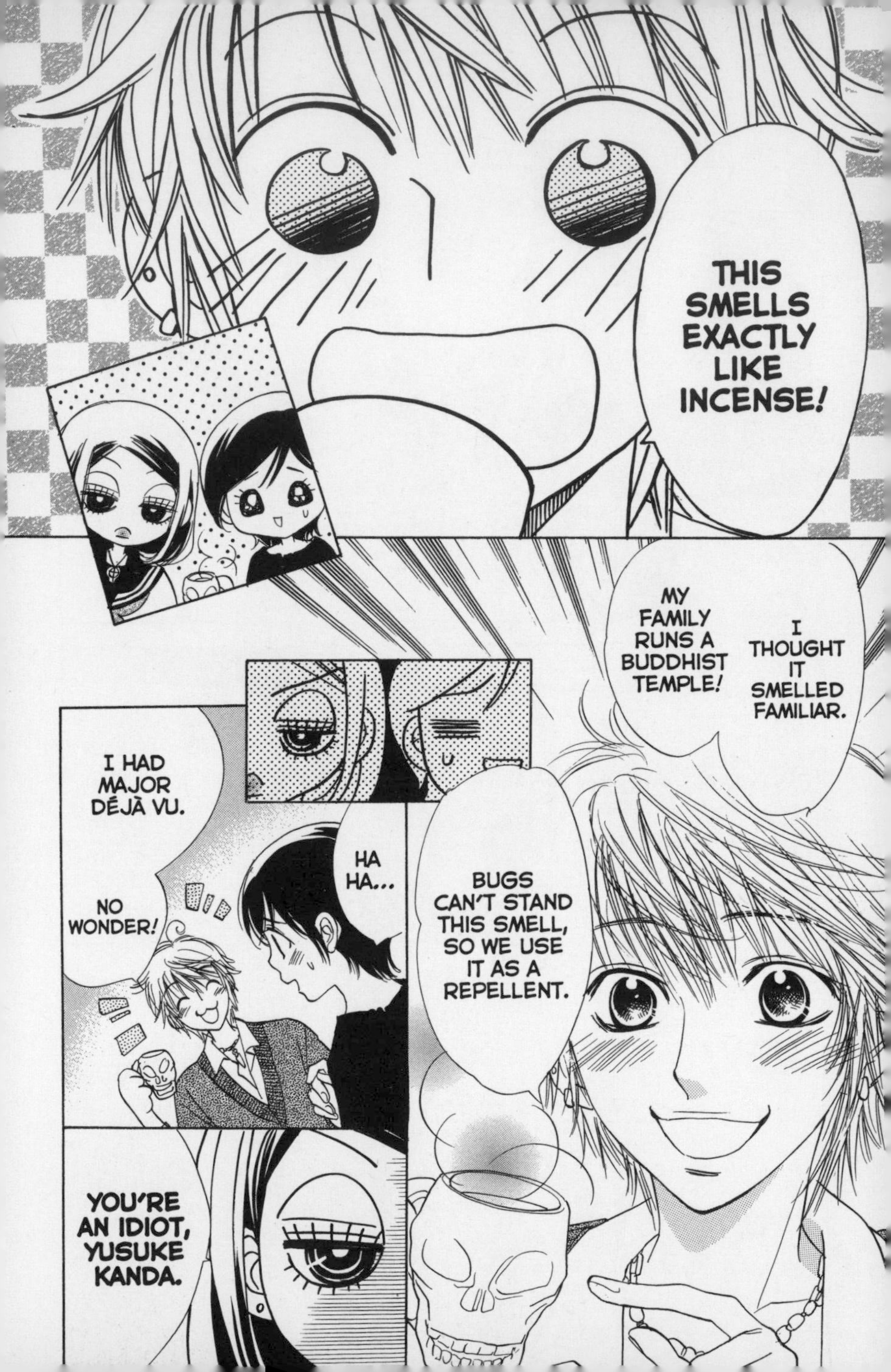
THIS SMELLS EXACTLY LIKE INCENSE!
MY FAMILY RUNS A BUDDHIST TEMPLE!
I THOUGHT IT SMELLED FAMILIAR.
BUGS CAN'T STAND THIS SMELL, SO WE USE IT AS A REPELLENT.
I HAD MAJOR DÉJÀ VU.
HA HA...
NO WONDER!
YOU'RE AN IDIOT, YUSUKE KANDA.

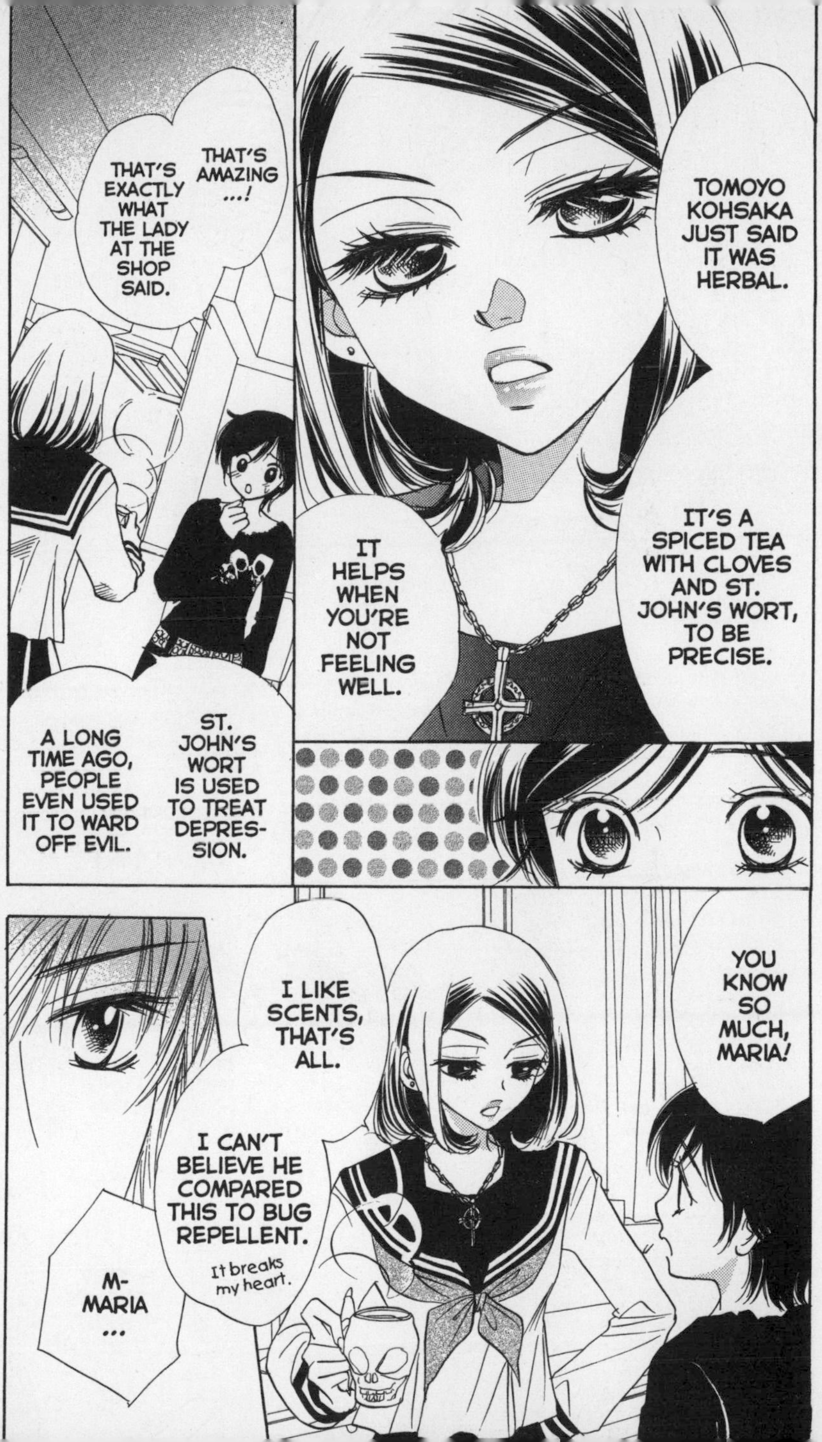
TOMOYO KOHSAKA JUST SAID IT WAS HERBAL.
IT'S A SPICED TEA WITH CLOVES AND ST. JOHN'S WORT, TO BE PRECISE.
IT HELPS WHEN YOU'RE NOT FEELING WELL.
THAT'S AMAZING...!
THAT'S EXACTLY WHAT THE LADY AT THE SHOP SAID.
ST. JOHN'S WORT IS USED TO TREAT DEPRESSION.
A LONG TIME AGO, PEOPLE EVEN USED IT TO WARD OFF EVIL.
YOU KNOW SO MUCH, MARIA!
I LIKE SCENTS, THAT'S ALL.
I CAN'T BELIEVE HE COMPARED THIS TO BUG REPELLENT.
It breaks my heart.
M-MARIA...

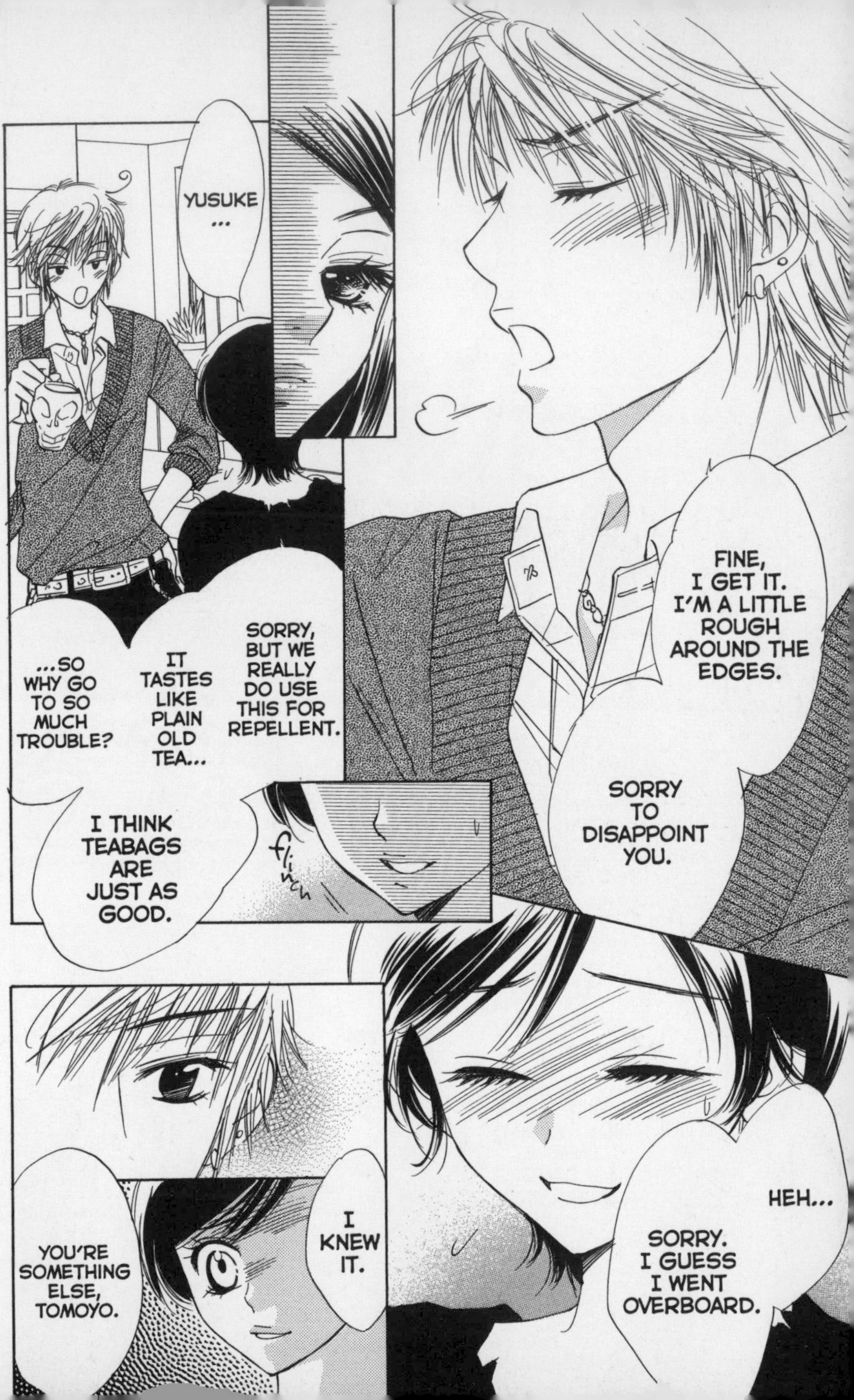
FINE, I GET IT. I'M A LITTLE ROUGH AROUND THE EDGES.
SORRY TO DISAPPOINT YOU.
YUSUKE ...
SORRY, BUT WE REALLY DO USE THIS FOR REPELLENT.
IT TASTES LIKE PLAIN OLD TEA...
...SO WHY GO TO SO MUCH TROUBLE?
flinch
I THINK TEABAGS ARE JUST AS GOOD.
HEH...
SORRY. I GUESS I WENT OVERBOARD.
I KNEW IT.
YOU'RE SOMETHING ELSE, TOMOYO.

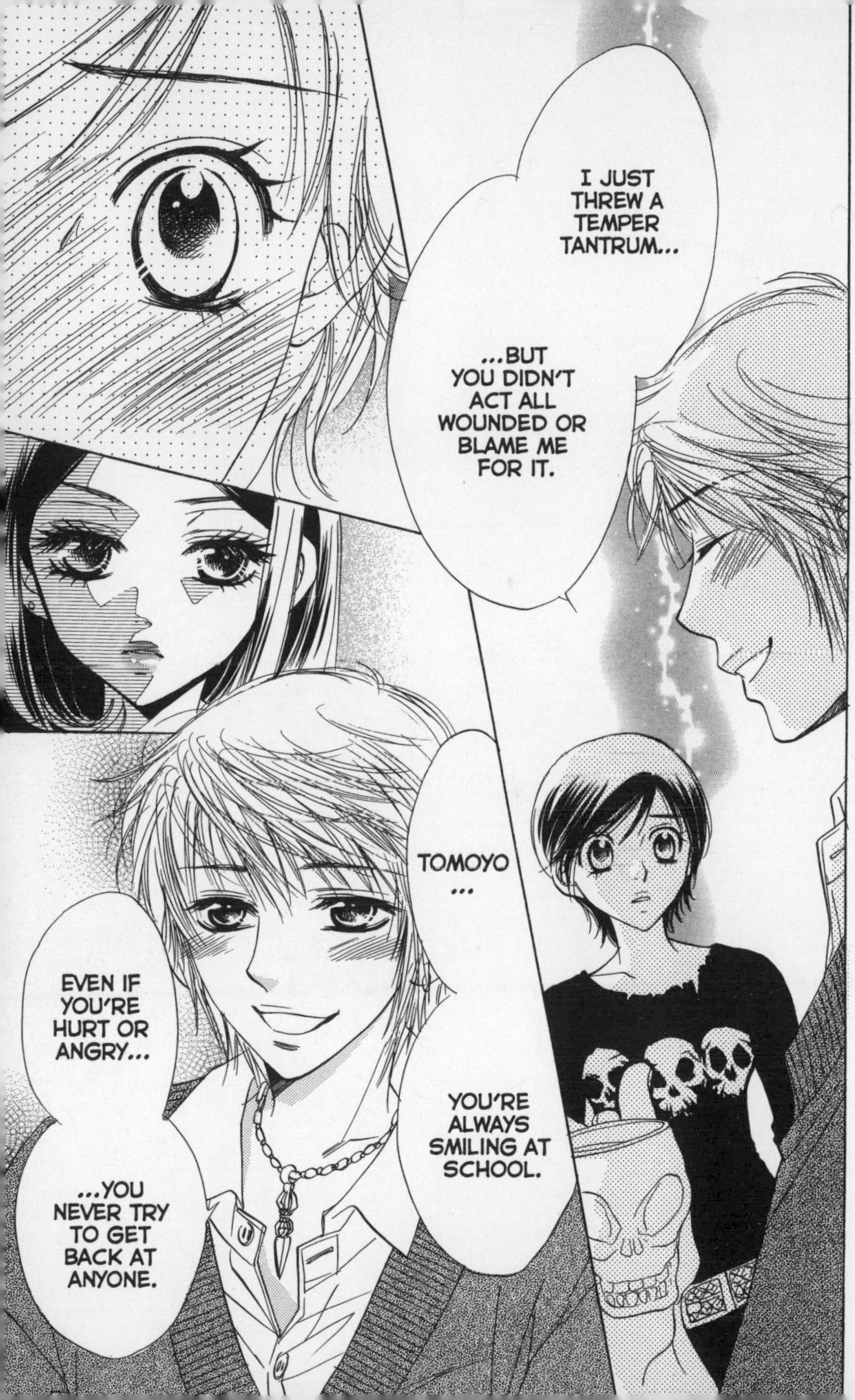
I JUST THREW A TEMPER TANTRUM...
...BUT YOU DIDN'T ACT ALL WOUNDED OR BLAME ME FOR IT.
TOMOYO...
YOU'RE ALWAYS SMILING AT SCHOOL.
EVEN IF YOU'RE HURT OR ANGRY...
...YOU NEVER TRY TO GET BACK AT ANYONE.

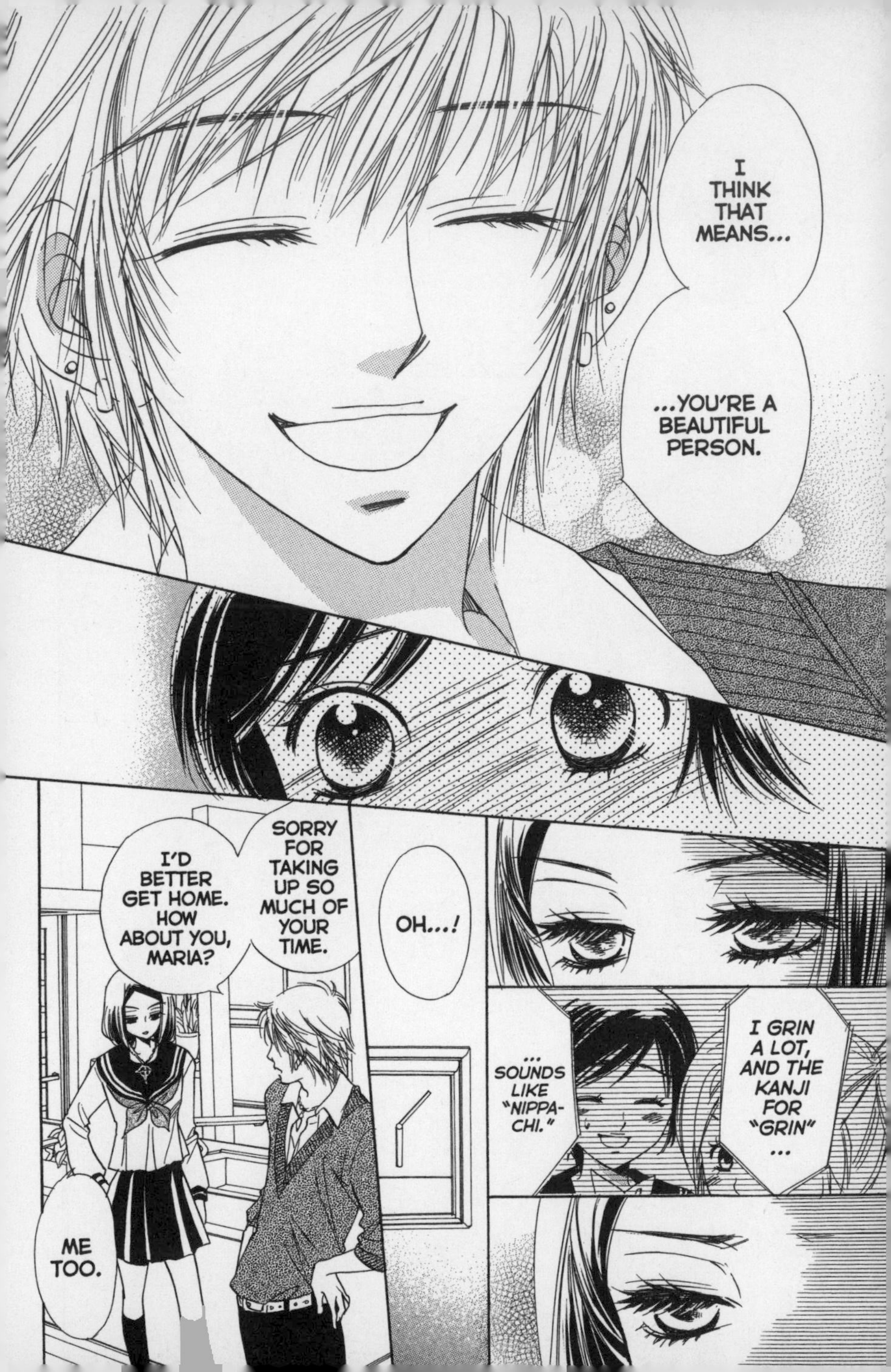
I THINK THAT MEANS...
...YOU'RE A BEAUTIFUL PERSON.
I GRIN A LOT, AND THE KANJI FOR "GRIN" ...
...SOUNDS LIKE "NIPPA-CHI."
OH...!
SORRY FOR TAKING UP SO MUCH OF YOUR TIME.
I'D BETTER GET HOME. HOW ABOUT YOU, MARIA?
ME TOO.

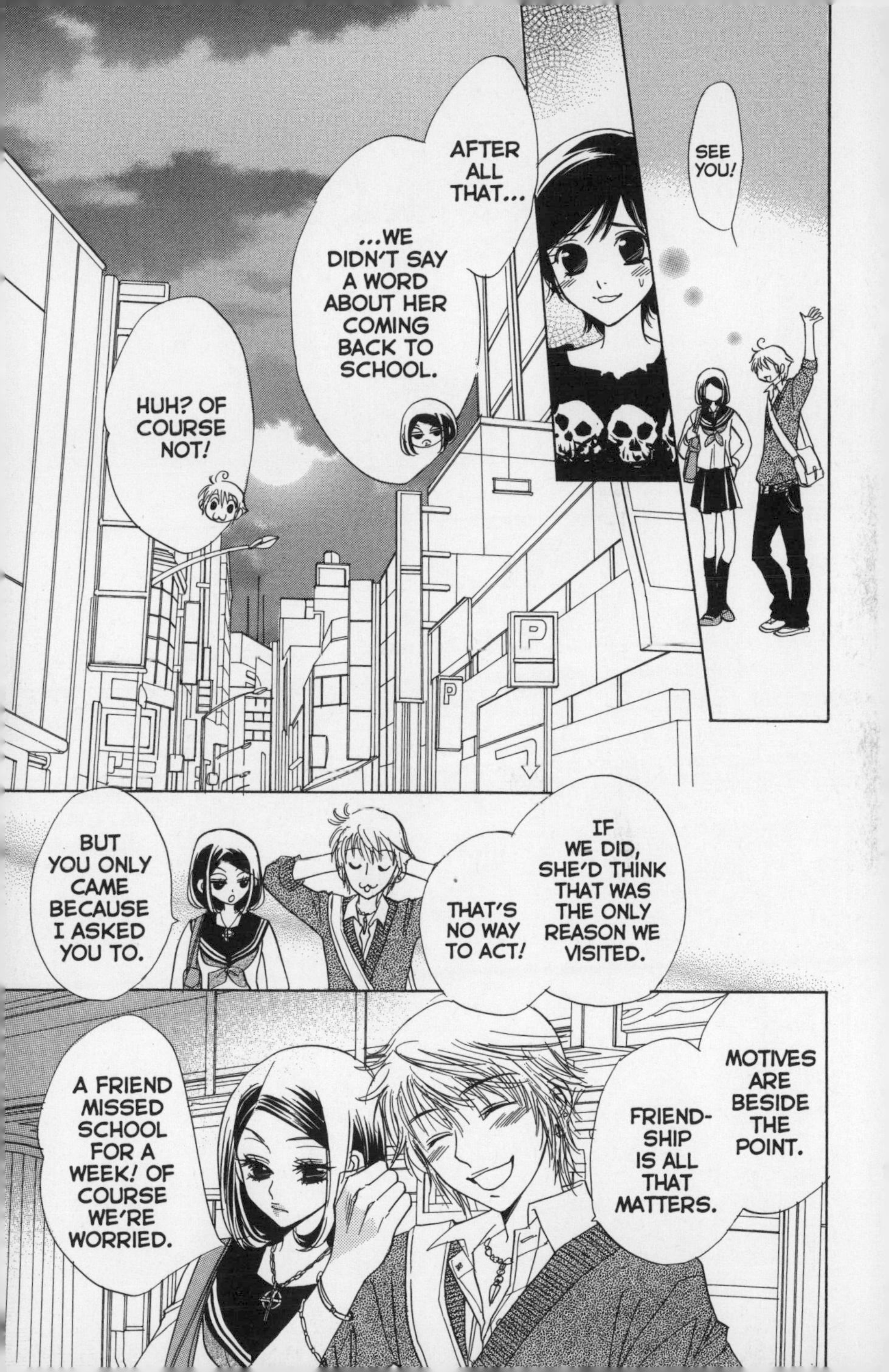
SEE YOU!
AFTER ALL THAT...
...WE DIDN'T SAY A WORD ABOUT HER COMING BACK TO SCHOOL.
HUH? OF COURSE NOT!
IF WE DID, SHE'D THINK THAT WAS THE ONLY REASON WE VISITED.
THAT'S NO WAY TO ACT!
BUT YOU ONLY CAME BECAUSE I ASKED YOU TO.
MOTIVES ARE BESIDE THE POINT.
FRIEND-SHIP IS ALL THAT MATTERS.
A FRIEND MISSED SCHOOL FOR A WEEK! OF COURSE WE'RE WORRIED.

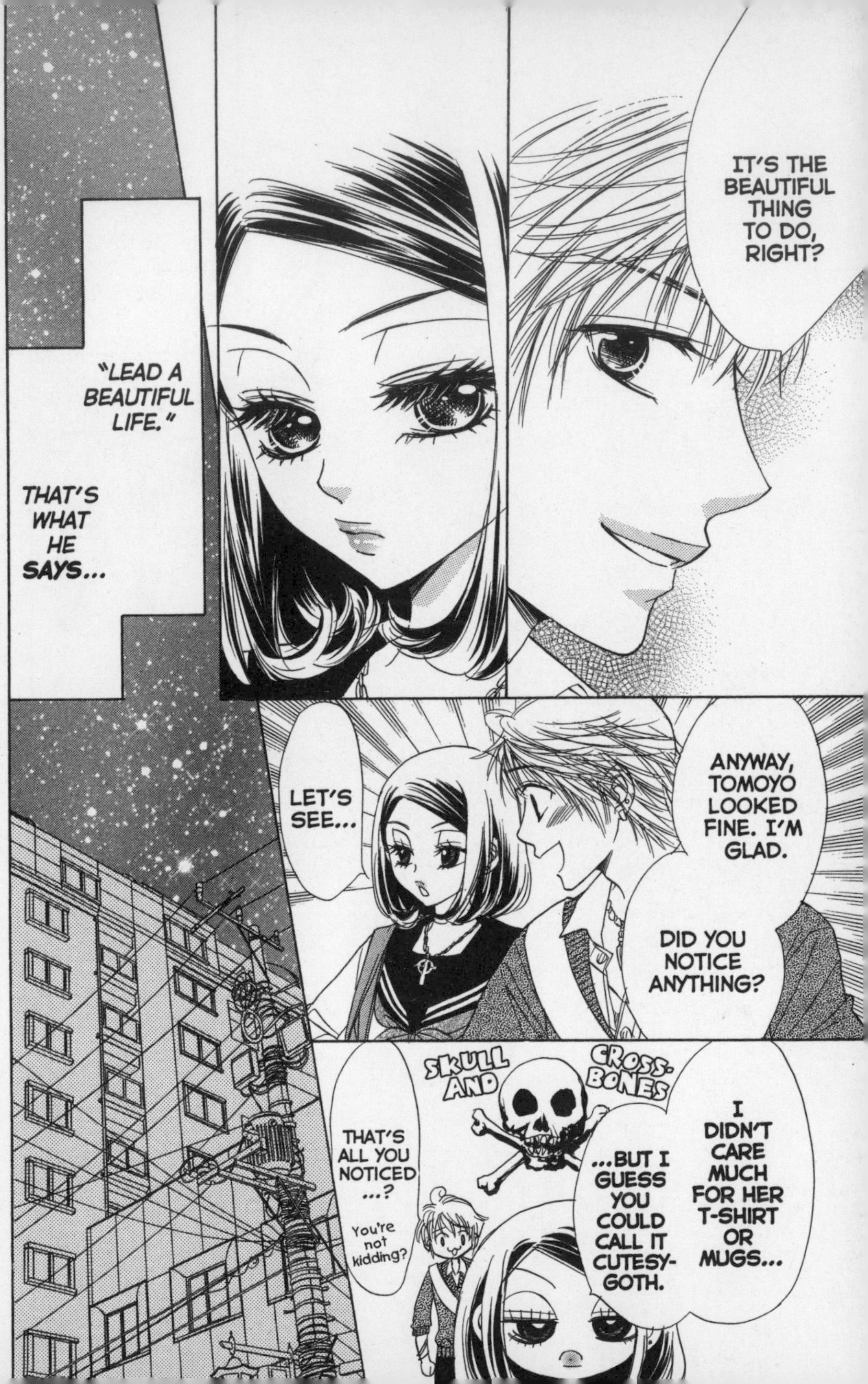
IT'S THE BEAUTIFUL THING TO DO, RIGHT?
ANYWAY, TOMOYO LOOKED FINE. I'M GLAD.
DID YOU NOTICE ANYTHING?
LET'S SEE...
I DIDN'T CARE MUCH FOR HER T-SHIRT OR MUGS...
...BUT I GUESS YOU COULD CALL IT CUTESY-GOTH.
CROSS-BONES
SKULL AND
THAT'S ALL YOU NOTICED...?
You're not kidding?
"LEAD A BEAUTIFUL LIFE."
THAT'S WHAT HE SAYS...

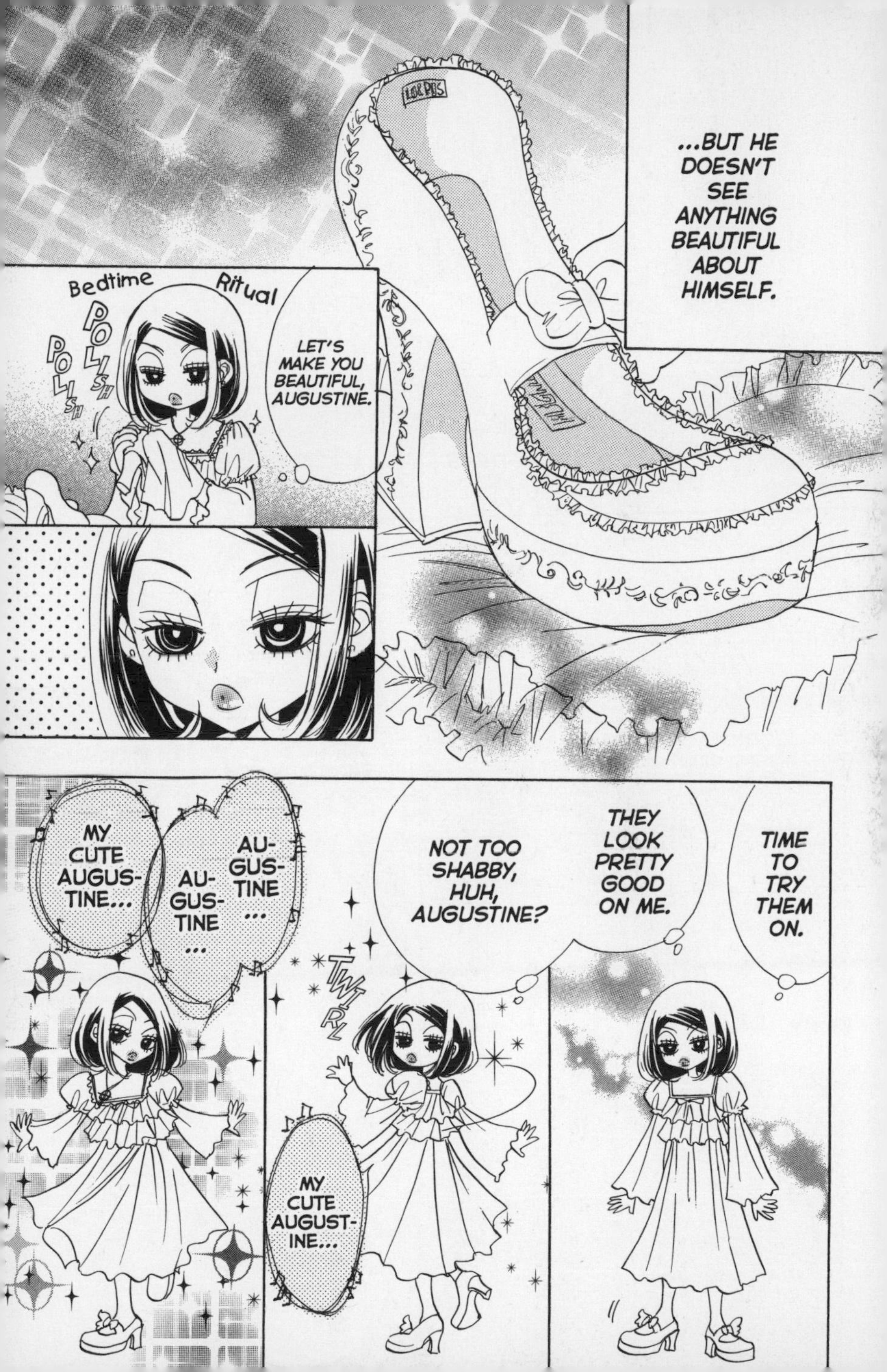
...BUT HE DOESN'T SEE ANYTHING BEAUTIFUL ABOUT HIMSELF.
Bedtime Ritual
POLISH POLISH
LET'S MAKE YOU BEAUTIFUL, AUGUSTINE.
TIME TO TRY THEM ON.
THEY LOOK PRETTY GOOD ON ME.
NOT TOO SHABBY, HUH, AUGUSTINE?
TWIRL
MY CUTE AUGUST-INE...
AU-GUS-TINE...
AU-GUS-TINE...
MY CUTE AUGUS-TINE...

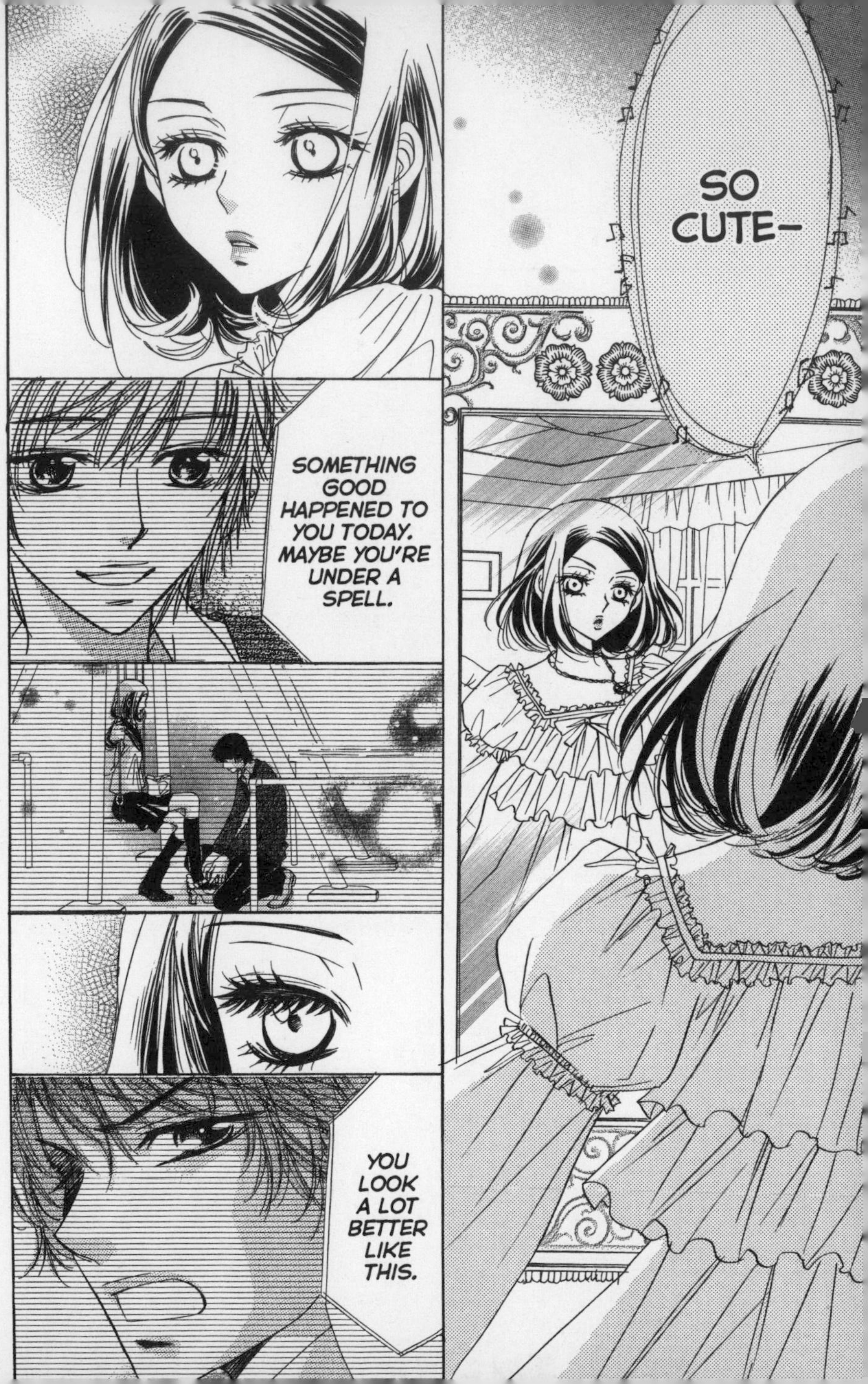
SO CUTE–
SOMETHING GOOD HAPPENED TO YOU TODAY. MAYBE YOU'RE UNDER A SPELL.
YOU LOOK A LOT BETTER LIKE THIS.

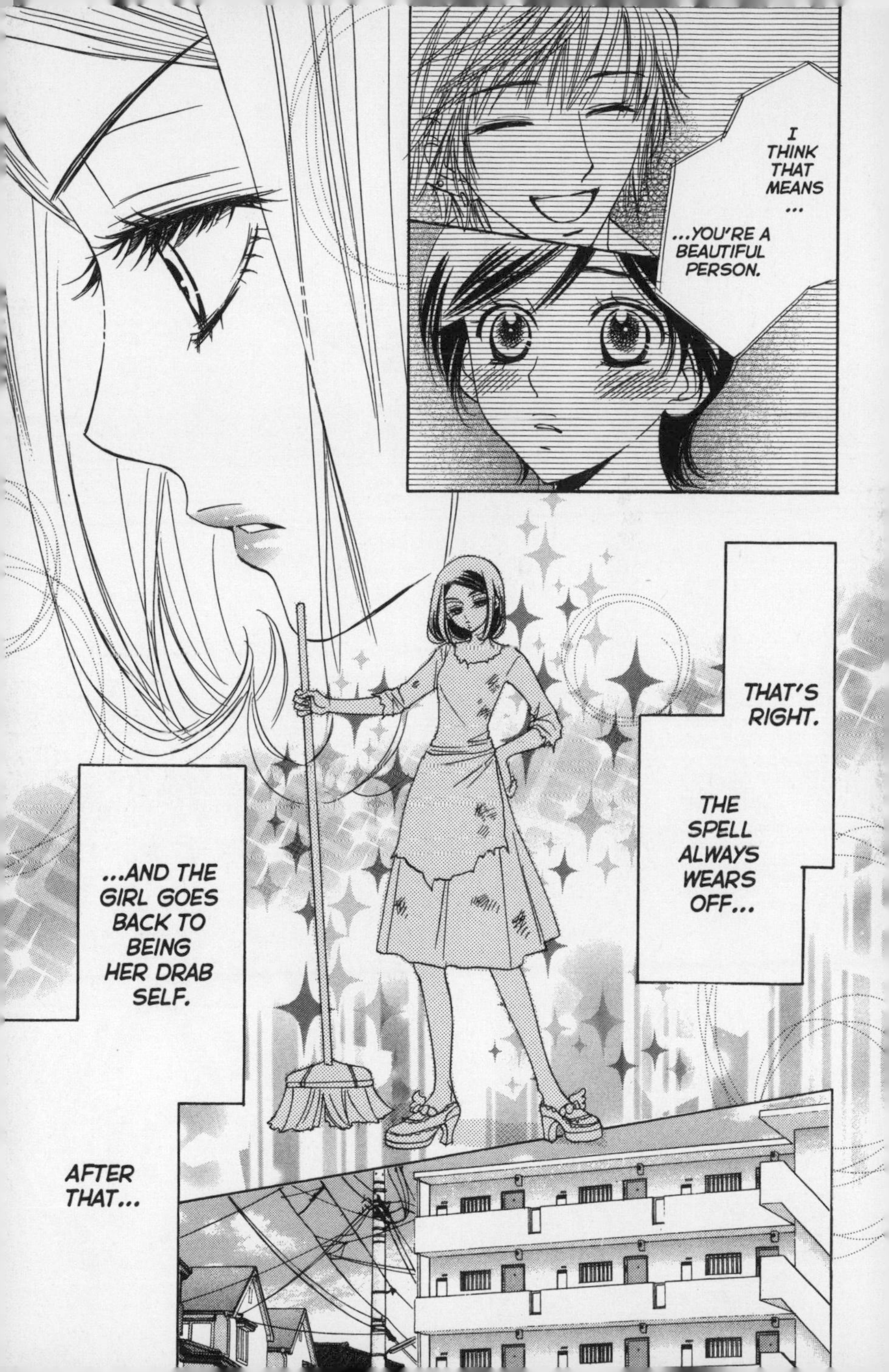

I THINK THAT MEANS ...
...YOU'RE A BEAUTIFUL PERSON.
THAT'S RIGHT.
THE SPELL ALWAYS WEARS OFF...
...AND THE GIRL GOES BACK TO BEING HER DRAB SELF.
AFTER THAT...

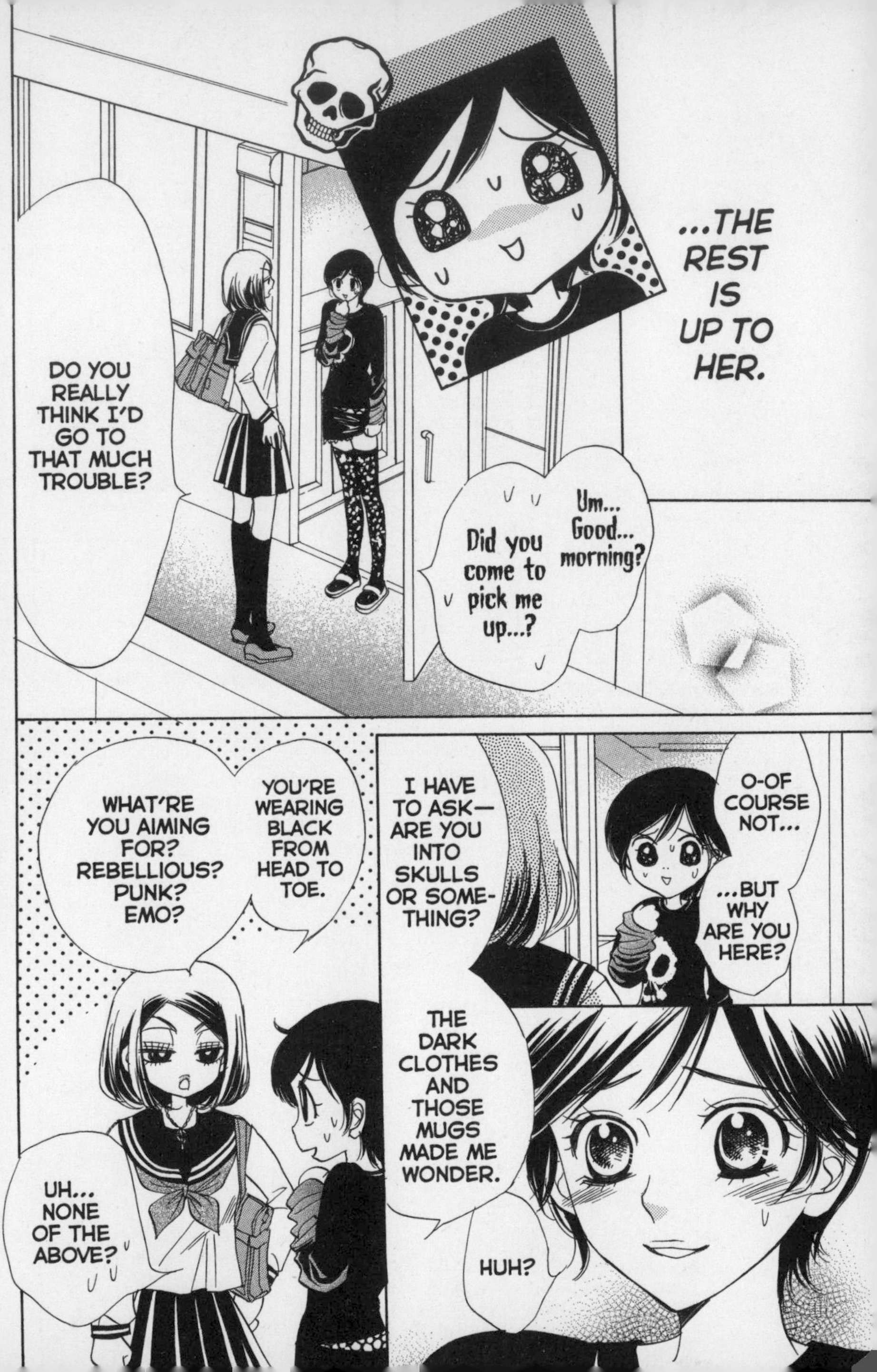
...THE REST IS UP TO HER.
Um... Good... morning?
Did you come to pick me up...?
DO YOU REALLY THINK I'D GO TO THAT MUCH TROUBLE?
O-OF COURSE NOT...
...BUT WHY ARE YOU HERE?
I HAVE TO ASK— ARE YOU INTO SKULLS OR SOME-THING?
THE DARK CLOTHES AND THOSE MUGS MADE ME WONDER.
HUH?
YOU'RE WEARING BLACK FROM HEAD TO TOE.
WHAT'RE YOU AIMING FOR? REBELLIOUS? PUNK? EMO?
UH... NONE OF THE ABOVE?

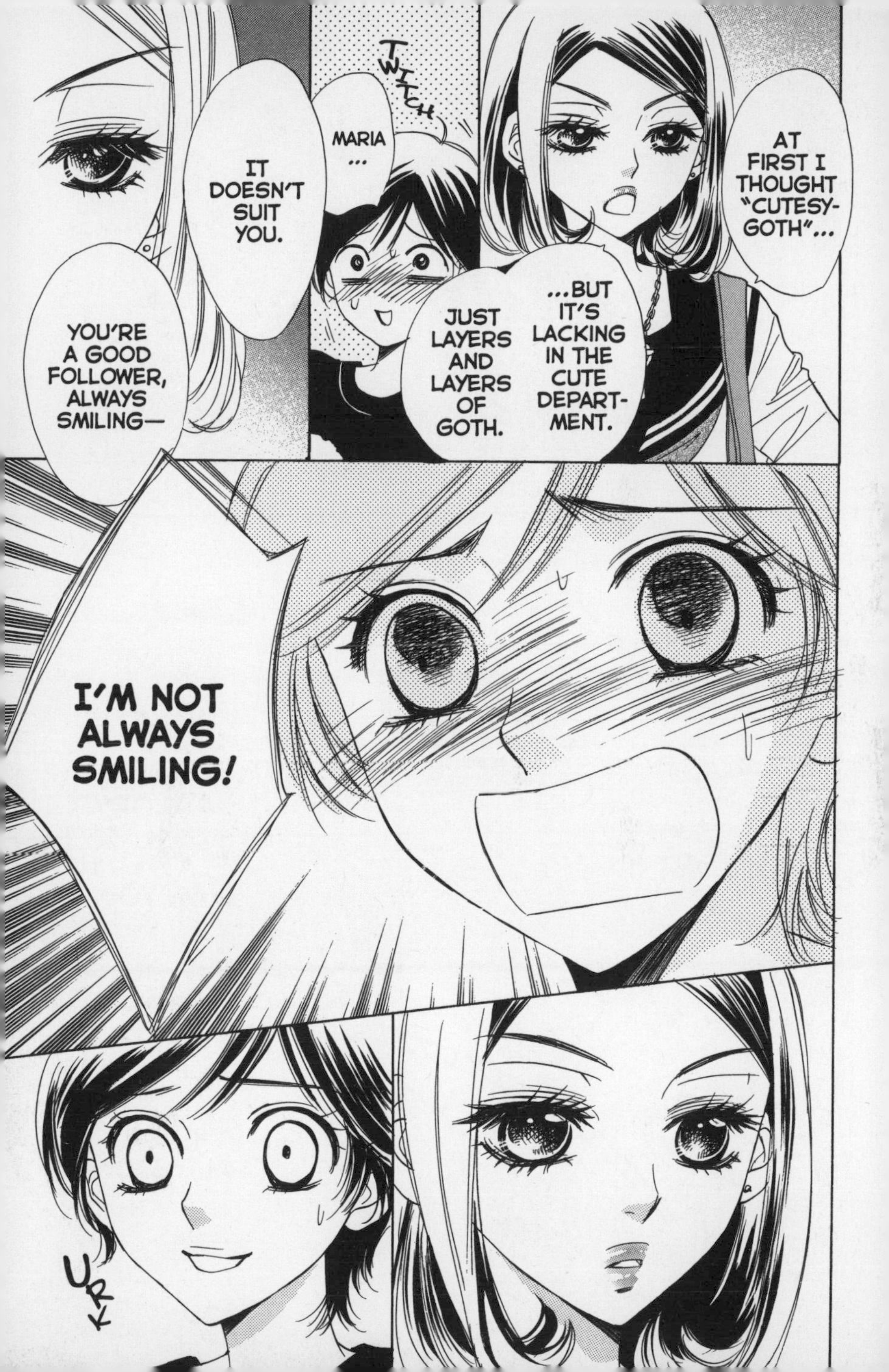
AT FIRST I THOUGHT "CUTESY-GOTH"...
...BUT IT'S LACKING IN THE CUTE DEPART-MENT.
JUST LAYERS AND LAYERS OF GOTH.
TWITCH
MARIA ...
IT DOESN'T SUIT YOU.
YOU'RE A GOOD FOLLOWER, ALWAYS SMILING—
I'M NOT ALWAYS SMILING!
URK

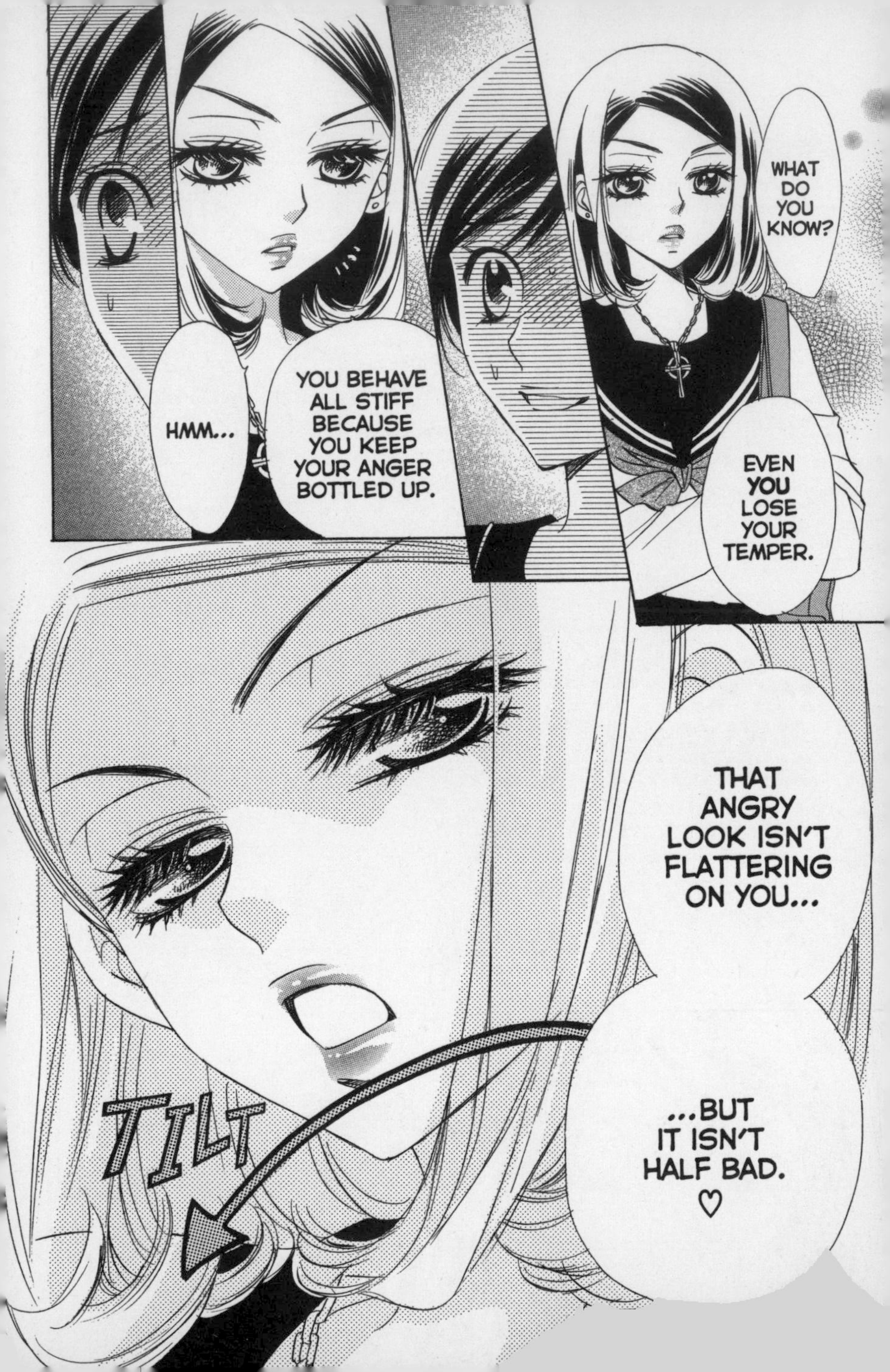
WHAT DO YOU KNOW?
EVEN YOU LOSE YOUR TEMPER.
YOU BEHAVE ALL STIFF BECAUSE YOU KEEP YOUR ANGER BOTTLED UP.
HMM...
THAT ANGRY LOOK ISN'T FLATTERING ON YOU...
...BUT IT ISN'T HALF BAD. ♡
TILT

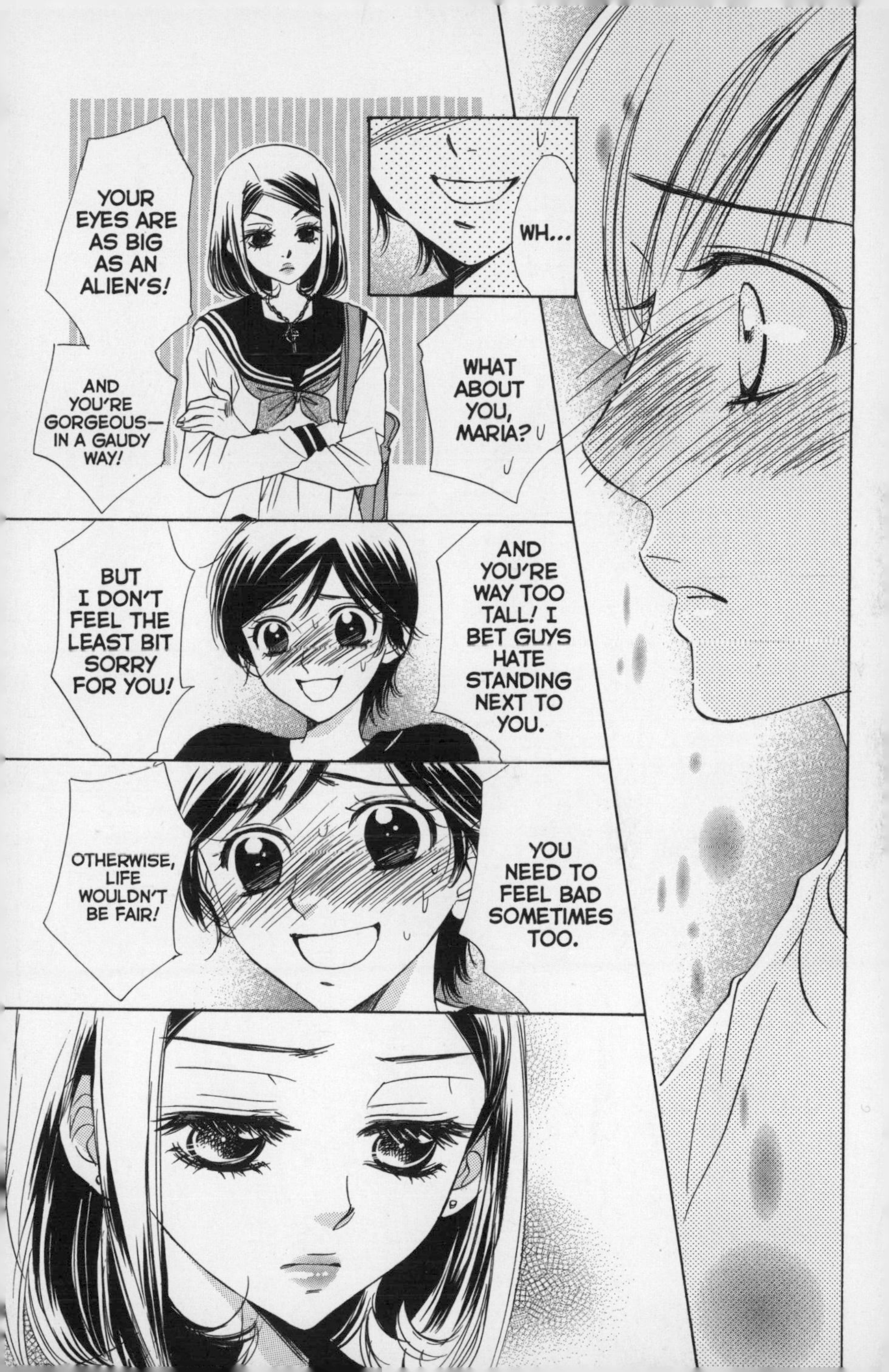
WH...
WHAT ABOUT YOU, MARIA?
YOUR EYES ARE AS BIG AS AN ALIEN'S!
AND YOU'RE GORGEOUS—IN A GAUDY WAY!
AND YOU'RE WAY TOO TALL! I BET GUYS HATE STANDING NEXT TO YOU.
BUT I DON'T FEEL THE LEAST BIT SORRY FOR YOU!
YOU NEED TO FEEL BAD SOMETIMES TOO.
OTHERWISE, LIFE WOULDN'T BE FAIR!

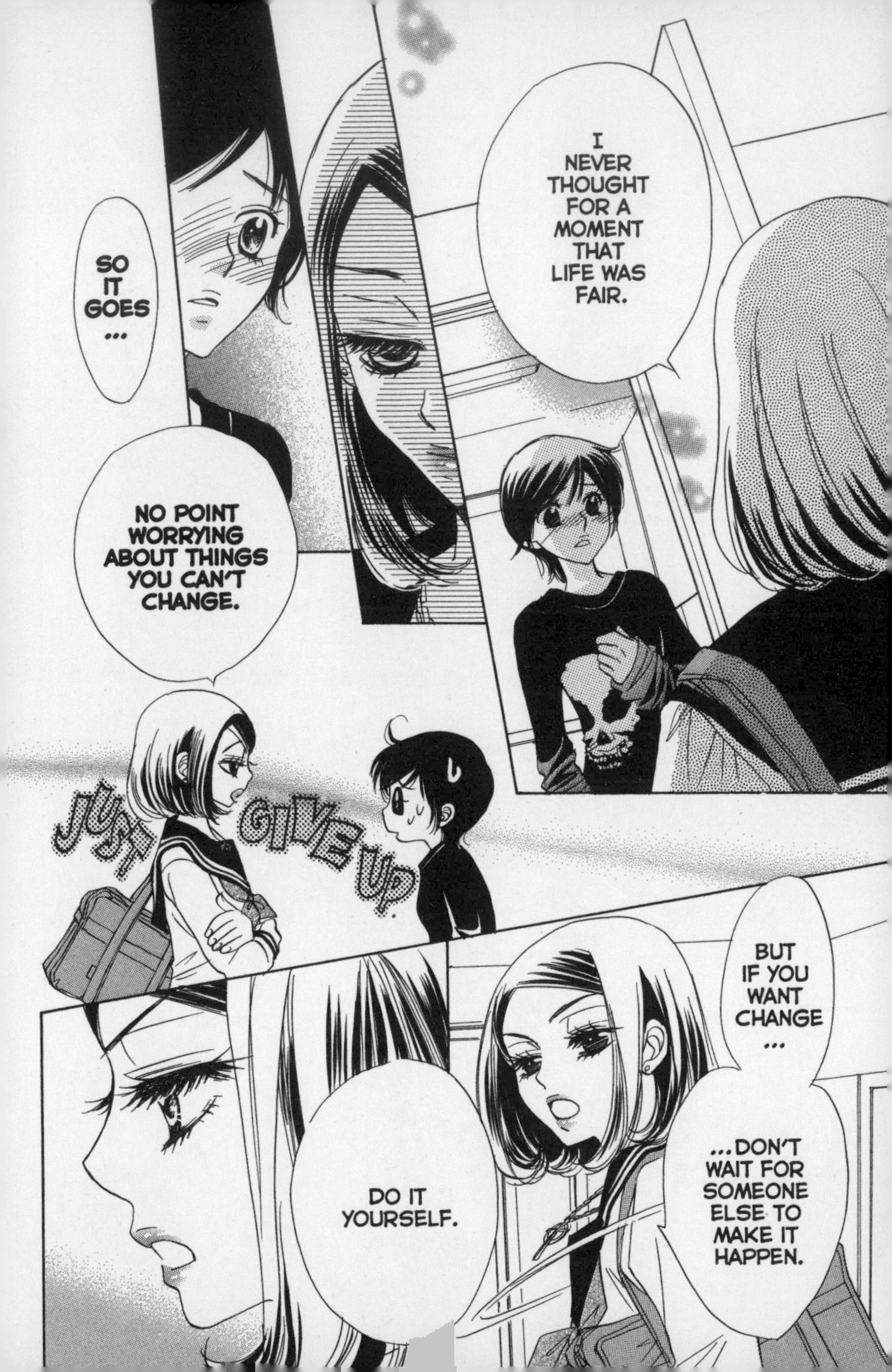
I NEVER THOUGHT FOR A MOMENT THAT LIFE WAS FAIR.
SO IT GOES...
NO POINT WORRYING ABOUT THINGS YOU CAN'T CHANGE.
JUST GIVE UP.
BUT IF YOU WANT CHANGE...
...DON'T WAIT FOR SOMEONE ELSE TO MAKE IT HAPPEN.
DO IT YOURSELF.

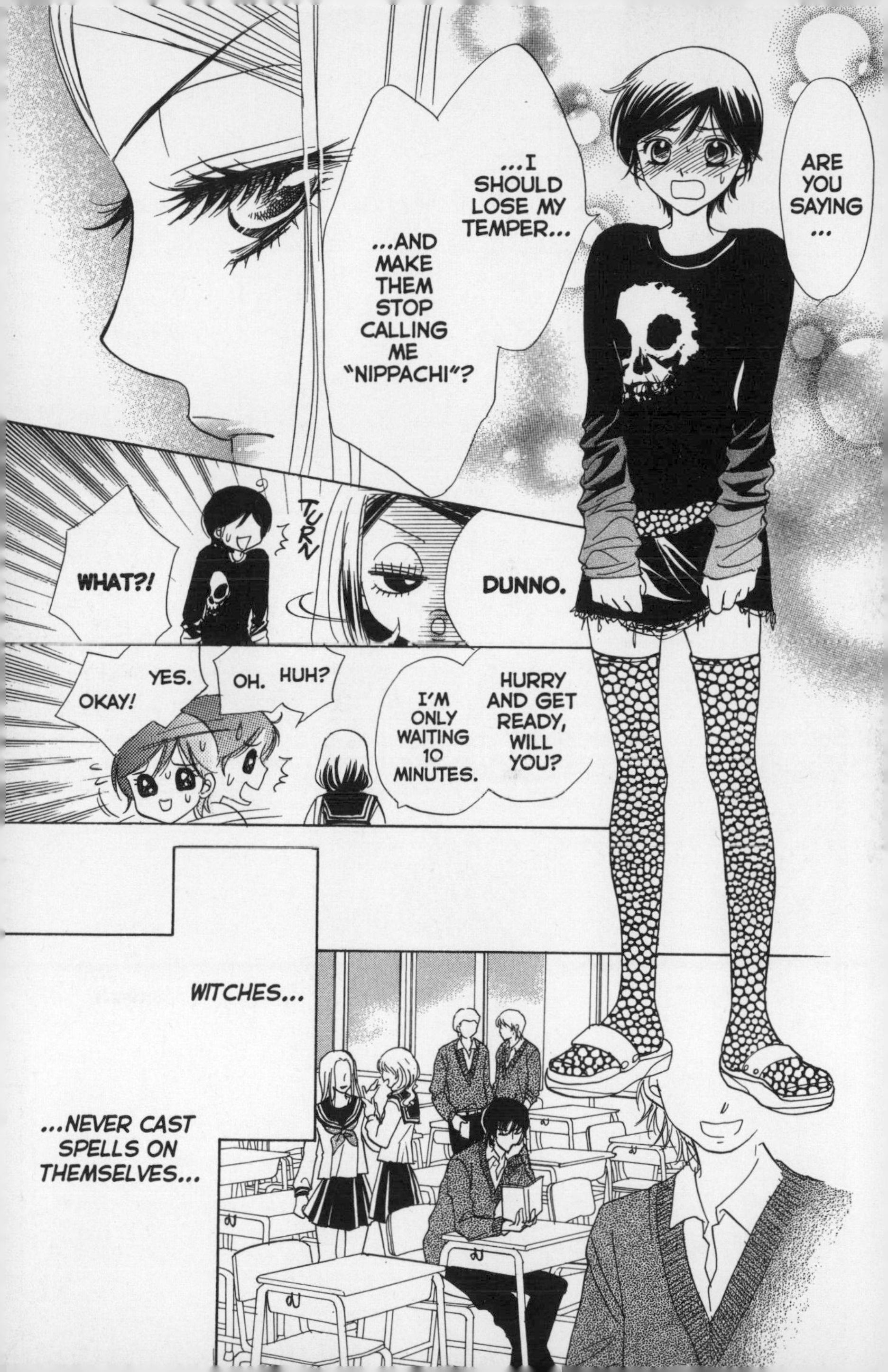
ARE YOU SAYING...
...I SHOULD LOSE MY TEMPER...
...AND MAKE THEM STOP CALLING ME "NIPPACHI"?
DUNNO.
TURN
WHAT?!
HURRY AND GET READY, WILL YOU?
I'M ONLY WAITING 10 MINUTES.
HUH?
OH.
YES.
OKAY!
WITCHES...
...NEVER CAST SPELLS ON THEMSELVES...

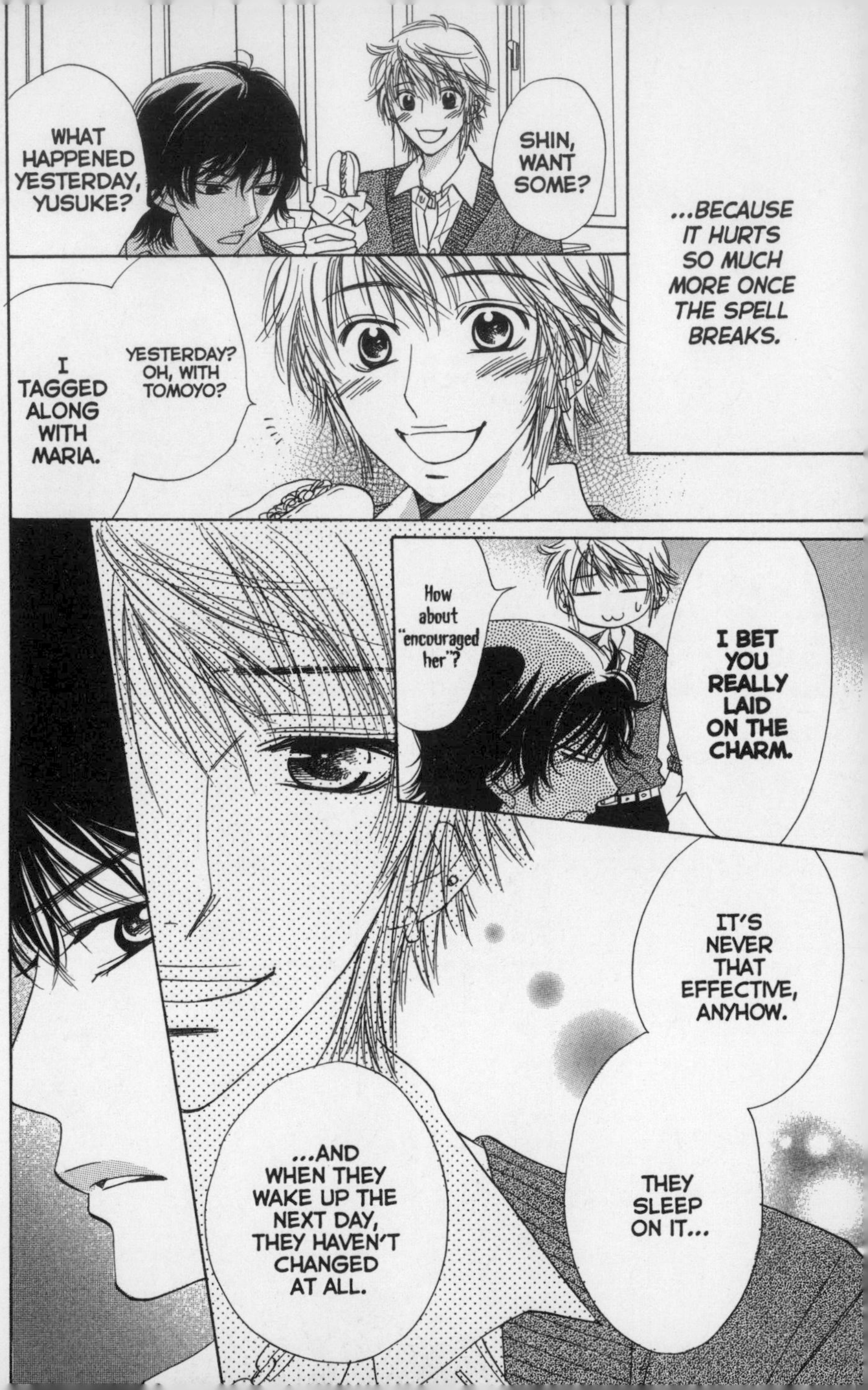
...BECAUSE IT HURTS SO MUCH MORE ONCE THE SPELL BREAKS.
SHIN, WANT SOME?
WHAT HAPPENED YESTERDAY, YUSUKE?
YESTERDAY? OH, WITH TOMOYO?
I TAGGED ALONG WITH MARIA.
I BET YOU REALLY LAID ON THE CHARM.
How about "encouraged her"?
IT'S NEVER THAT EFFECTIVE, ANYHOW.
THEY SLEEP ON IT...
...AND WHEN THEY WAKE UP THE NEXT DAY, THEY HAVEN'T CHANGED AT ALL.

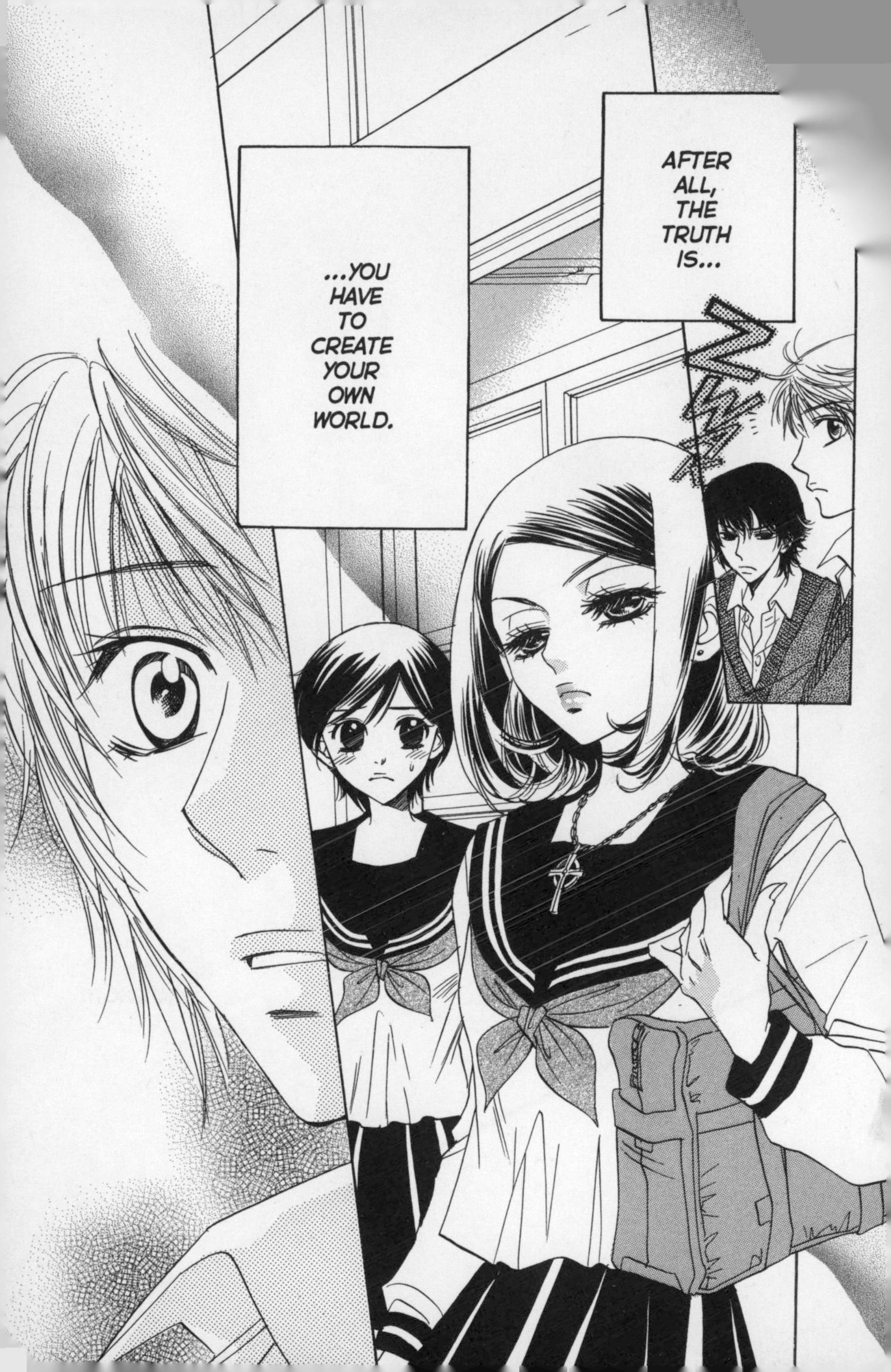
AFTER ALL, THE TRUTH IS...
...YOU HAVE TO CREATE YOUR OWN WORLD.

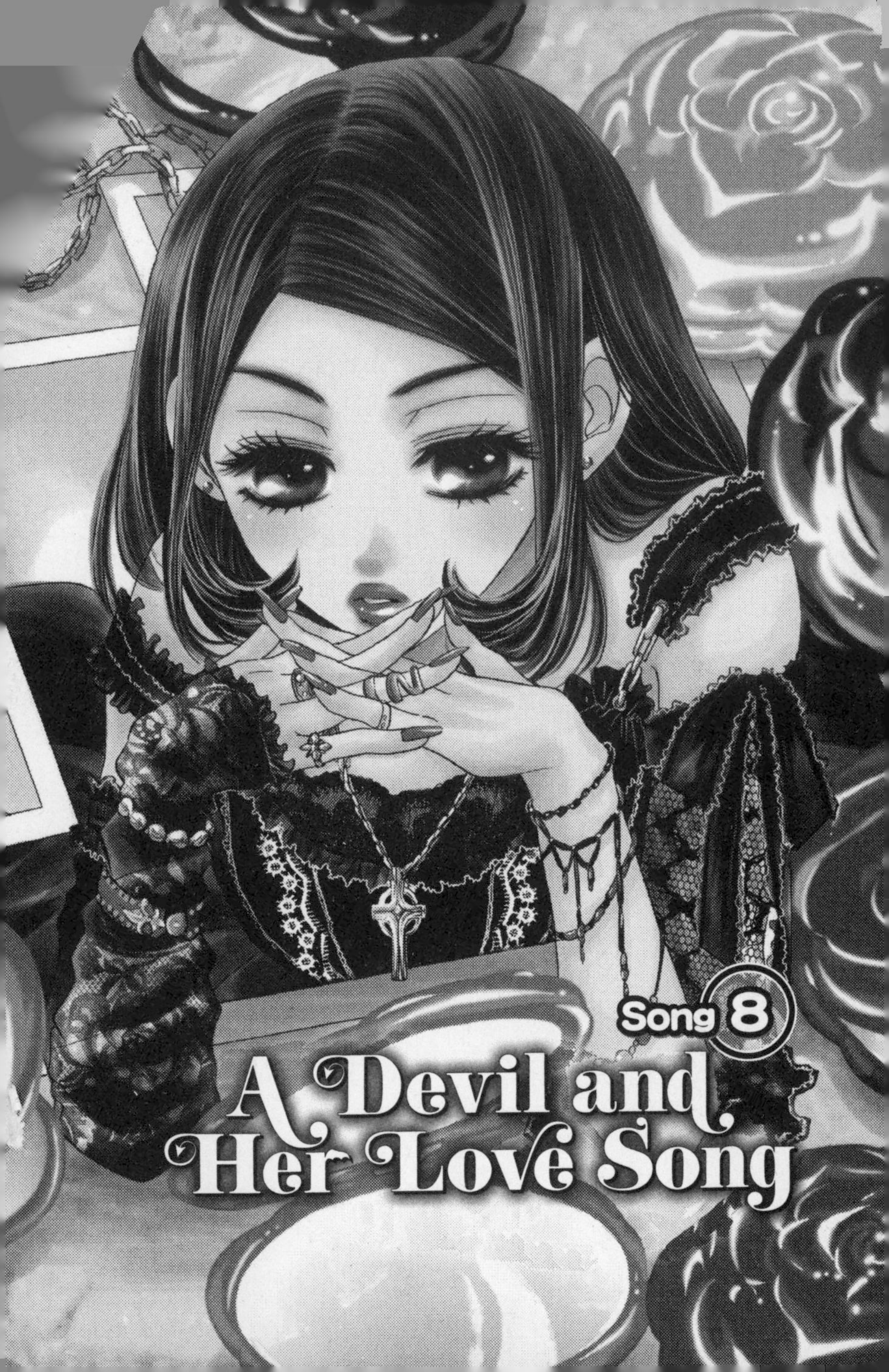
Song 8
A Devil and Her Love Song

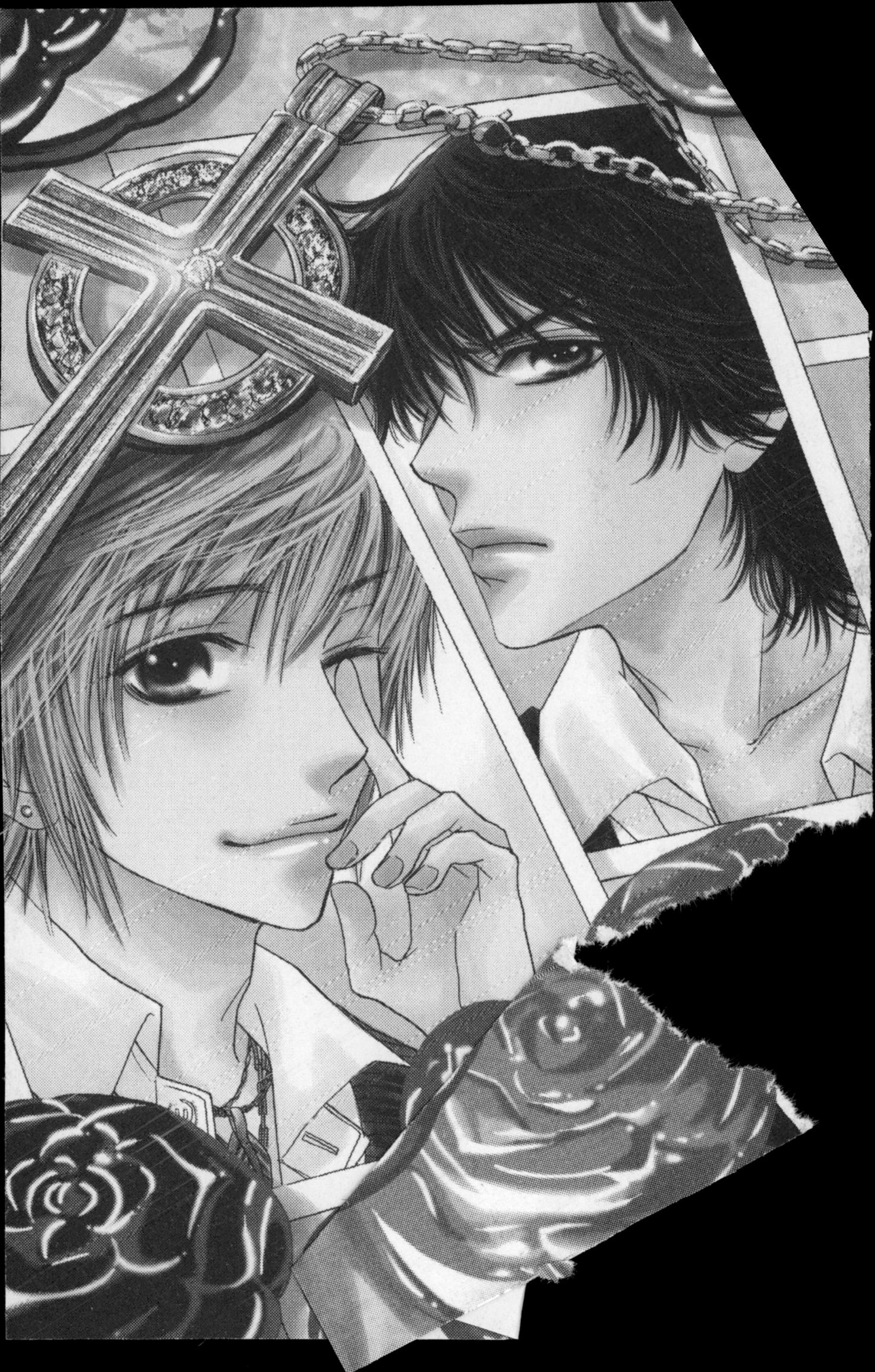

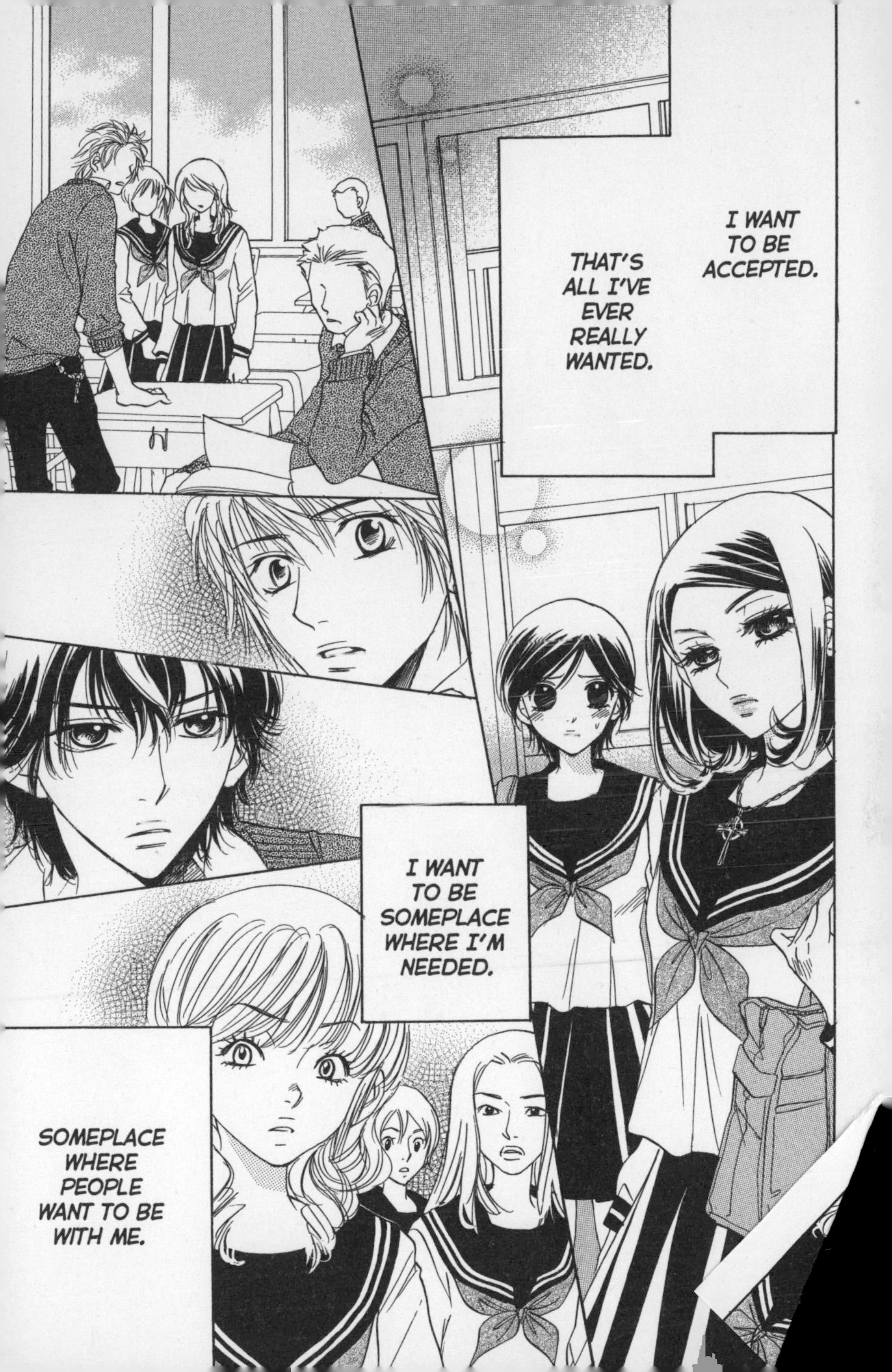
I WANT TO BE ACCEPTED.
THAT'S ALL I'VE EVER REALLY WANTED.
I WANT TO BE SOMEPLACE WHERE I'M NEEDED.
SOMEPLACE WHERE PEOPLE WANT TO BE WITH ME.

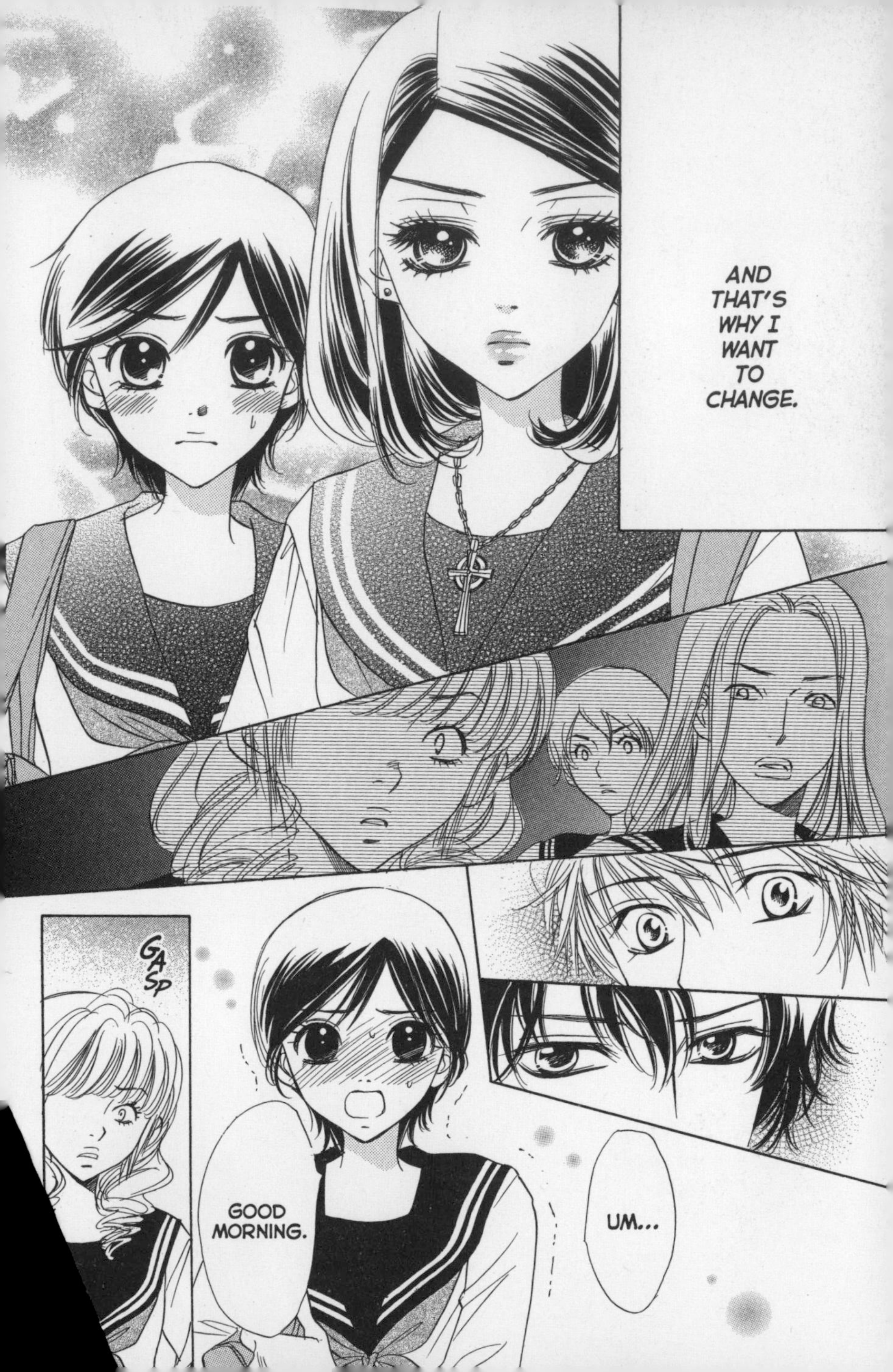
AND THAT'S WHY I WANT TO CHANGE.
UM...
GOOD MORNING.
GASP

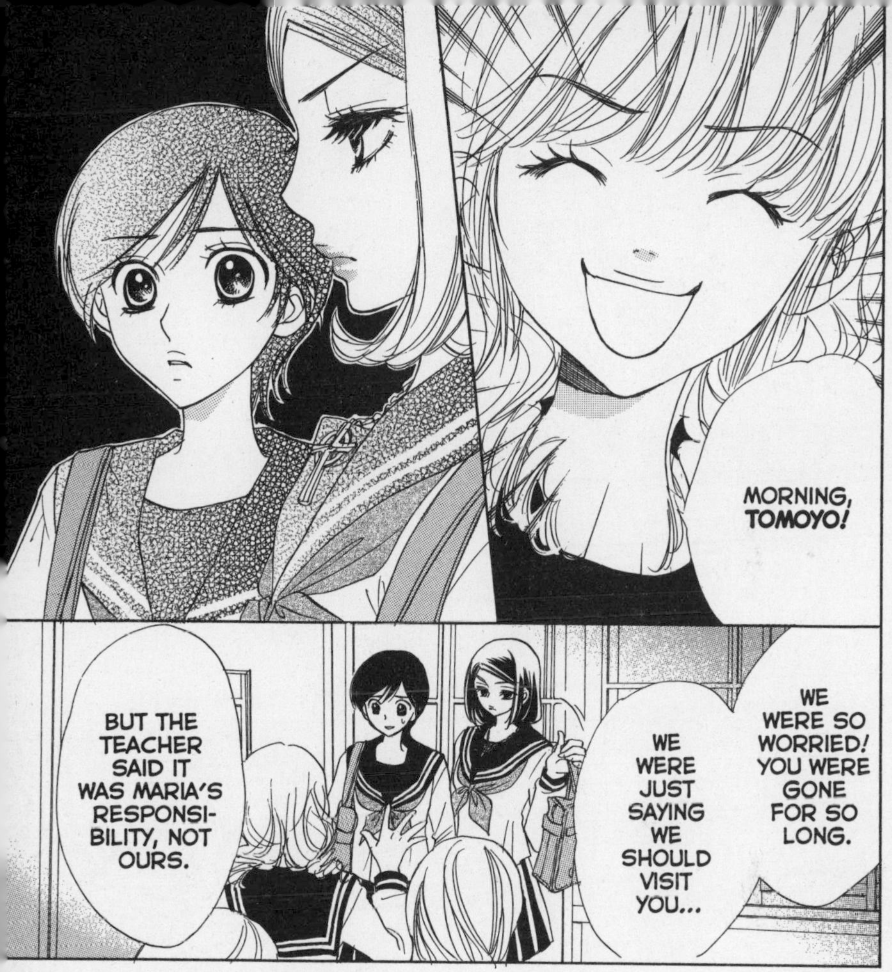
MORNING, TOMOYO!
WE WERE SO WORRIED! YOU WERE GONE FOR SO LONG.
WE WERE JUST SAYING WE SHOULD VISIT YOU...
BUT THE TEACHER SAID IT WAS MARIA'S RESPONSI-BILITY, NOT OURS.

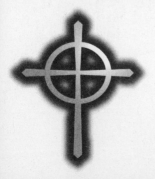

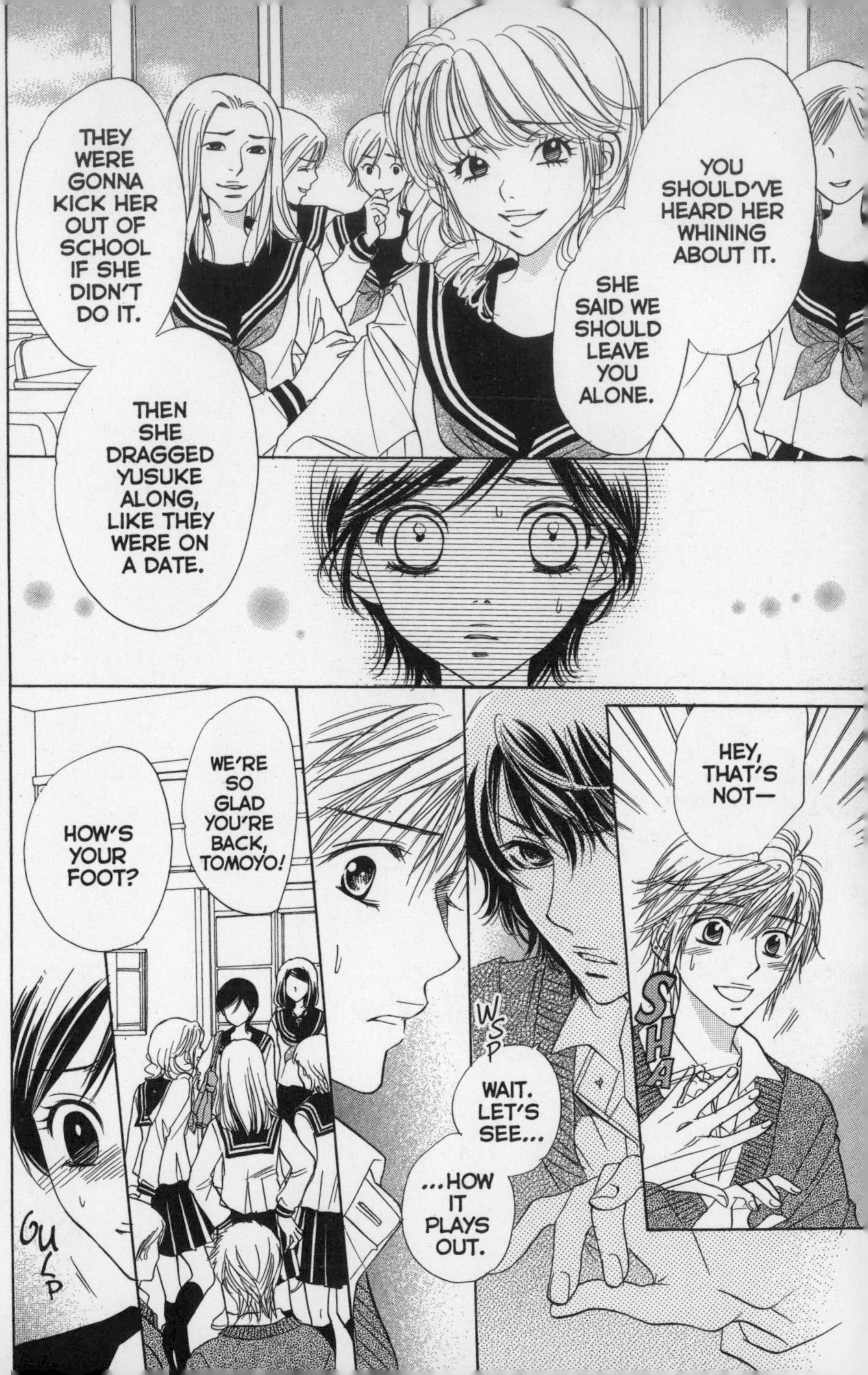
YOU SHOULD'VE HEARD HER WHINING ABOUT IT.
SHE SAID WE SHOULD LEAVE YOU ALONE.
THEY WERE GONNA KICK HER OUT OF SCHOOL IF SHE DIDN'T DO IT.
THEN SHE DRAGGED YUSUKE ALONG, LIKE THEY WERE ON A DATE.
HEY, THAT'S NOT—
SHA
WSP
WAIT. LET'S SEE...
...HOW IT PLAYS OUT.
WE'RE SO GLAD YOU'RE BACK, TOMOYO!
HOW'S YOUR FOOT?
GULP

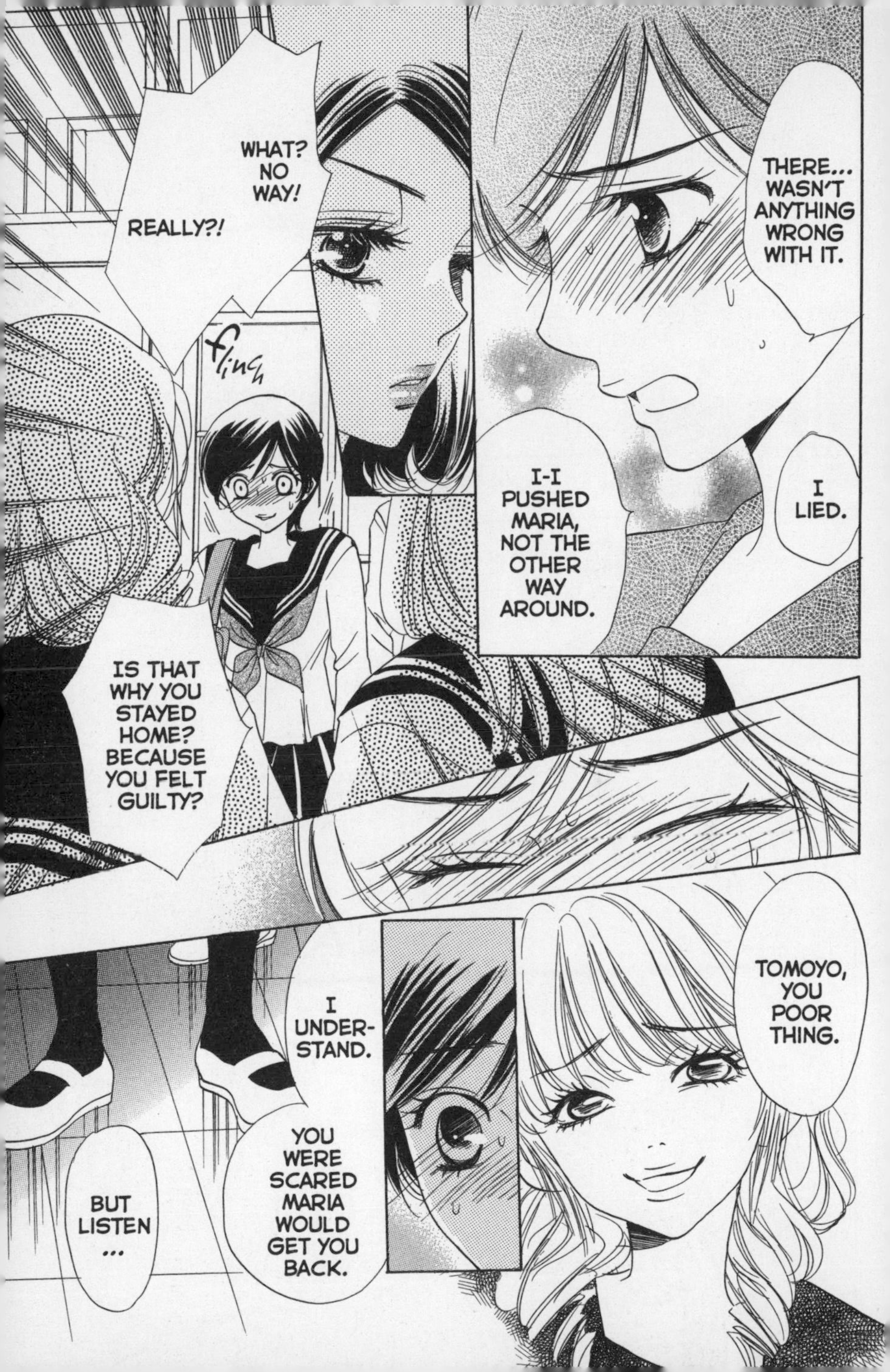
THERE... WASN'T ANYTHING WRONG WITH IT.
I LIED.
I-I PUSHED MARIA, NOT THE OTHER WAY AROUND.
WHAT? NO WAY!
REALLY?!
flinch
IS THAT WHY YOU STAYED HOME? BECAUSE YOU FELT GUILTY?
TOMOYO, YOU POOR THING.
I UNDER-STAND.
YOU WERE SCARED MARIA WOULD GET YOU BACK.
BUT LISTEN...

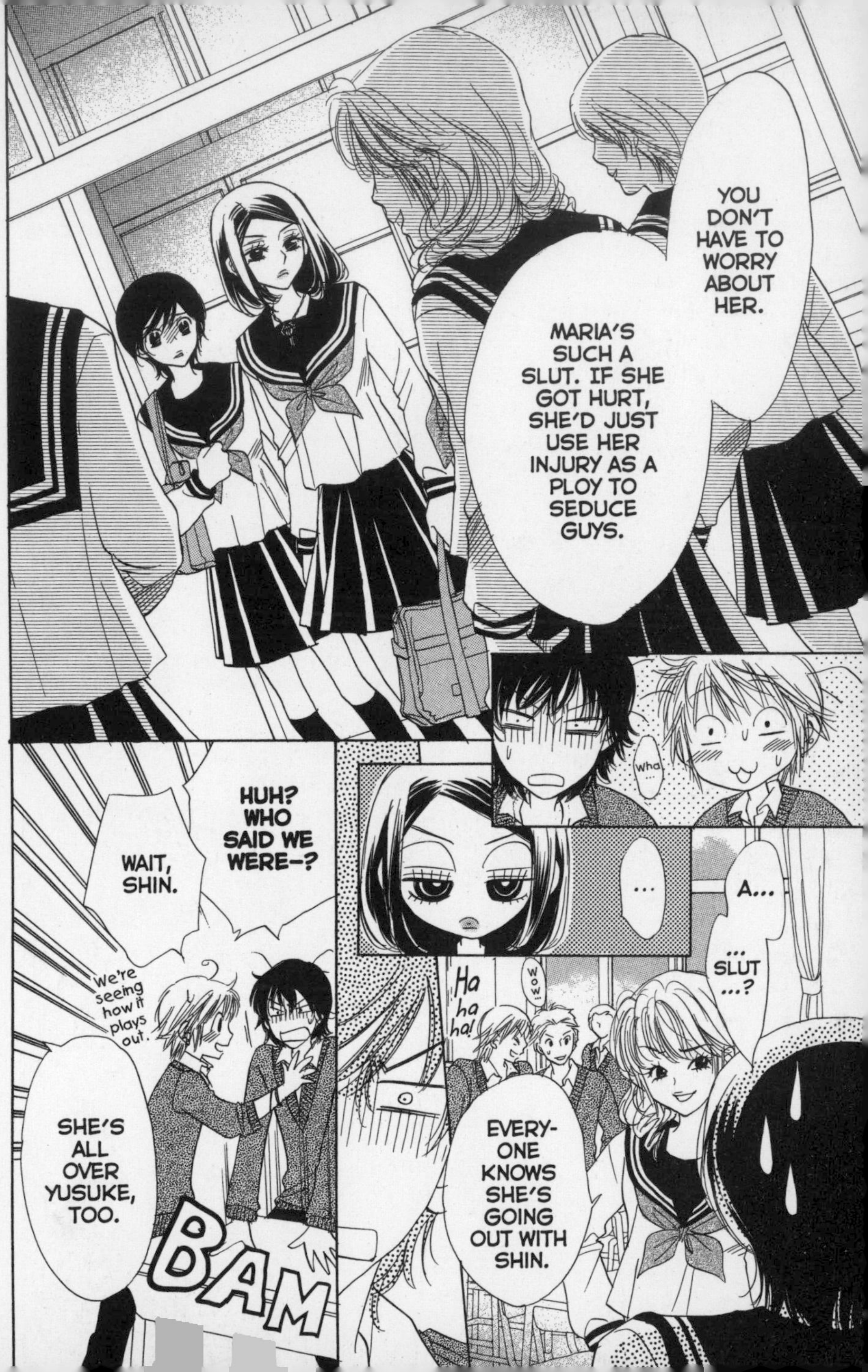
YOU DON'T HAVE TO WORRY ABOUT HER.
MARIA'S SUCH A SLUT. IF SHE GOT HURT, SHE'D JUST USE HER INJURY AS A PLOY TO SEDUCE GUYS.
Wha...
A... ...SLUT ...?
...
Wow...
Ha ha ha!
EVERY-ONE KNOWS SHE'S GOING OUT WITH SHIN.
HUH? WHO SAID WE WERE--?
WAIT, SHIN.
We're seeing how it plays out.
SHE'S ALL OVER YUSUKE, TOO.
BAM

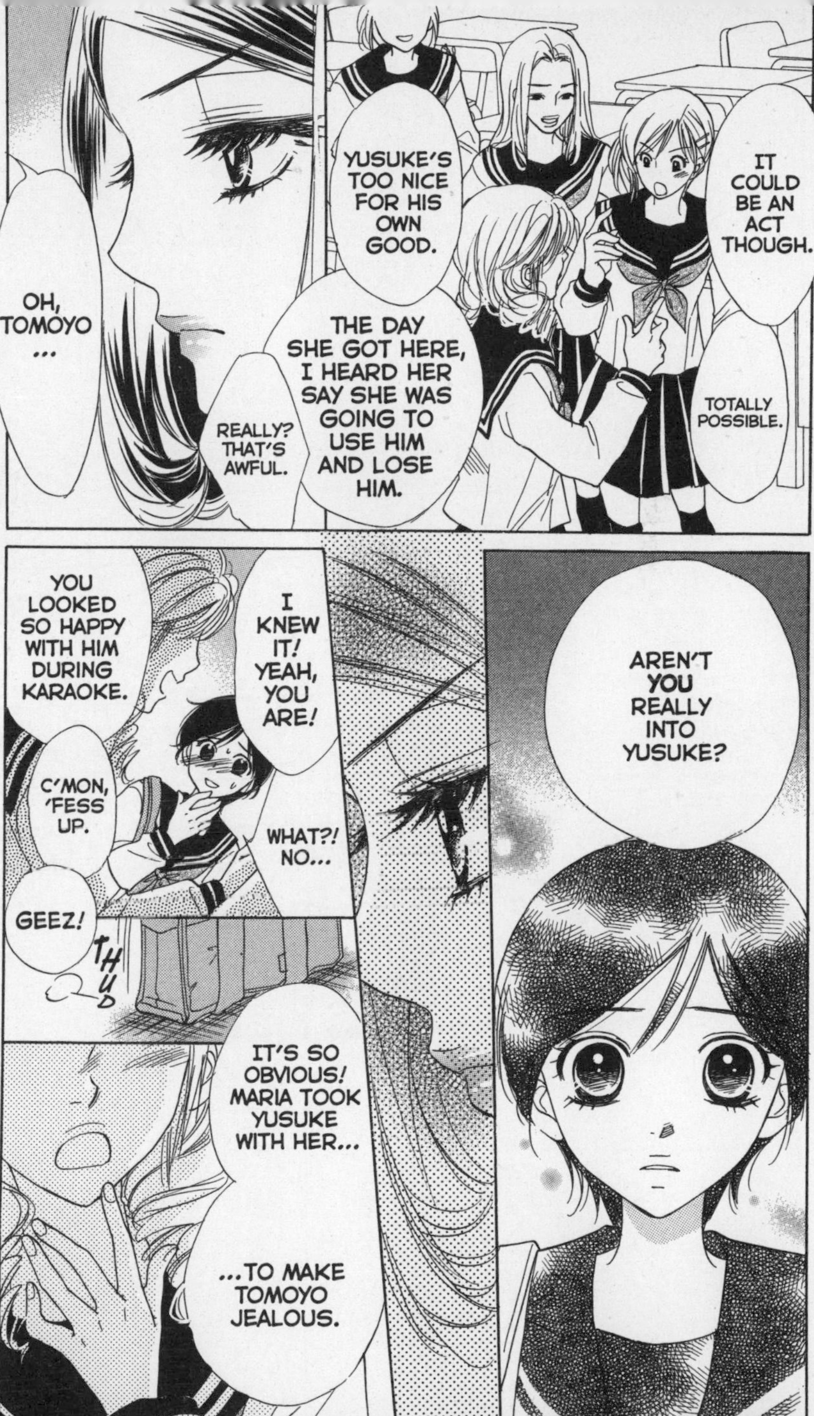
YUSUKE'S TOO NICE FOR HIS OWN GOOD.
IT COULD BE AN ACT THOUGH.
TOTALLY POSSIBLE.
THE DAY SHE GOT HERE, I HEARD HER SAY SHE WAS GOING TO USE HIM AND LOSE HIM.
REALLY? THAT'S AWFUL.
OH, TOMOYO ...
AREN'T YOU REALLY INTO YUSUKE?
I KNEW IT! YEAH, YOU ARE!
YOU LOOKED SO HAPPY WITH HIM DURING KARAOKE.
WHAT?! NO...
C'MON, 'FESS UP.
GEEZ!
THUD
IT'S SO OBVIOUS! MARIA TOOK YUSUKE WITH HER...
...TO MAKE TOMOYO JEALOUS.

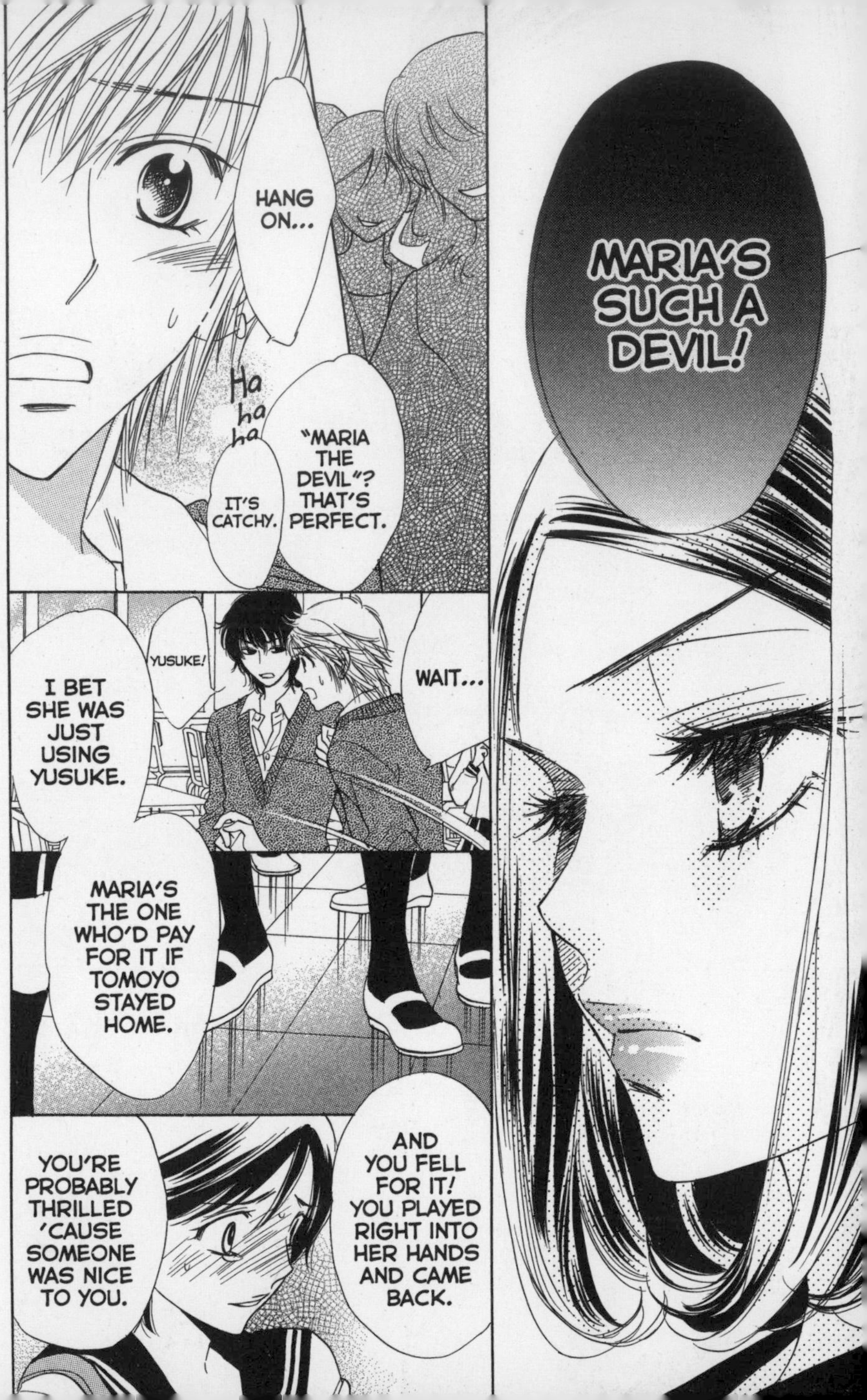
MARIA'S SUCH A DEVIL!
HANG ON...
"MARIA THE DEVIL"? THAT'S PERFECT.
Ha ha ha
IT'S CATCHY.
WAIT...
YUSUKE!
I BET SHE WAS JUST USING YUSUKE.
MARIA'S THE ONE WHO'D PAY FOR IT IF TOMOYO STAYED HOME.
AND YOU FELL FOR IT! YOU PLAYED RIGHT INTO HER HANDS AND CAME BACK.
YOU'RE PROBABLY THRILLED 'CAUSE SOMEONE WAS NICE TO YOU.

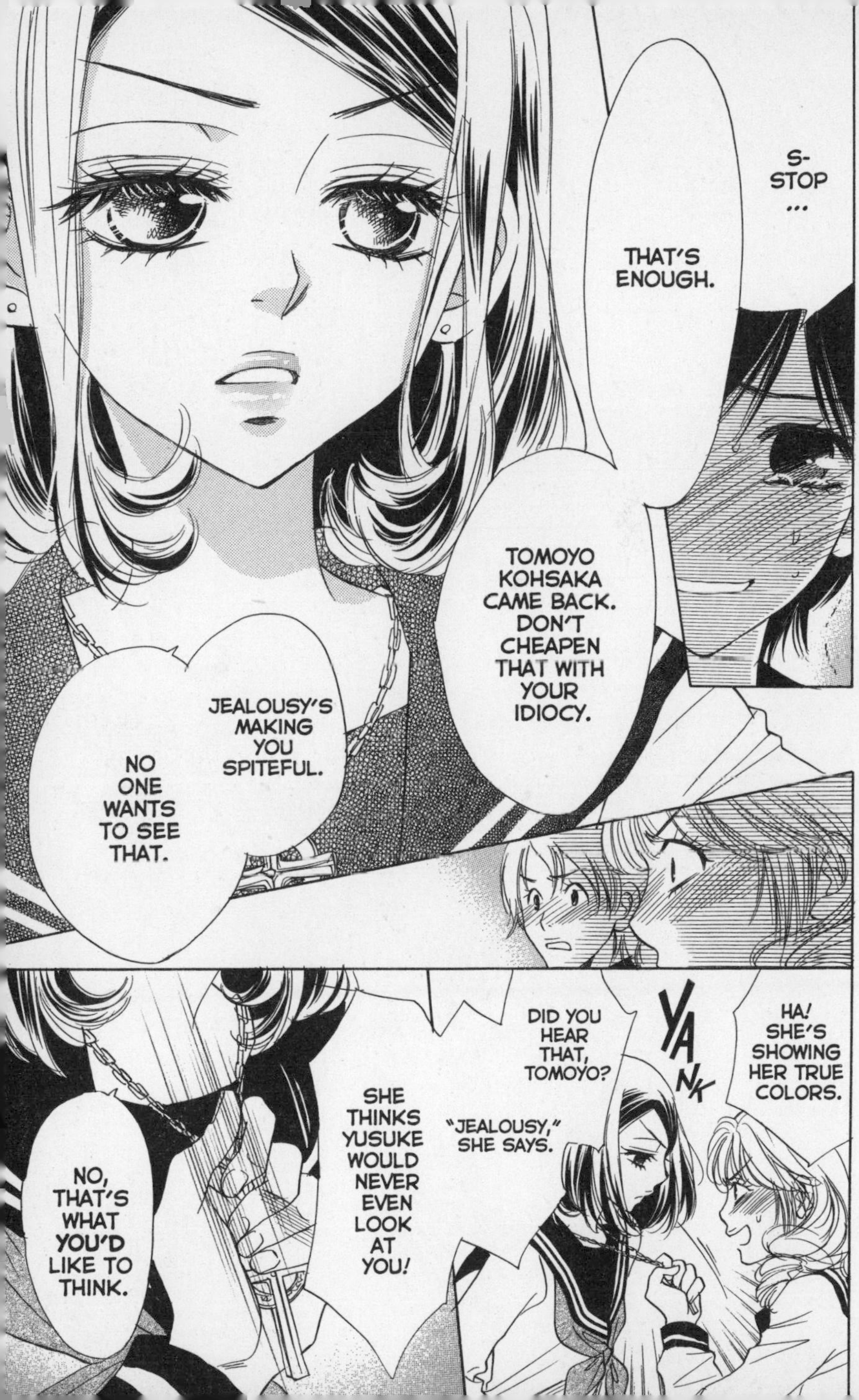
S-STOP...
THAT'S ENOUGH.
TOMOYO KOHSAKA CAME BACK. DON'T CHEAPEN THAT WITH YOUR IDIOCY.
JEALOUSY'S MAKING YOU SPITEFUL.
NO ONE WANTS TO SEE THAT.
HA! SHE'S SHOWING HER TRUE COLORS.
YANK
DID YOU HEAR THAT, TOMOYO?
"JEALOUSY," SHE SAYS.
SHE THINKS YUSUKE WOULD NEVER EVEN LOOK AT YOU!
NO, THAT'S WHAT YOU'D LIKE TO THINK.

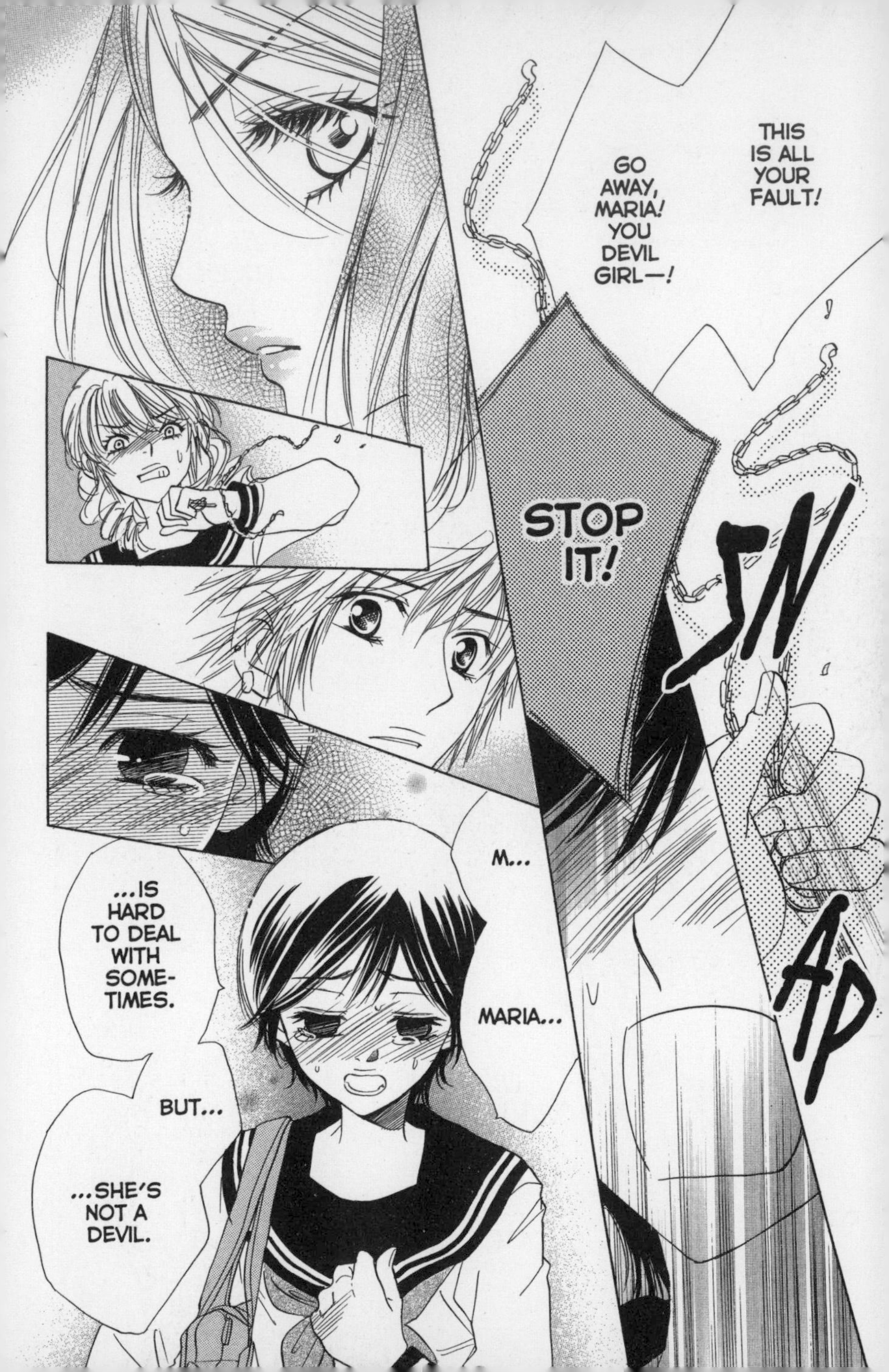
THIS IS ALL YOUR FAULT!
GO AWAY, MARIA! YOU DEVIL GIRL—!
STOP IT!
SNAP
M...
MARIA...
...IS HARD TO DEAL WITH SOME-TIMES.
BUT...
...SHE'S NOT A DEVIL.

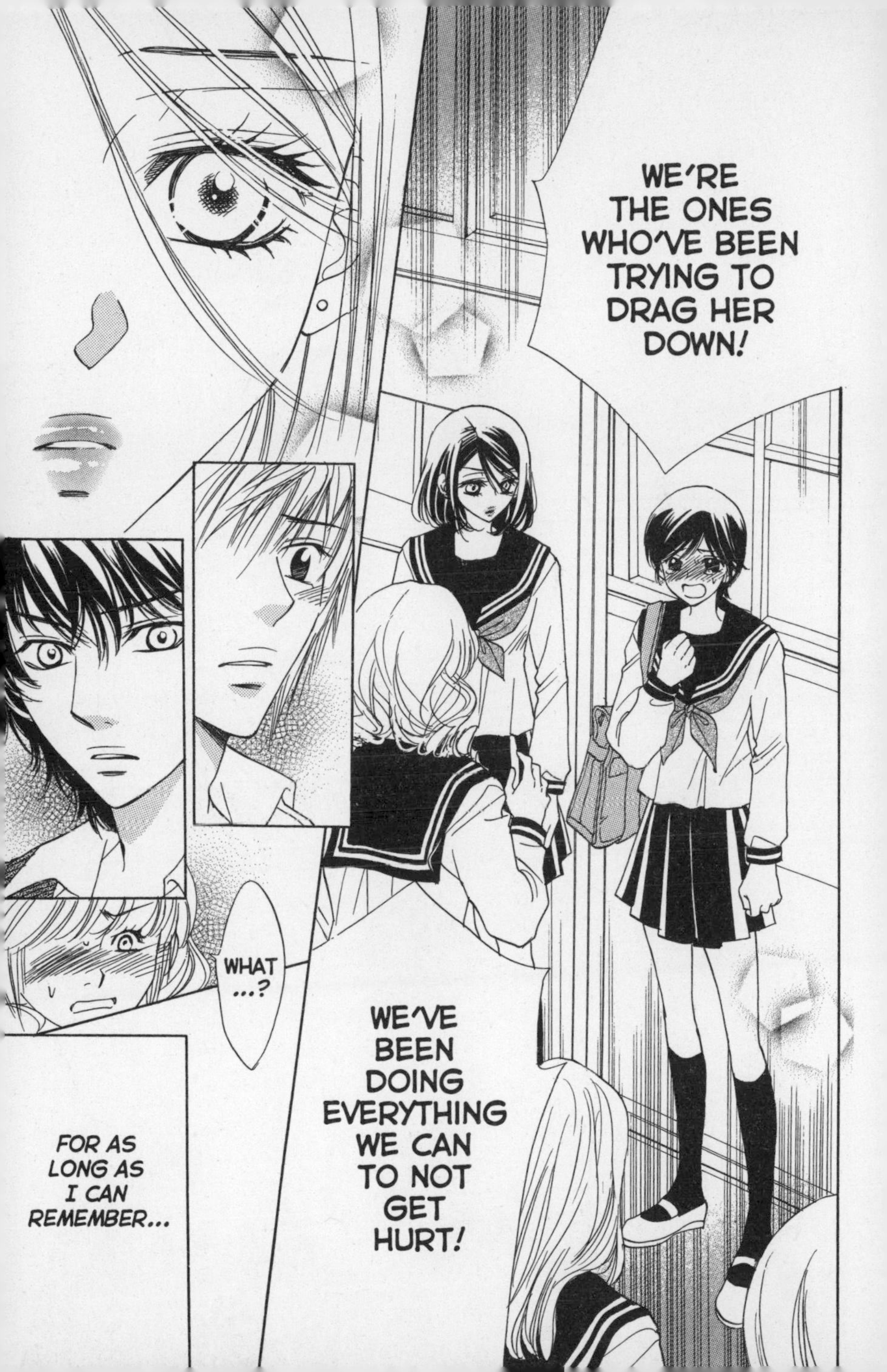
WE'RE THE ONES WHO'VE BEEN TRYING TO DRAG HER DOWN!
WE'VE BEEN DOING EVERYTHING WE CAN TO NOT GET HURT!
WHAT ...?
FOR AS LONG AS I CAN REMEMBER...

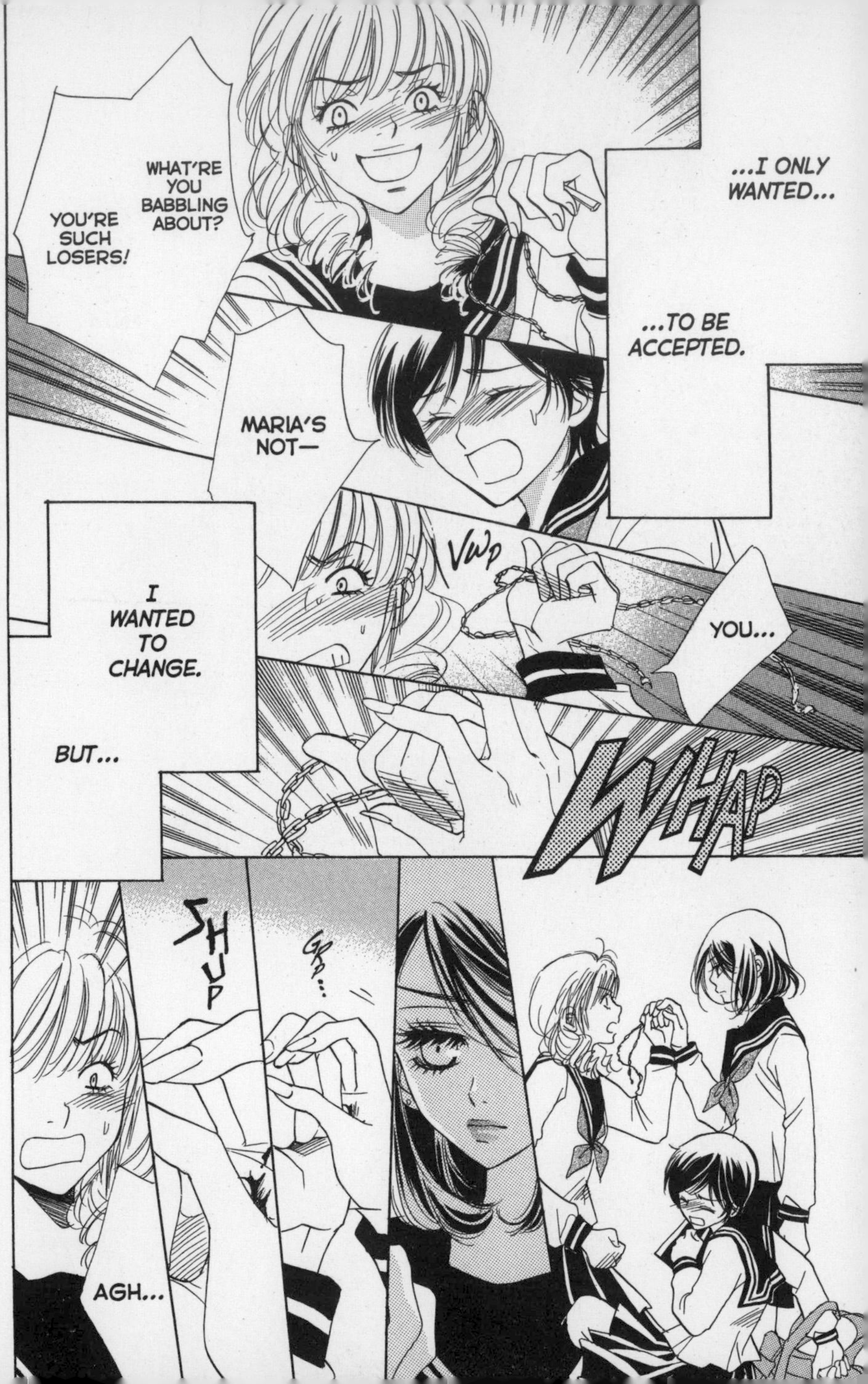
...I ONLY WANTED...
...TO BE ACCEPTED.
WHAT'RE YOU BABBLING ABOUT?
YOU'RE SUCH LOSERS!
MARIA'S NOT—
YOU...
VWP
I WANTED TO CHANGE.
BUT...
WHAP
GRP...
SHUP
AGH...

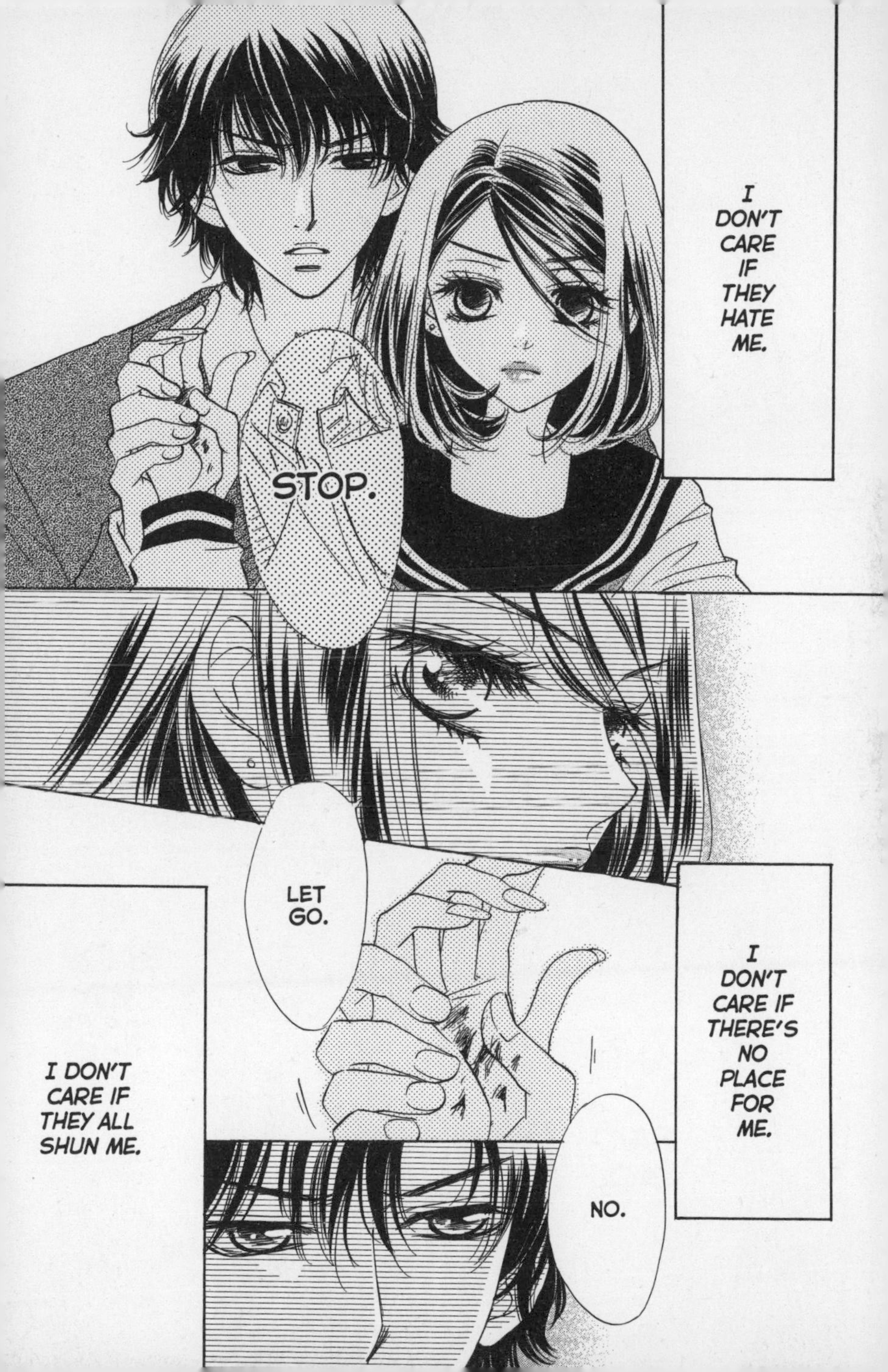
I DON'T CARE IF THEY HATE ME.
STOP.
LET GO.
I DON'T CARE IF THERE'S NO PLACE FOR ME.
NO.
I DON'T CARE IF THEY ALL SHUN ME.

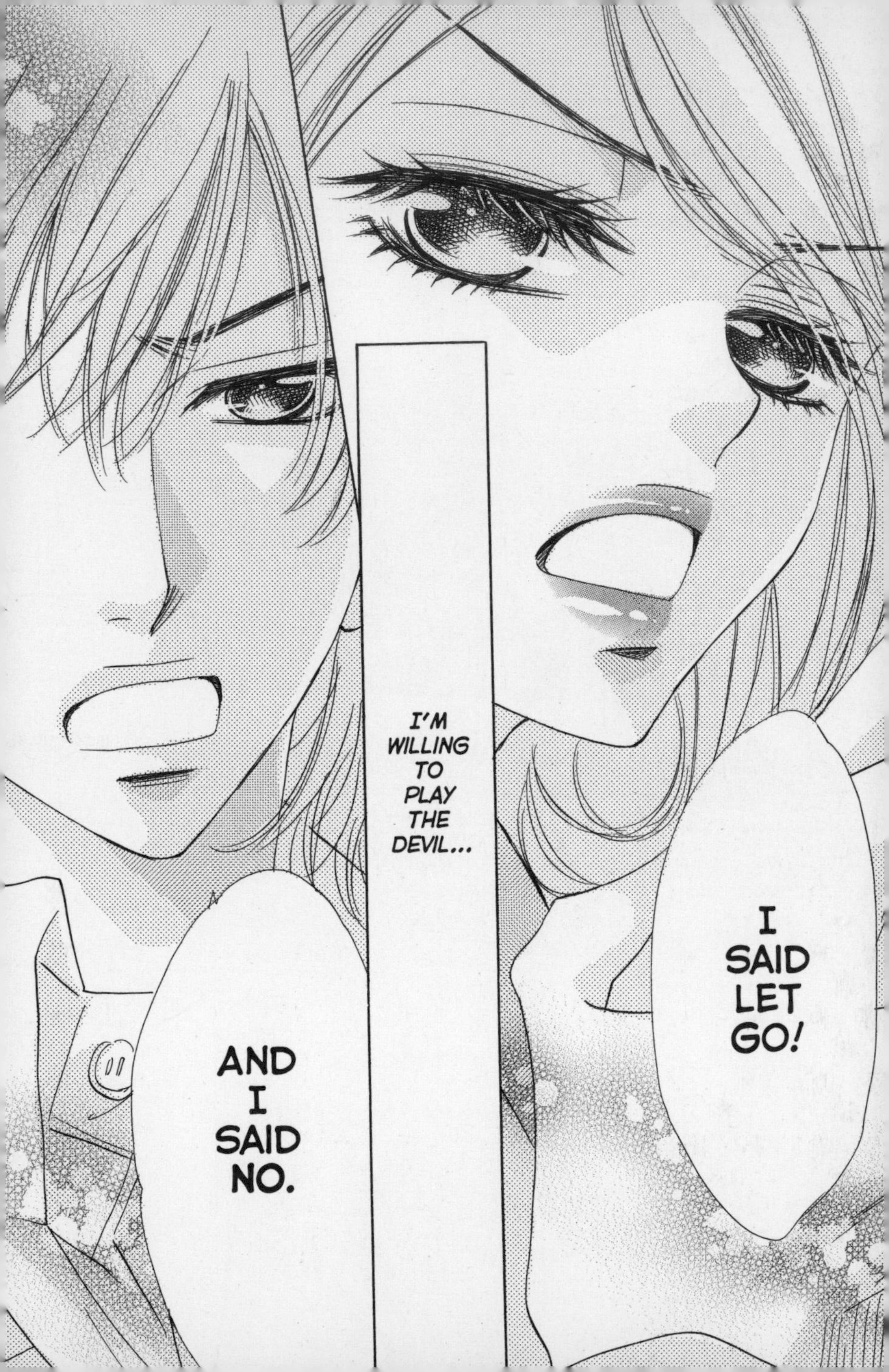
I SAID LET GO!
I'M WILLING TO PLAY THE DEVIL...
AND I SAID NO.

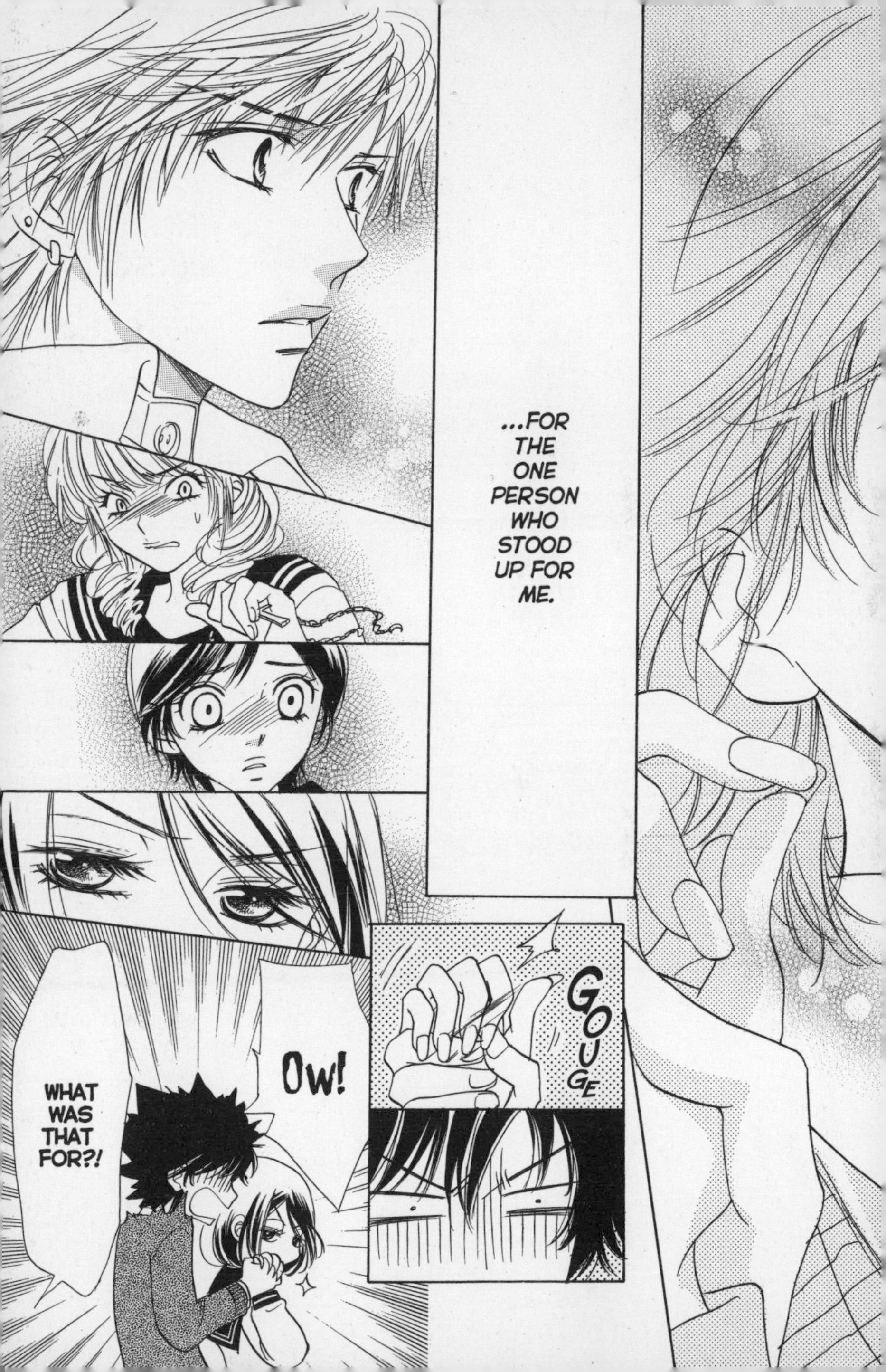
...FOR THE ONE PERSON WHO STOOD UP FOR ME.
GOUGE
Ow!
WHAT WAS THAT FOR?!

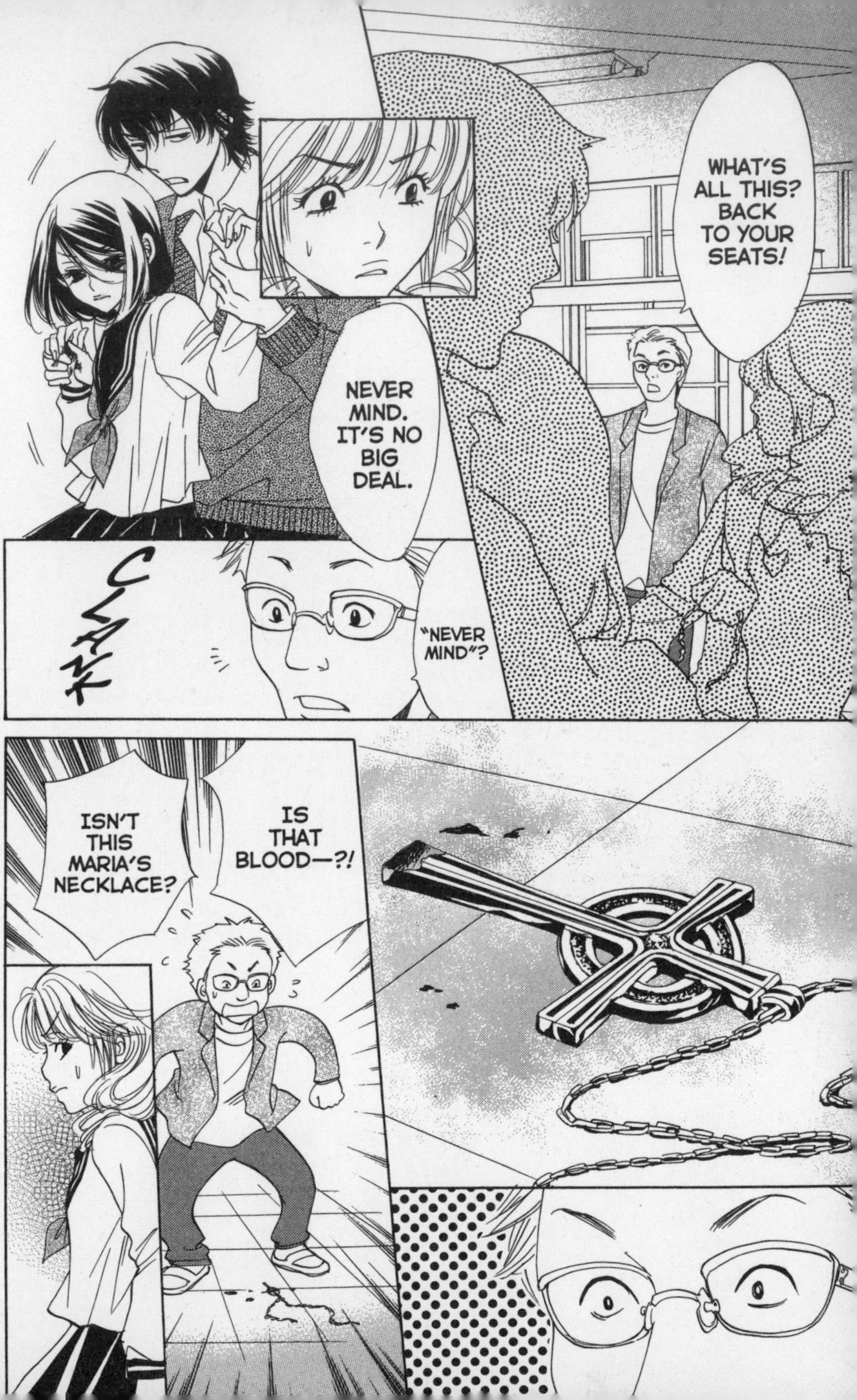
WHAT'S ALL THIS? BACK TO YOUR SEATS!
NEVER MIND. IT'S NO BIG DEAL.
"NEVER MIND"?
CLANK
IS THAT BLOOD—?!
ISN'T THIS MARIA'S NECKLACE?

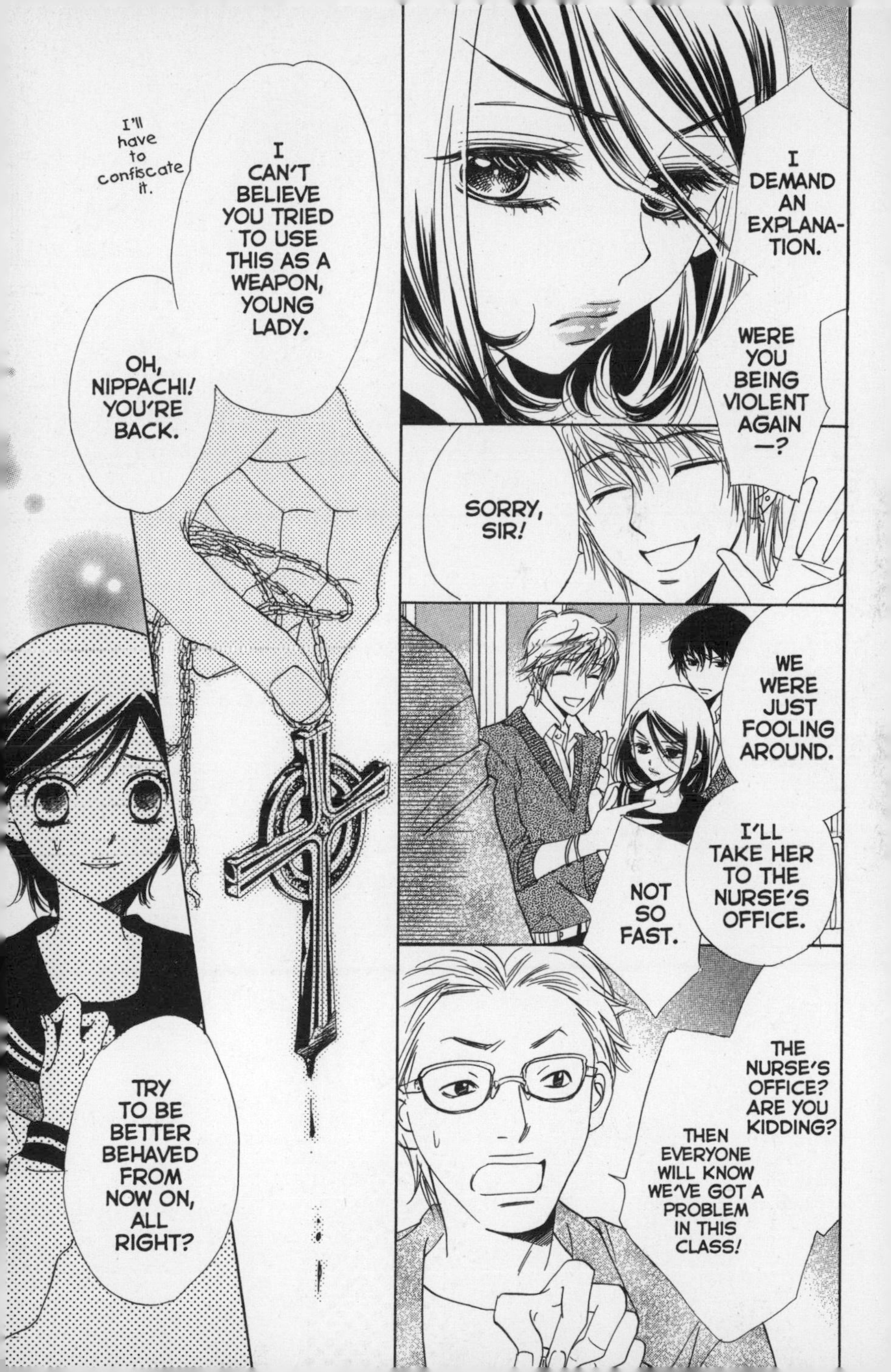
I DEMAND AN EXPLANATION.
WERE YOU BEING VIOLENT AGAIN—?
SORRY, SIR!
WE WERE JUST FOOLING AROUND.
I'LL TAKE HER TO THE NURSE'S OFFICE.
NOT SO FAST.
THE NURSE'S OFFICE? ARE YOU KIDDING?
THEN EVERYONE WILL KNOW WE'VE GOT A PROBLEM IN THIS CLASS!
I CAN'T BELIEVE YOU TRIED TO USE THIS AS A WEAPON, YOUNG LADY.
I'll have to confiscate it.
OH, NIPPACHI! YOU'RE BACK.
TRY TO BE BETTER BEHAVED FROM NOW ON, ALL RIGHT?

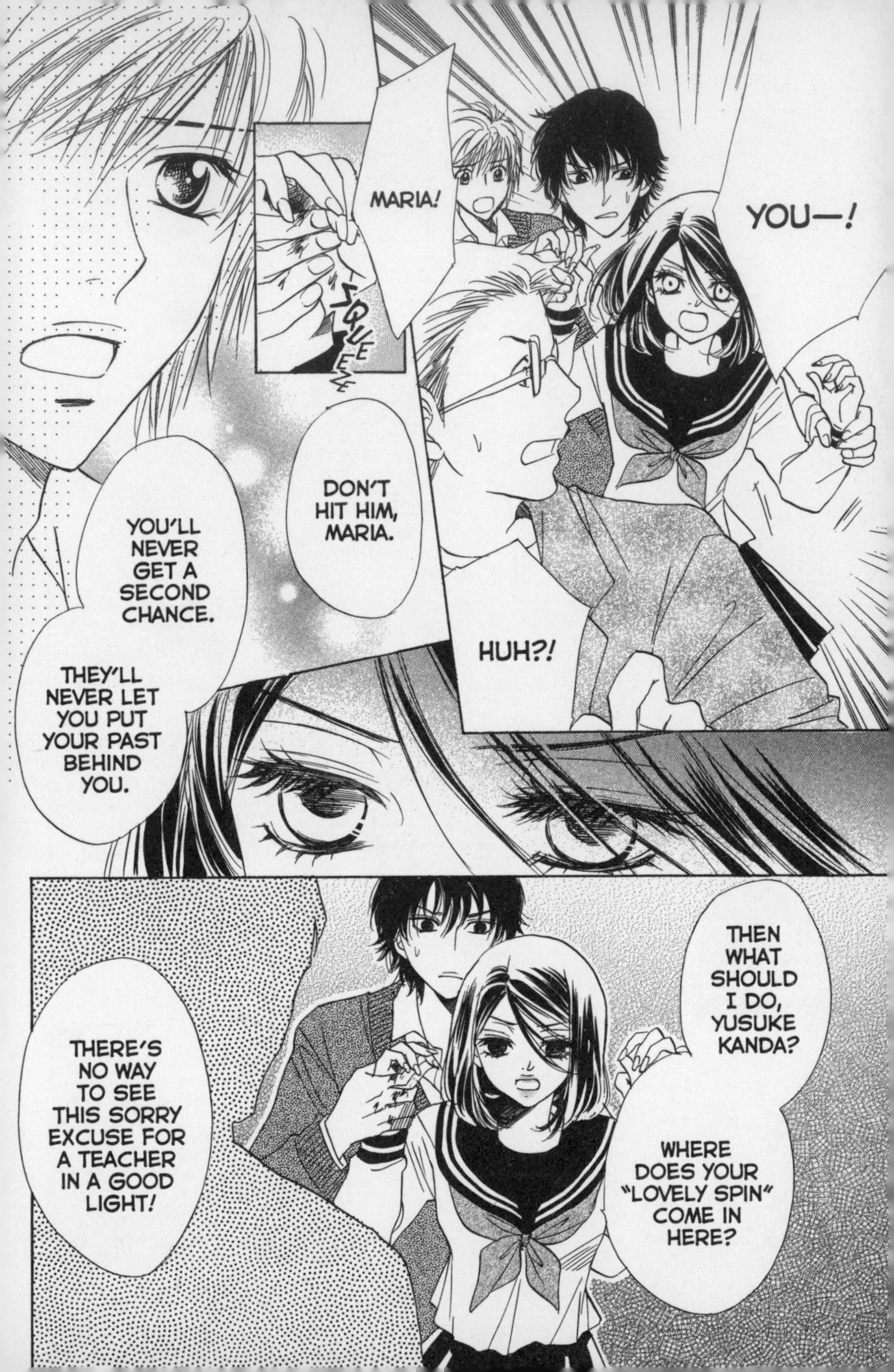
YOU—!
MARIA!
SQUEEZE
DON'T HIT HIM, MARIA.
HUH?!
YOU'LL NEVER GET A SECOND CHANCE.
THEY'LL NEVER LET YOU PUT YOUR PAST BEHIND YOU.
THEN WHAT SHOULD I DO, YUSUKE KANDA?
WHERE DOES YOUR "LOVELY SPIN" COME IN HERE?
THERE'S NO WAY TO SEE THIS SORRY EXCUSE FOR A TEACHER IN A GOOD LIGHT!

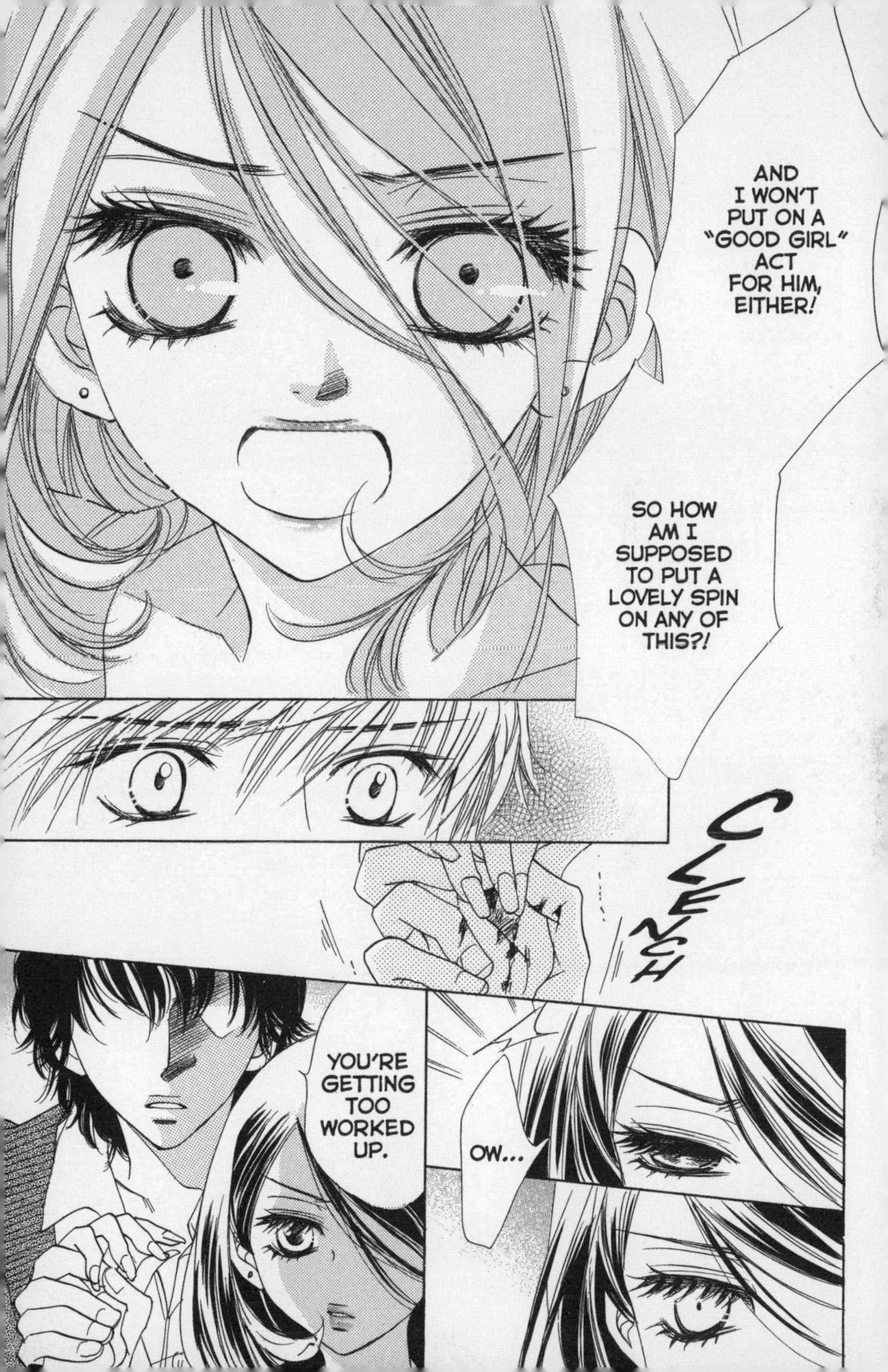
AND I WON'T PUT ON A "GOOD GIRL" ACT FOR HIM, EITHER!
SO HOW AM I SUPPOSED TO PUT A LOVELY SPIN ON ANY OF THIS?!
CLENCH
OW...
YOU'RE GETTING TOO WORKED UP.

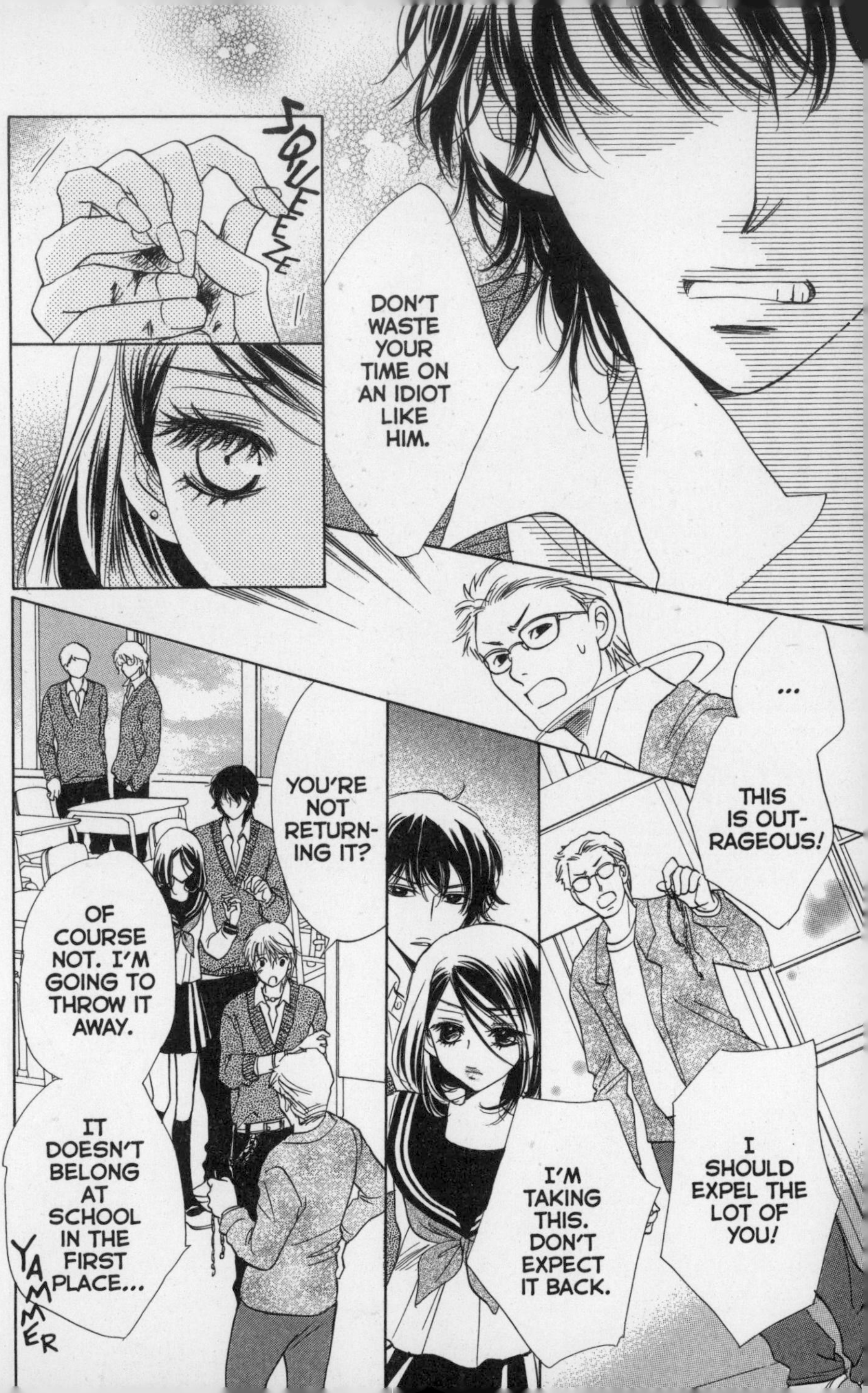
DON'T WASTE YOUR TIME ON AN IDIOT LIKE HIM.
SQUEEEZE
...
THIS IS OUT-RAGEOUS!
I SHOULD EXPEL THE LOT OF YOU!
I'M TAKING THIS. DON'T EXPECT IT BACK.
YOU'RE NOT RETURNING IT?
OF COURSE NOT. I'M GOING TO THROW IT AWAY.
IT DOESN'T BELONG AT SCHOOL IN THE FIRST PLACE...
YAMMER

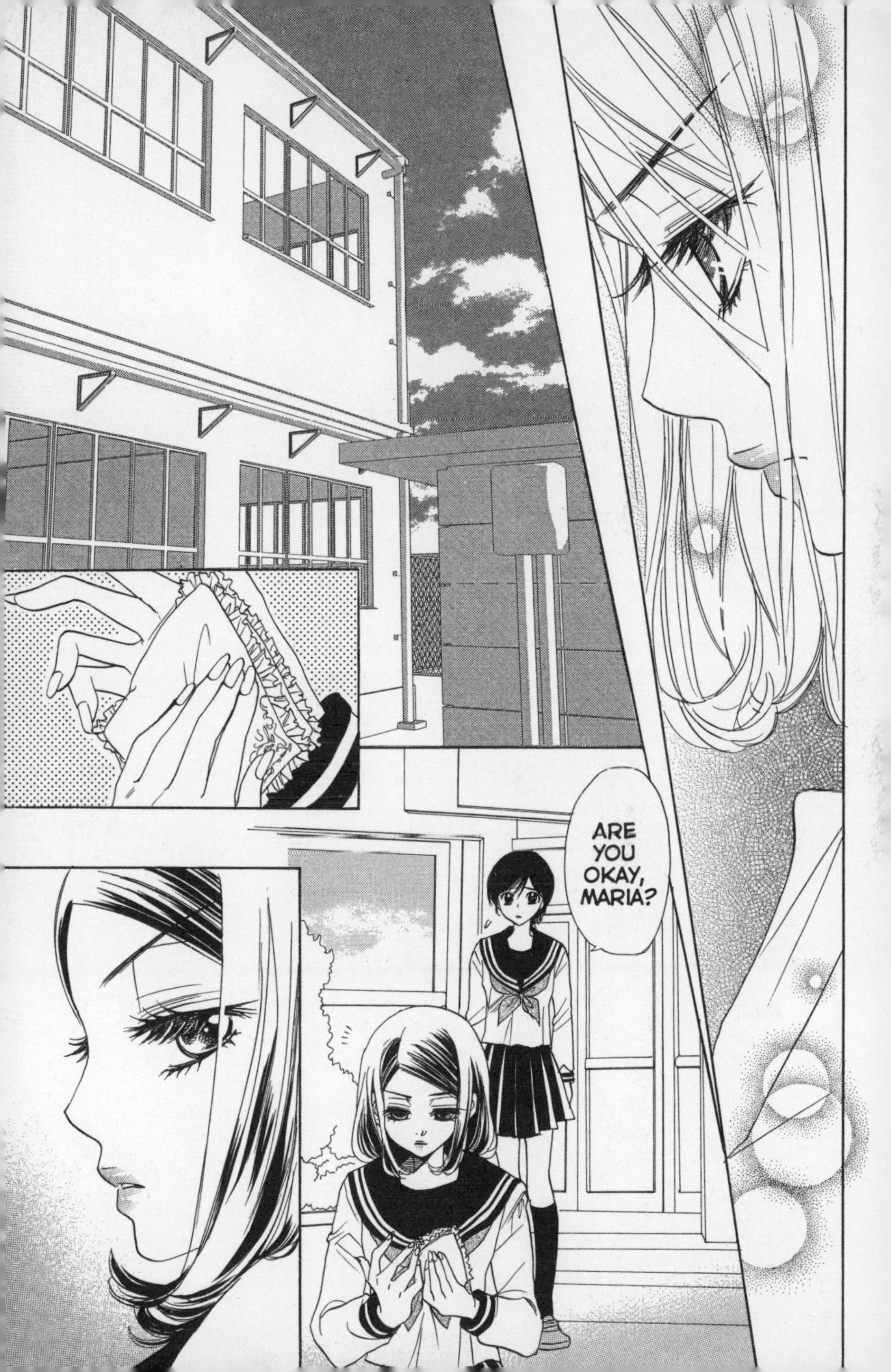
ARE YOU OKAY, MARIA?

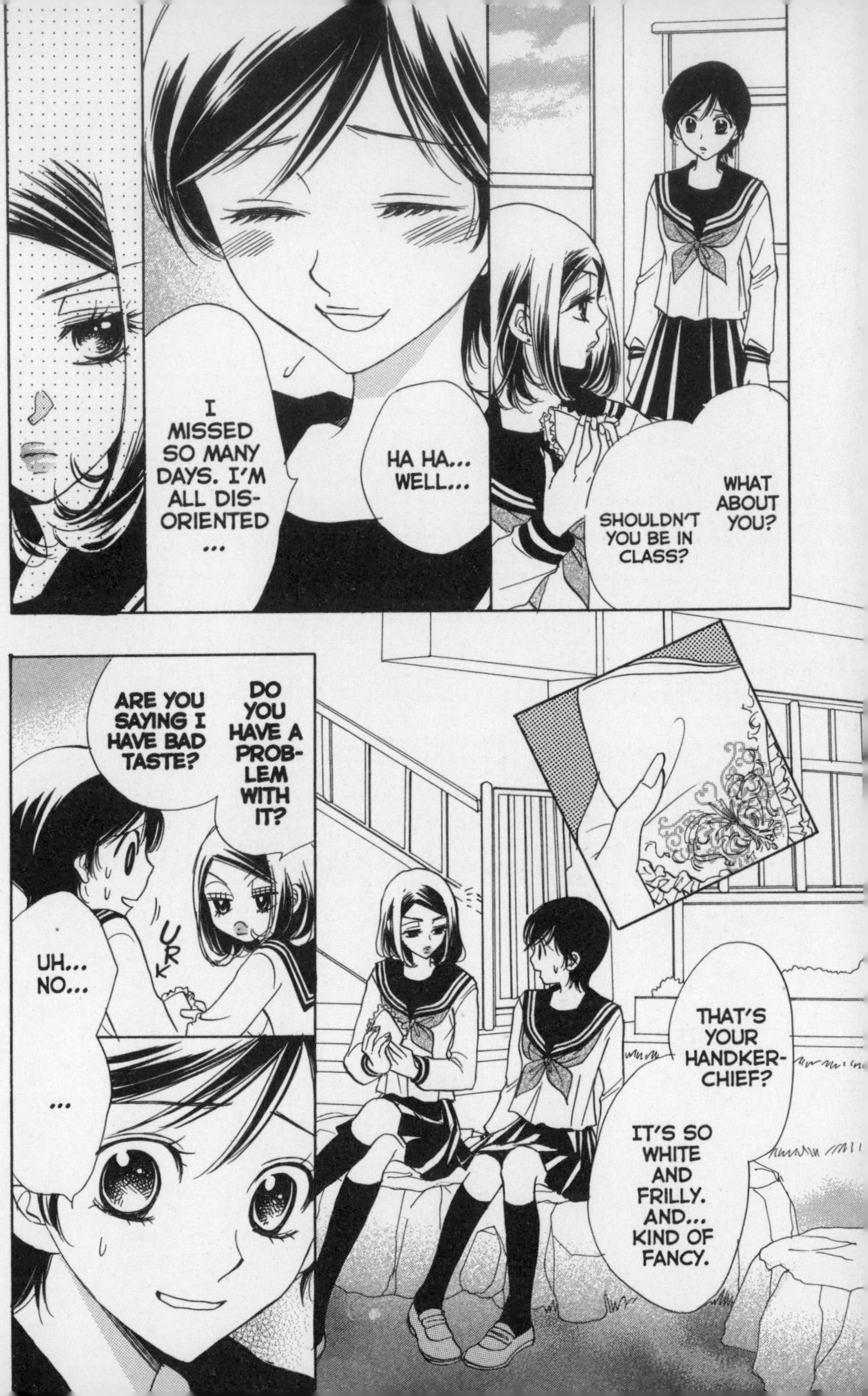
WHAT ABOUT YOU?
SHOULDN'T YOU BE IN CLASS?
HA HA... WELL...
I MISSED SO MANY DAYS. I'M ALL DIS-ORIENTED ...
THAT'S YOUR HANDKER-CHIEF?
IT'S SO WHITE AND FRILLY. AND... KIND OF FANCY.
DO YOU HAVE A PROB-LEM WITH IT?
ARE YOU SAYING I HAVE BAD TASTE?
URK
UH... NO...
...

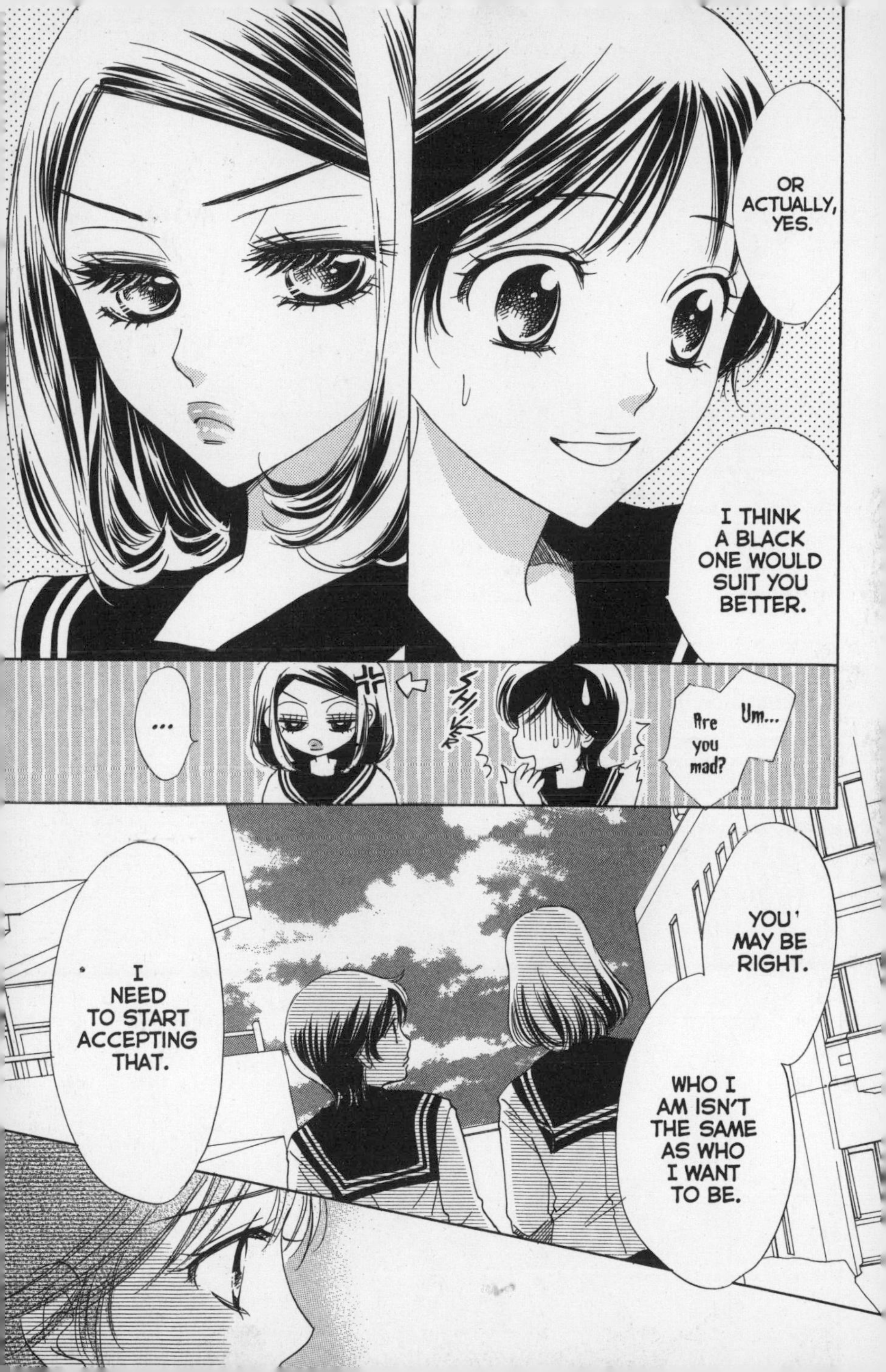
OR ACTUALLY, YES.
I THINK A BLACK ONE WOULD SUIT YOU BETTER.
Um...
Are you mad?
SHIVER
...
YOU MAY BE RIGHT.
WHO I AM ISN'T THE SAME AS WHO I WANT TO BE.
I NEED TO START ACCEPTING THAT.

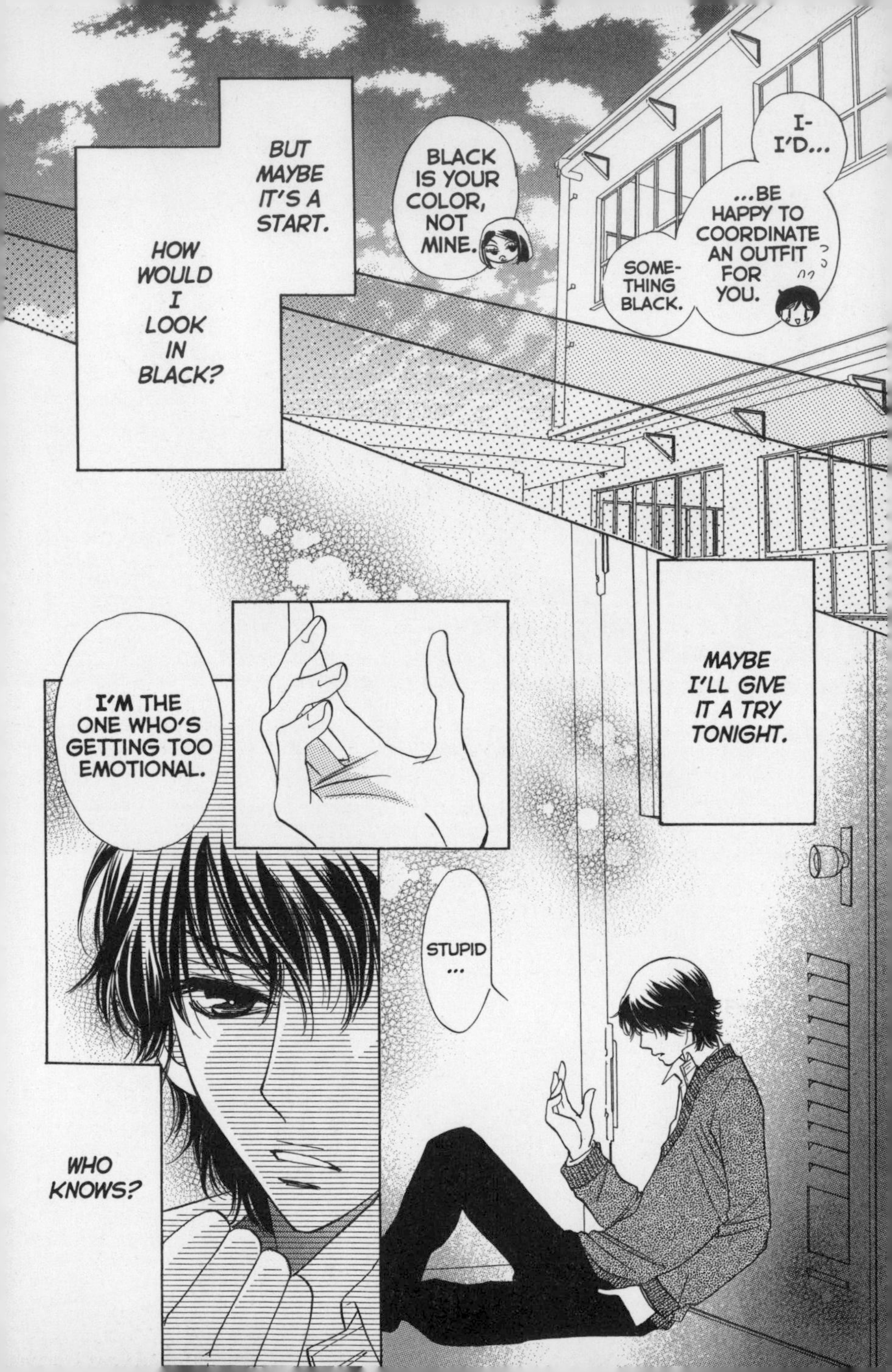
I- I'D...
...BE HAPPY TO COORDINATE AN OUTFIT FOR YOU.
SOME-THING BLACK.
BLACK IS YOUR COLOR, NOT MINE.
BUT MAYBE IT'S A START.
HOW WOULD I LOOK IN BLACK?
MAYBE I'LL GIVE IT A TRY TONIGHT.
STUPID...
I'M THE ONE WHO'S GETTING TOO EMOTIONAL.
WHO KNOWS?

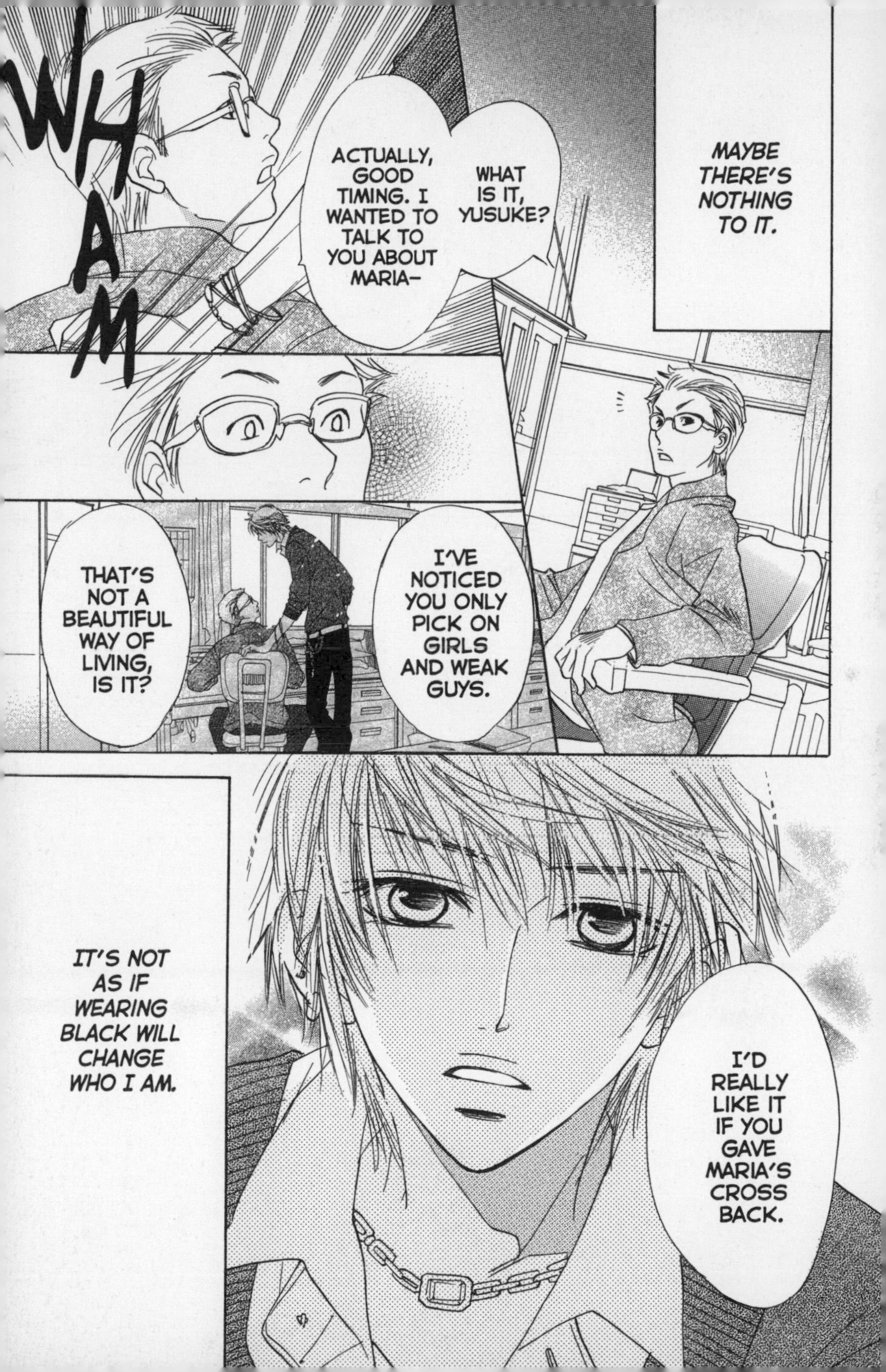
MAYBE THERE'S NOTHING TO IT.
WHAM
WHAT IS IT, YUSUKE?
ACTUALLY, GOOD TIMING. I WANTED TO TALK TO YOU ABOUT MARIA—
I'VE NOTICED YOU ONLY PICK ON GIRLS AND WEAK GUYS.
THAT'S NOT A BEAUTIFUL WAY OF LIVING, IS IT?
I'D REALLY LIKE IT IF YOU GAVE MARIA'S CROSS BACK.
IT'S NOT AS IF WEARING BLACK WILL CHANGE WHO I AM.

A Devil and
Her Love Song

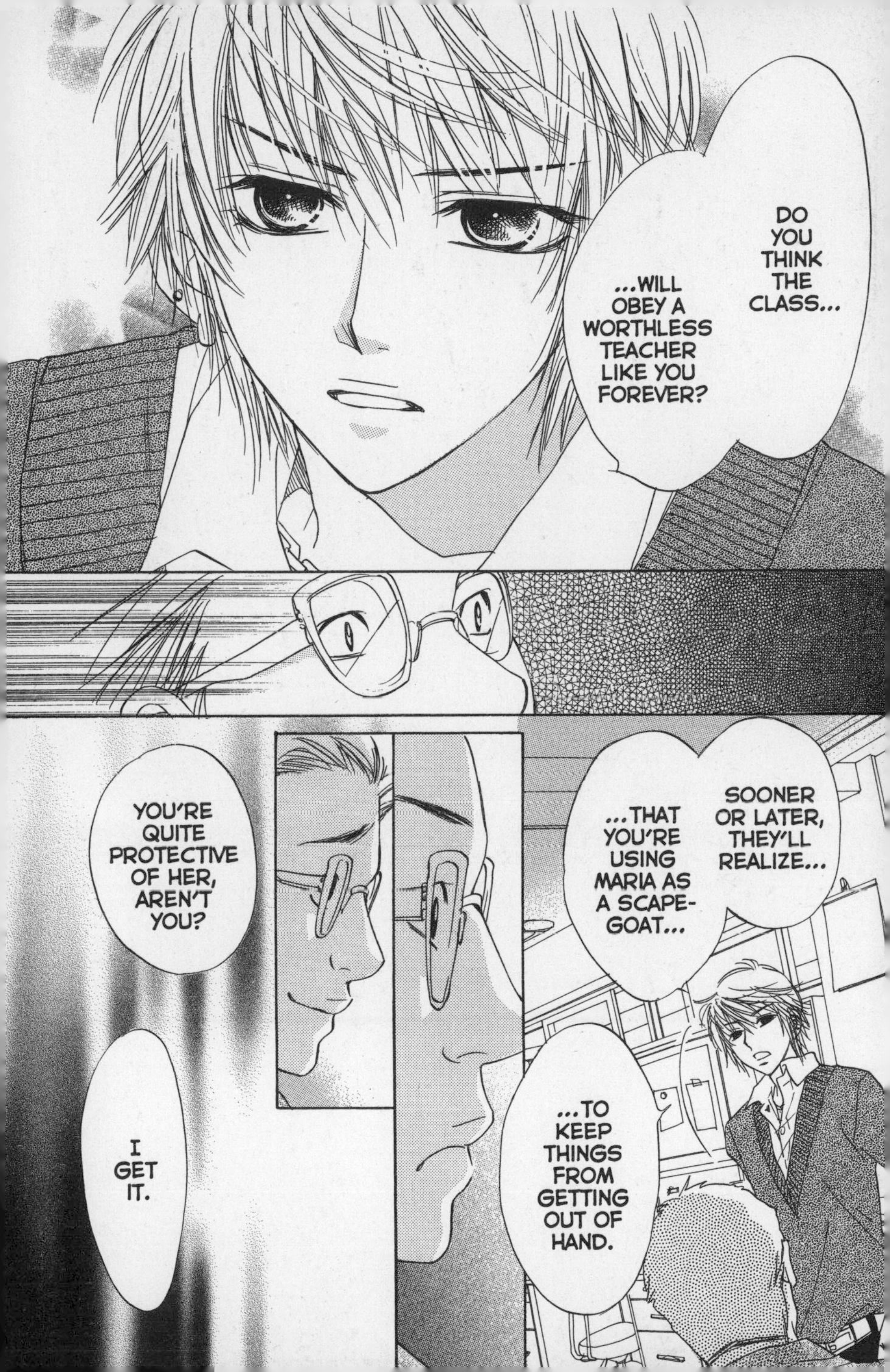
DO YOU THINK THE CLASS...
...WILL OBEY A WORTHLESS TEACHER LIKE YOU FOREVER?
SOONER OR LATER, THEY'LL REALIZE...
...THAT YOU'RE USING MARIA AS A SCAPE-GOAT...
...TO KEEP THINGS FROM GETTING OUT OF HAND.
YOU'RE QUITE PROTECTIVE OF HER, AREN'T YOU?
I GET IT.

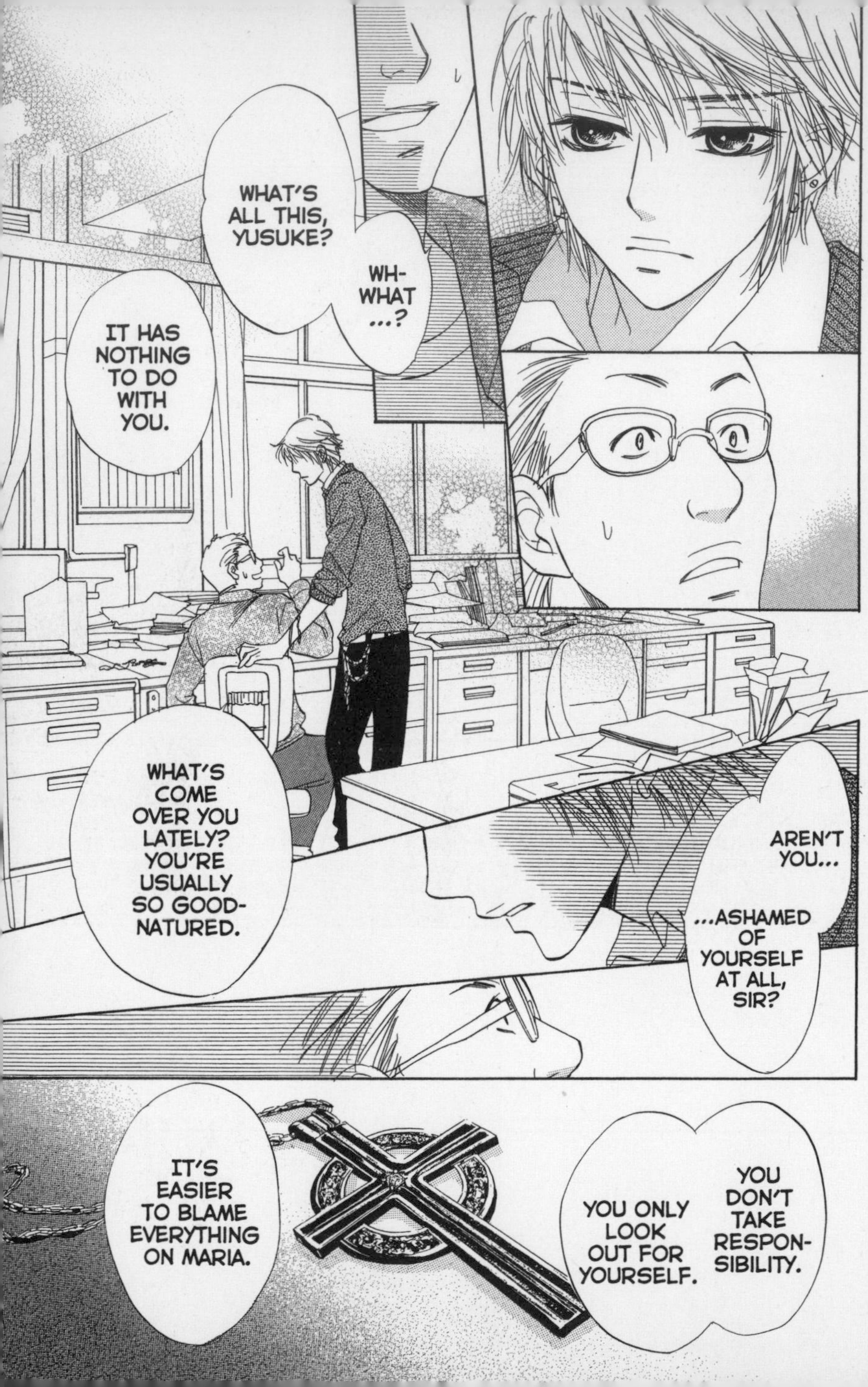
WHAT'S ALL THIS, YUSUKE?
WH-WHAT ...?
IT HAS NOTHING TO DO WITH YOU.
WHAT'S COME OVER YOU LATELY? YOU'RE USUALLY SO GOOD-NATURED.
AREN'T YOU...
...ASHAMED OF YOURSELF AT ALL, SIR?
YOU DON'T TAKE RESPON-SIBILITY.
YOU ONLY LOOK OUT FOR YOURSELF.
IT'S EASIER TO BLAME EVERYTHING ON MARIA.

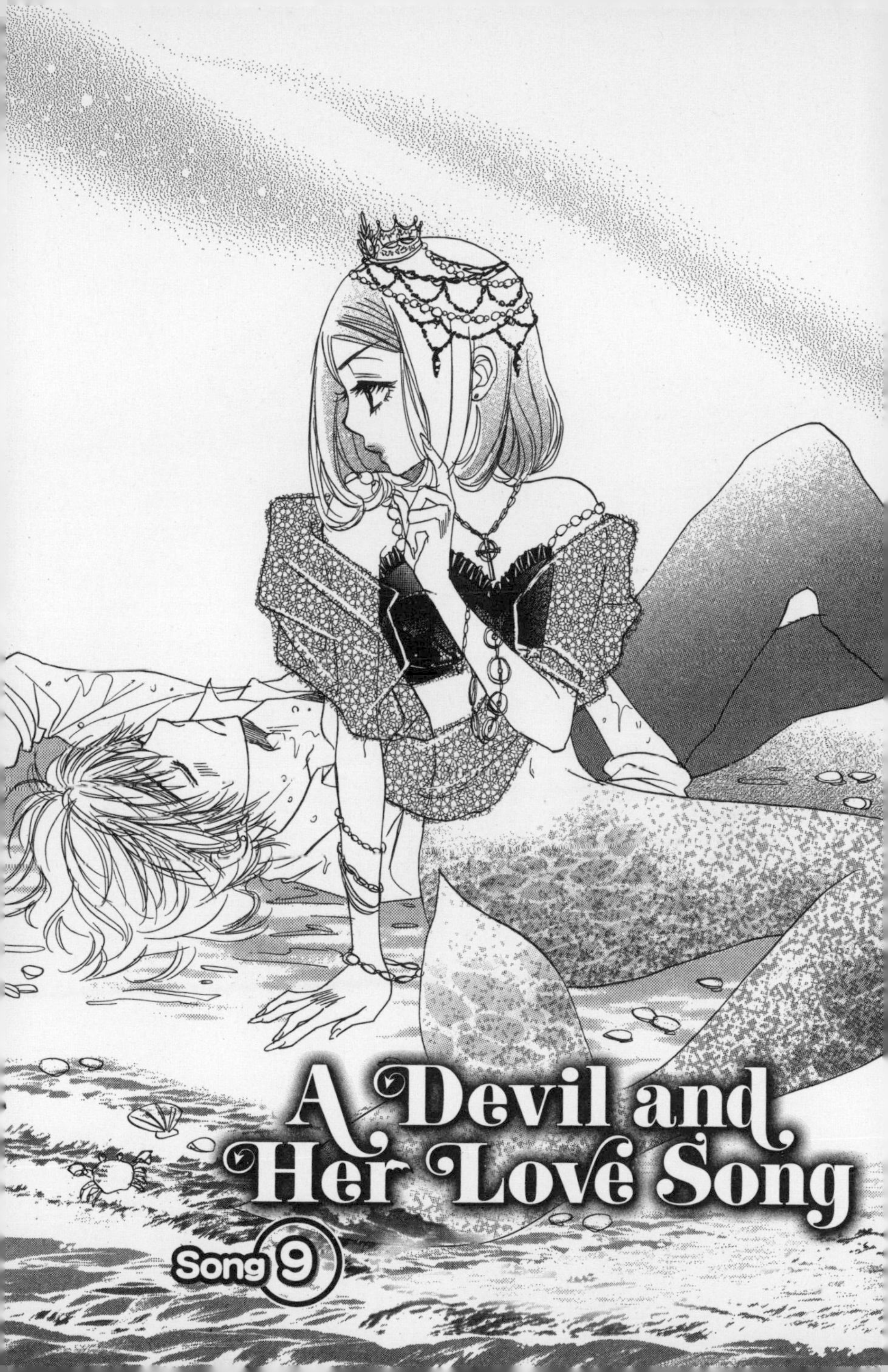
A Devil and Her Love Song
Song 9

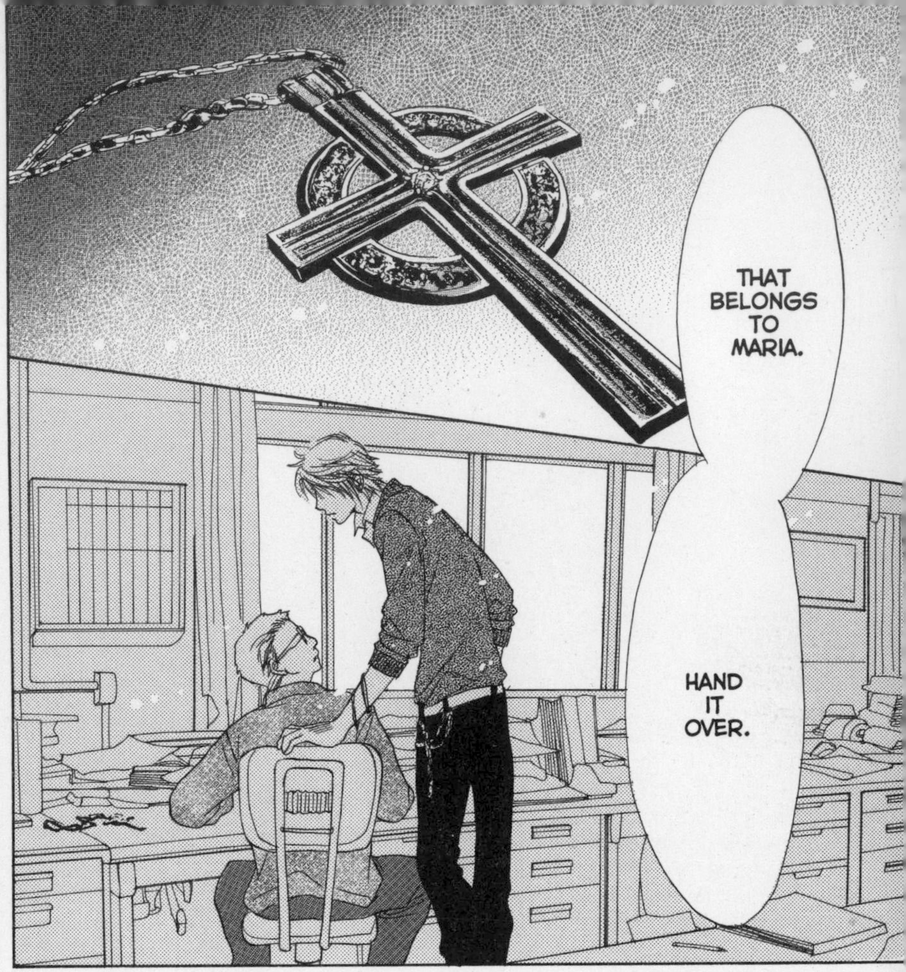
THAT BELONGS TO MARIA.
HAND IT OVER.

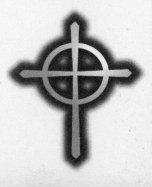

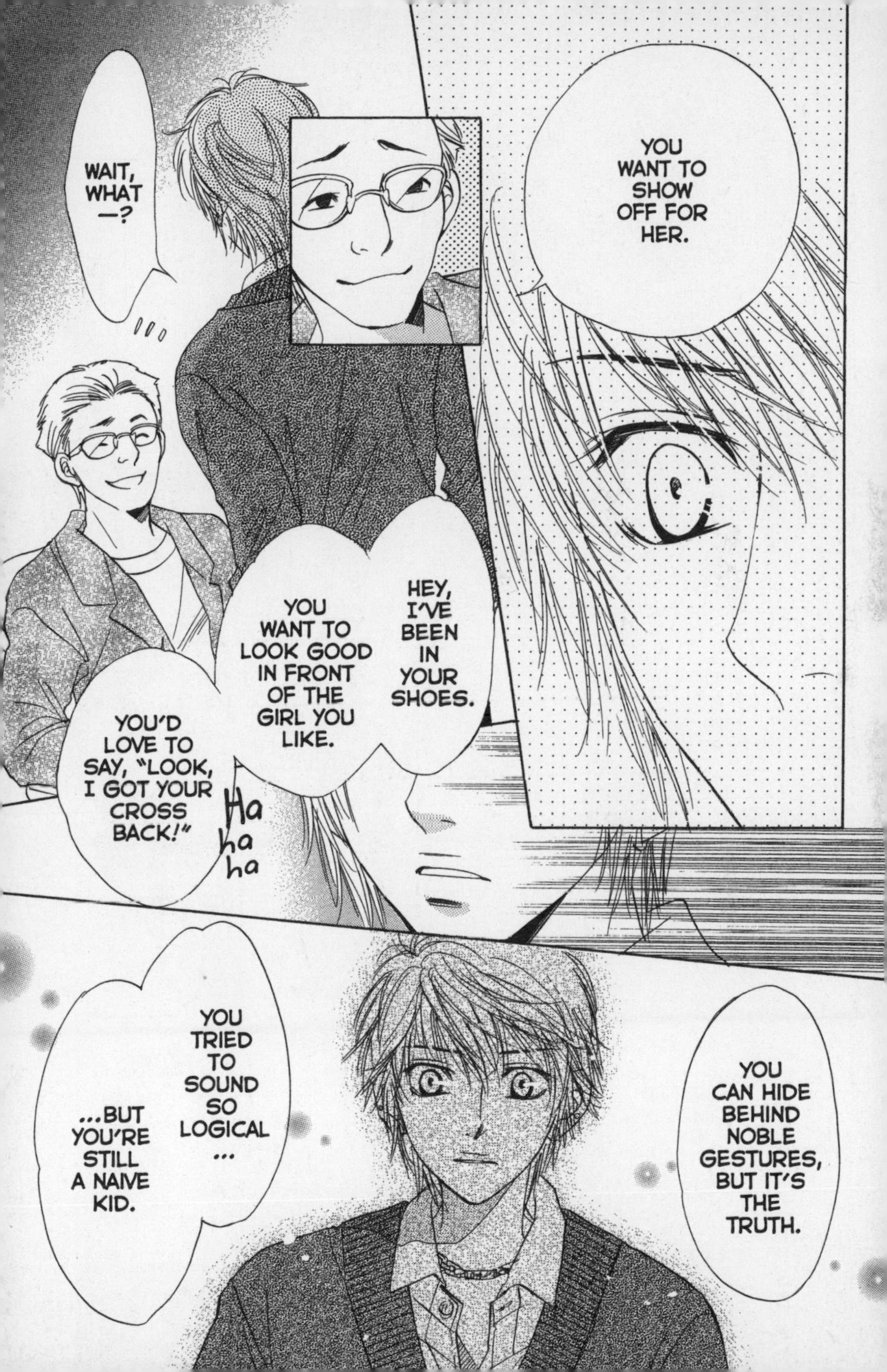
YOU WANT TO SHOW OFF FOR HER.
WAIT, WHAT —?
HEY, I'VE BEEN IN YOUR SHOES.
YOU WANT TO LOOK GOOD IN FRONT OF THE GIRL YOU LIKE.
YOU'D LOVE TO SAY, "LOOK, I GOT YOUR CROSS BACK!"
Ha ha ha
YOU CAN HIDE BEHIND NOBLE GESTURES, BUT IT'S THE TRUTH.
YOU TRIED TO SOUND SO LOGICAL ...
...BUT YOU'RE STILL A NAIVE KID.

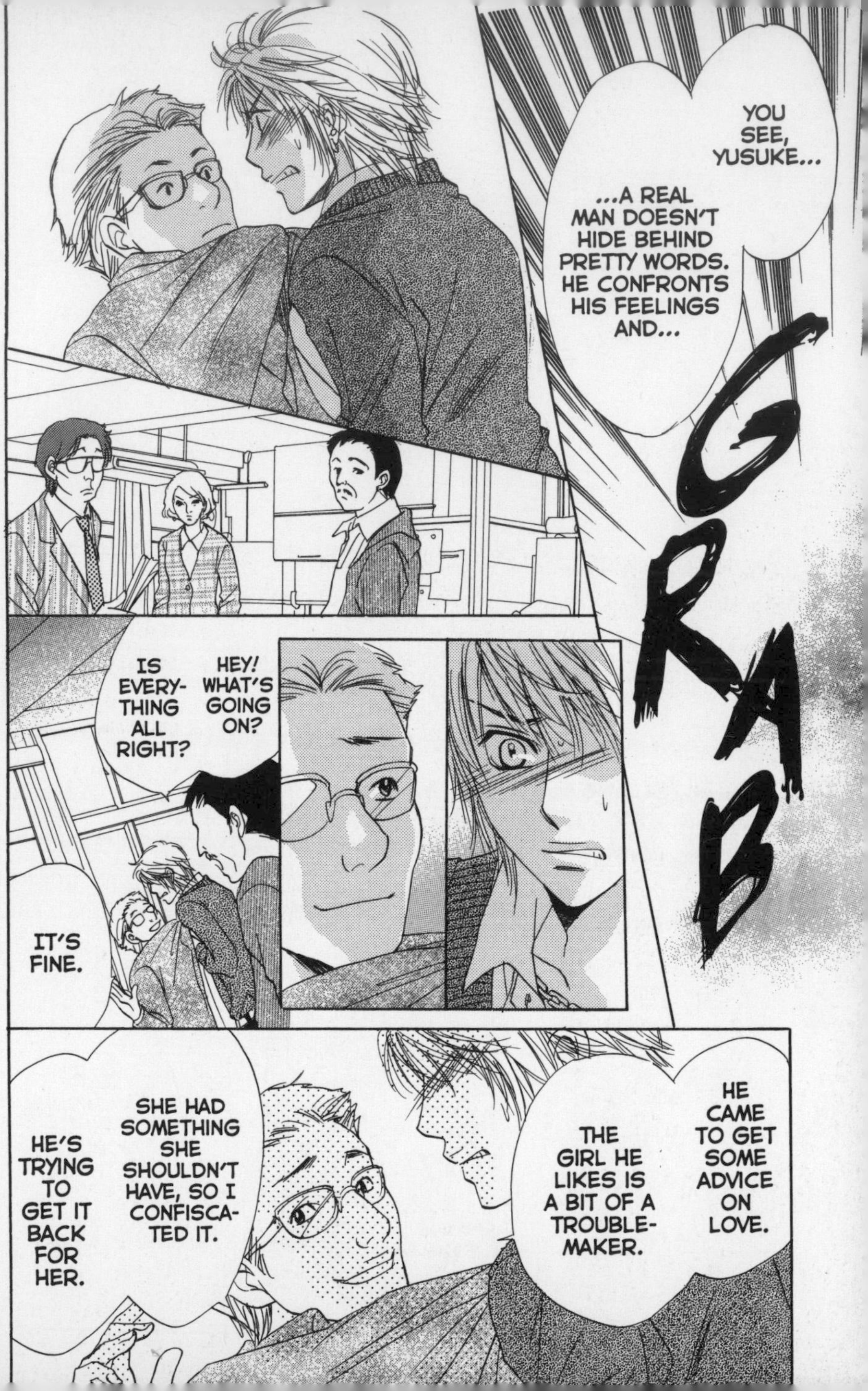
YOU SEE, YUSUKE...
...A REAL MAN DOESN'T HIDE BEHIND PRETTY WORDS. HE CONFRONTS HIS FEELINGS AND...
GRAB
HEY! WHAT'S GOING ON?
IS EVERYTHING ALL RIGHT?
IT'S FINE.
HE CAME TO GET SOME ADVICE ON LOVE.
THE GIRL HE LIKES IS A BIT OF A TROUBLE-MAKER.
SHE HAD SOMETHING SHE SHOULDN'T HAVE, SO I CONFISCA-TED IT.
HE'S TRYING TO GET IT BACK FOR HER.

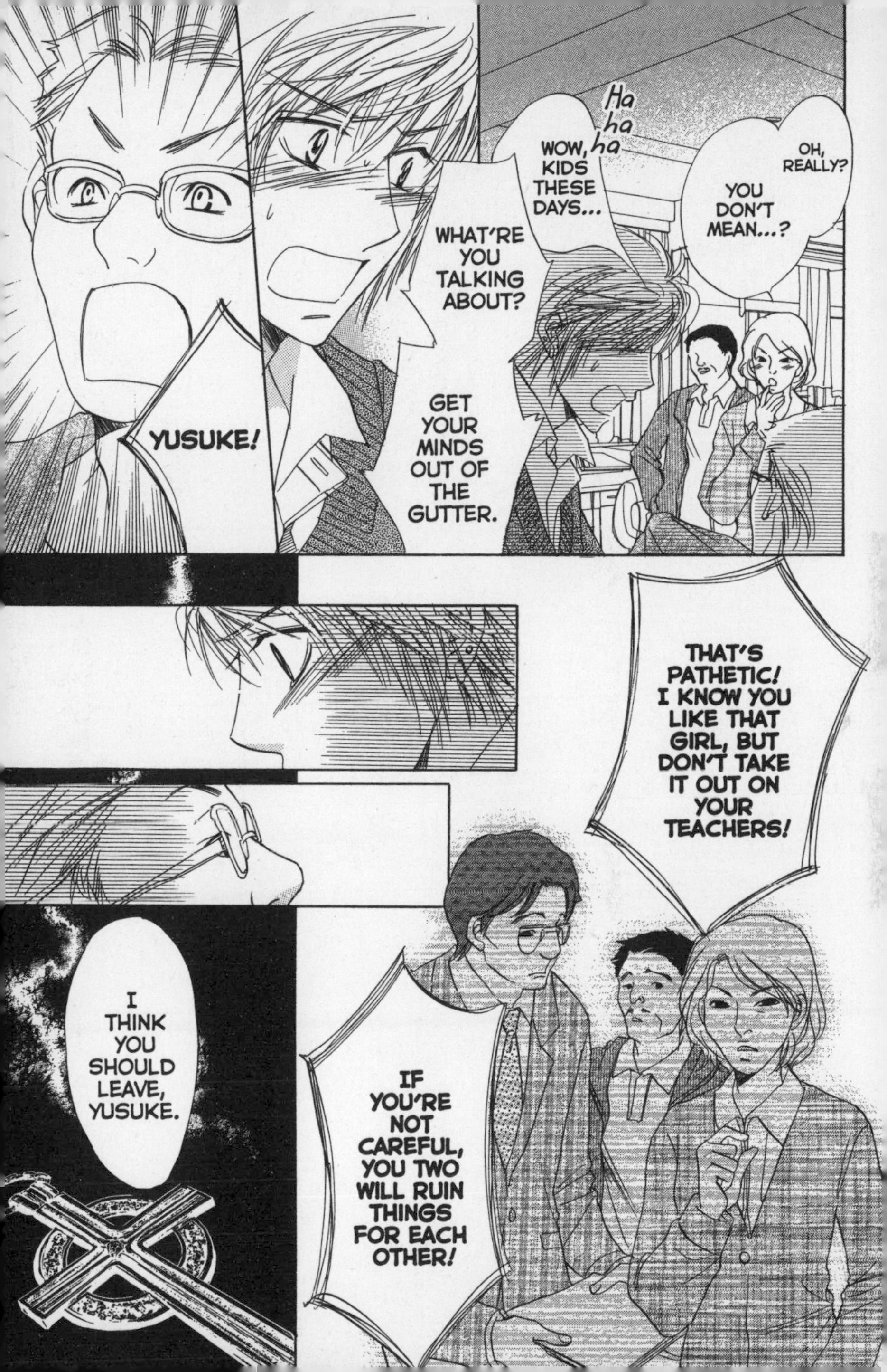
OH, REALLY?
YOU DON'T MEAN...?
Ha ha ha
WOW, KIDS THESE DAYS...
WHAT'RE YOU TALKING ABOUT?
GET YOUR MINDS OUT OF THE GUTTER.
YUSUKE!
THAT'S PATHETIC! I KNOW YOU LIKE THAT GIRL, BUT DON'T TAKE IT OUT ON YOUR TEACHERS!
IF YOU'RE NOT CAREFUL, YOU TWO WILL RUIN THINGS FOR EACH OTHER!
I THINK YOU SHOULD LEAVE, YUSUKE.

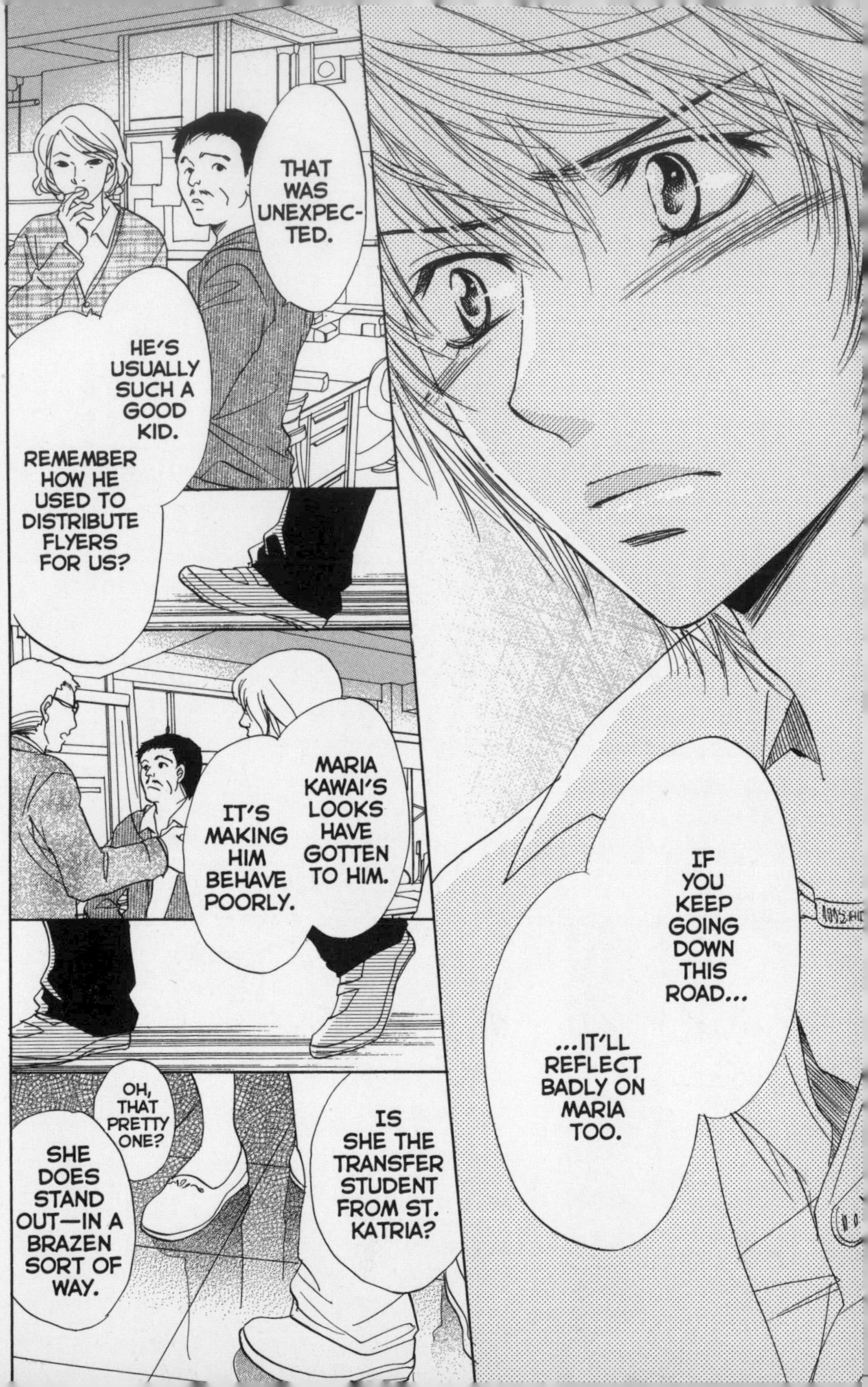
IF YOU KEEP GOING DOWN THIS ROAD...
...IT'LL REFLECT BADLY ON MARIA TOO.
THAT WAS UNEXPEC-TED.
HE'S USUALLY SUCH A GOOD KID.
REMEMBER HOW HE USED TO DISTRIBUTE FLYERS FOR US?
MARIA KAWAI'S LOOKS HAVE GOTTEN TO HIM.
IT'S MAKING HIM BEHAVE POORLY.
IS SHE THE TRANSFER STUDENT FROM ST. KATRIA?
OH, THAT PRETTY ONE?
SHE DOES STAND OUT—IN A BRAZEN SORT OF WAY.

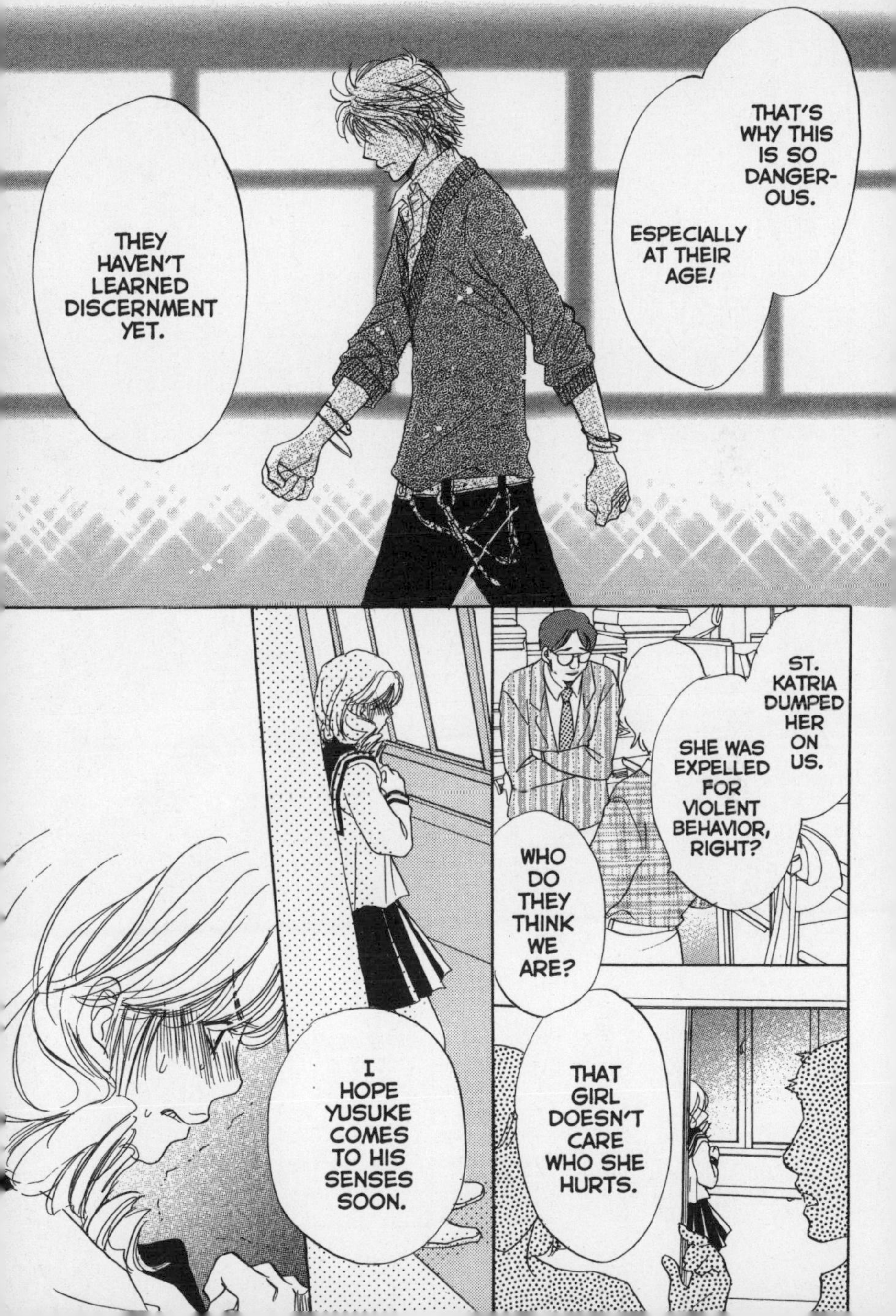
THAT'S WHY THIS IS SO DANGER-OUS.
ESPECIALLY AT THEIR AGE!
THEY HAVEN'T LEARNED DISCERNMENT YET.
ST. KATRIA DUMPED HER ON US.
SHE WAS EXPELLED FOR VIOLENT BEHAVIOR, RIGHT?
WHO DO THEY THINK WE ARE?
THAT GIRL DOESN'T CARE WHO SHE HURTS.
I HOPE YUSUKE COMES TO HIS SENSES SOON.

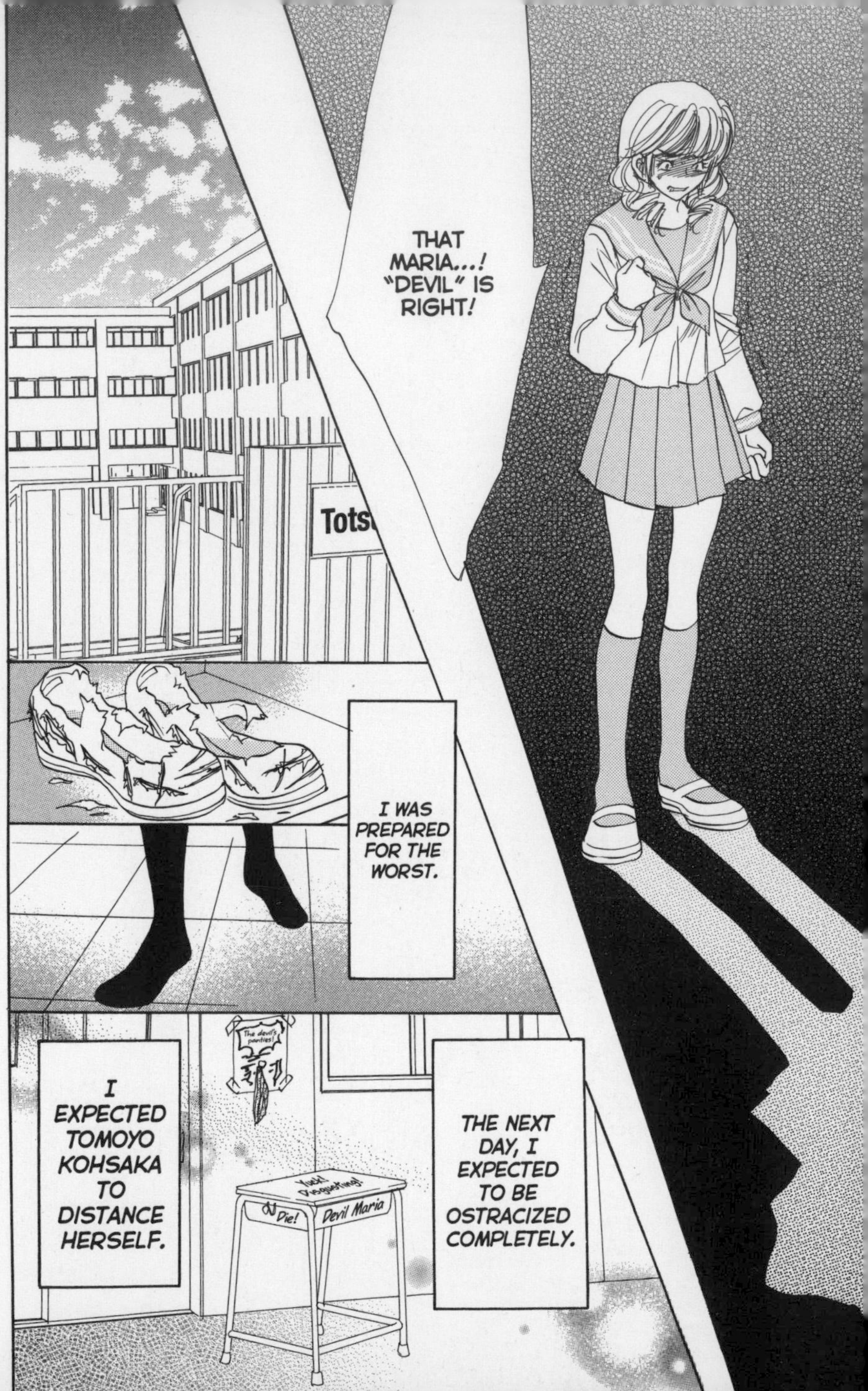
THAT MARIA...! "DEVIL" IS RIGHT!
I WAS PREPARED FOR THE WORST.
THE NEXT DAY, I EXPECTED TO BE OSTRACIZED COMPLETELY.
I EXPECTED TOMOYO KOHSAKA TO DISTANCE HERSELF.
The devil's panties!
Yuck! Disgusting!
Die!
Devil Maria

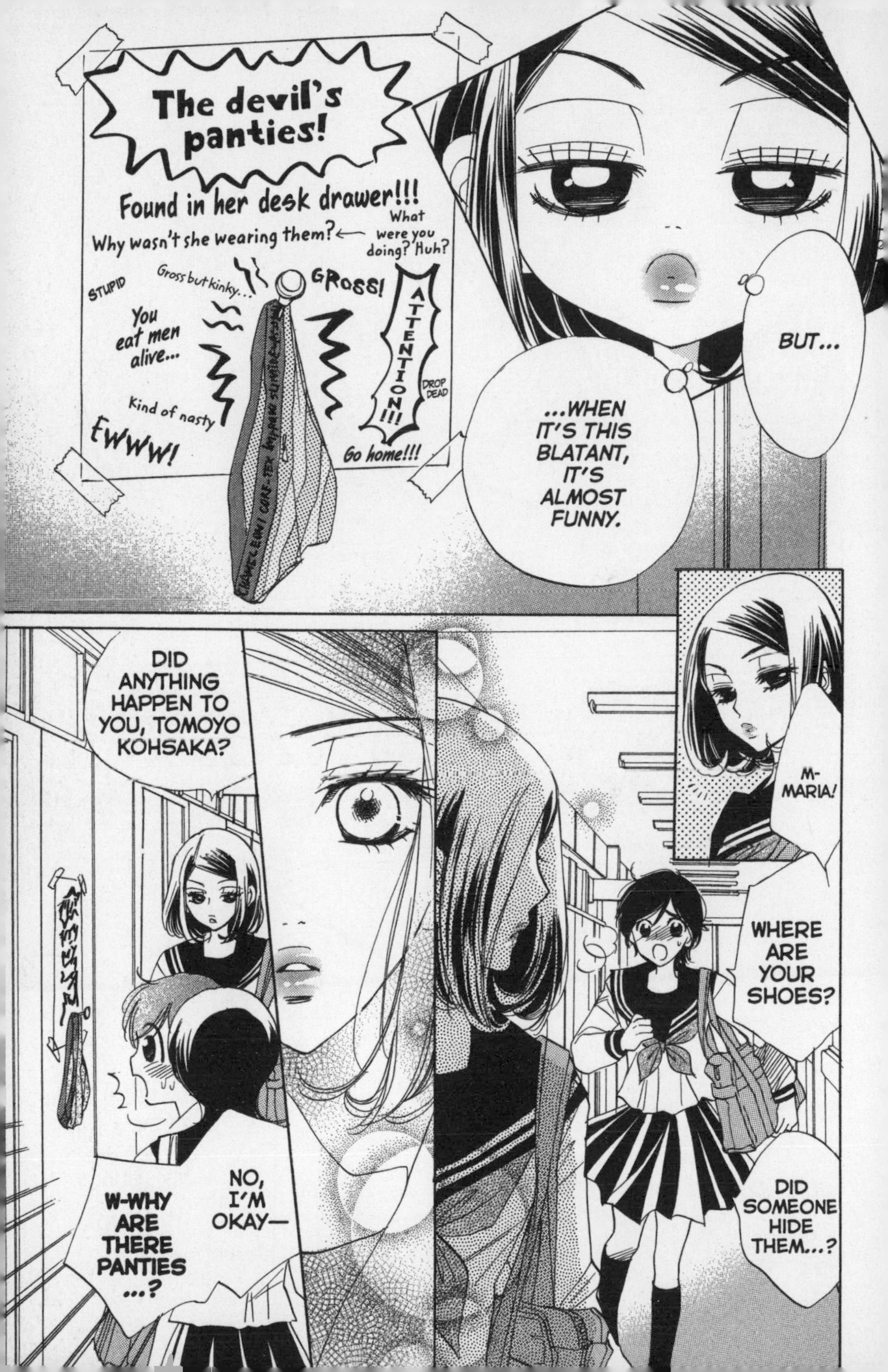
BUT...
...WHEN IT'S THIS BLATANT, IT'S ALMOST FUNNY.
The devil's panties!
Found in her desk drawer!!!
What were you doing? Huh?
Why wasn't she wearing them?
GROSS!
Gross but kinky...
STUPID
ATTENTION!!!
You eat men alive...
DROP DEAD
Kind of nasty
EWWW!
Go home!!!
M-MARIA!
WHERE ARE YOUR SHOES?
DID SOMEONE HIDE THEM...?
DID ANYTHING HAPPEN TO YOU, TOMOYO KOHSAKA?
NO, I'M OKAY—
W-WHY ARE THERE PANTIES ...?

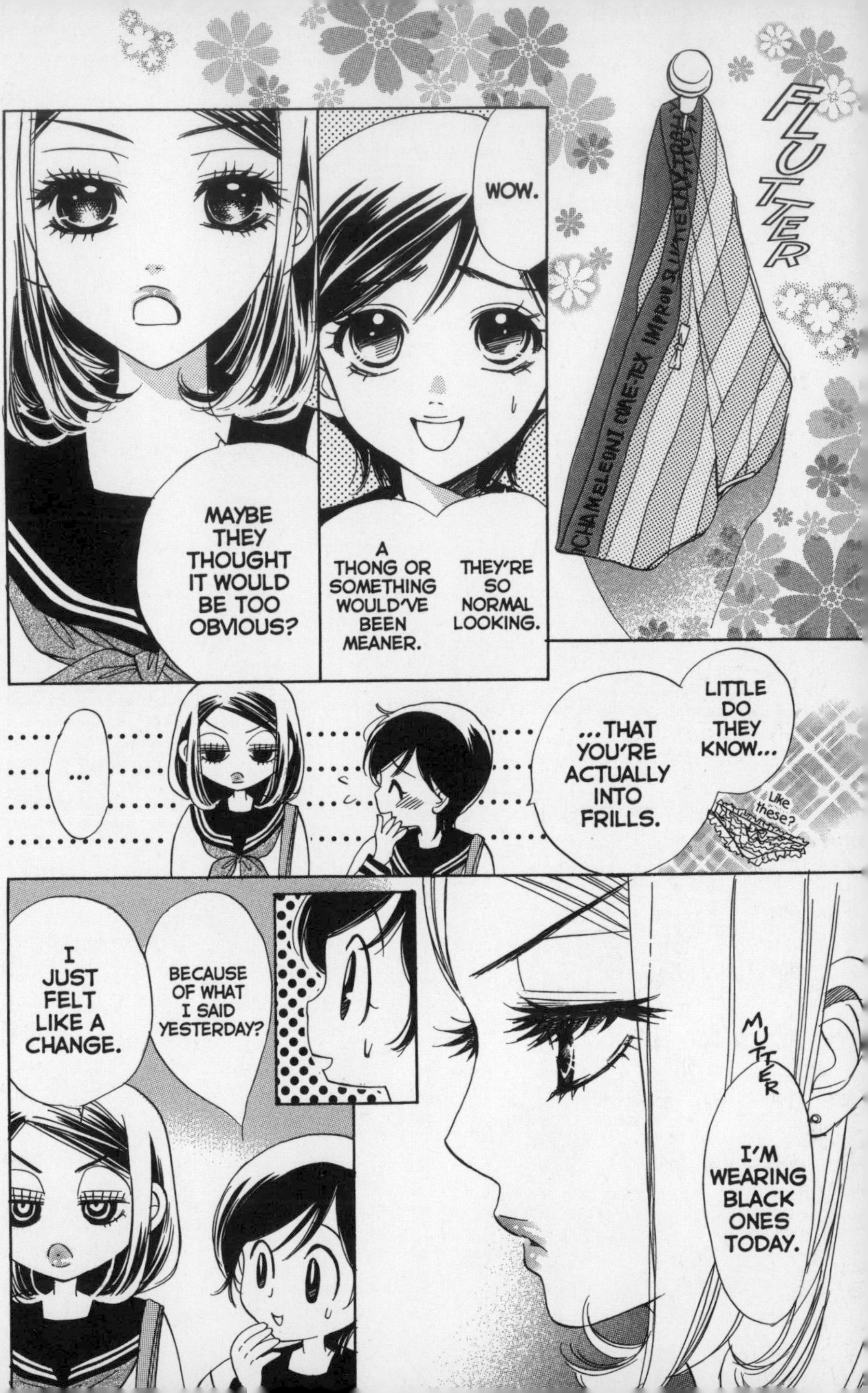
FLUTTER
WOW.
THEY'RE SO NORMAL LOOKING.
A THONG OR SOMETHING WOULD'VE BEEN MEANER.
MAYBE THEY THOUGHT IT WOULD BE TOO OBVIOUS?
LITTLE DO THEY KNOW...
...THAT YOU'RE ACTUALLY INTO FRILLS.
Like these?
...
MUTTER
I'M WEARING BLACK ONES TODAY.
BECAUSE OF WHAT I SAID YESTERDAY?
I JUST FELT LIKE A CHANGE.

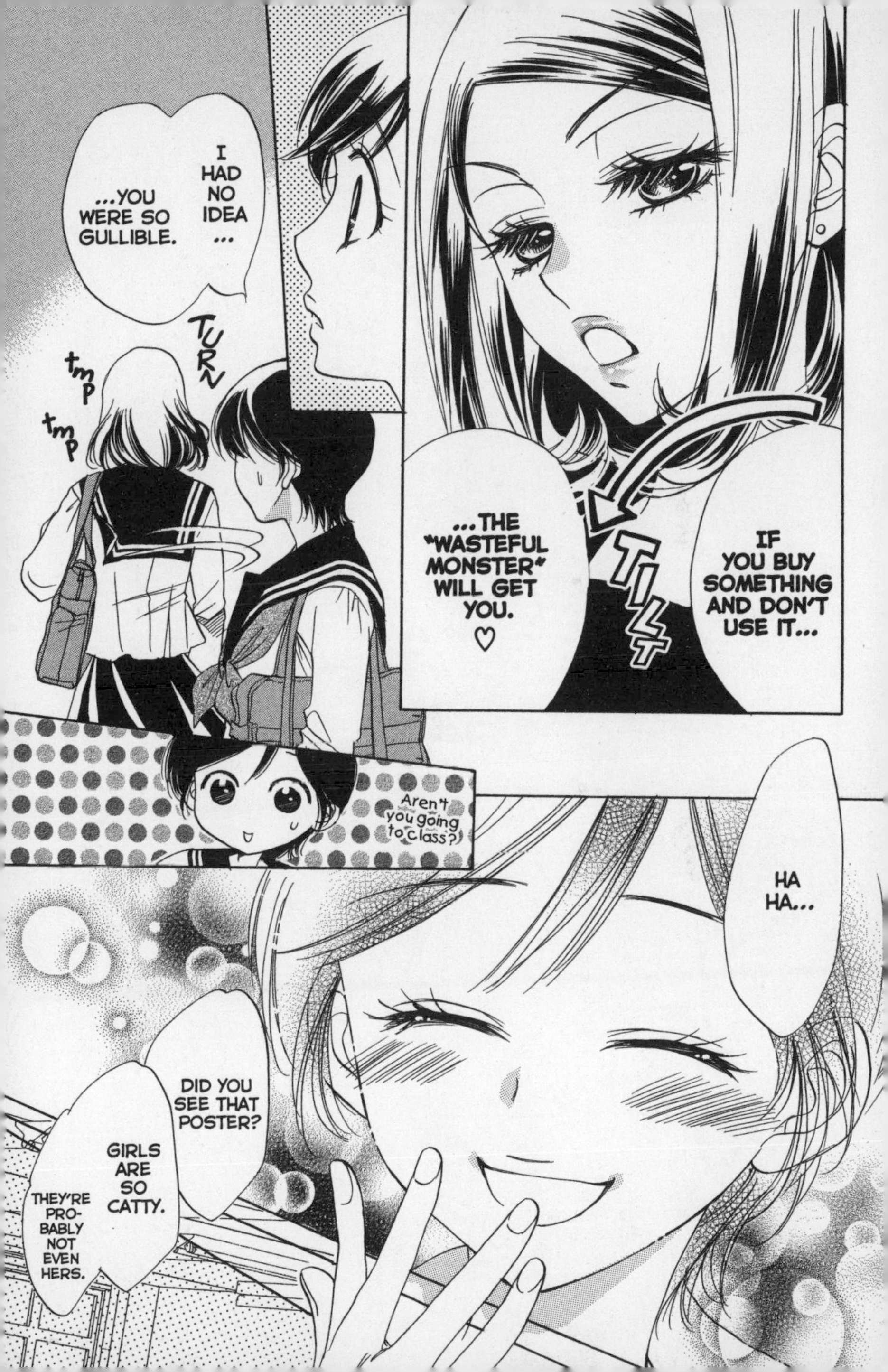
IF YOU BUY SOMETHING AND DON'T USE IT...
...THE "WASTEFUL MONSTER" WILL GET YOU. ♡
TILT
I HAD NO IDEA...
...YOU WERE SO GULLIBLE.
TURN
tmp
tmp
Aren't you going to class?
HA HA...
DID YOU SEE THAT POSTER?
GIRLS ARE SO CATTY.
THEY'RE PRO-BABLY NOT EVEN HERS.

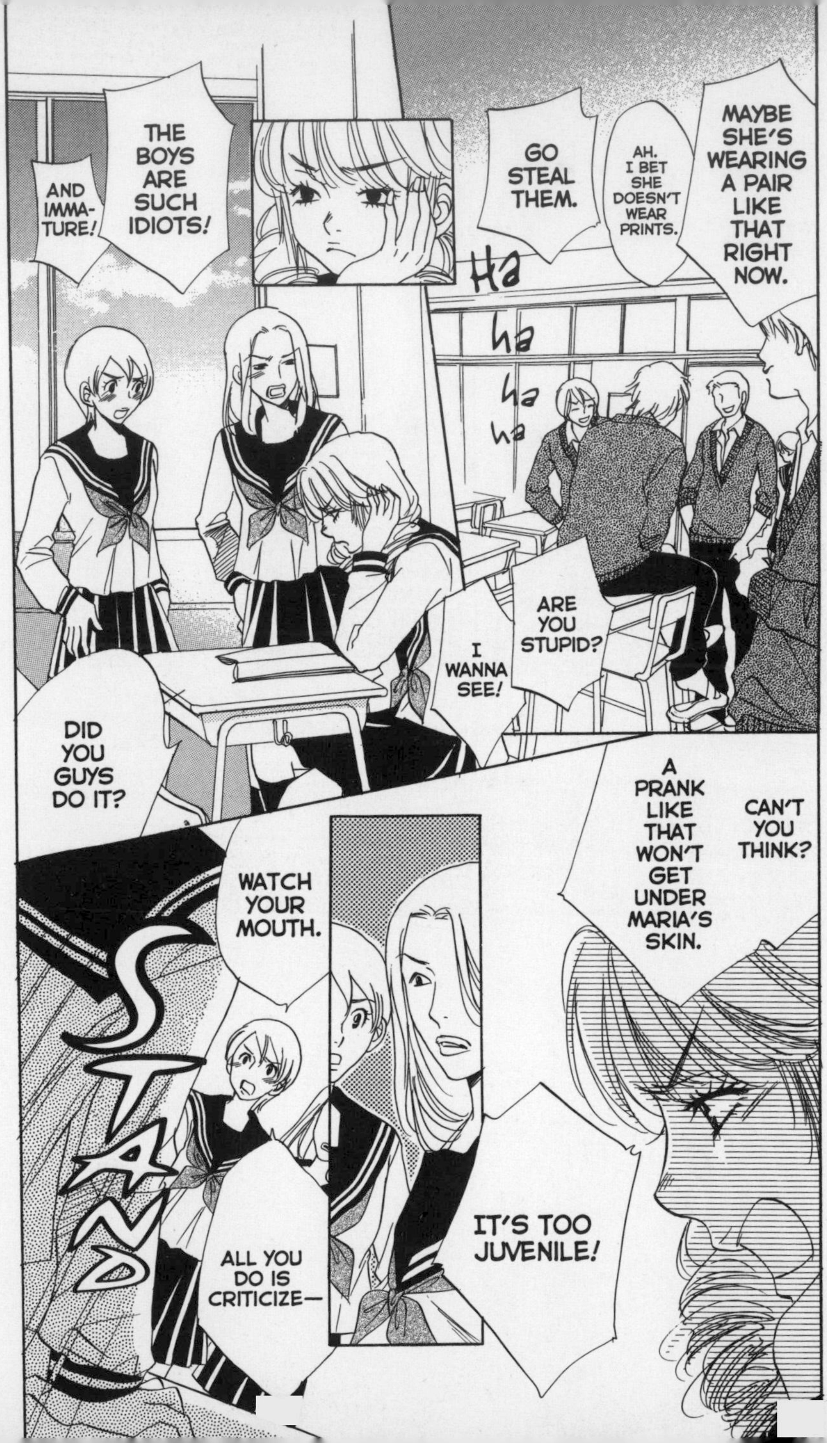
MAYBE SHE'S WEARING A PAIR LIKE THAT RIGHT NOW.
AH. I BET SHE DOESN'T WEAR PRINTS.
GO STEAL THEM.
Ha ha ha ha
ARE YOU STUPID?
I WANNA SEE!
THE BOYS ARE SUCH IDIOTS!
AND IMMA-TURE!
DID YOU GUYS DO IT?
CAN'T YOU THINK?
A PRANK LIKE THAT WON'T GET UNDER MARIA'S SKIN.
IT'S TOO JUVENILE!
WATCH YOUR MOUTH.
ALL YOU DO IS CRITICIZE—
STAND

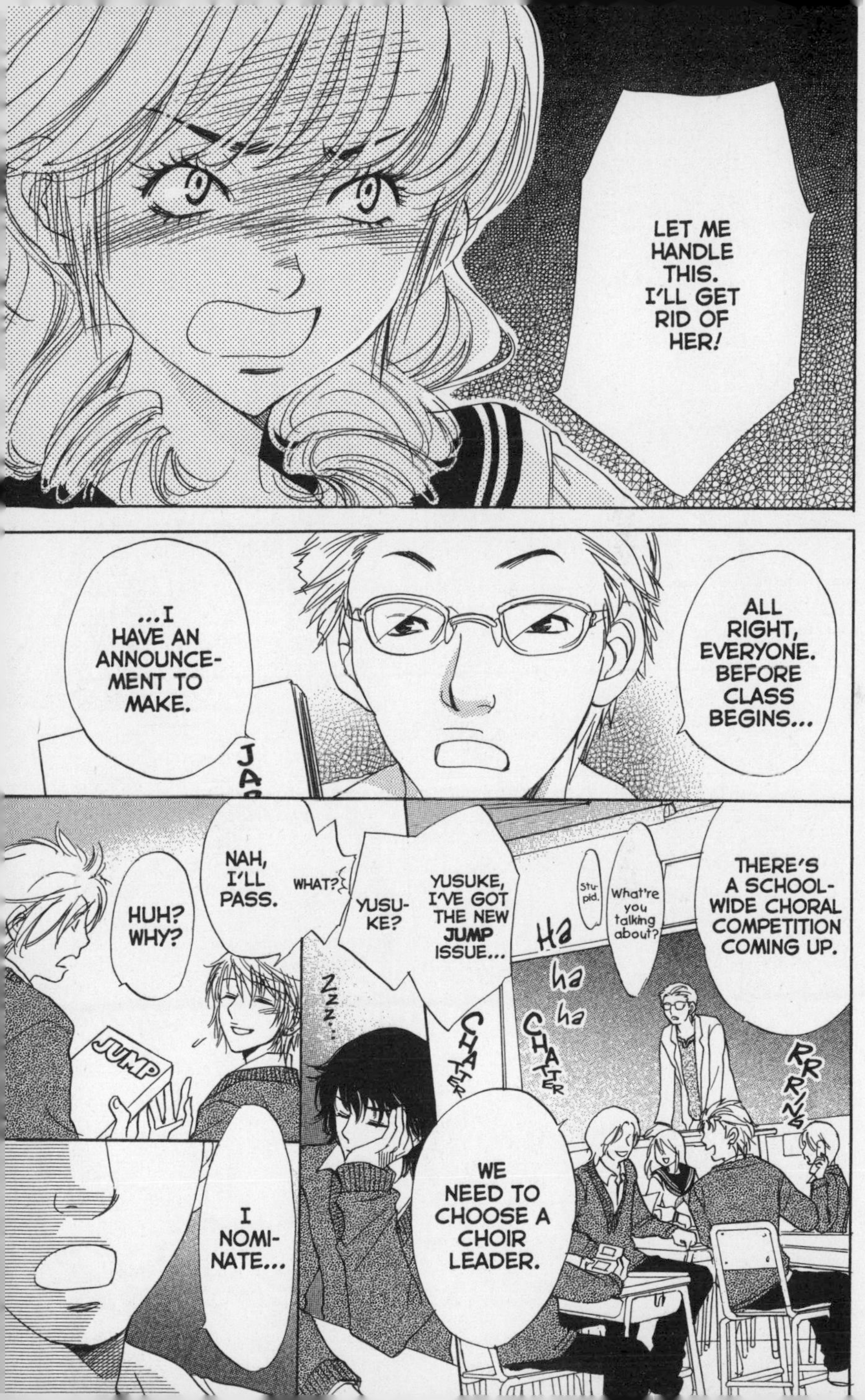
LET ME HANDLE THIS. I'LL GET RID OF HER!
ALL RIGHT, EVERYONE. BEFORE CLASS BEGINS...
...I HAVE AN ANNOUNCEMENT TO MAKE.
THERE'S A SCHOOL-WIDE CHORAL COMPETITION COMING UP.
RRRING
What're you talking about?
Stu-pid.
Ha ha ha
CHATTER CHATTER
YUSUKE, I'VE GOT THE NEW JUMP ISSUE...
YUSU-KE?
WHAT?
Zzz...
WE NEED TO CHOOSE A CHOIR LEADER.
NAH, I'LL PASS.
HUH? WHY?
JUMP
I NOMI-NATE...

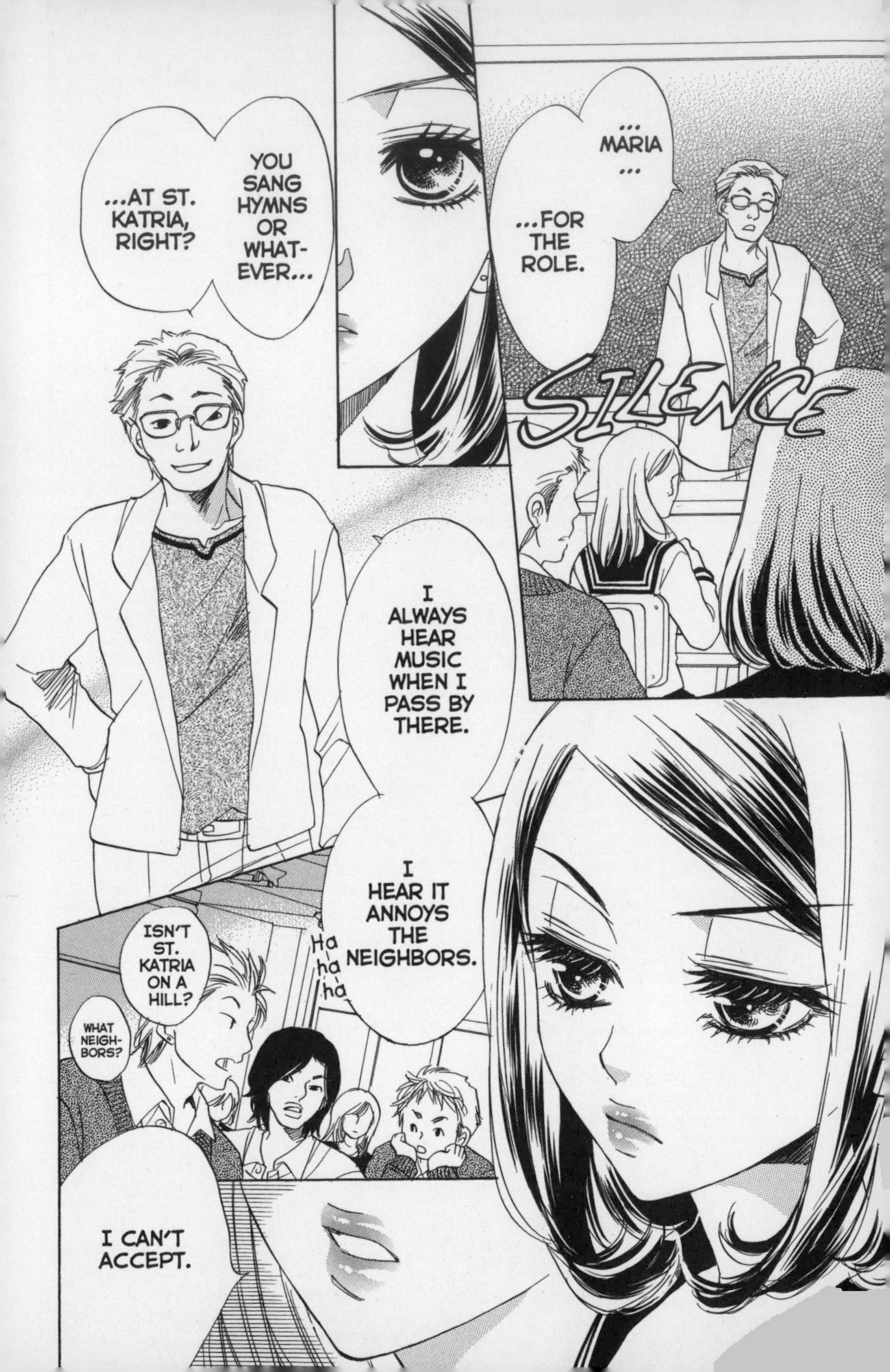
...MARIA...
...FOR THE ROLE.
SILENCE
YOU SANG HYMNS OR WHATEVER...
...AT ST. KATRIA, RIGHT?
I ALWAYS HEAR MUSIC WHEN I PASS BY THERE.
I HEAR IT ANNOYS THE NEIGHBORS.
Ha ha ha
ISN'T ST. KATRIA ON A HILL?
WHAT NEIGHBORS?
I CAN'T ACCEPT.

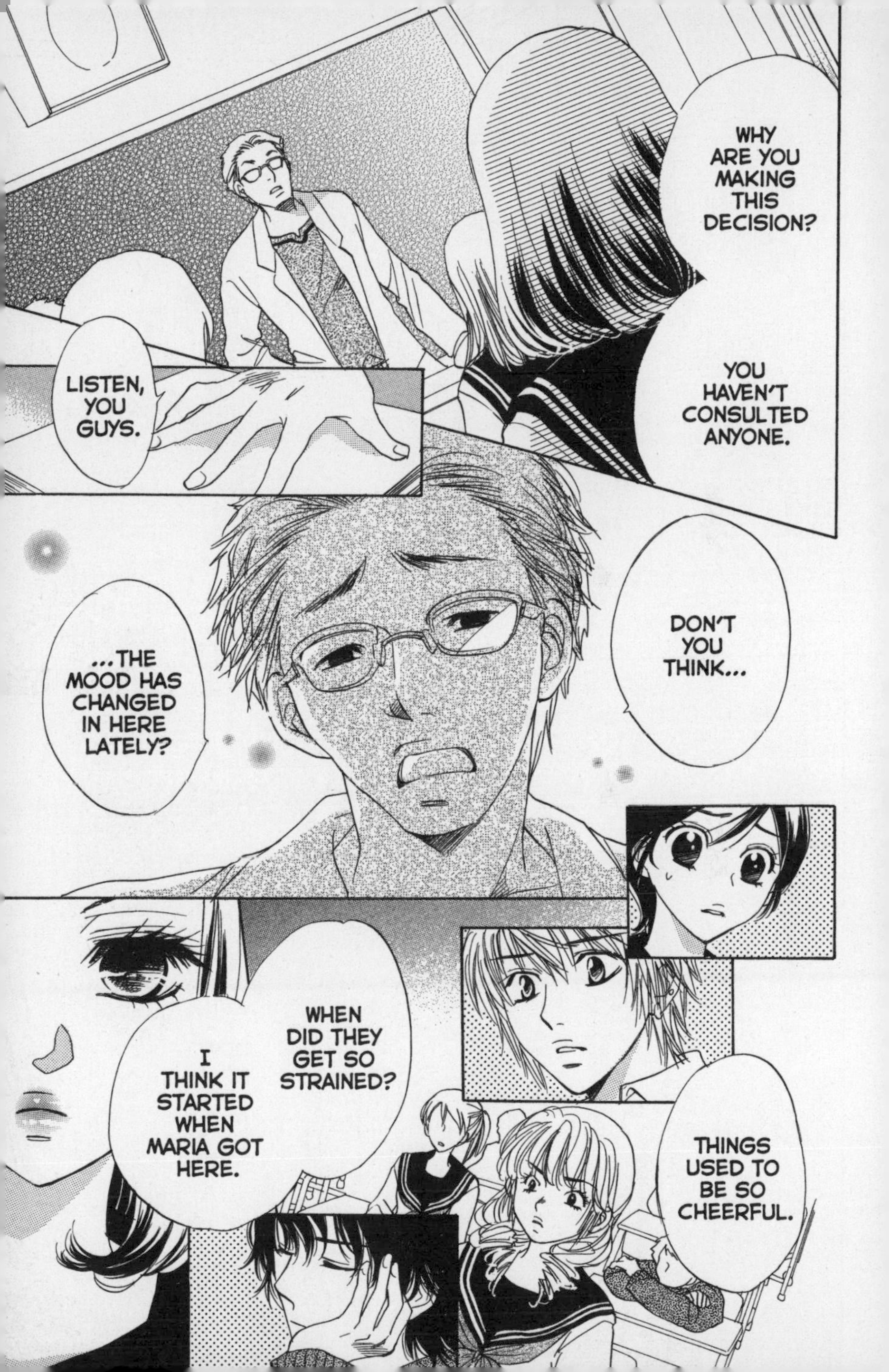
WHY ARE YOU MAKING THIS DECISION?
YOU HAVEN'T CONSULTED ANYONE.
LISTEN, YOU GUYS.
DON'T YOU THINK...
...THE MOOD HAS CHANGED IN HERE LATELY?
THINGS USED TO BE SO CHEERFUL.
WHEN DID THEY GET SO STRAINED?
I THINK IT STARTED WHEN MARIA GOT HERE.

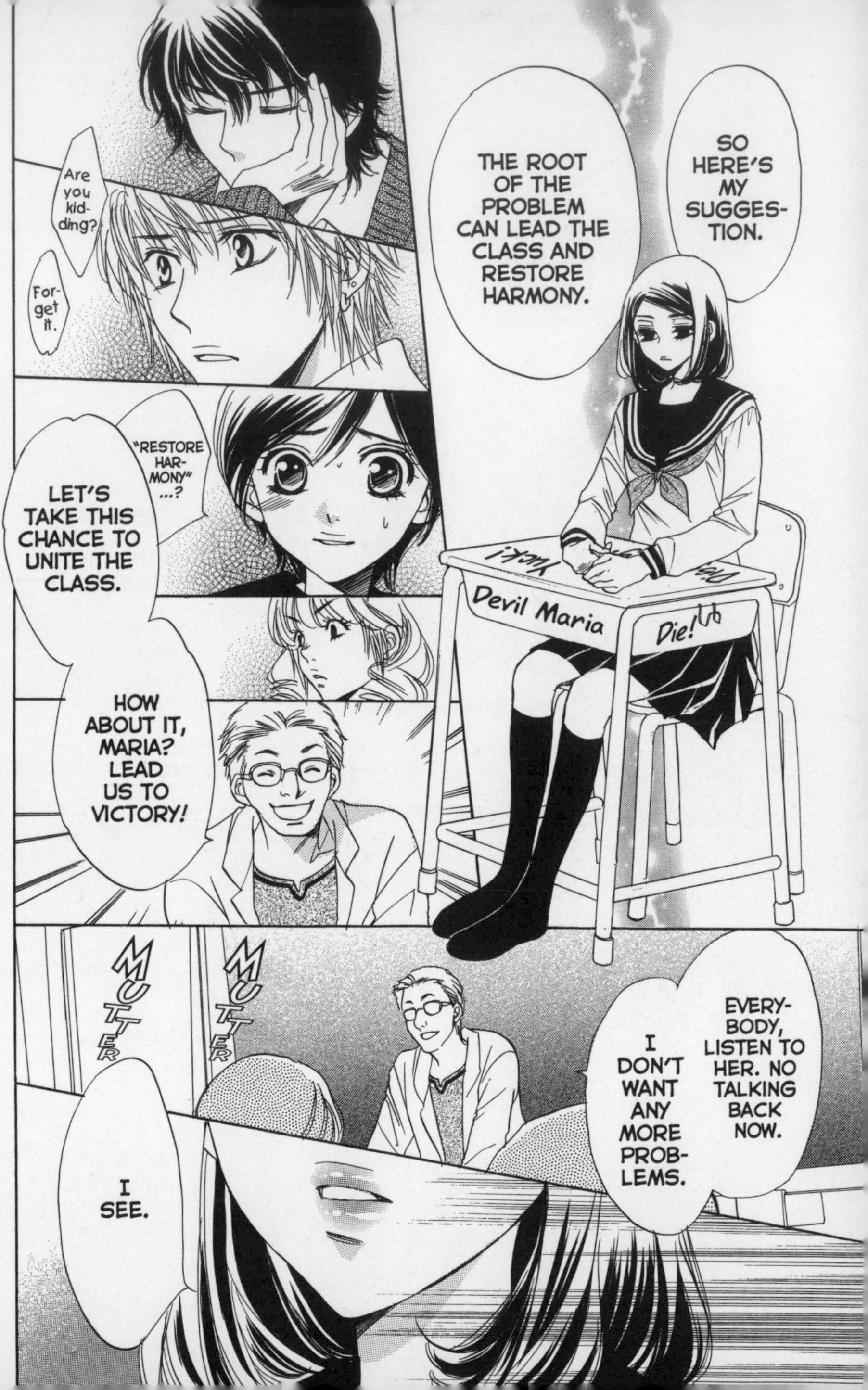
SO HERE'S MY SUGGESTION.
THE ROOT OF THE PROBLEM CAN LEAD THE CLASS AND RESTORE HARMONY.
Yuck!
Devil Maria
Die!
Are you kidding?
Forget it.
"RESTORE HARMONY"...?
LET'S TAKE THIS CHANCE TO UNITE THE CLASS.
HOW ABOUT IT, MARIA? LEAD US TO VICTORY!
EVERYBODY, LISTEN TO HER. NO TALKING BACK NOW.
I DON'T WANT ANY MORE PROBLEMS.
MUTTER
MUTTER
I SEE.

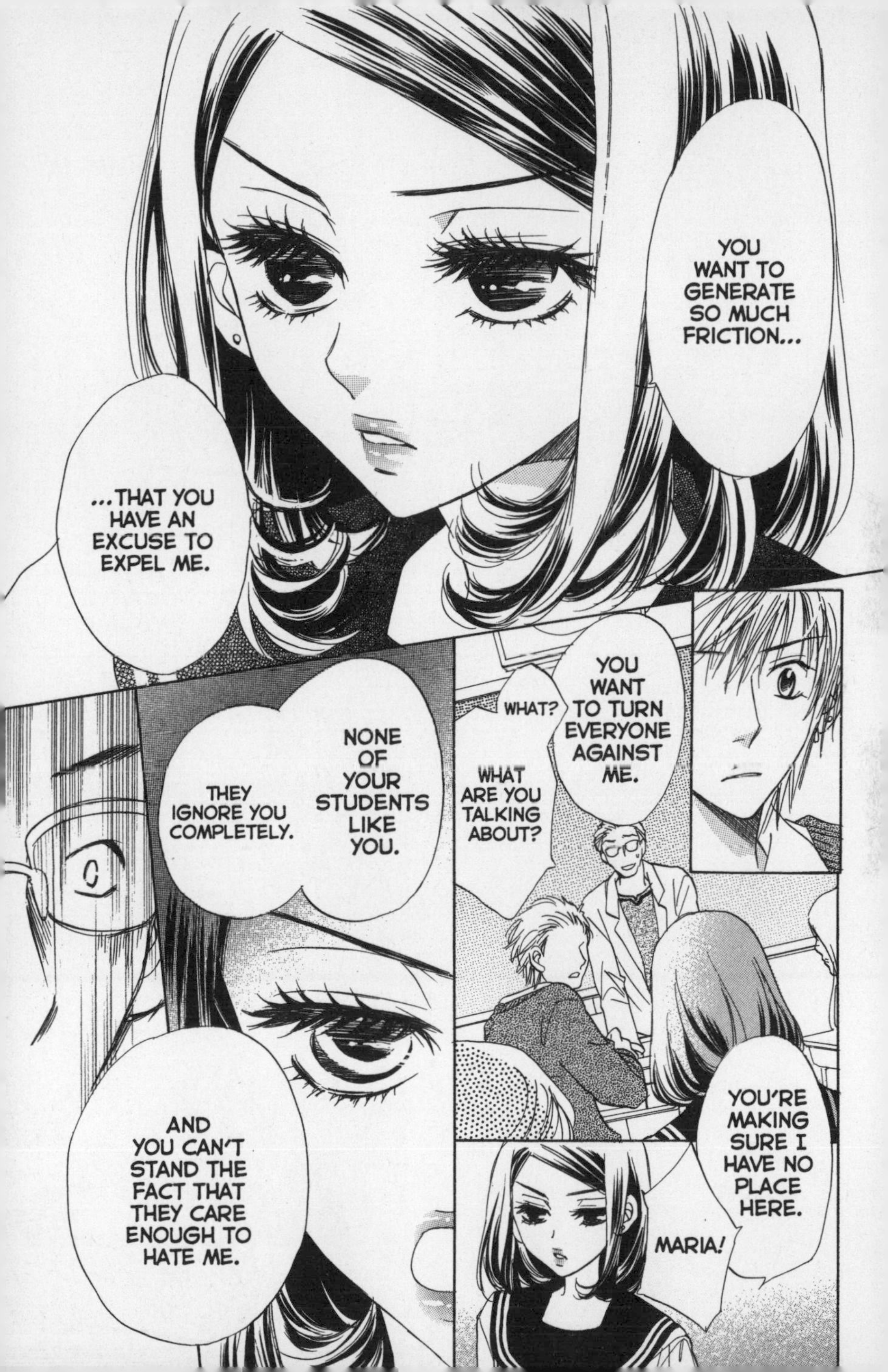
YOU WANT TO GENERATE SO MUCH FRICTION...
...THAT YOU HAVE AN EXCUSE TO EXPEL ME.
YOU WANT TO TURN EVERYONE AGAINST ME.
WHAT?
WHAT ARE YOU TALKING ABOUT?
YOU'RE MAKING SURE I HAVE NO PLACE HERE.
MARIA!
NONE OF YOUR STUDENTS LIKE YOU.
THEY IGNORE YOU COMPLETELY.
AND YOU CAN'T STAND THE FACT THAT THEY CARE ENOUGH TO HATE ME.

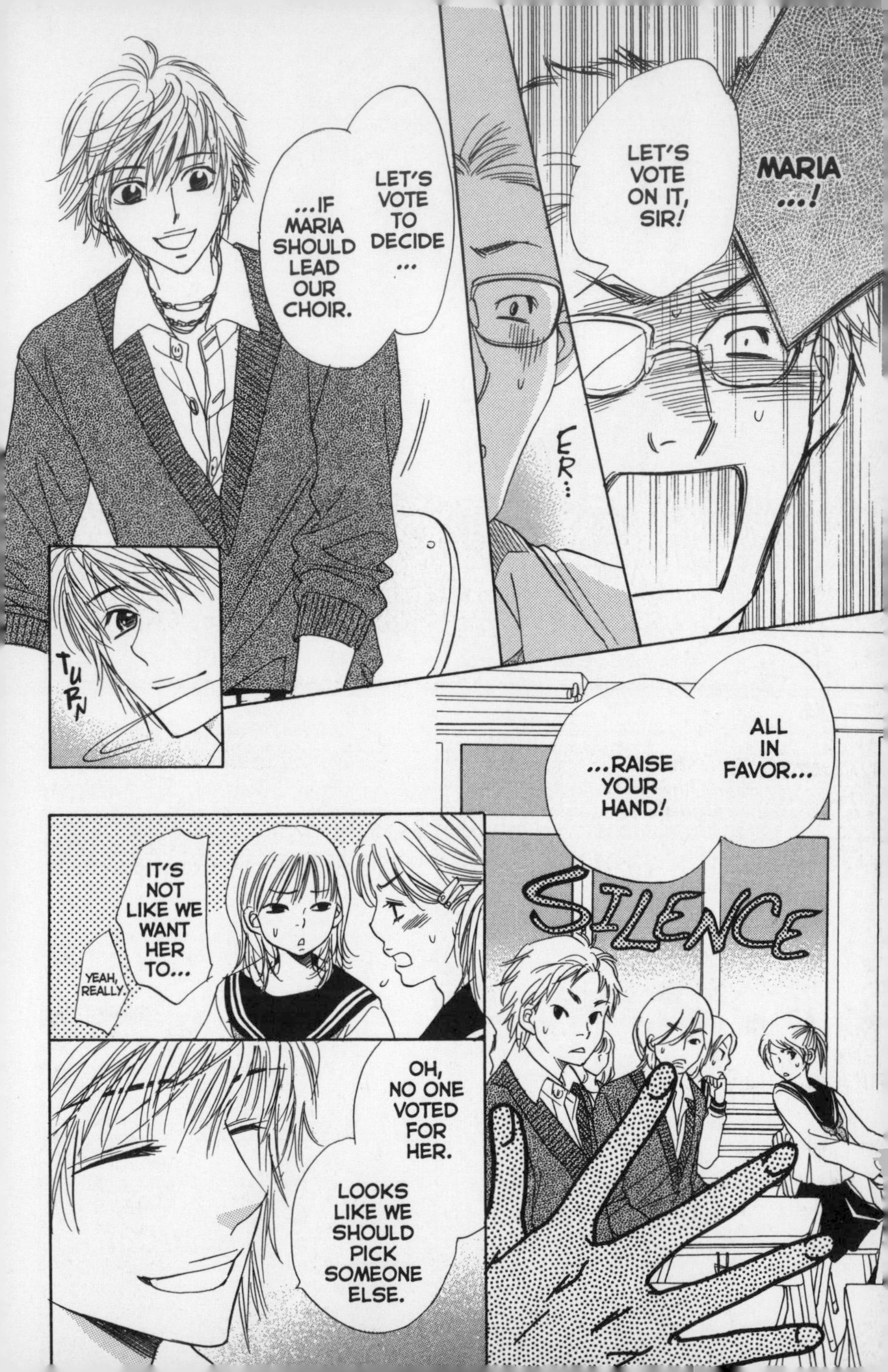
MARIA ...!
LET'S VOTE ON IT, SIR!
ER...
LET'S VOTE TO DECIDE...
...IF MARIA SHOULD LEAD OUR CHOIR.
TURN
ALL IN FAVOR...
...RAISE YOUR HAND!
SILENCE
IT'S NOT LIKE WE WANT HER TO...
YEAH, REALLY.
OH, NO ONE VOTED FOR HER.
LOOKS LIKE WE SHOULD PICK SOMEONE ELSE.

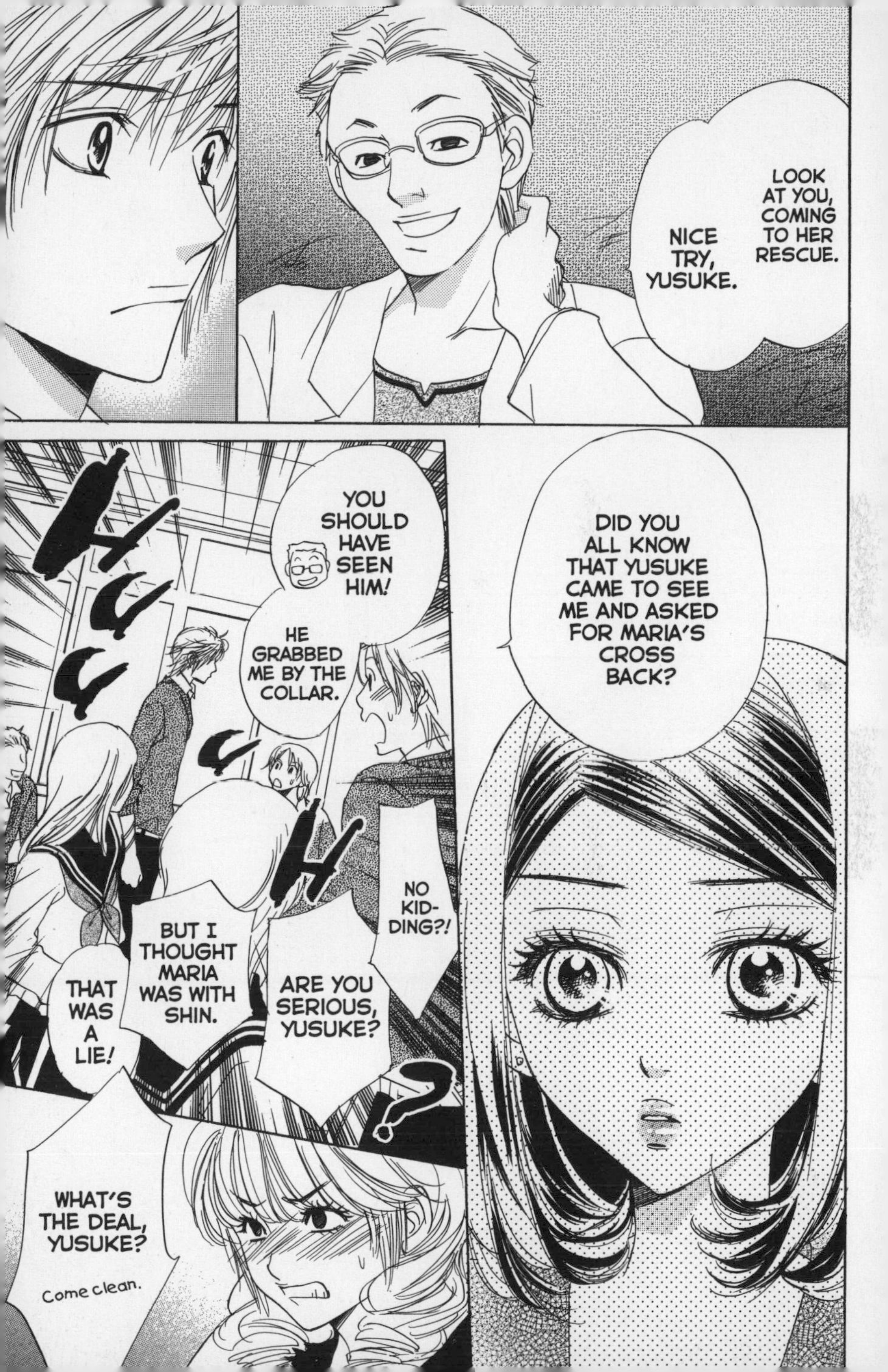
LOOK AT YOU, COMING TO HER RESCUE.
NICE TRY, YUSUKE.
DID YOU ALL KNOW THAT YUSUKE CAME TO SEE ME AND ASKED FOR MARIA'S CROSS BACK?
YOU SHOULD HAVE SEEN HIM!
HE GRABBED ME BY THE COLLAR.
NO KID-DING?!
ARE YOU SERIOUS, YUSUKE?
BUT I THOUGHT MARIA WAS WITH SHIN.
THAT WAS A LIE!
WHAT'S THE DEAL, YUSUKE?
Come clean.

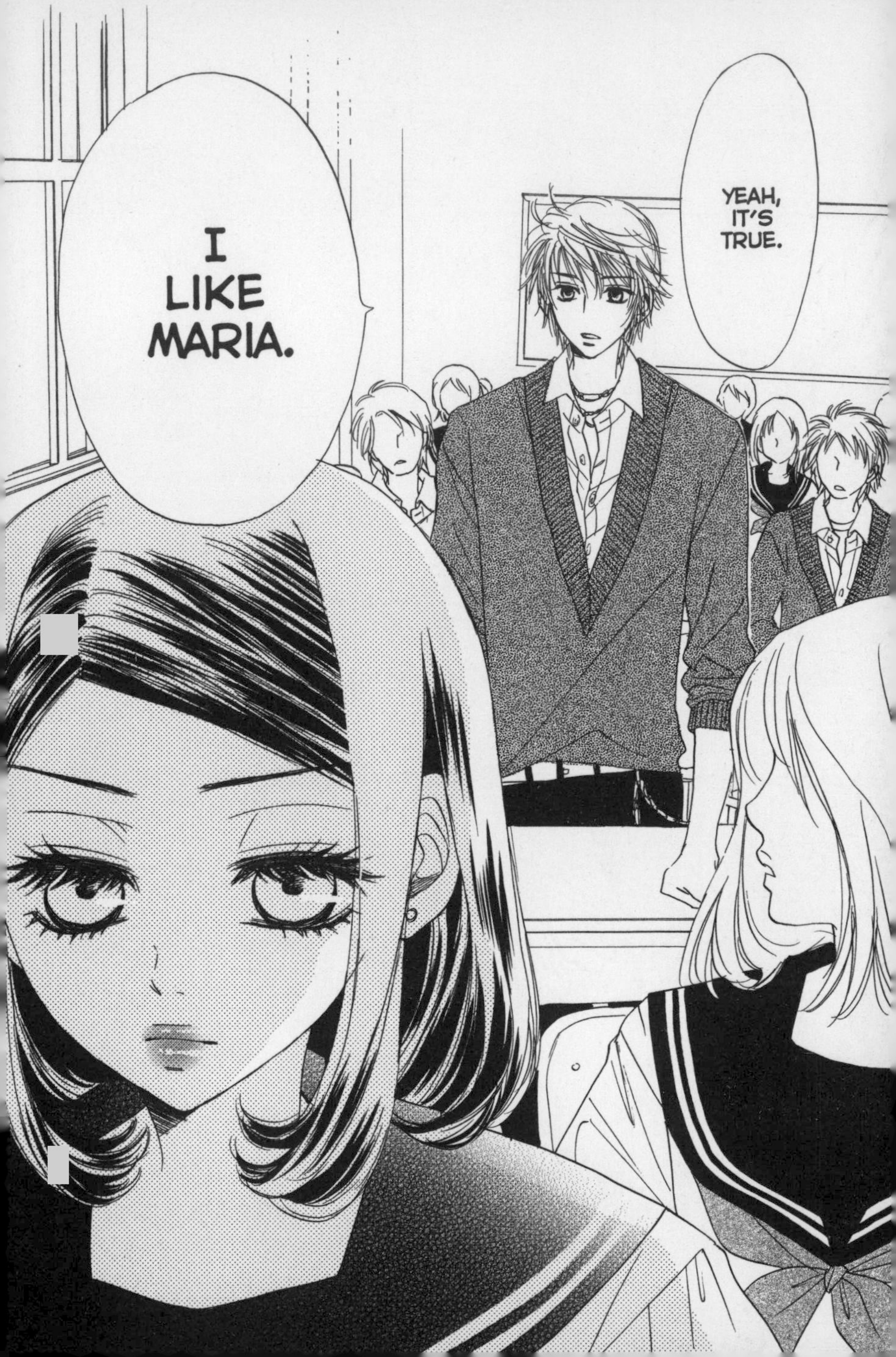
YEAH, IT'S TRUE.
I LIKE MARIA.

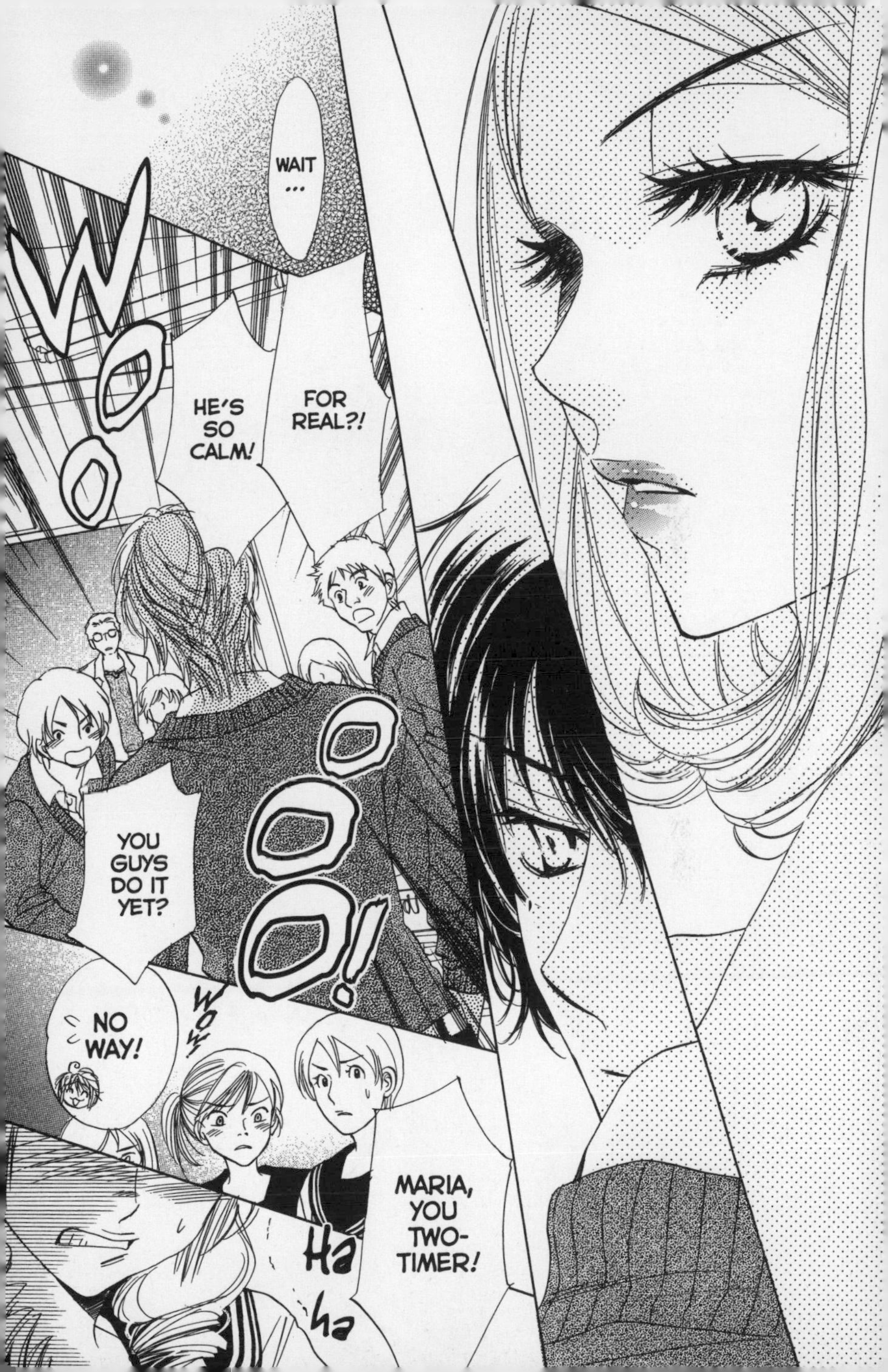
WAIT ...
FOR REAL?!
HE'S SO CALM!
WOOOOOO!
YOU GUYS DO IT YET?
MARIA, YOU TWO-TIMER!
NO WAY!
WOW
Ha ha

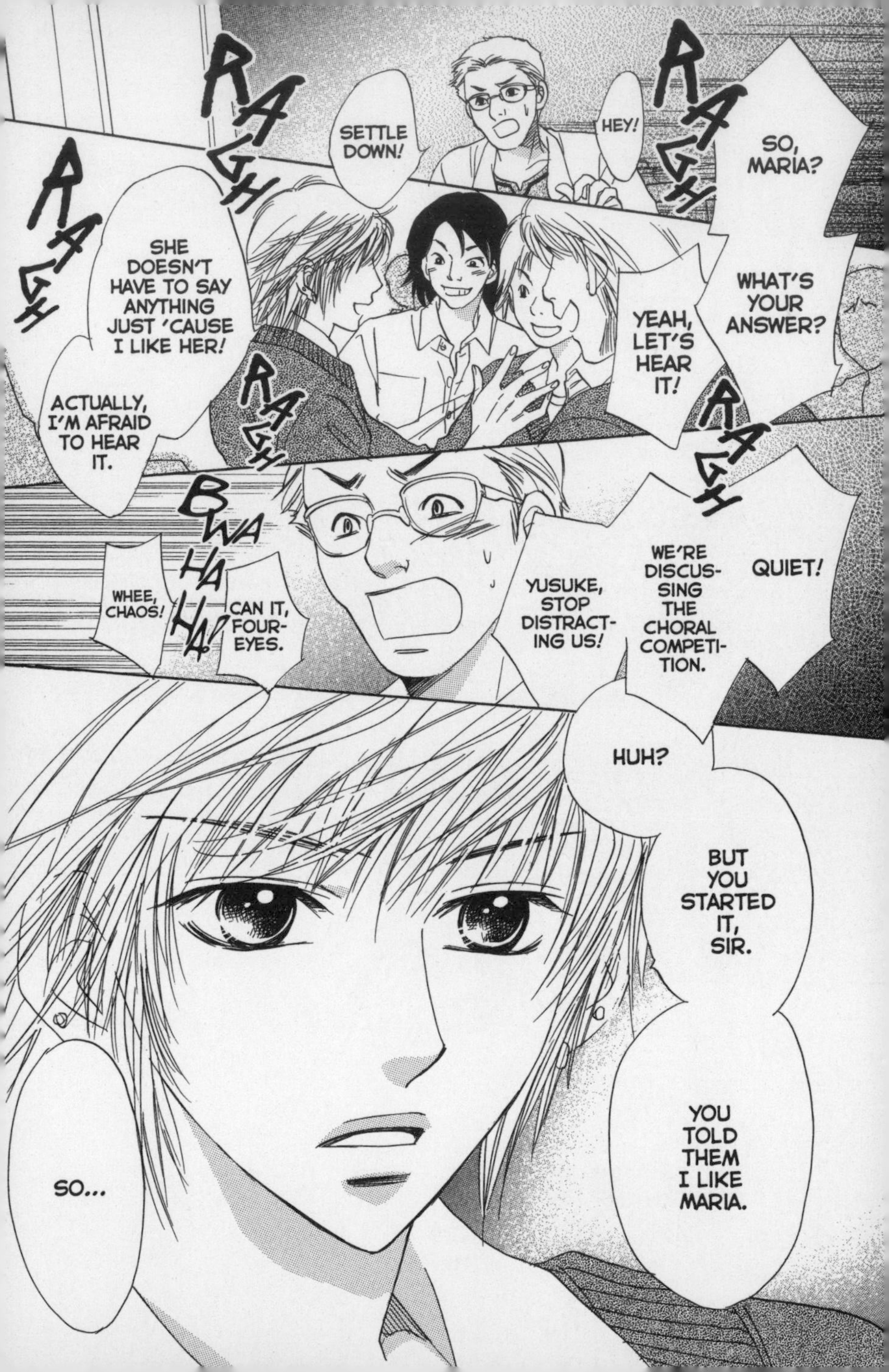
RAGH
SO, MARIA?
HEY!
SETTLE DOWN!
RAGH
WHAT'S YOUR ANSWER?
YEAH, LET'S HEAR IT!
SHE DOESN'T HAVE TO SAY ANYTHING JUST 'CAUSE I LIKE HER!
RAGH
ACTUALLY, I'M AFRAID TO HEAR IT.
RAGH
RAGH
QUIET!
WE'RE DISCUS-SING THE CHORAL COMPETI-TION.
YUSUKE, STOP DISTRACT-ING US!
CAN IT, FOUR-EYES.
BWAHAHAHA!
WHEE, CHAOS!
HUH?
BUT YOU STARTED IT, SIR.
YOU TOLD THEM I LIKE MARIA.
SO...

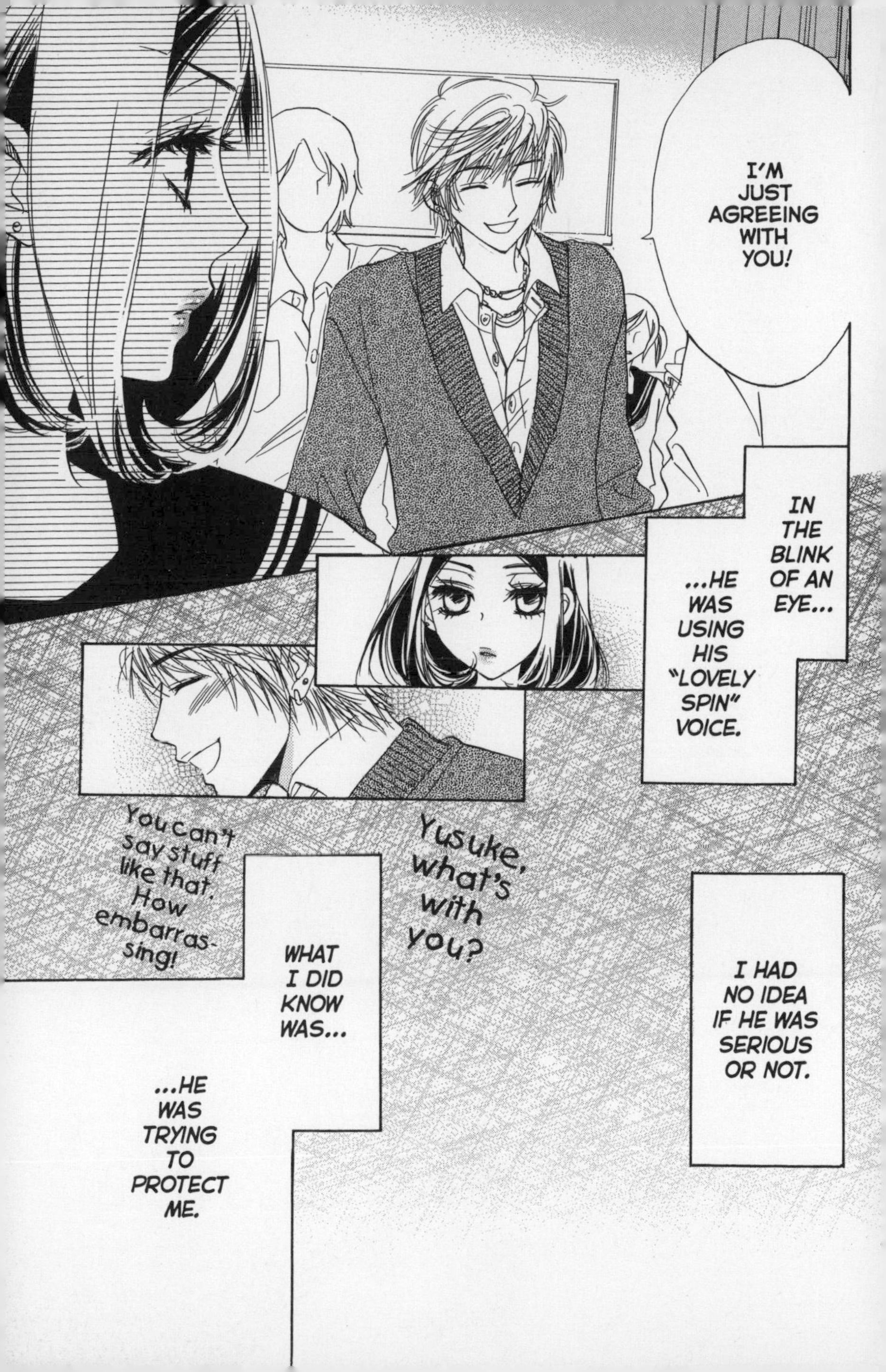
I'M JUST AGREEING WITH YOU!
IN THE BLINK OF AN EYE...
...HE WAS USING HIS "LOVELY SPIN" VOICE.
I HAD NO IDEA IF HE WAS SERIOUS OR NOT.
Yusuke, what's with you?
You can't say stuff like that. How embarras-sing!
WHAT I DID KNOW WAS...
...HE WAS TRYING TO PROTECT ME.

A Devil and
Her Love Song

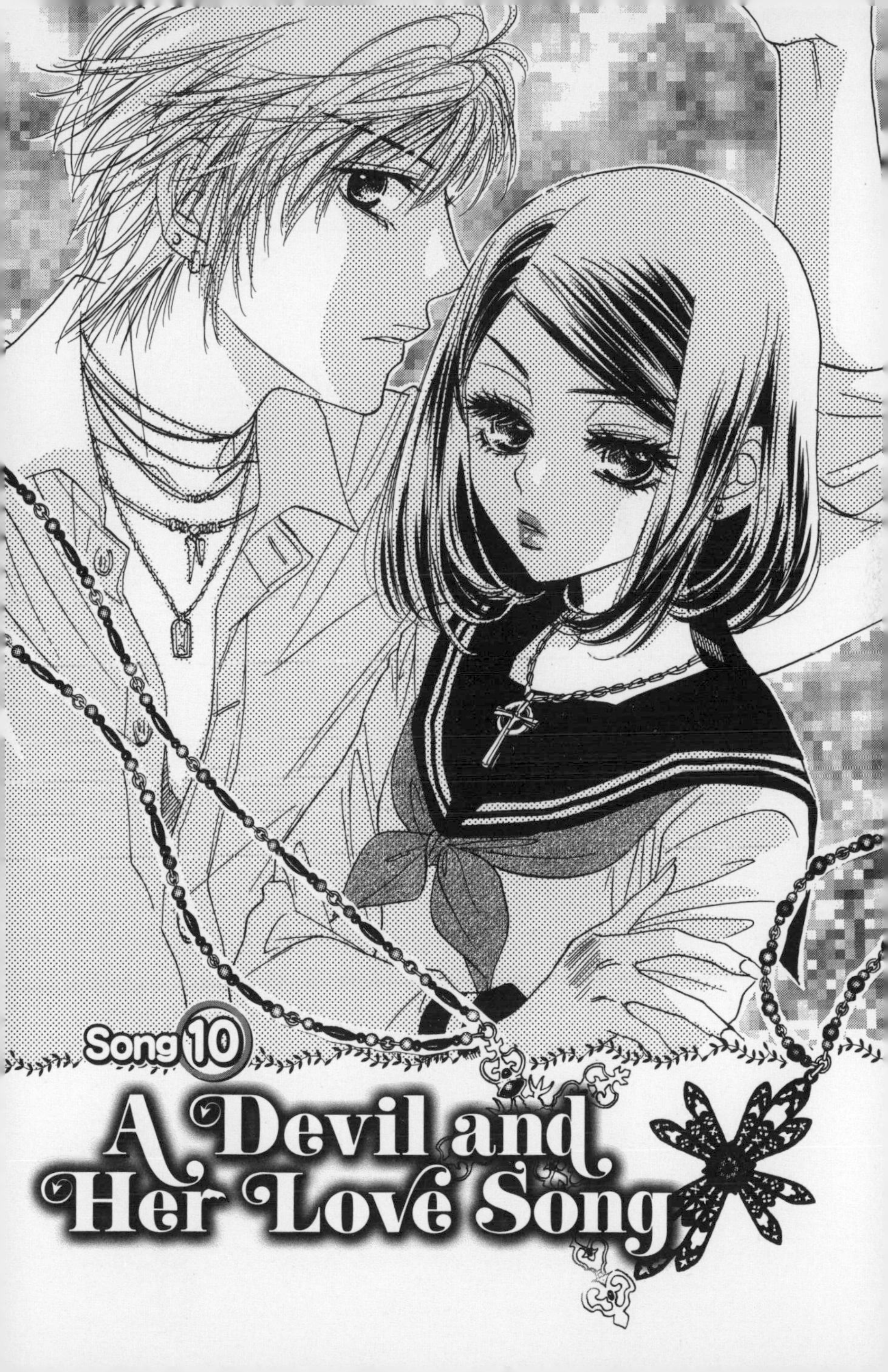
Song 10
A Devil and Her Love Song

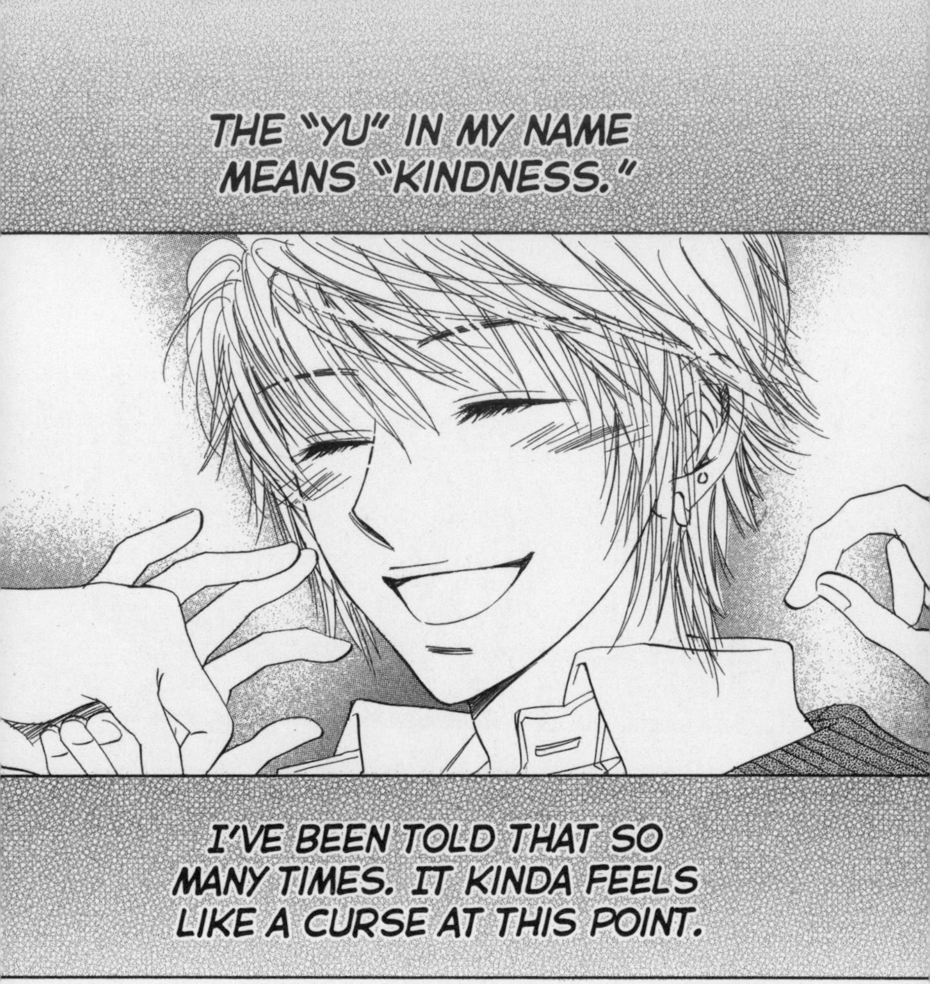
THE "YU" IN MY NAME MEANS "KINDNESS."
I'VE BEEN TOLD THAT SO MANY TIMES. IT KINDA FEELS LIKE A CURSE AT THIS POINT.

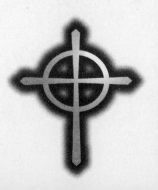

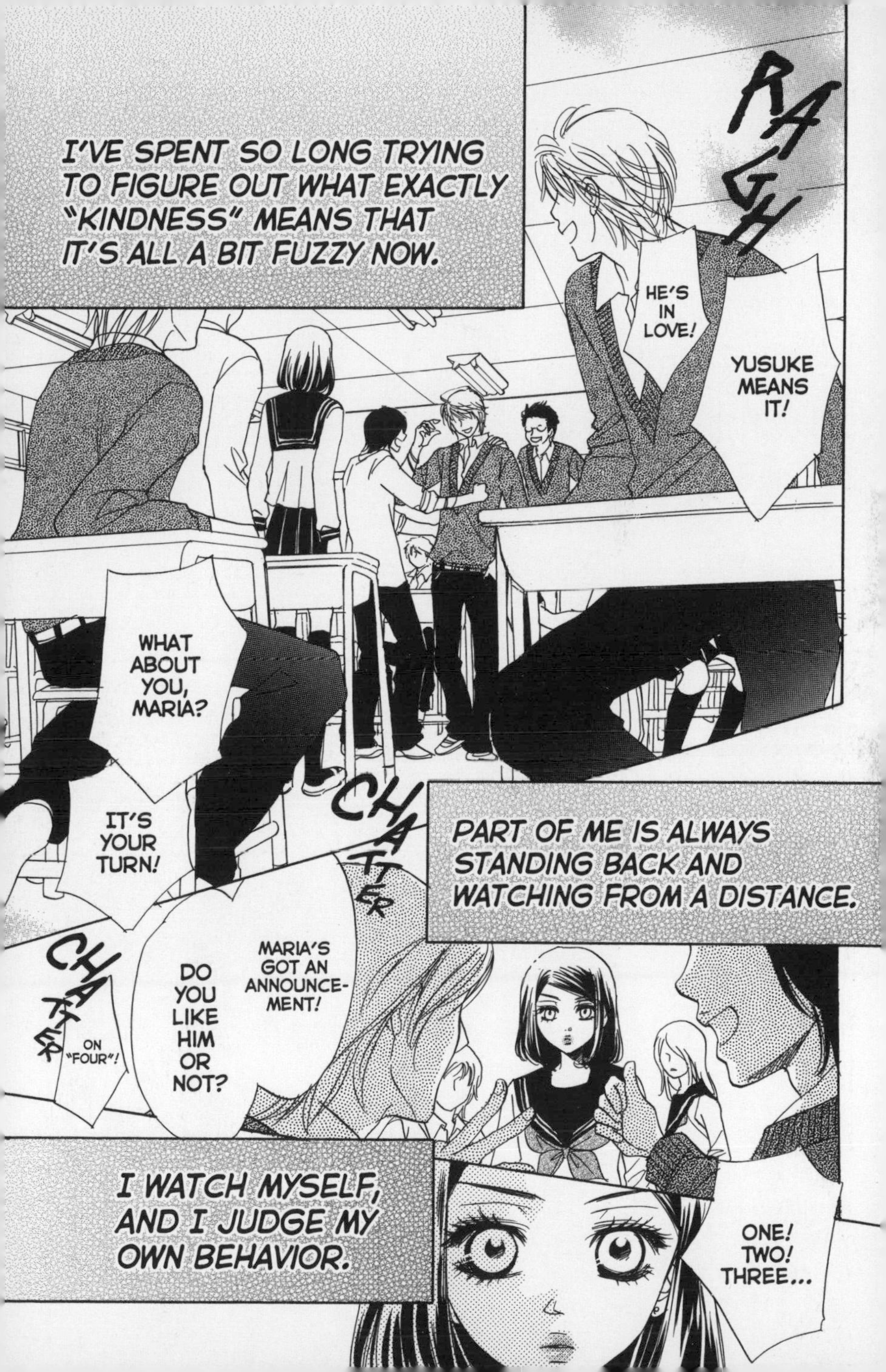
RAGH
HE'S IN LOVE!
YUSUKE MEANS IT!
I'VE SPENT SO LONG TRYING TO FIGURE OUT WHAT EXACTLY "KINDNESS" MEANS THAT IT'S ALL A BIT FUZZY NOW.
WHAT ABOUT YOU, MARIA?
IT'S YOUR TURN!
CHATTER
PART OF ME IS ALWAYS STANDING BACK AND WATCHING FROM A DISTANCE.
MARIA'S GOT AN ANNOUNCE-MENT!
DO YOU LIKE HIM OR NOT?
CHATTER
ON "FOUR"!
ONE! TWO! THREE...
I WATCH MYSELF, AND I JUDGE MY OWN BEHAVIOR.

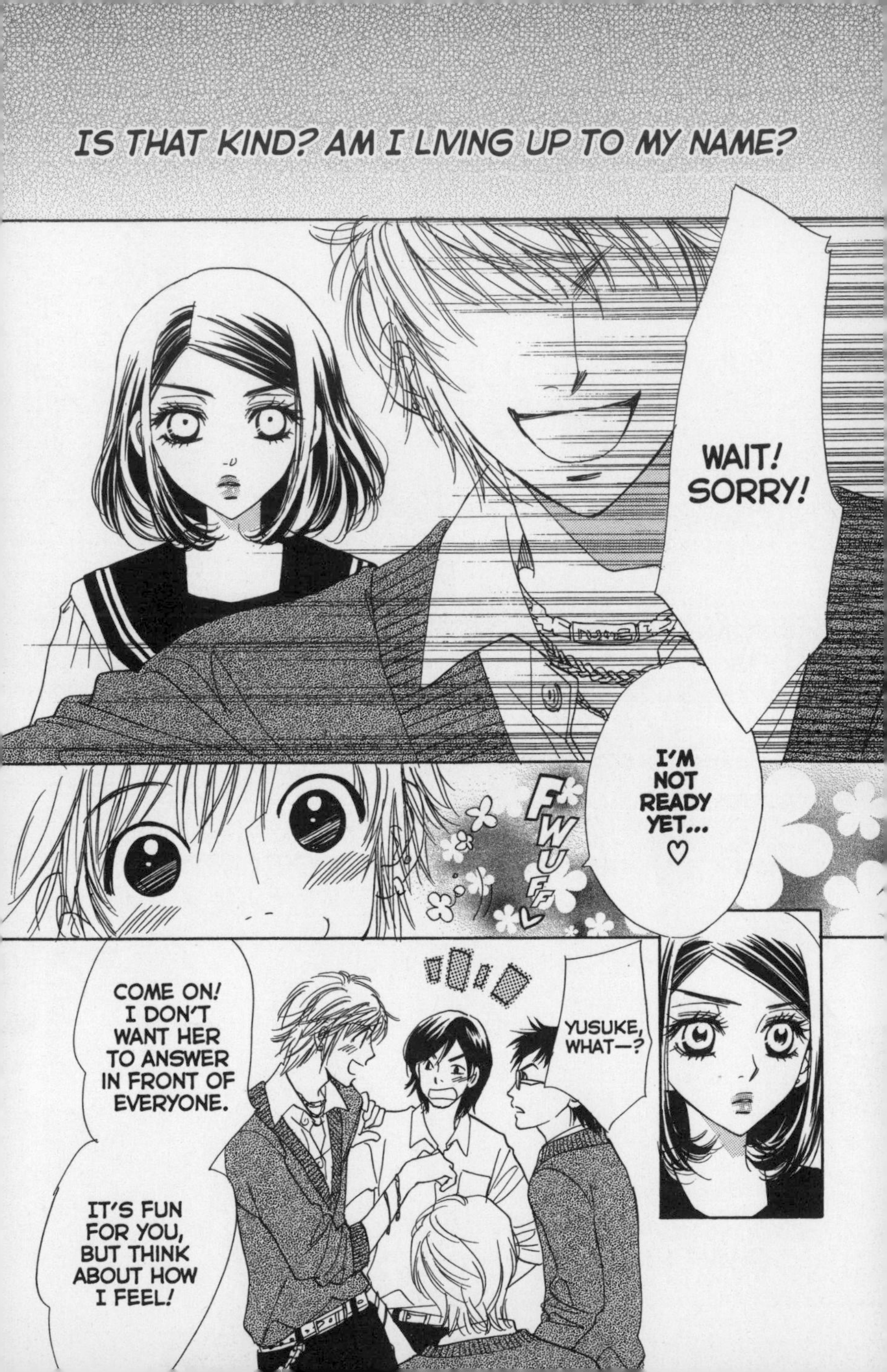
IS THAT KIND? AM I LIVING UP TO MY NAME?
WAIT! SORRY!
I'M NOT READY YET... ♡
FWUFF♡
YUSUKE, WHAT—?
COME ON! I DON'T WANT HER TO ANSWER IN FRONT OF EVERYONE.
IT'S FUN FOR YOU, BUT THINK ABOUT HOW I FEEL!

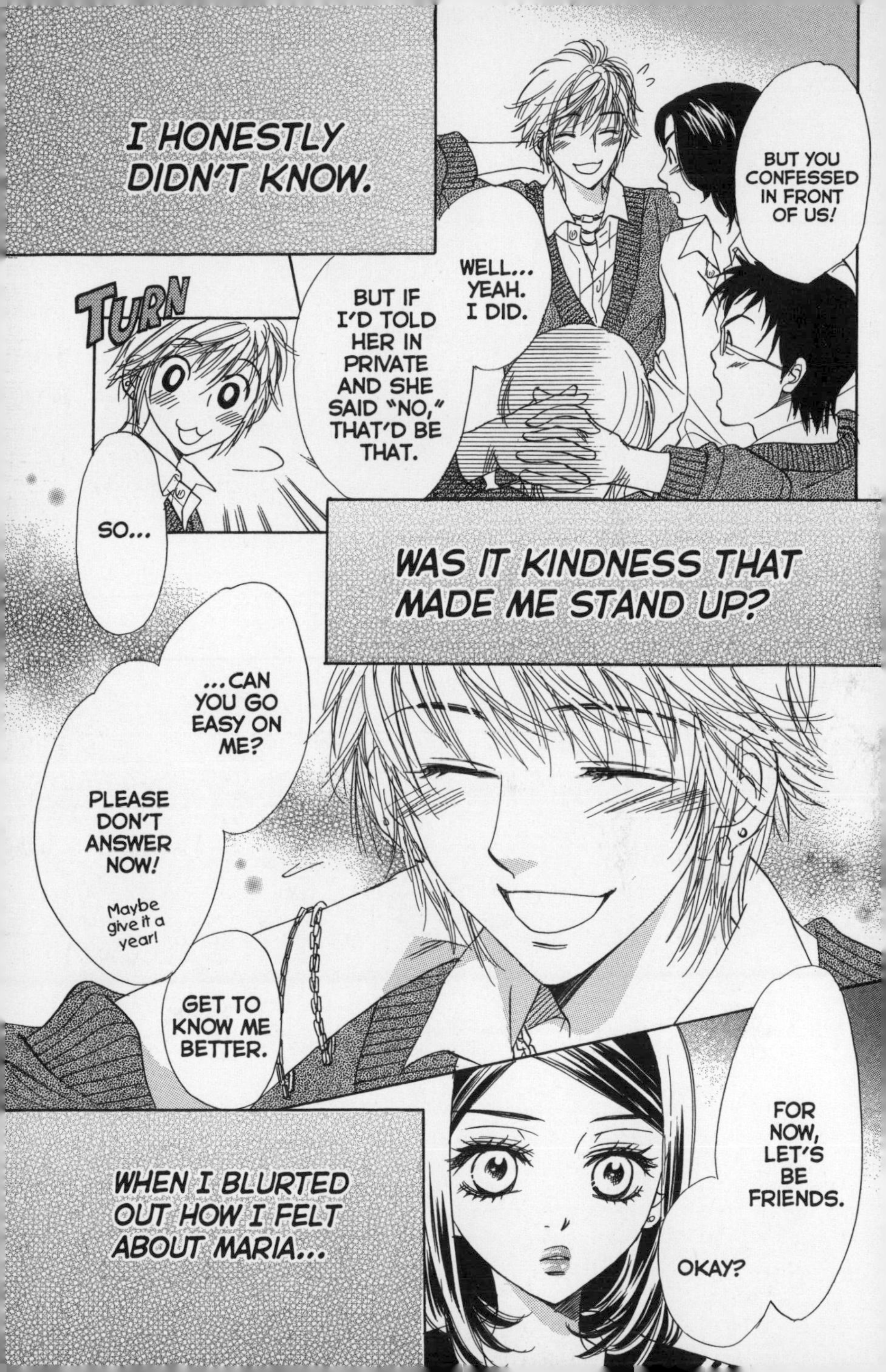
BUT YOU CONFESSED IN FRONT OF US!
WELL... YEAH. I DID.
BUT IF I'D TOLD HER IN PRIVATE AND SHE SAID "NO," THAT'D BE THAT.
I HONESTLY DIDN'T KNOW.
TURN
SO...
WAS IT KINDNESS THAT MADE ME STAND UP?
...CAN YOU GO EASY ON ME?
PLEASE DON'T ANSWER NOW!
Maybe give it a year!
GET TO KNOW ME BETTER.
FOR NOW, LET'S BE FRIENDS.
OKAY?
WHEN I BLURTED OUT HOW I FELT ABOUT MARIA...

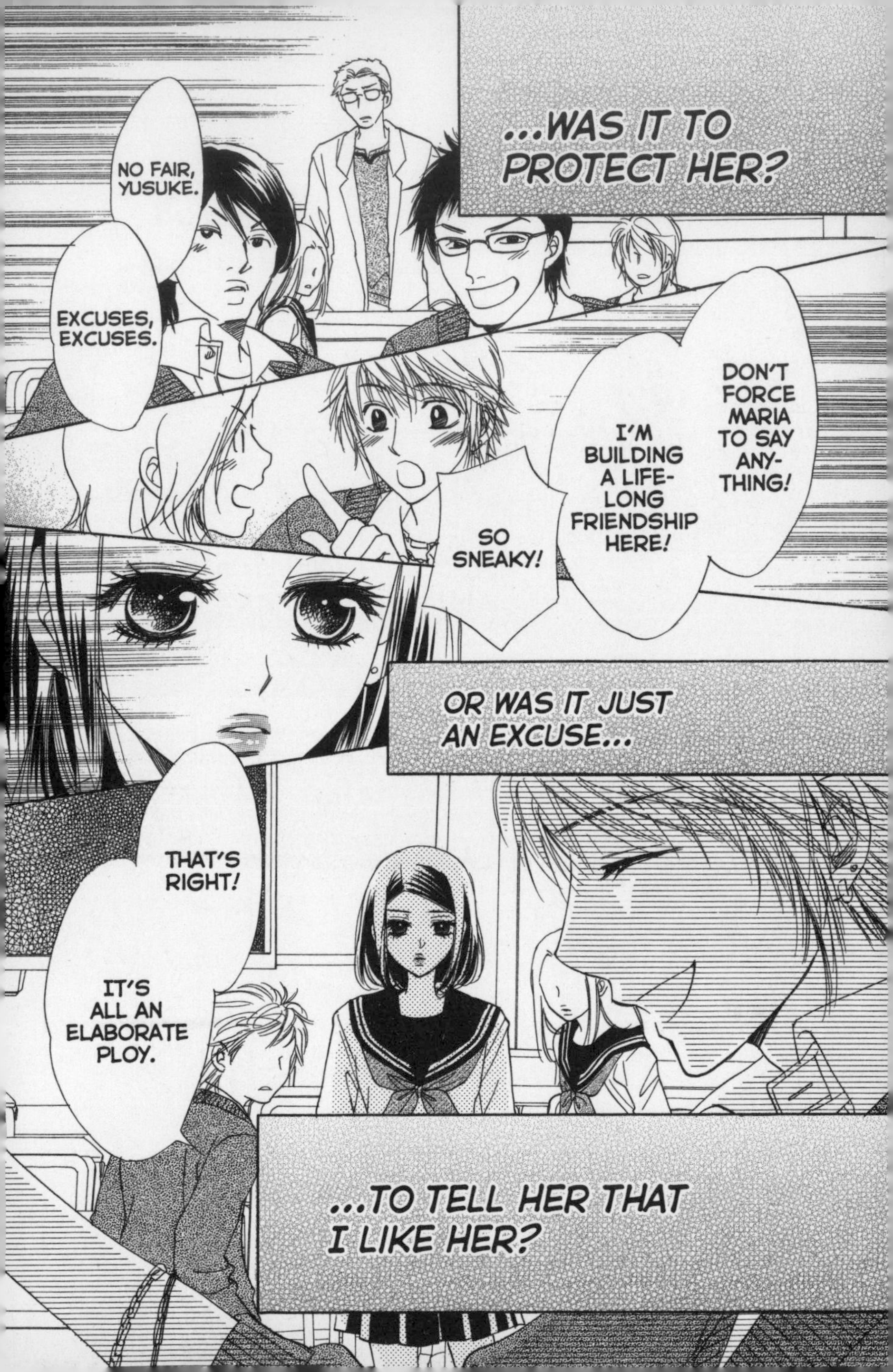
...WAS IT TO PROTECT HER?
NO FAIR, YUSUKE.
EXCUSES, EXCUSES.
DON'T FORCE MARIA TO SAY ANYTHING!
I'M BUILDING A LIFELONG FRIENDSHIP HERE!
SO SNEAKY!
OR WAS IT JUST AN EXCUSE...
THAT'S RIGHT!
IT'S ALL AN ELABORATE PLOY.
...TO TELL HER THAT I LIKE HER?

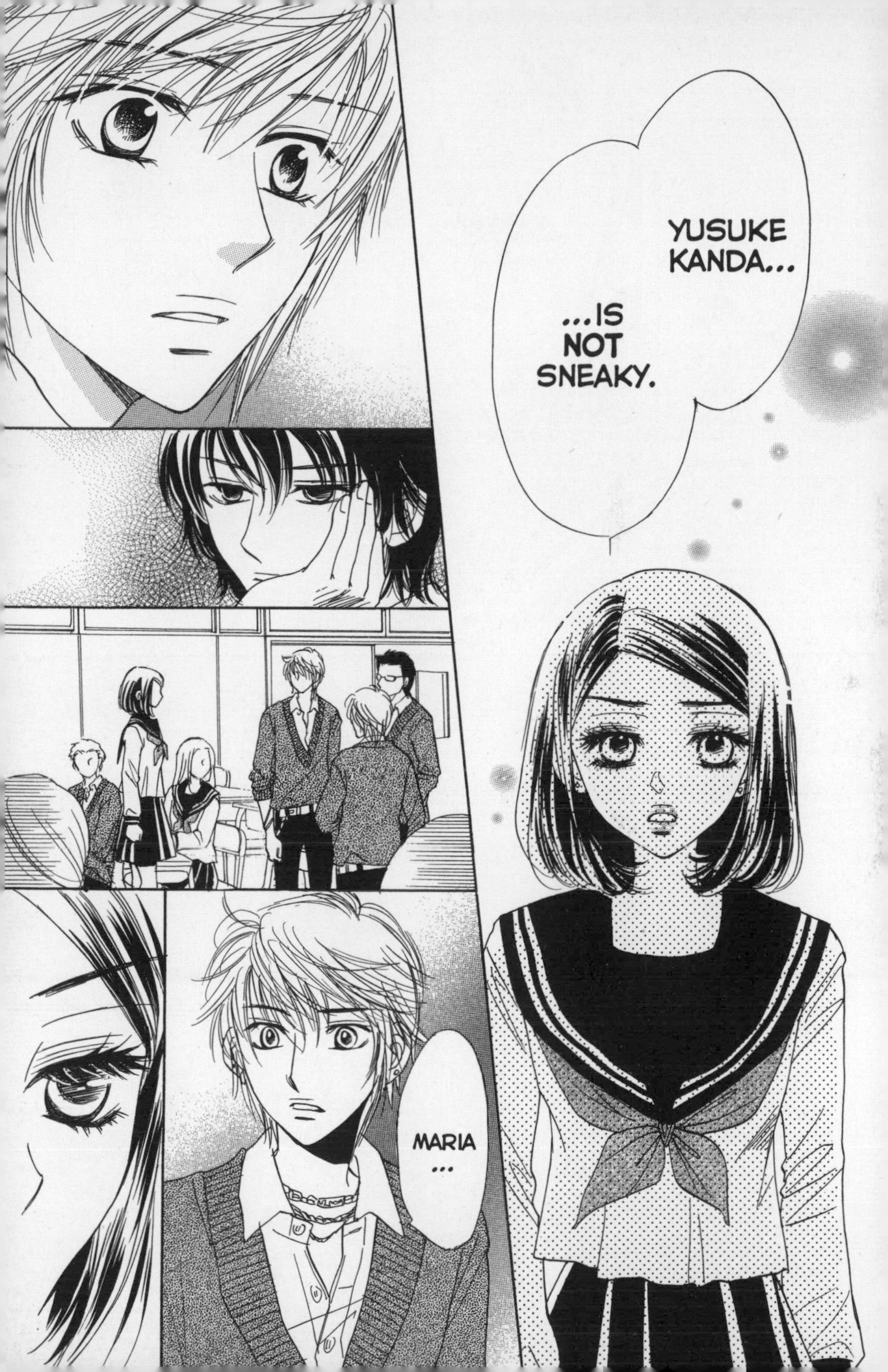
YUSUKE KANDA...
...IS NOT SNEAKY.
MARIA ...

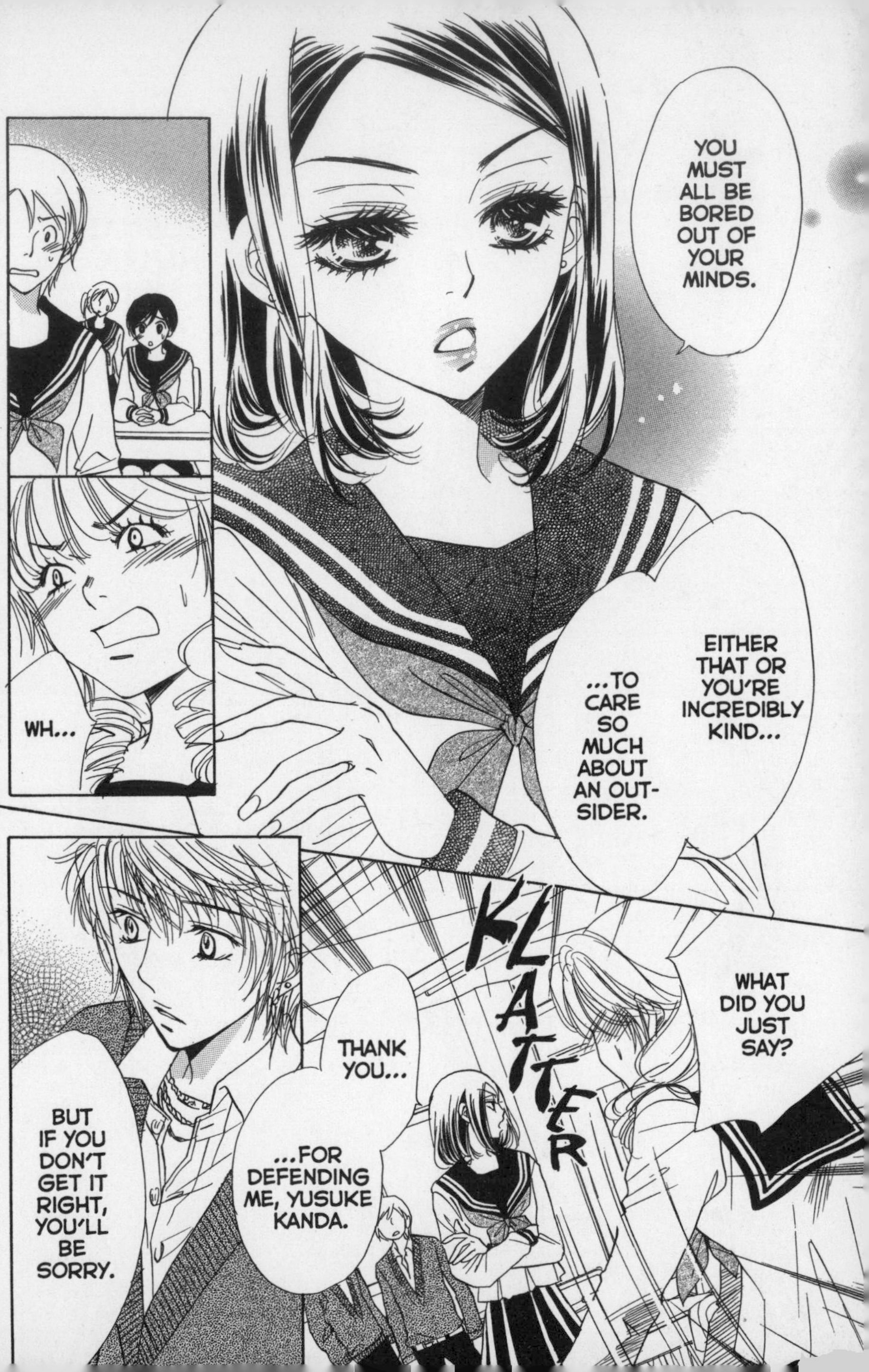
YOU MUST ALL BE BORED OUT OF YOUR MINDS.
EITHER THAT OR YOU'RE INCREDIBLY KIND...
...TO CARE SO MUCH ABOUT AN OUT-SIDER.
WH...
KLATTER
WHAT DID YOU JUST SAY?
THANK YOU...
...FOR DEFENDING ME, YUSUKE KANDA.
BUT IF YOU DON'T GET IT RIGHT, YOU'LL BE SORRY.

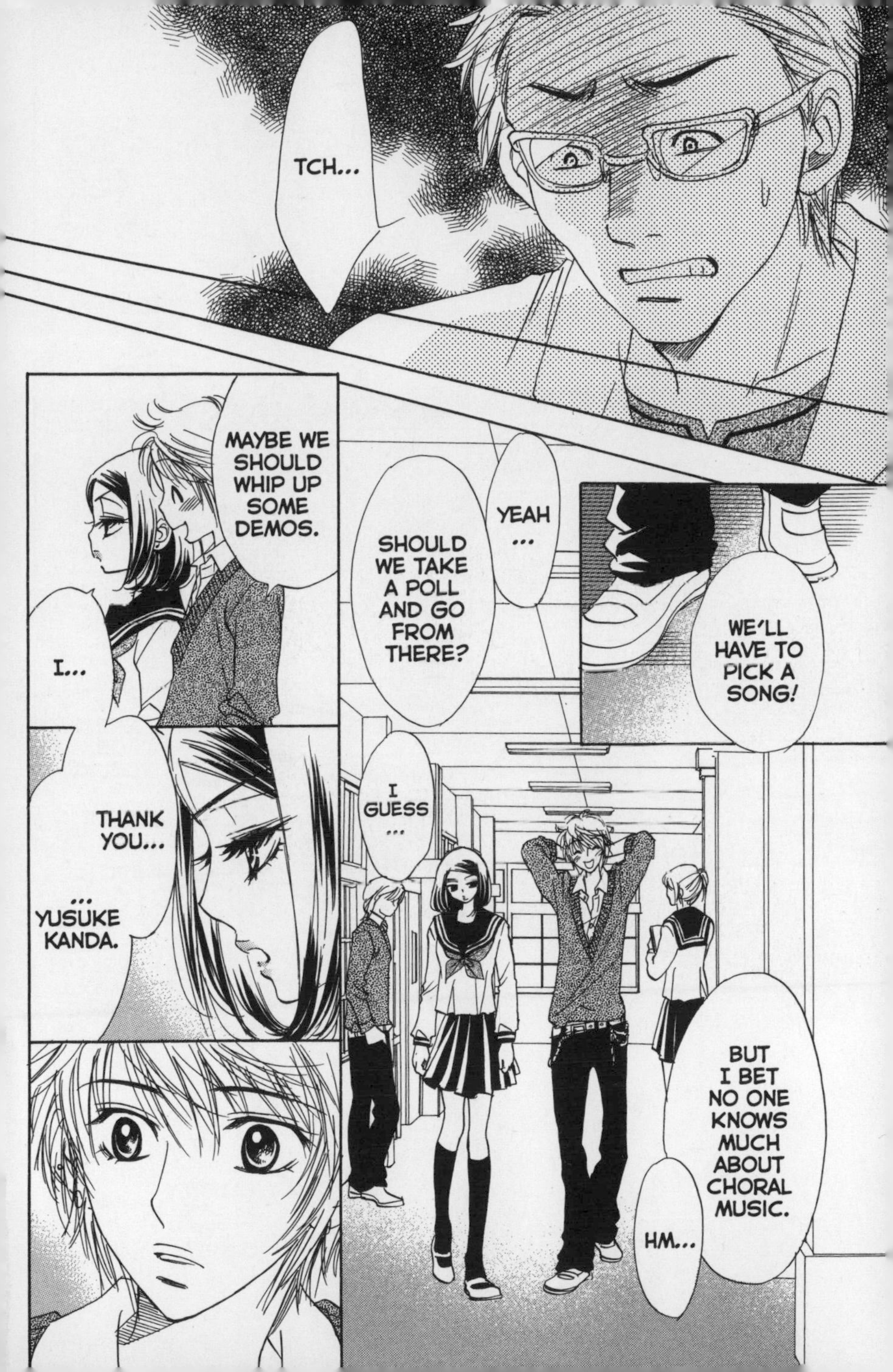
TCH...
WE'LL HAVE TO PICK A SONG!
YEAH ...
SHOULD WE TAKE A POLL AND GO FROM THERE?
BUT I BET NO ONE KNOWS MUCH ABOUT CHORAL MUSIC.
HM...
I GUESS ...
MAYBE WE SHOULD WHIP UP SOME DEMOS.
I...
THANK YOU...
... YUSUKE KANDA.

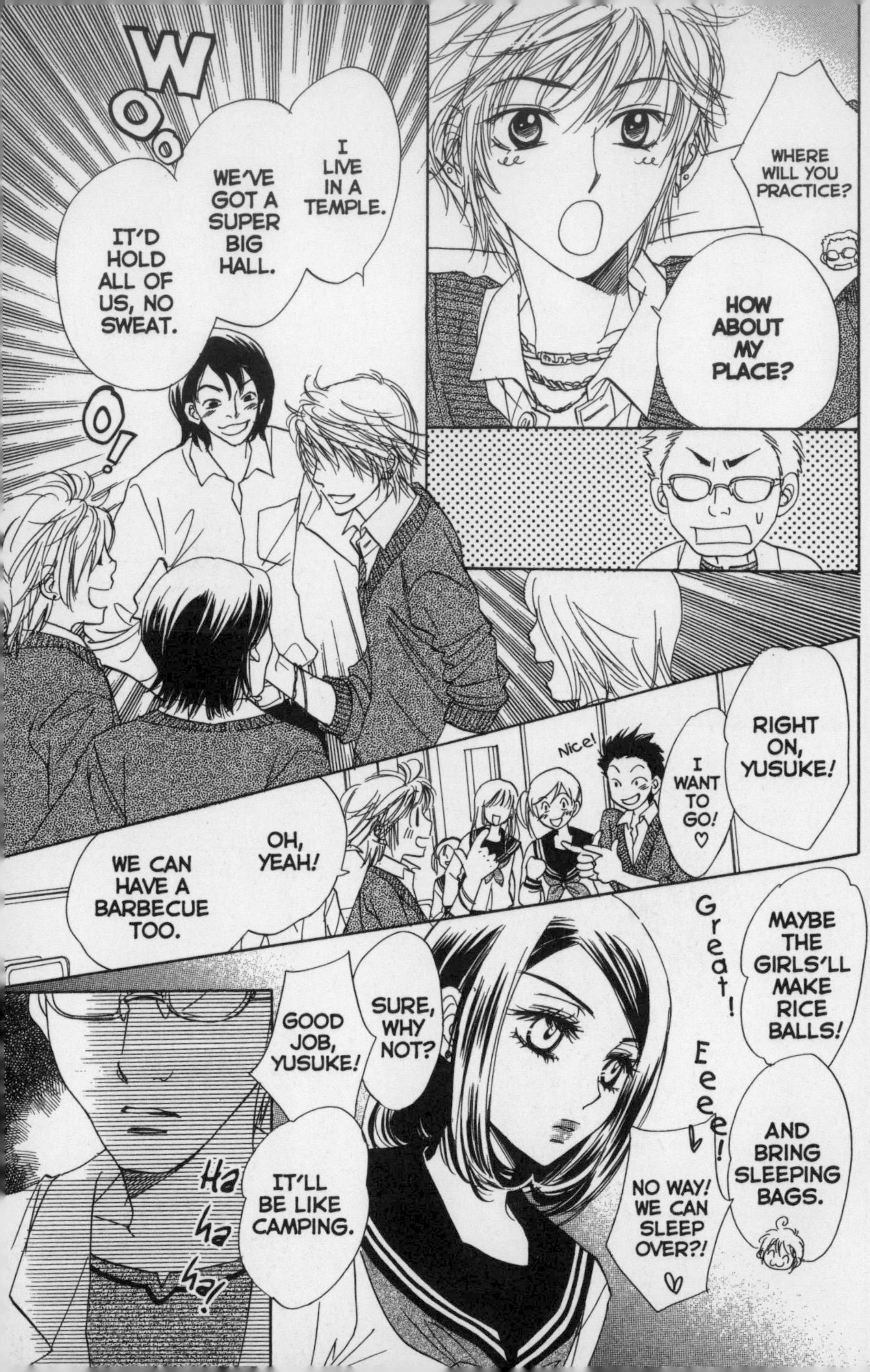
WHERE WILL YOU PRACTICE?
HOW ABOUT MY PLACE?
I LIVE IN A TEMPLE.
WE'VE GOT A SUPER BIG HALL.
IT'D HOLD ALL OF US, NO SWEAT.
WOO
O!
RIGHT ON, YUSUKE!
I WANT TO GO! ♡
Nice!
OH, YEAH!
WE CAN HAVE A BARBECUE TOO.
MAYBE THE GIRLS'LL MAKE RICE BALLS!
Great!
AND BRING SLEEPING BAGS.
Eeee!
NO WAY! WE CAN SLEEP OVER?! ♡
SURE, WHY NOT?
GOOD JOB, YUSUKE!
IT'LL BE LIKE CAMPING.
Ha ha ha!

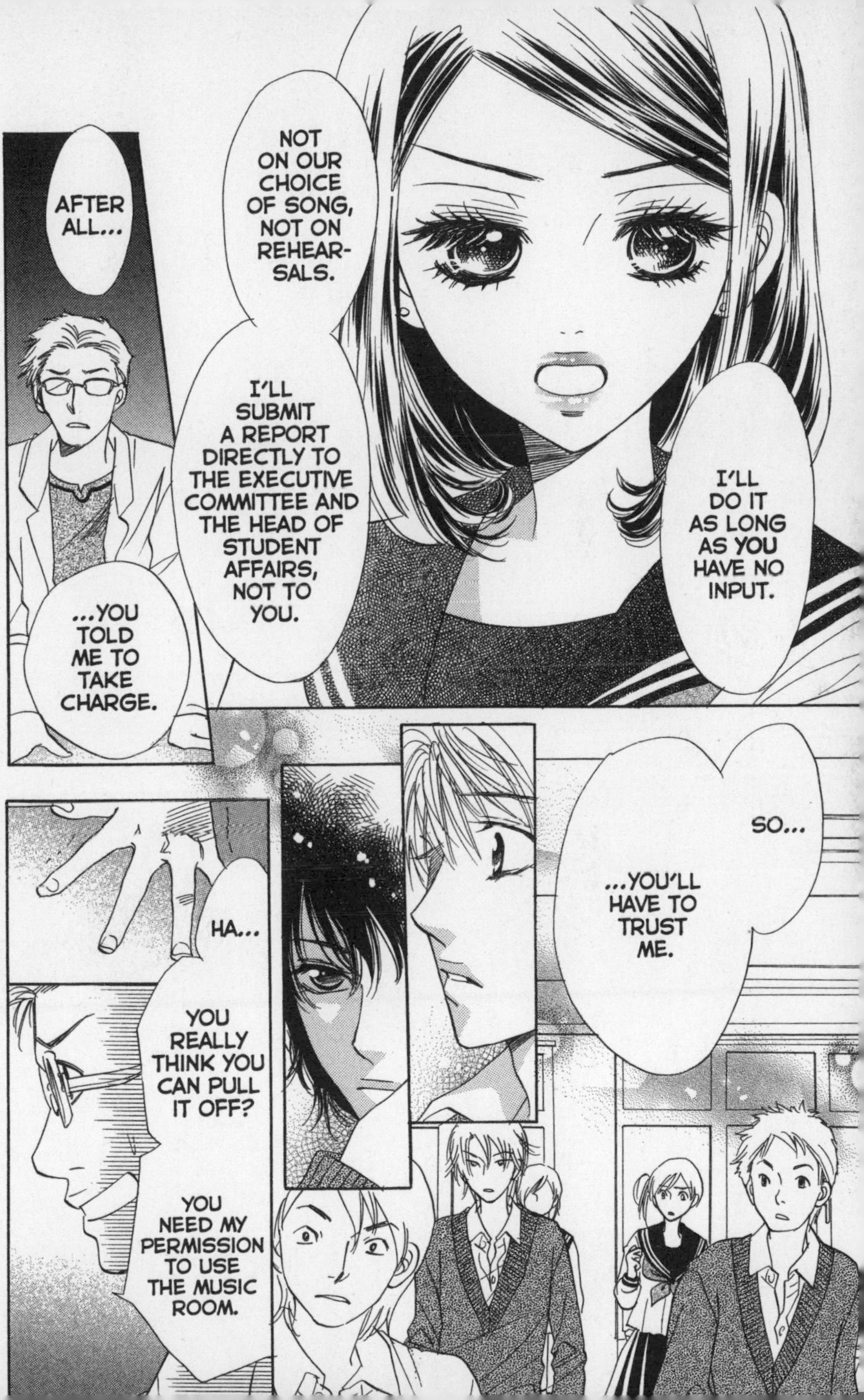
I'LL DO IT AS LONG AS YOU HAVE NO INPUT.
NOT ON OUR CHOICE OF SONG, NOT ON REHEAR-SALS.
I'LL SUBMIT A REPORT DIRECTLY TO THE EXECUTIVE COMMITTEE AND THE HEAD OF STUDENT AFFAIRS, NOT TO YOU.
AFTER ALL...
...YOU TOLD ME TO TAKE CHARGE.
SO...
...YOU'LL HAVE TO TRUST ME.
HA...
YOU REALLY THINK YOU CAN PULL IT OFF?
YOU NEED MY PERMISSION TO USE THE MUSIC ROOM.

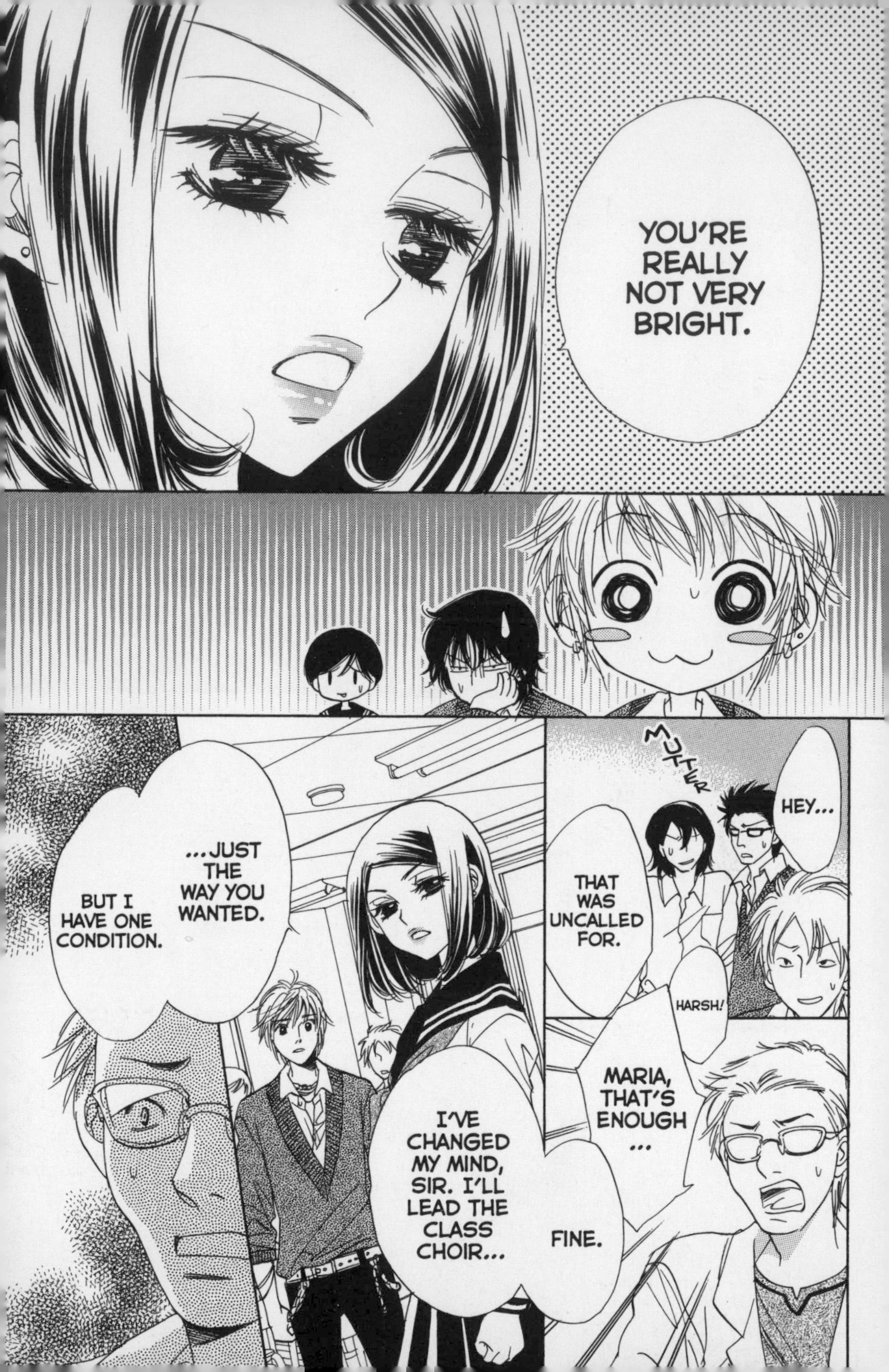

YOU'RE REALLY NOT VERY BRIGHT.
MUTTER
HEY...
THAT WAS UNCALLED FOR.
HARSH!
MARIA, THAT'S ENOUGH ...
FINE.
I'VE CHANGED MY MIND, SIR. I'LL LEAD THE CLASS CHOIR...
...JUST THE WAY YOU WANTED.
BUT I HAVE ONE CONDITION.

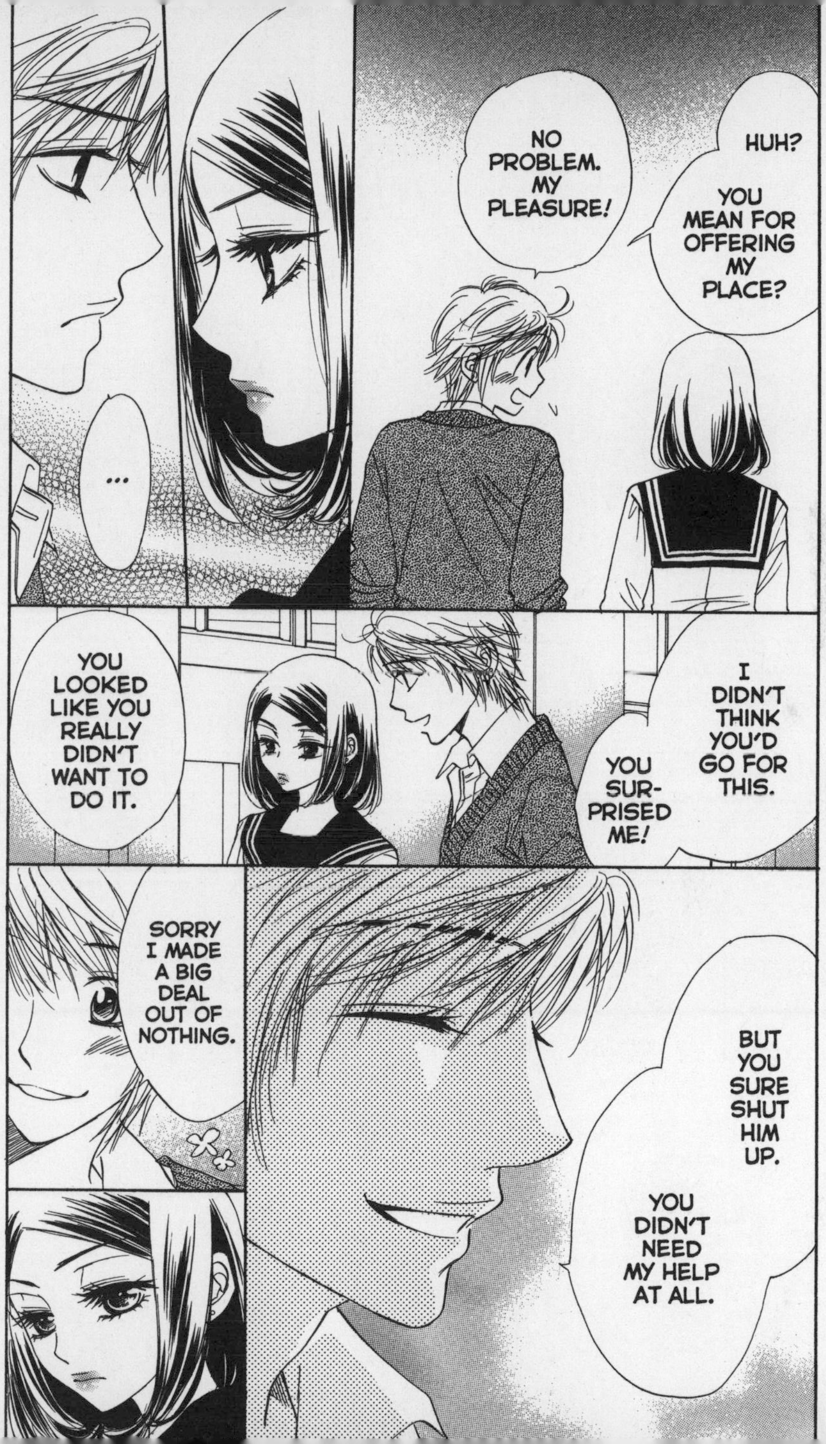
HUH?
YOU MEAN FOR OFFERING MY PLACE?
NO PROBLEM. MY PLEASURE!
...
I DIDN'T THINK YOU'D GO FOR THIS.
YOU SUR-PRISED ME!
YOU LOOKED LIKE YOU REALLY DIDN'T WANT TO DO IT.
BUT YOU SURE SHUT HIM UP.
YOU DIDN'T NEED MY HELP AT ALL.
SORRY I MADE A BIG DEAL OUT OF NOTHING.

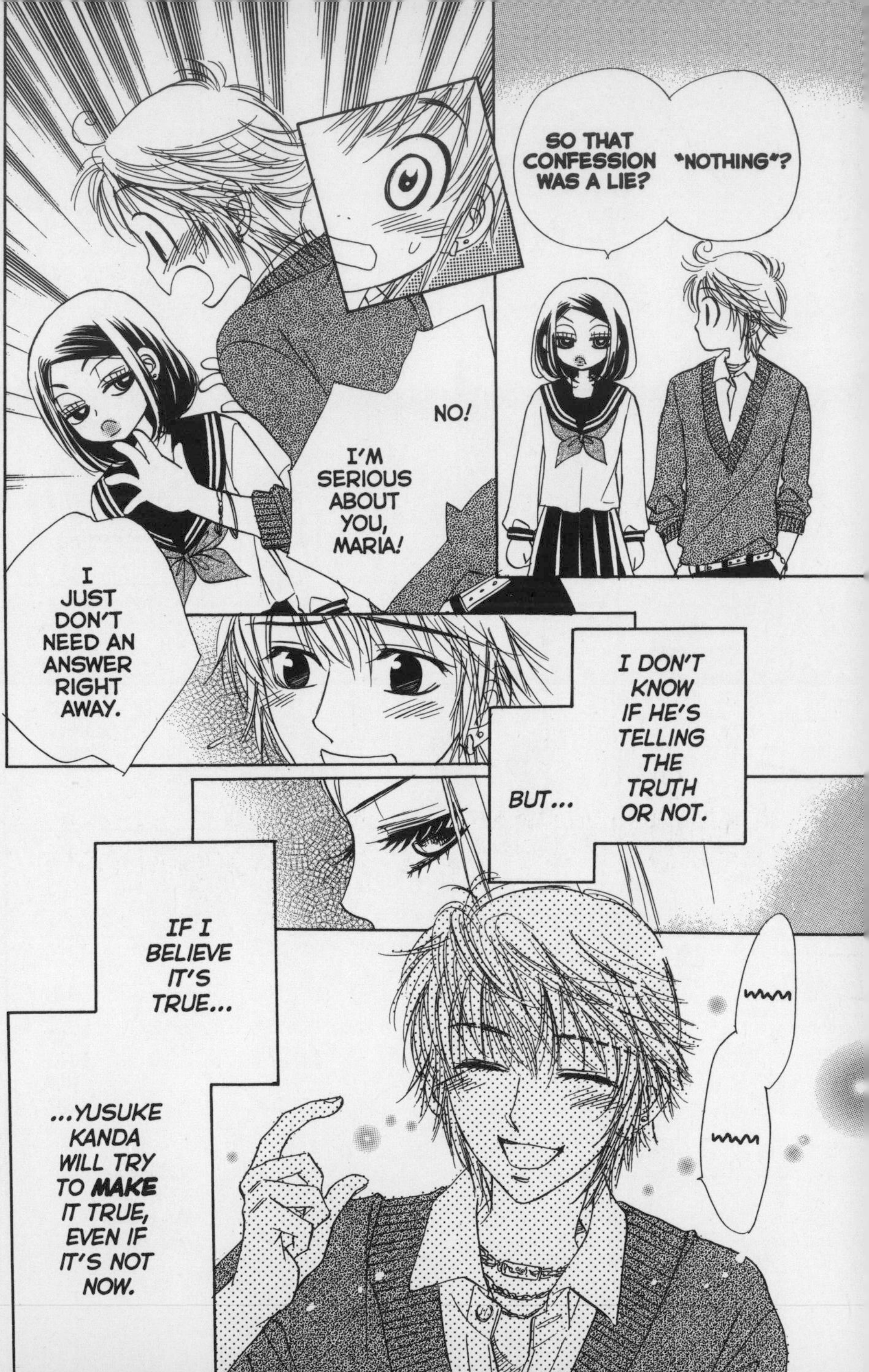
"NOTHING"?
SO THAT CONFESSION WAS A LIE?
NO!
I'M SERIOUS ABOUT YOU, MARIA!
I JUST DON'T NEED AN ANSWER RIGHT AWAY.
I DON'T KNOW IF HE'S TELLING THE TRUTH OR NOT.
BUT...
IF I BELIEVE IT'S TRUE...
...YUSUKE KANDA WILL TRY TO **MAKE** IT TRUE, EVEN IF IT'S NOT NOW.

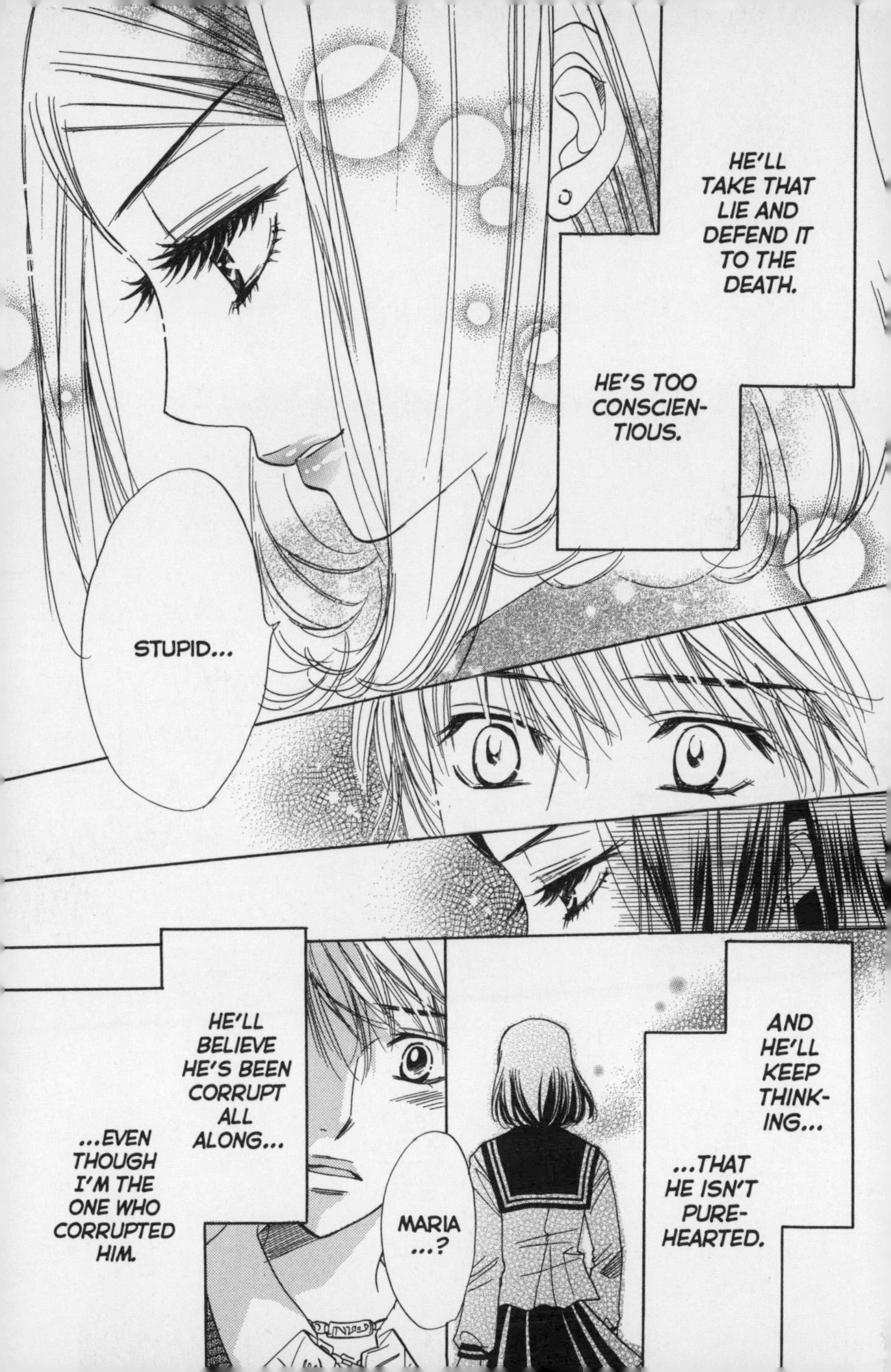
HE'LL TAKE THAT LIE AND DEFEND IT TO THE DEATH.
HE'S TOO CONSCIEN-TIOUS.
STUPID...
AND HE'LL KEEP THINK-ING...
...THAT HE ISN'T PURE-HEARTED.
MARIA ...?
HE'LL BELIEVE HE'S BEEN CORRUPT ALL ALONG...
...EVEN THOUGH I'M THE ONE WHO CORRUPTED HIM.

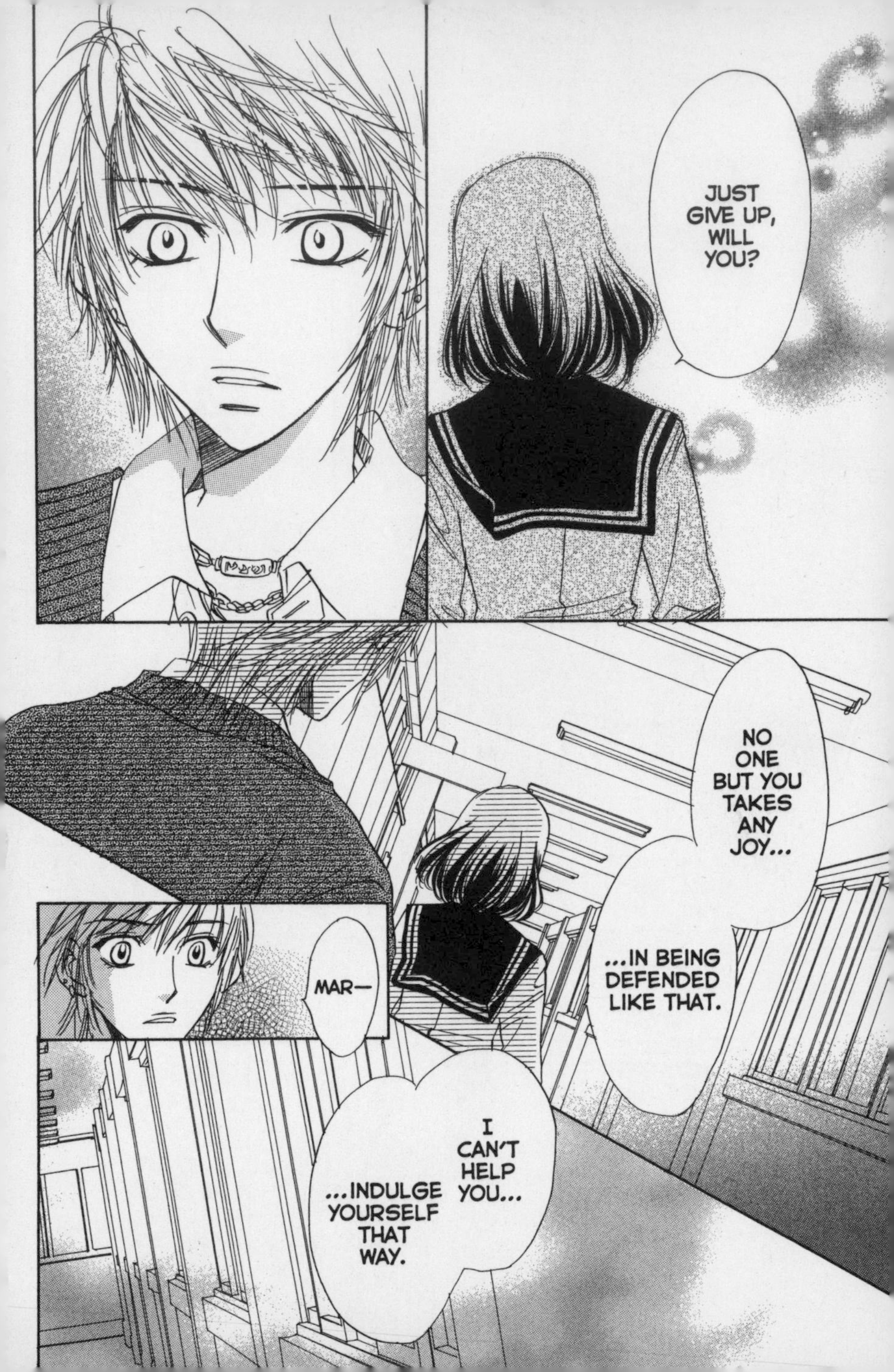
JUST GIVE UP, WILL YOU?
NO ONE BUT YOU TAKES ANY JOY...
...IN BEING DEFENDED LIKE THAT.
MAR—
I CAN'T HELP YOU...
...INDULGE YOURSELF THAT WAY.

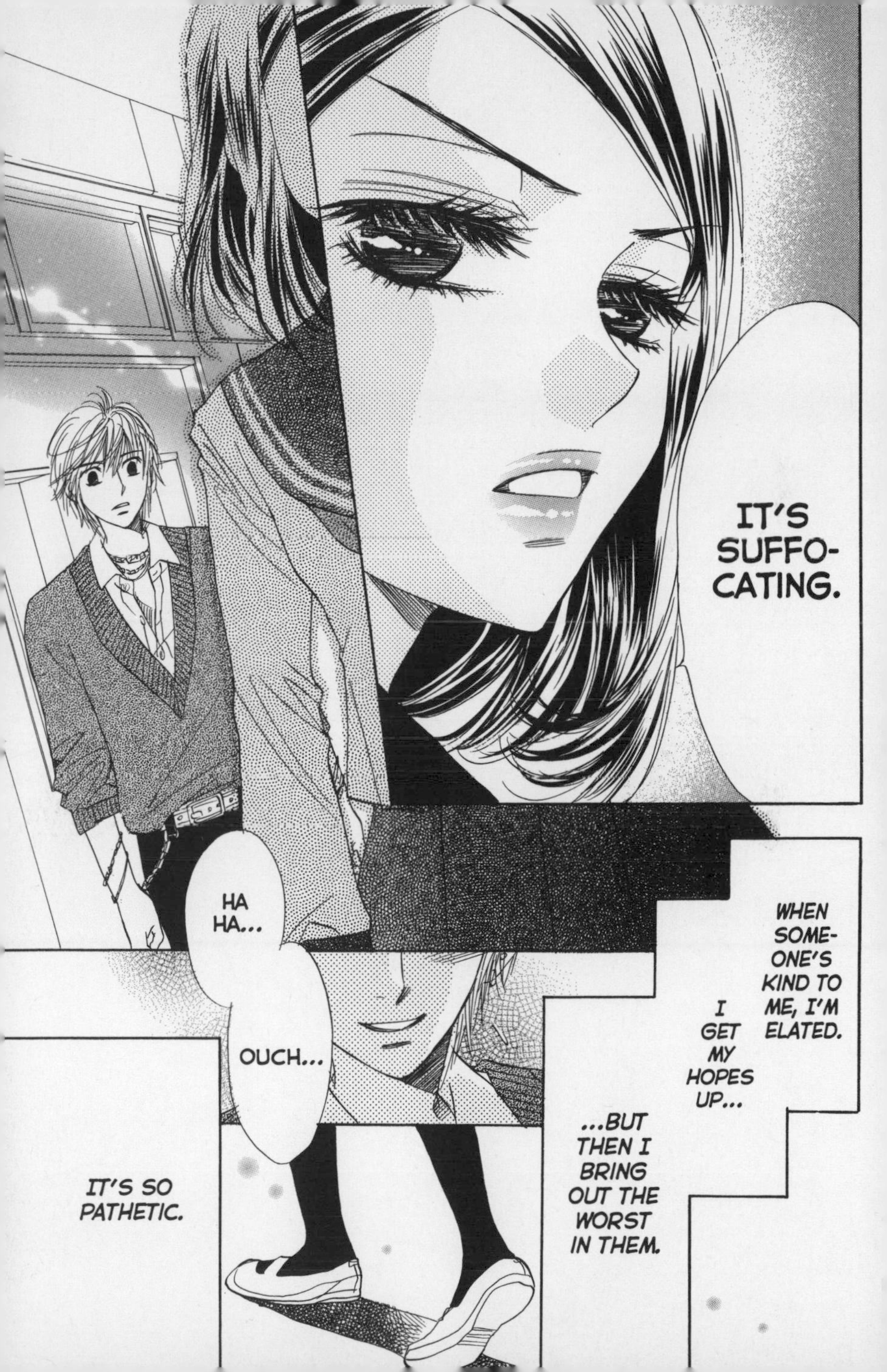
IT'S SUFFO-CATING.
HA HA...
WHEN SOME-ONE'S KIND TO ME, I'M ELATED.
I GET MY HOPES UP...
OUCH...
...BUT THEN I BRING OUT THE WORST IN THEM.
IT'S SO PATHETIC.

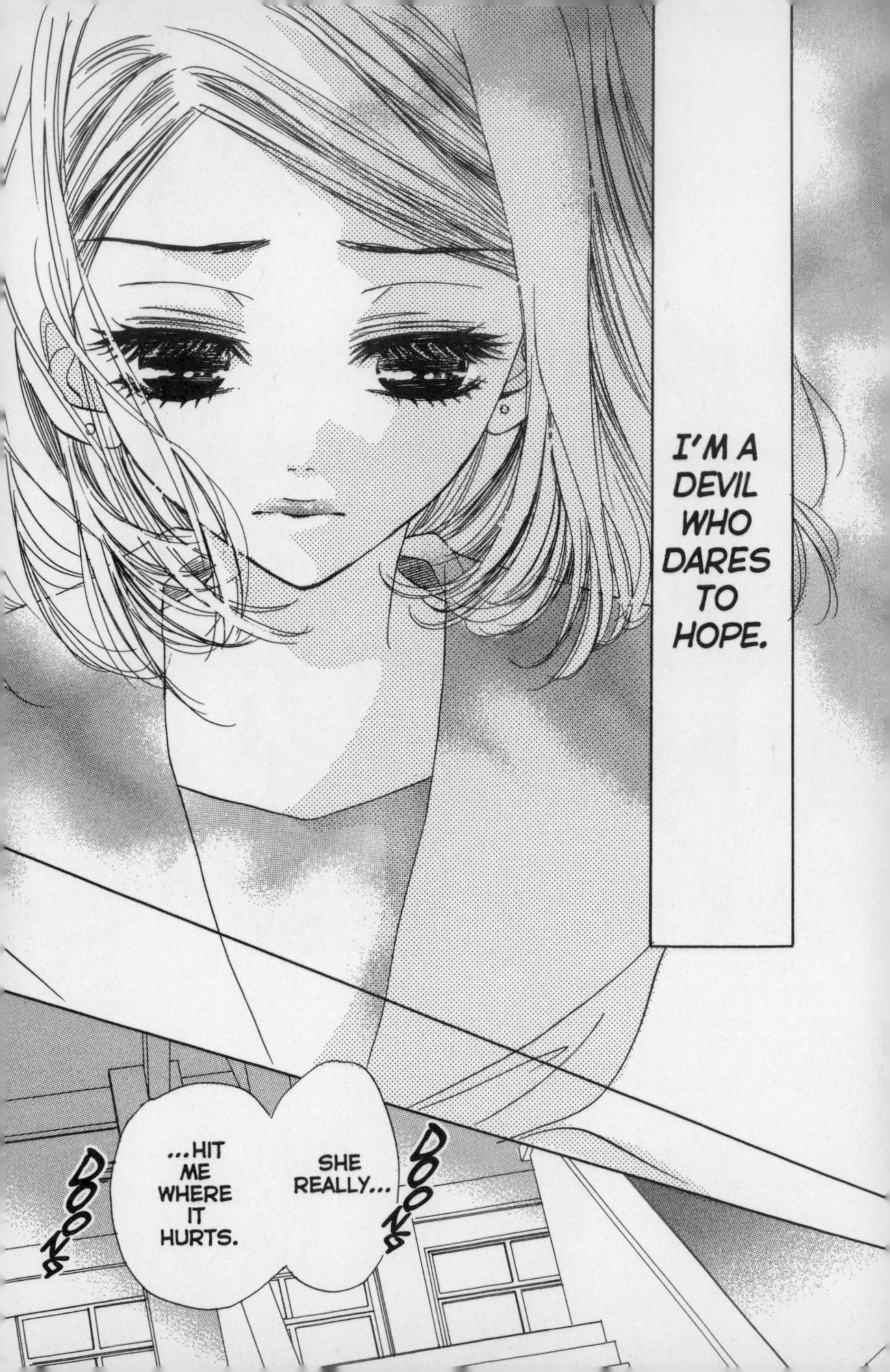
I'M A DEVIL WHO DARES TO HOPE.
DOOONG
SHE REALLY...
...HIT ME WHERE IT HURTS.
DOONG

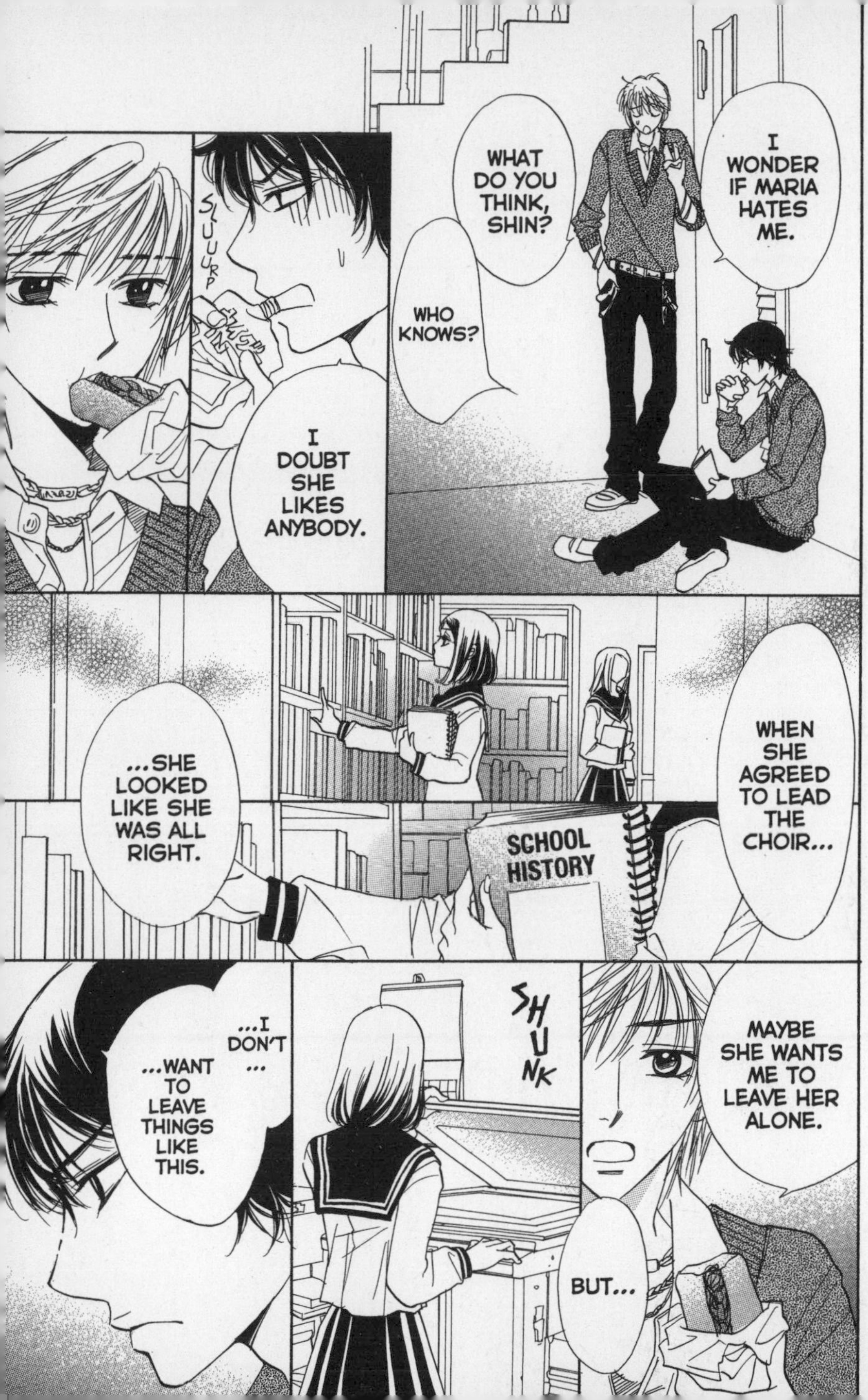
I WONDER IF MARIA HATES ME.
WHAT DO YOU THINK, SHIN?
WHO KNOWS?
SLUUURP
I DOUBT SHE LIKES ANYBODY.
WHEN SHE AGREED TO LEAD THE CHOIR...
SCHOOL HISTORY
...SHE LOOKED LIKE SHE WAS ALL RIGHT.
MAYBE SHE WANTS ME TO LEAVE HER ALONE.
BUT...
SHUNK
...I DON'T ...
...WANT TO LEAVE THINGS LIKE THIS.

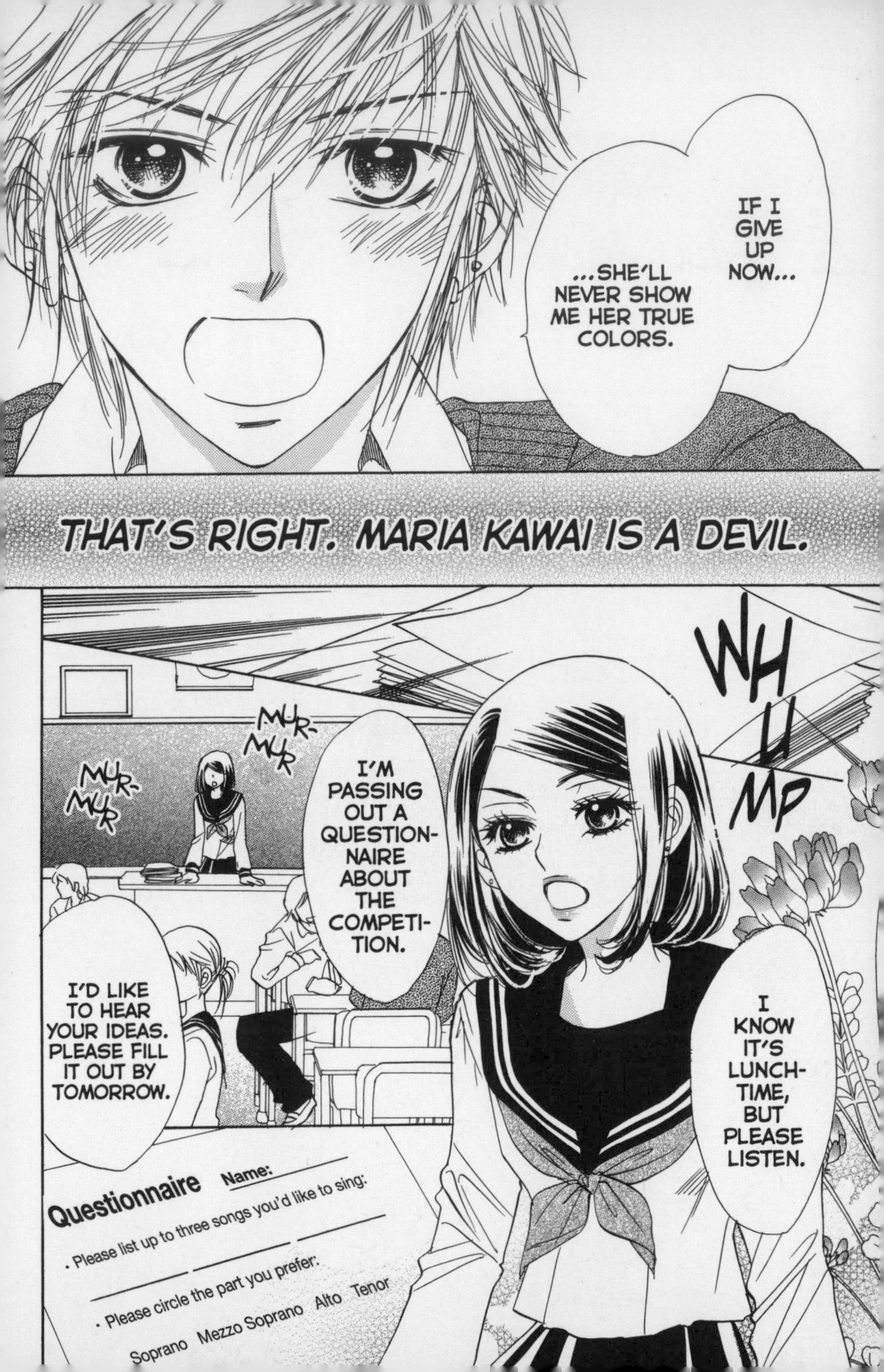
IF I GIVE UP NOW...
...SHE'LL NEVER SHOW ME HER TRUE COLORS.
THAT'S RIGHT. MARIA KAWAI IS A DEVIL.
WHUMP
I KNOW IT'S LUNCH-TIME, BUT PLEASE LISTEN.
I'M PASSING OUT A QUESTION-NAIRE ABOUT THE COMPETI-TION.
MUR-MUR
MUR-MUR
I'D LIKE TO HEAR YOUR IDEAS. PLEASE FILL IT OUT BY TOMORROW.
Questionnaire Name:
· Please list up to three songs you'd like to sing:
· Please circle the part you prefer:
Soprano Mezzo Soprano Alto Tenor

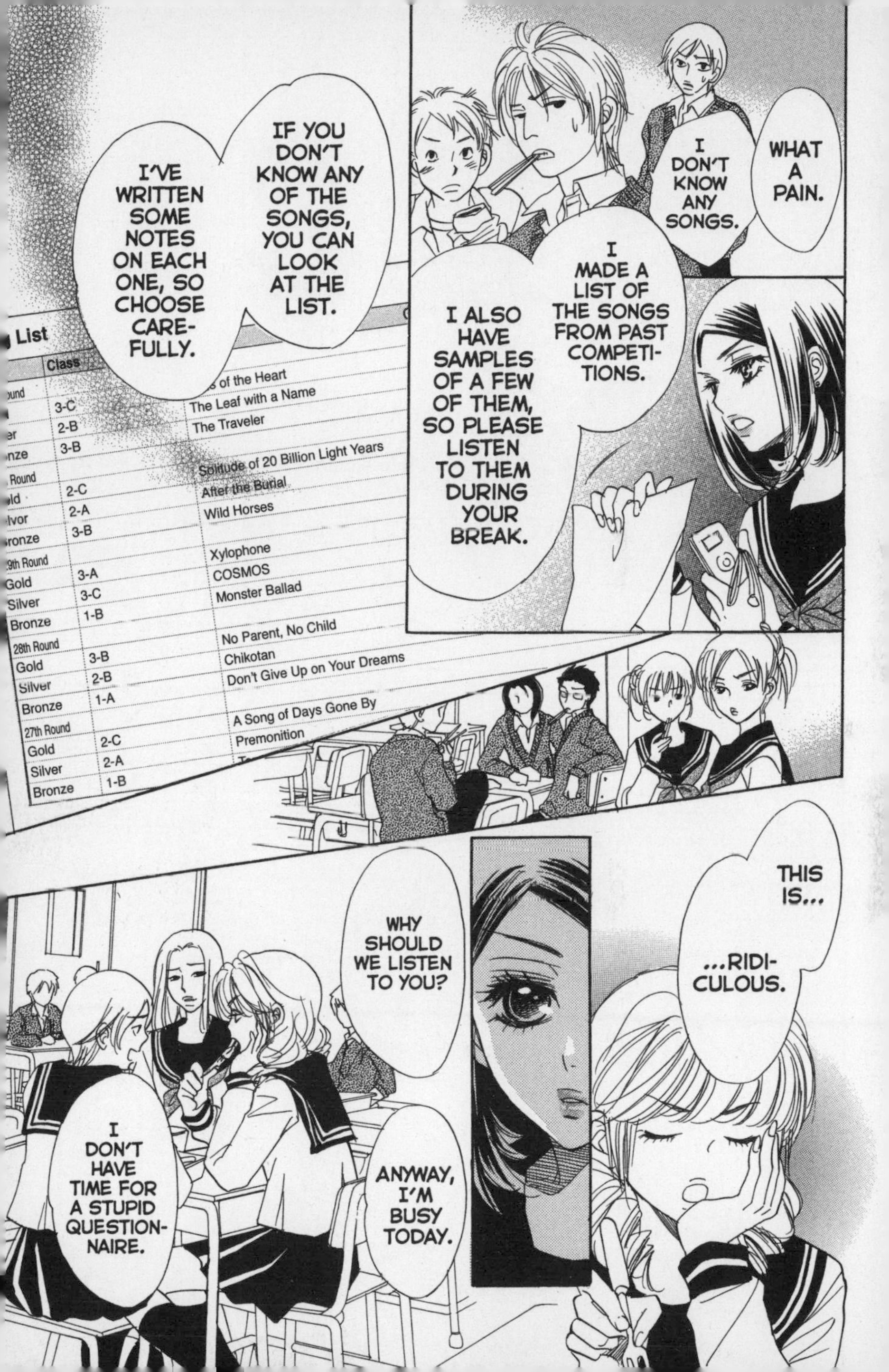
WHAT A PAIN.
I DON'T KNOW ANY SONGS.
I MADE A LIST OF THE SONGS FROM PAST COMPETITIONS.
I ALSO HAVE SAMPLES OF A FEW OF THEM, SO PLEASE LISTEN TO THEM DURING YOUR BREAK.
IF YOU DON'T KNOW ANY OF THE SONGS, YOU CAN LOOK AT THE LIST.
I'VE WRITTEN SOME NOTES ON EACH ONE, SO CHOOSE CAREFULLY.
List
Class
3-C The Leaf with a Name
2-B The Traveler
3-B
Solitude of 20 Billion Light Years
2-C After the Burial
2-A Wild Horses
Bronze 3-B
Xylophone
Gold 3-A COSMOS
Silver 3-C Monster Ballad
Bronze 1-B
28th Round No Parent, No Child
Gold 3-B Chikotan
Silver 2-B Don't Give Up on Your Dreams
Bronze 1-A
A Song of Days Gone By
27th Round Premonition
Gold 2-C
Silver 2-A
Bronze 1-B
THIS IS...
...RIDICULOUS.
WHY SHOULD WE LISTEN TO YOU?
ANYWAY, I'M BUSY TODAY.
I DON'T HAVE TIME FOR A STUPID QUESTIONNAIRE.

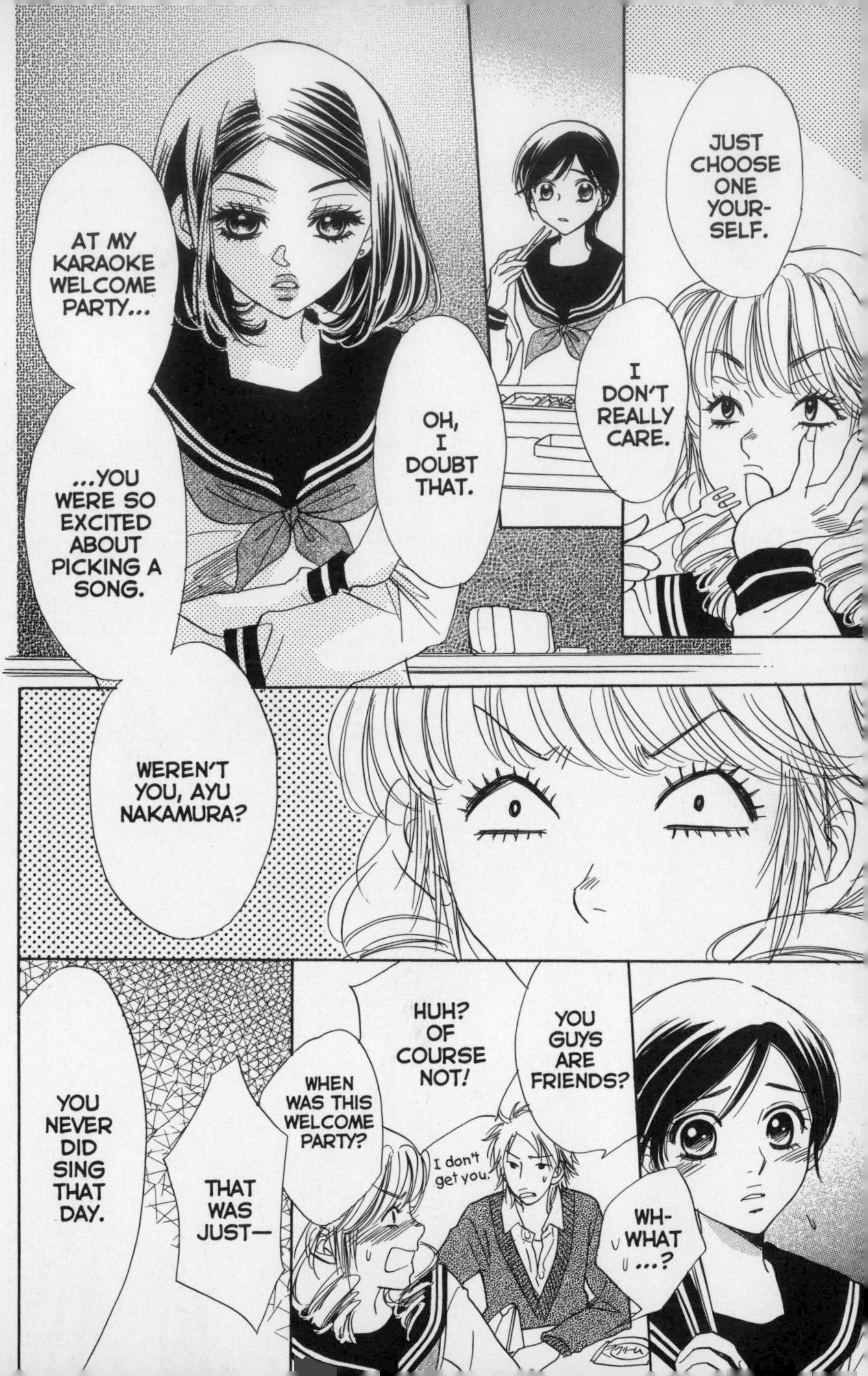

JUST CHOOSE ONE YOURSELF.
I DON'T REALLY CARE.
OH, I DOUBT THAT.
AT MY KARAOKE WELCOME PARTY...
...YOU WERE SO EXCITED ABOUT PICKING A SONG.
WEREN'T YOU, AYU NAKAMURA?
YOU GUYS ARE FRIENDS?
HUH? OF COURSE NOT!
WH-WHAT...?
WHEN WAS THIS WELCOME PARTY?
I don't get you.
THAT WAS JUST—
YOU NEVER DID SING THAT DAY.

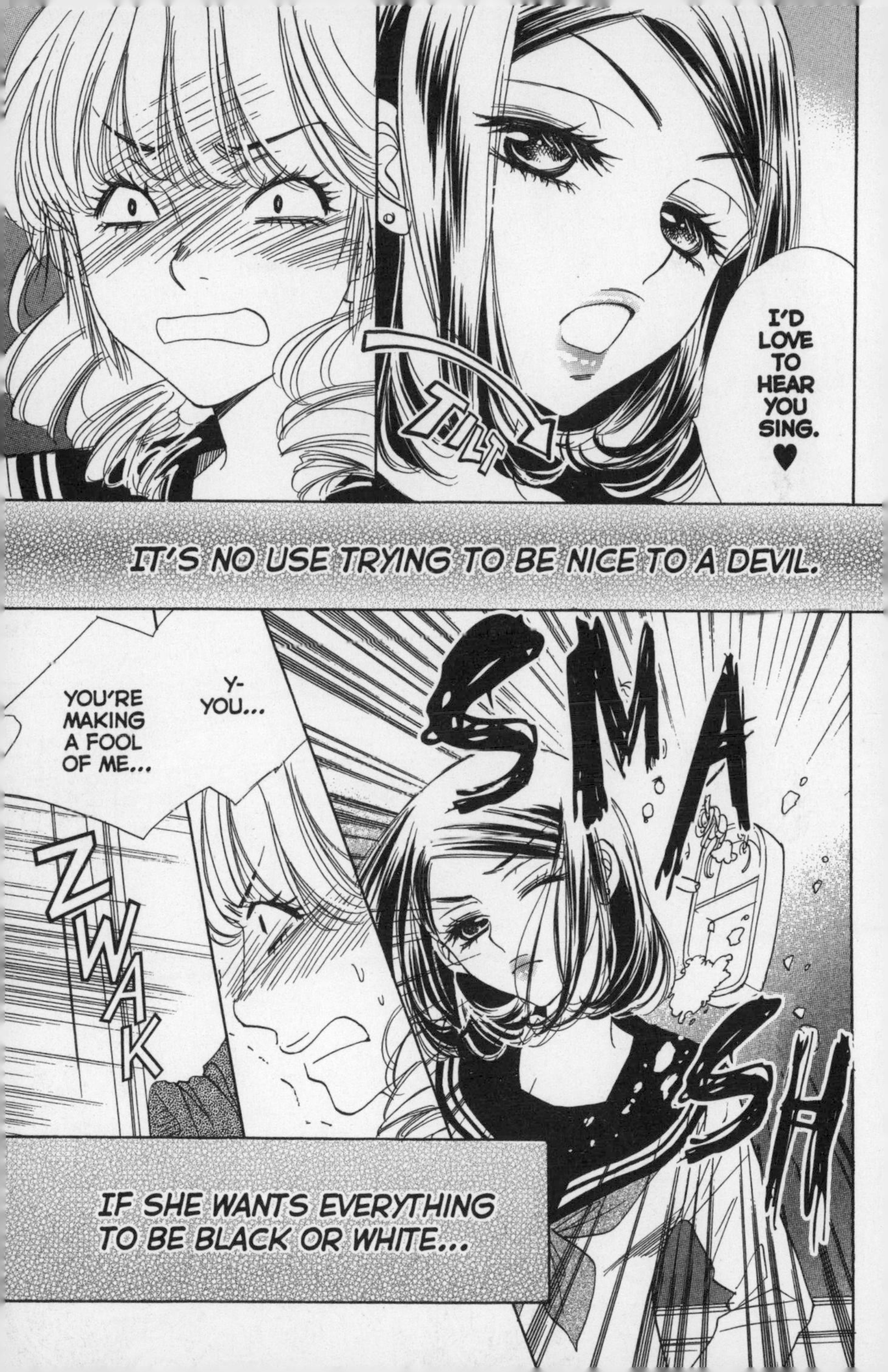
I'D LOVE TO HEAR YOU SING. ♥
TILT
IT'S NO USE TRYING TO BE NICE TO A DEVIL.
SMASH
Y-YOU...
YOU'RE MAKING A FOOL OF ME...
ZWAK
IF SHE WANTS EVERYTHING TO BE BLACK OR WHITE...

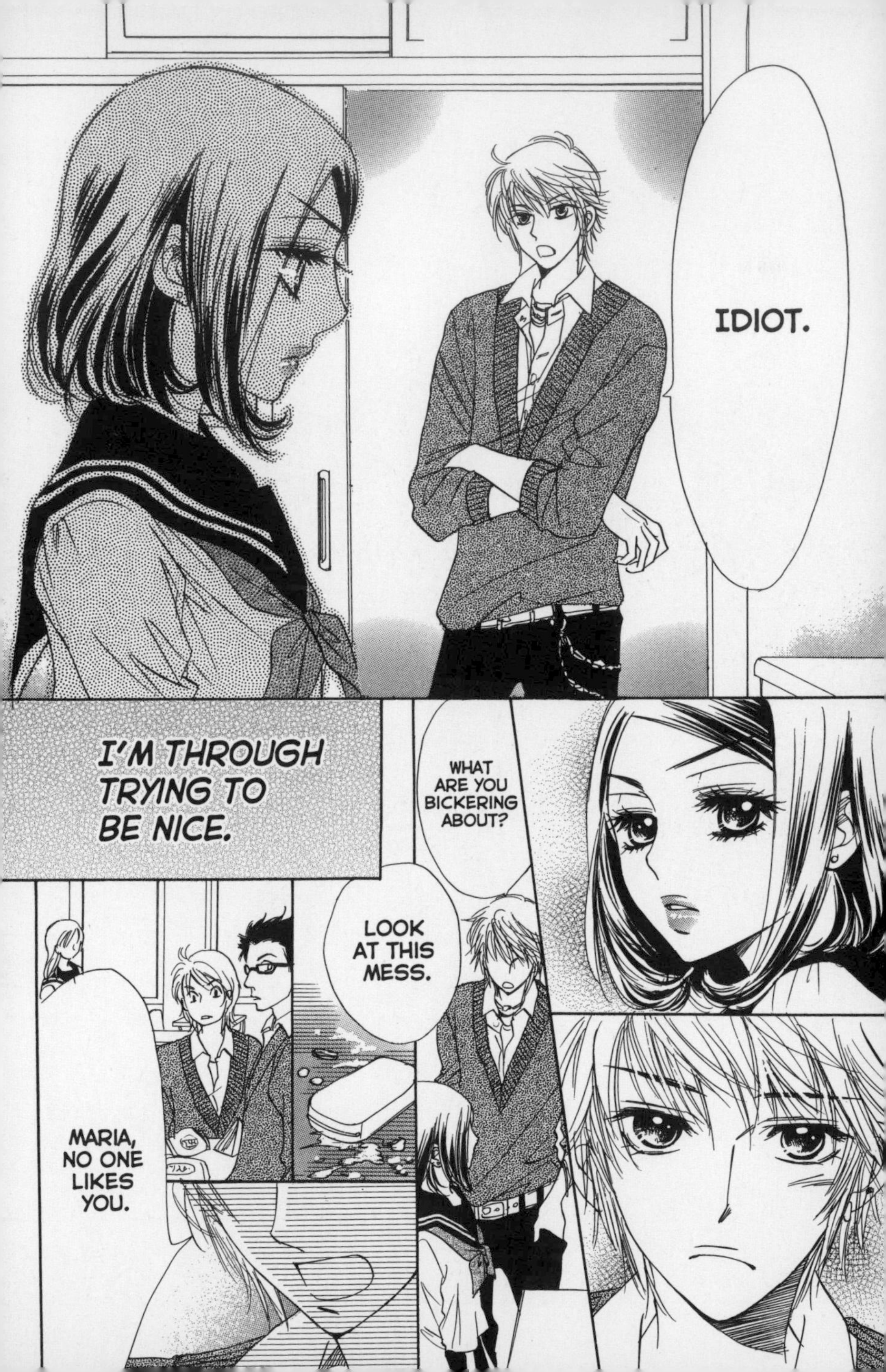
IDIOT.
WHAT ARE YOU BICKERING ABOUT?
LOOK AT THIS MESS.
I'M THROUGH TRYING TO BE NICE.
MARIA, NO ONE LIKES YOU.

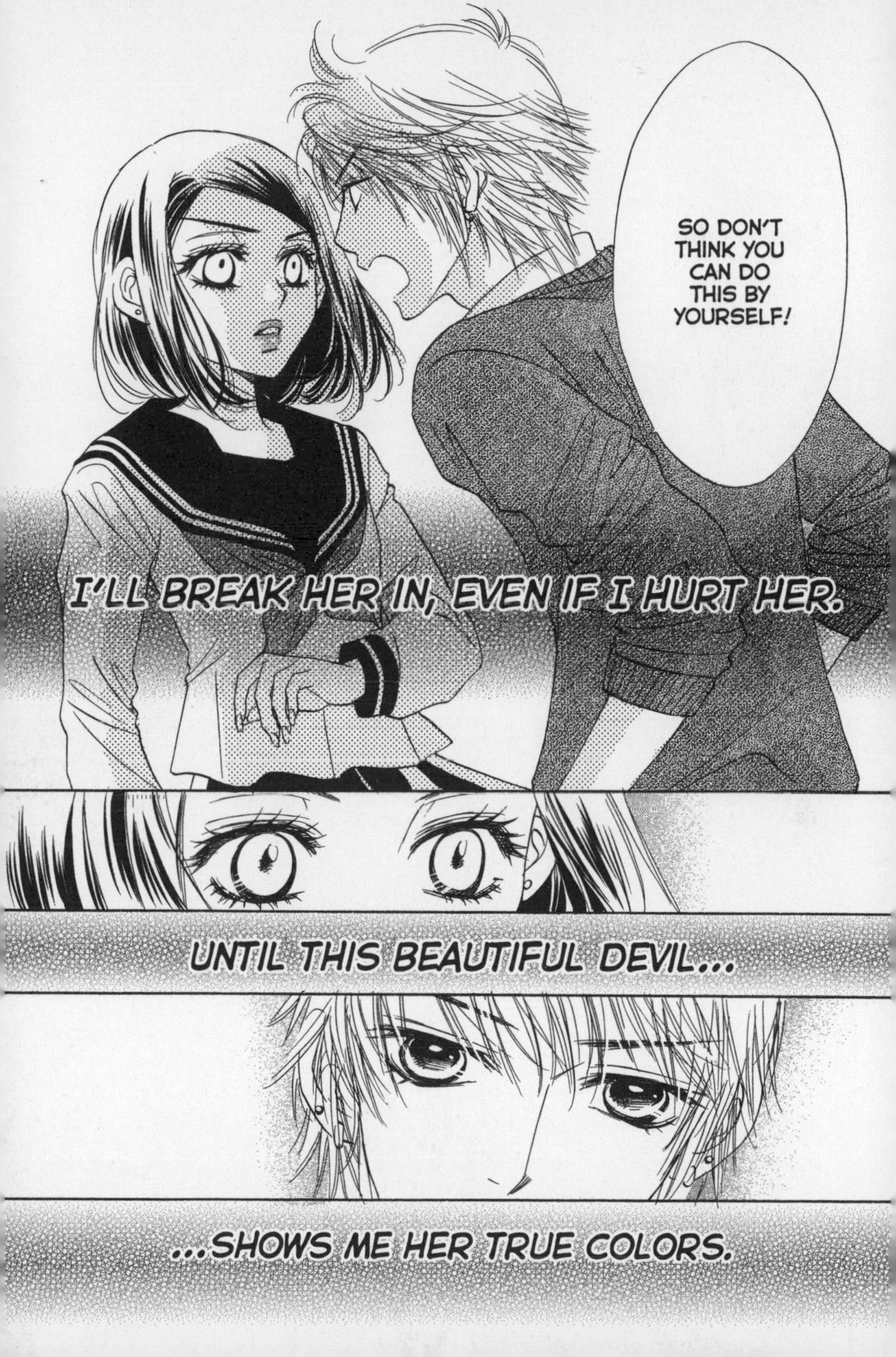
SO DON'T THINK YOU CAN DO THIS BY YOURSELF!
I'LL BREAK HER IN, EVEN IF I HURT HER.
UNTIL THIS BEAUTIFUL DEVIL...
...SHOWS ME HER TRUE COLORS.

A Devil and Her Love Song

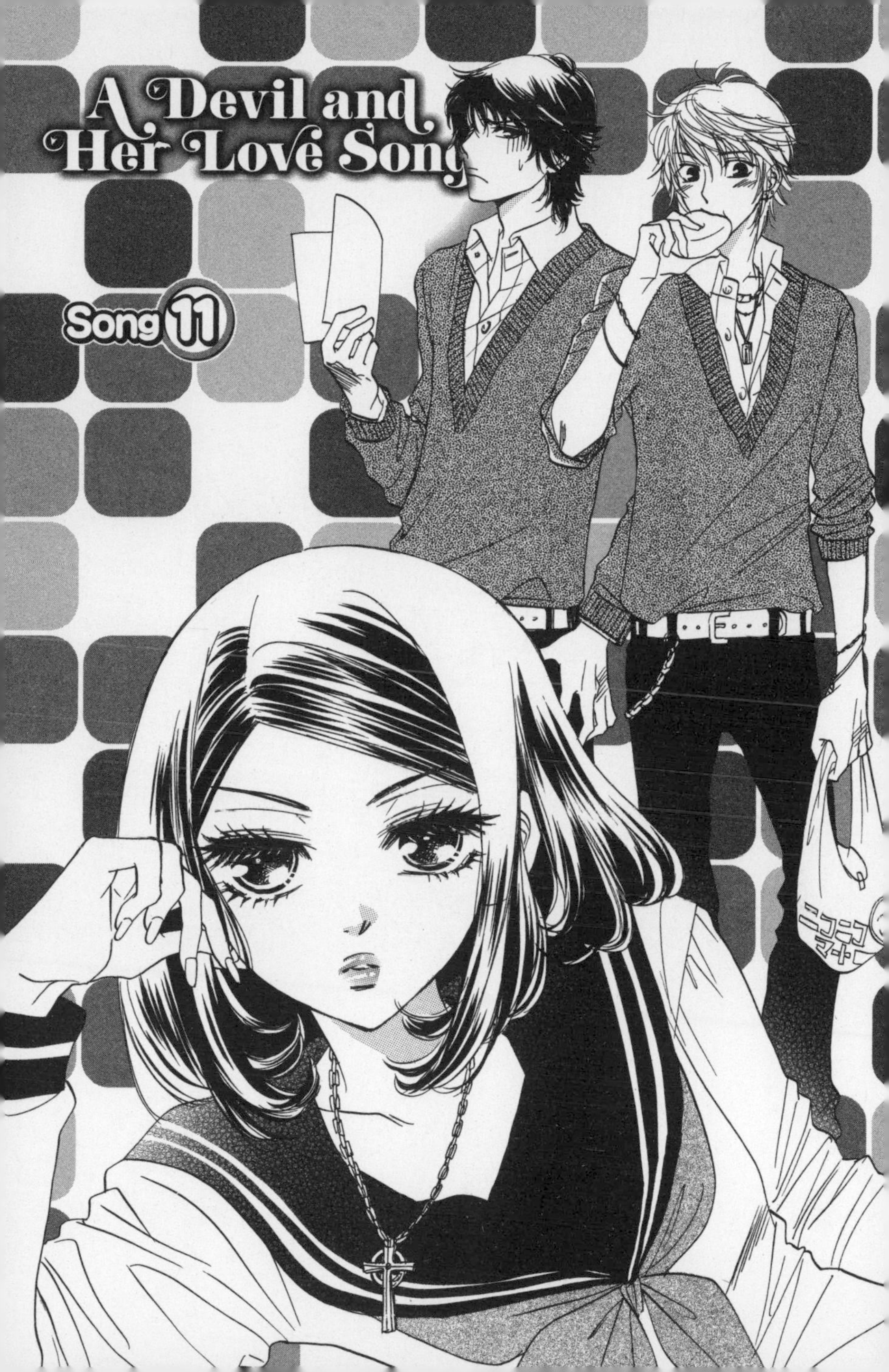
A Devil and
Her Love Song
Song 11

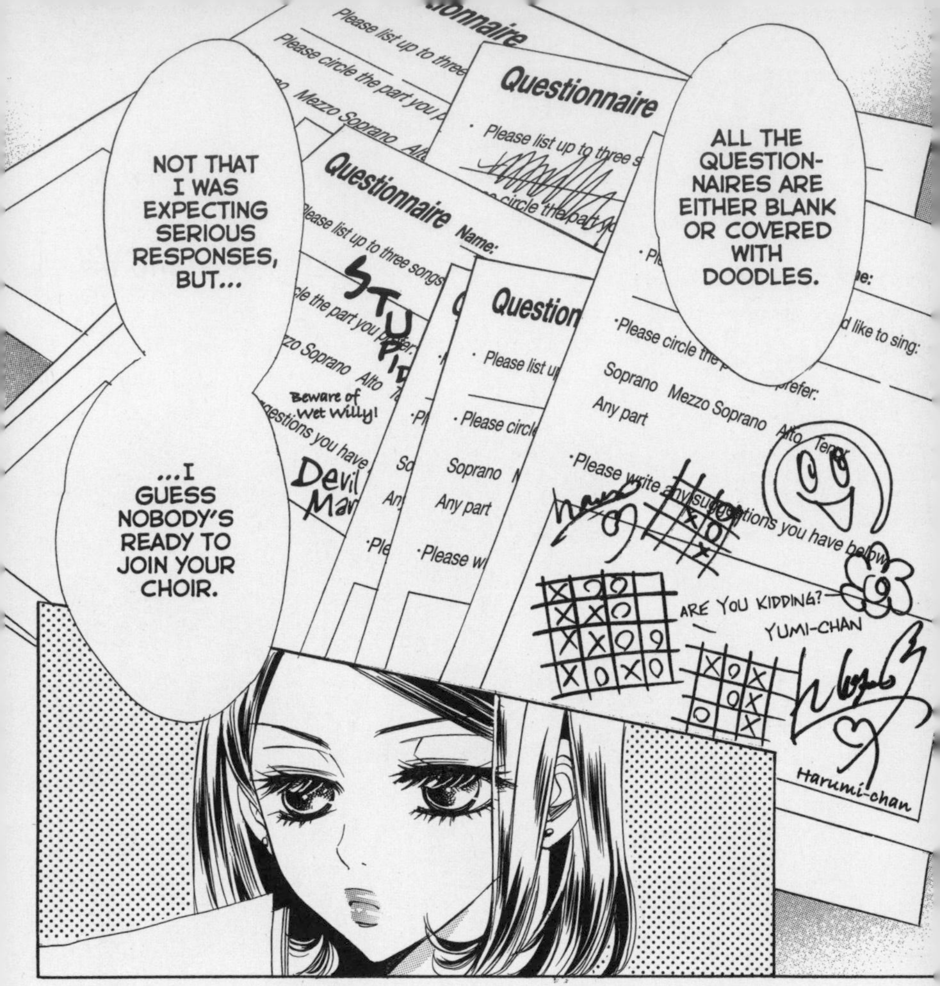
ALL THE QUESTIONNAIRES ARE EITHER BLANK OR COVERED WITH DOODLES.
NOT THAT I WAS EXPECTING SERIOUS RESPONSES, BUT...
...I GUESS NOBODY'S READY TO JOIN YOUR CHOIR.
Questionnaire
Please circle the part you prefer:
Soprano Mezzo Soprano Alto
Any part
Beware of Wet Willy!
ARE YOU KIDDING?
YUMI-CHAN
Harumi-chan

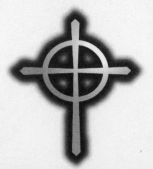

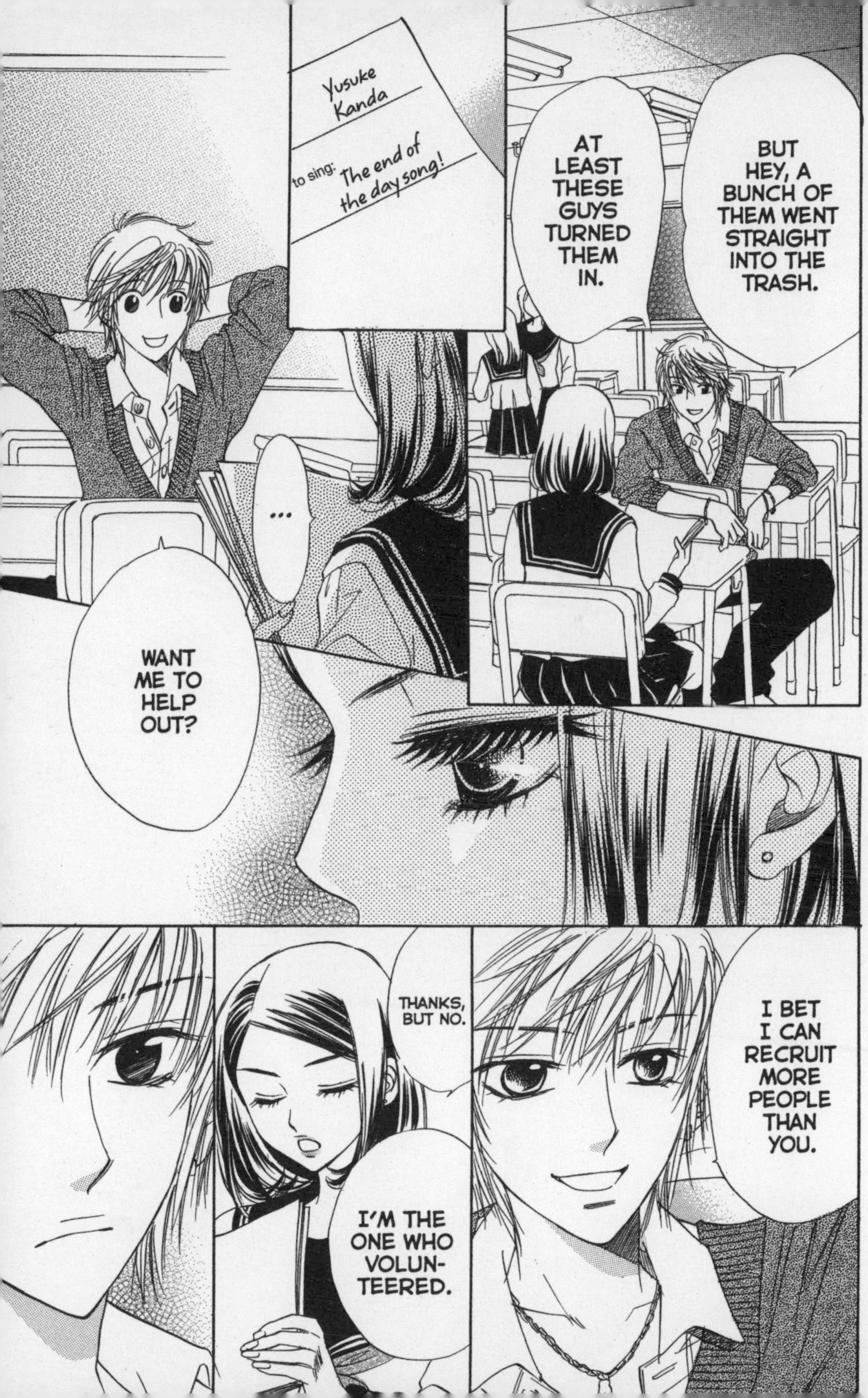
BUT HEY, A BUNCH OF THEM WENT STRAIGHT INTO THE TRASH.
AT LEAST THESE GUYS TURNED THEM IN.
Yusuke Kanda
to sing: The end of the day song!
...
WANT ME TO HELP OUT?
I BET I CAN RECRUIT MORE PEOPLE THAN YOU.
THANKS, BUT NO.
I'M THE ONE WHO VOLUNTEERED.

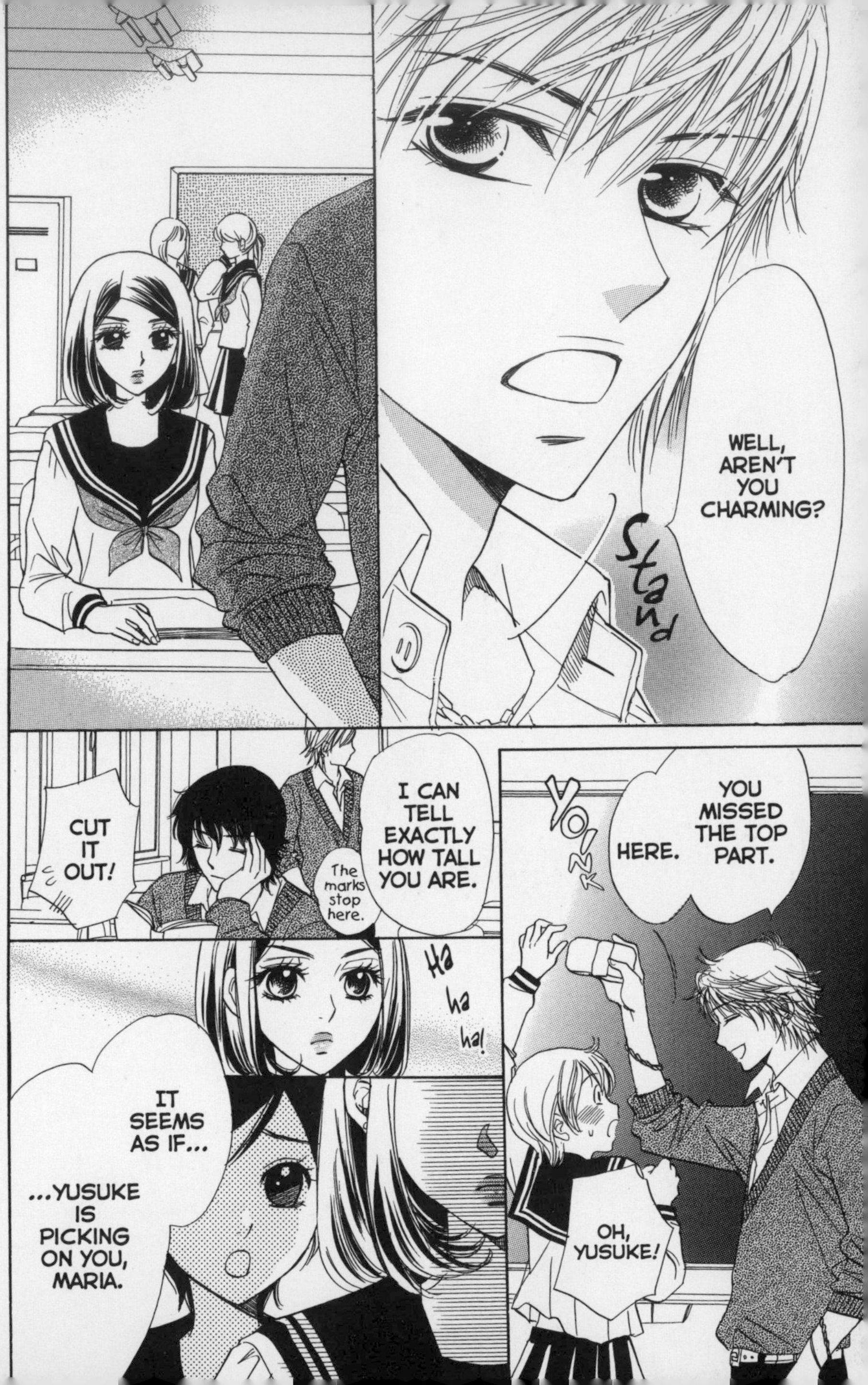
WELL, AREN'T YOU CHARMING?
Stand
YOU MISSED THE TOP PART.
HERE.
YONK
OH, YUSUKE!
I CAN TELL EXACTLY HOW TALL YOU ARE.
The marks stop here.
CUT IT OUT!
Ha ha ha!
IT SEEMS AS IF...
...YUSUKE IS PICKING ON YOU, MARIA.

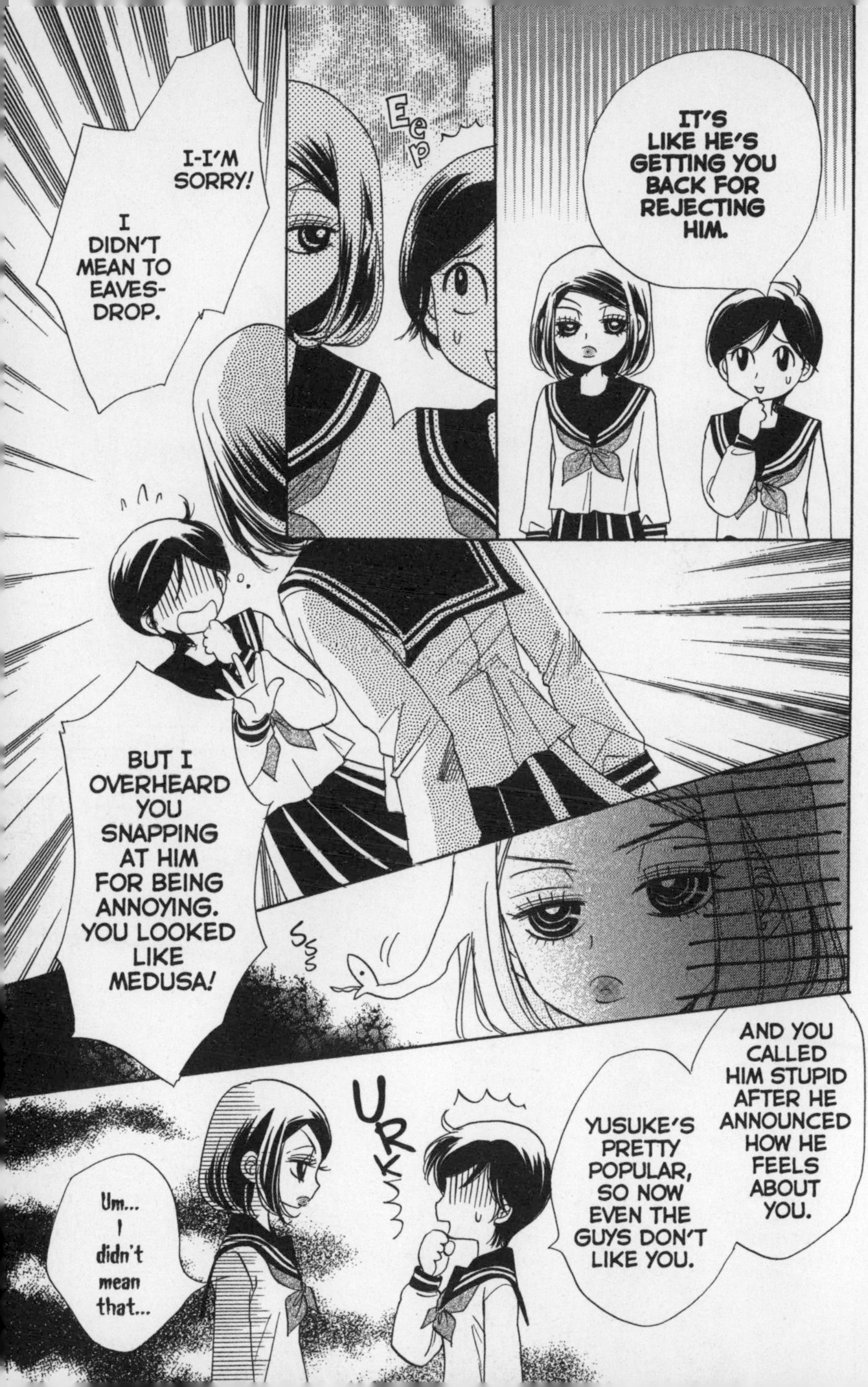
IT'S LIKE HE'S GETTING YOU BACK FOR REJECTING HIM.
Eep
I-I'M SORRY!
I DIDN'T MEAN TO EAVES-DROP.
BUT I OVERHEARD YOU SNAPPING AT HIM FOR BEING ANNOYING. YOU LOOKED LIKE MEDUSA!
SSS
AND YOU CALLED HIM STUPID AFTER HE ANNOUNCED HOW HE FEELS ABOUT YOU.
YUSUKE'S PRETTY POPULAR, SO NOW EVEN THE GUYS DON'T LIKE YOU.
URK
Um... I didn't mean that...

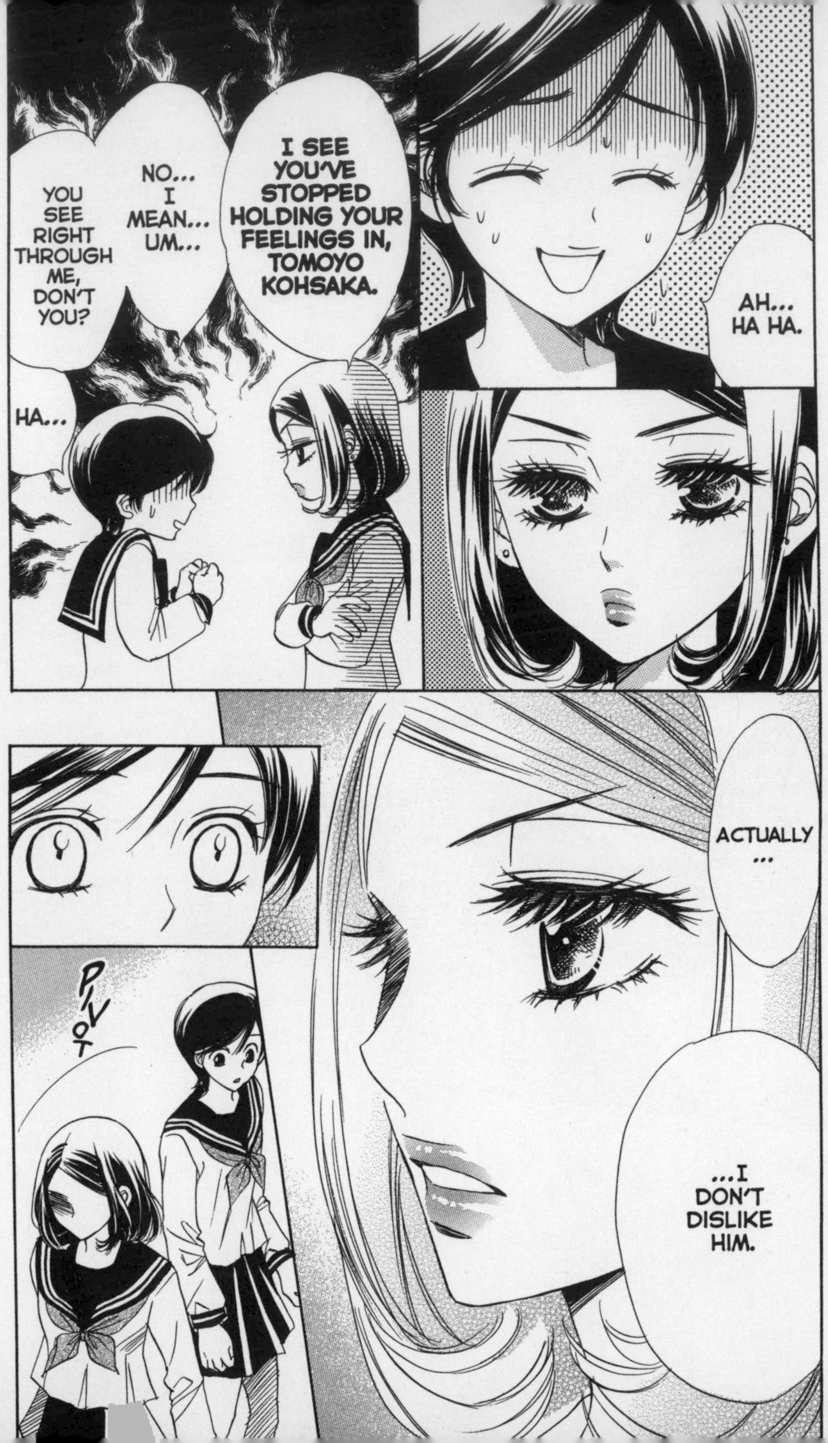
AH... HA HA.
I SEE YOU'VE STOPPED HOLDING YOUR FEELINGS IN, TOMOYO KOHSAKA.
NO... I MEAN... UM...
YOU SEE RIGHT THROUGH ME, DON'T YOU?
HA...
ACTUALLY ...
...I DON'T DISLIKE HIM.
PIVOT

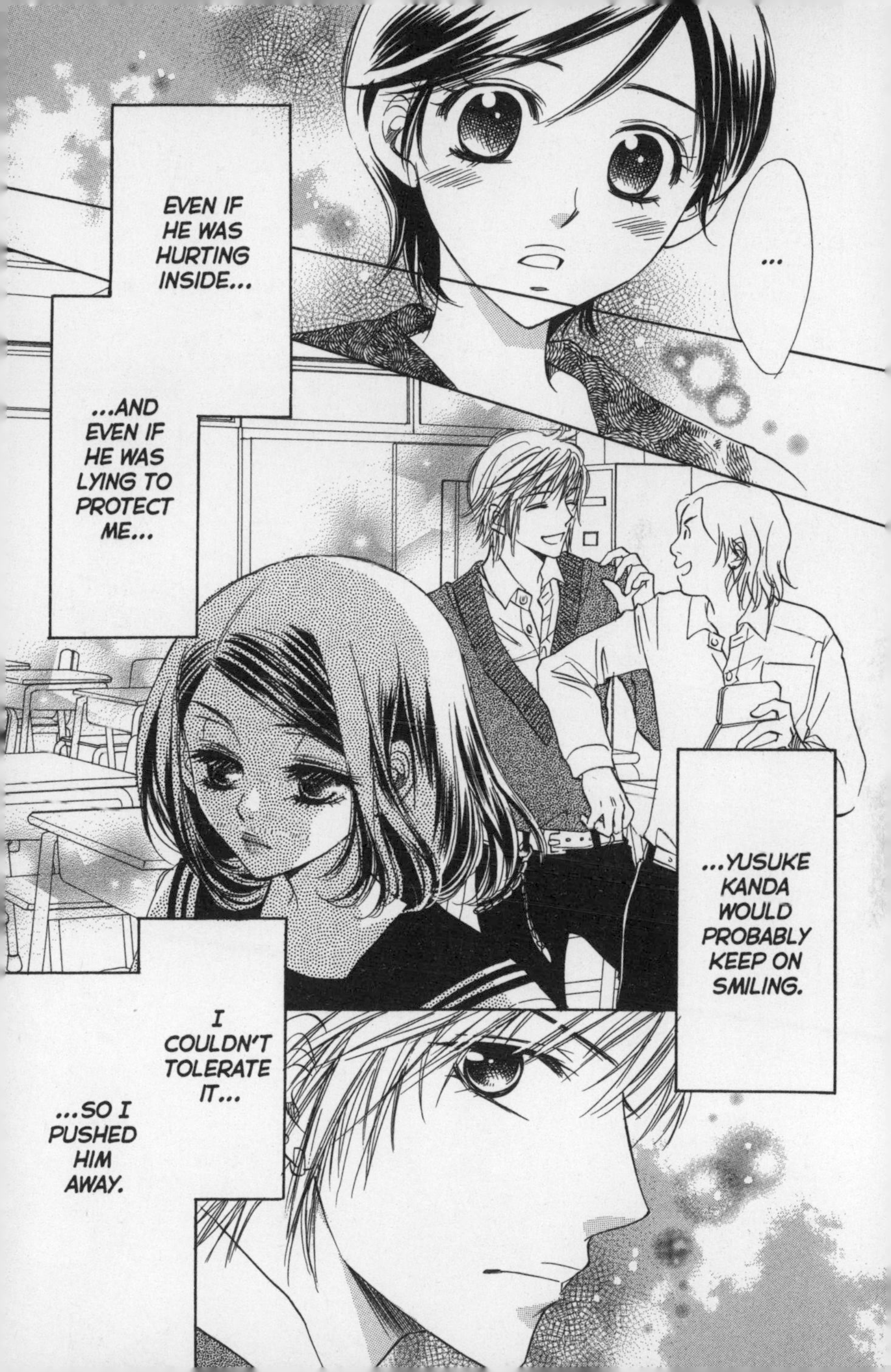
...
EVEN IF HE WAS HURTING INSIDE...
...AND EVEN IF HE WAS LYING TO PROTECT ME...
...YUSUKE KANDA WOULD PROBABLY KEEP ON SMILING.
I COULDN'T TOLERATE IT...
...SO I PUSHED HIM AWAY.

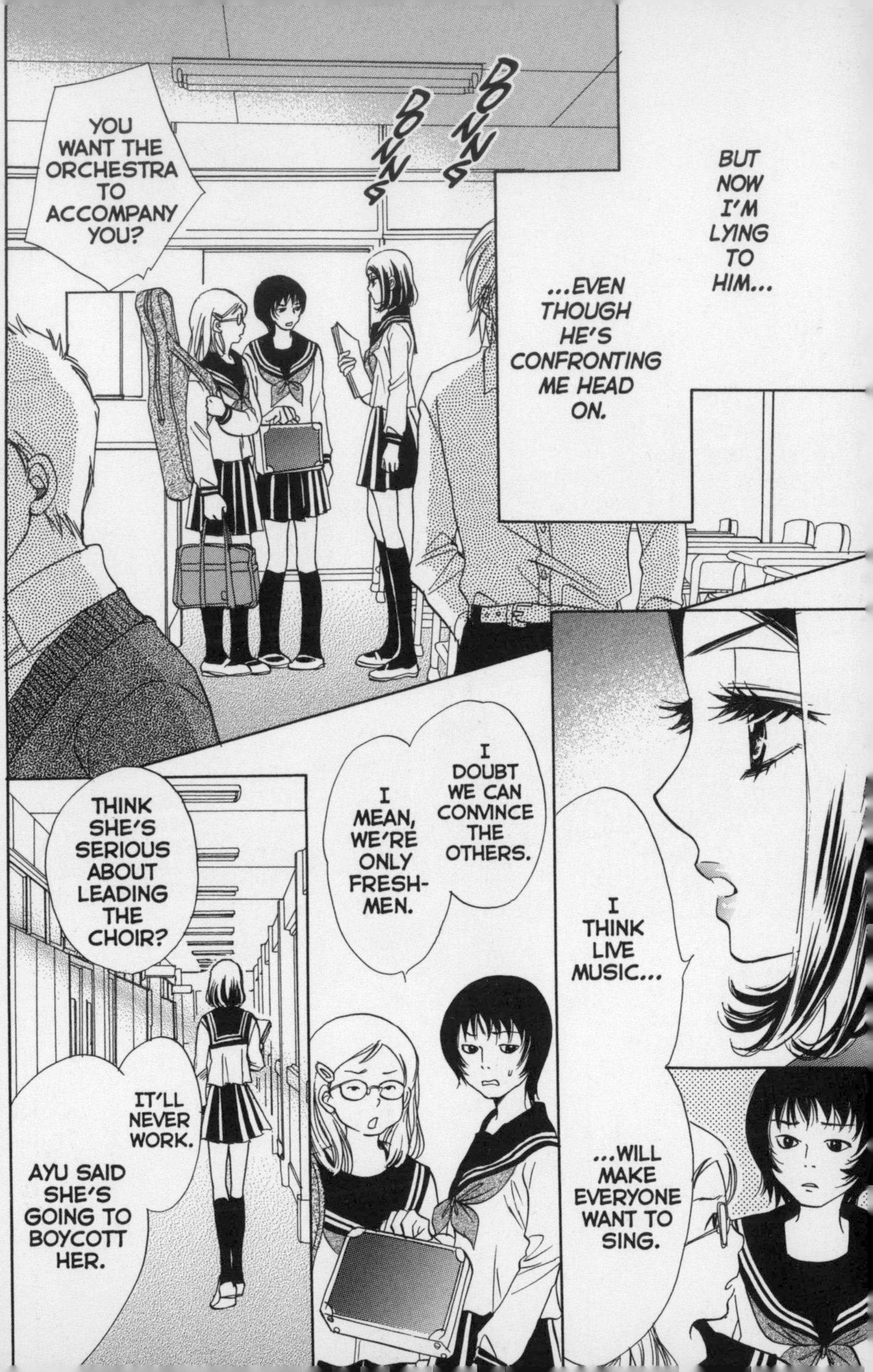
BUT NOW I'M LYING TO HIM...
...EVEN THOUGH HE'S CONFRONTING ME HEAD ON.
DONNG
DONNG
YOU WANT THE ORCHESTRA TO ACCOMPANY YOU?
I THINK LIVE MUSIC...
...WILL MAKE EVERYONE WANT TO SING.
I DOUBT WE CAN CONVINCE THE OTHERS.
I MEAN, WE'RE ONLY FRESH-MEN.
THINK SHE'S SERIOUS ABOUT LEADING THE CHOIR?
IT'LL NEVER WORK.
AYU SAID SHE'S GOING TO BOYCOTT HER.

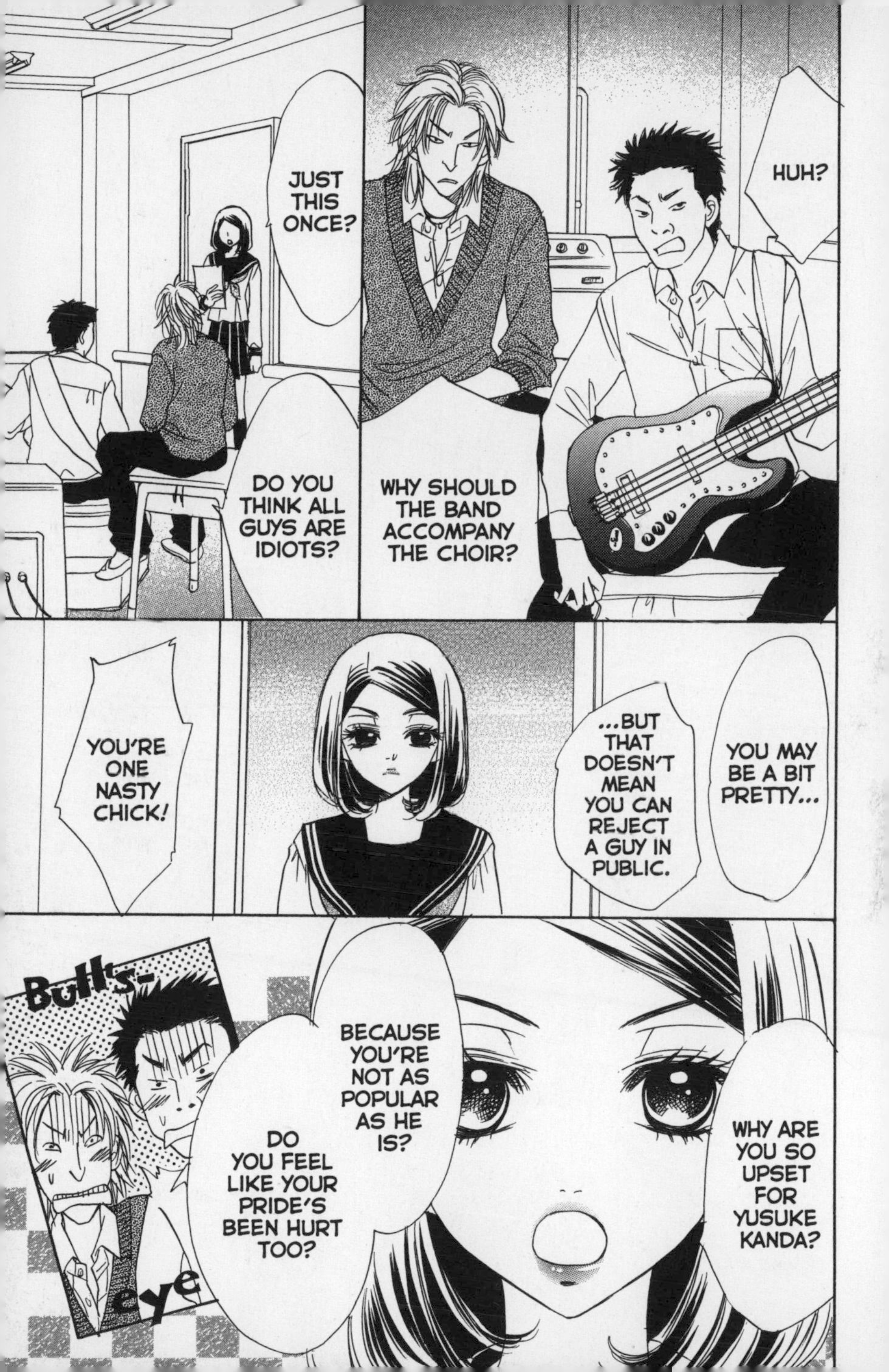
HUH?
WHY SHOULD THE BAND ACCOMPANY THE CHOIR?
JUST THIS ONCE?
DO YOU THINK ALL GUYS ARE IDIOTS?
YOU MAY BE A BIT PRETTY...
...BUT THAT DOESN'T MEAN YOU CAN REJECT A GUY IN PUBLIC.
YOU'RE ONE NASTY CHICK!
WHY ARE YOU SO UPSET FOR YUSUKE KANDA?
BECAUSE YOU'RE NOT AS POPULAR AS HE IS?
DO YOU FEEL LIKE YOUR PRIDE'S BEEN HURT TOO?
Bull's-eye

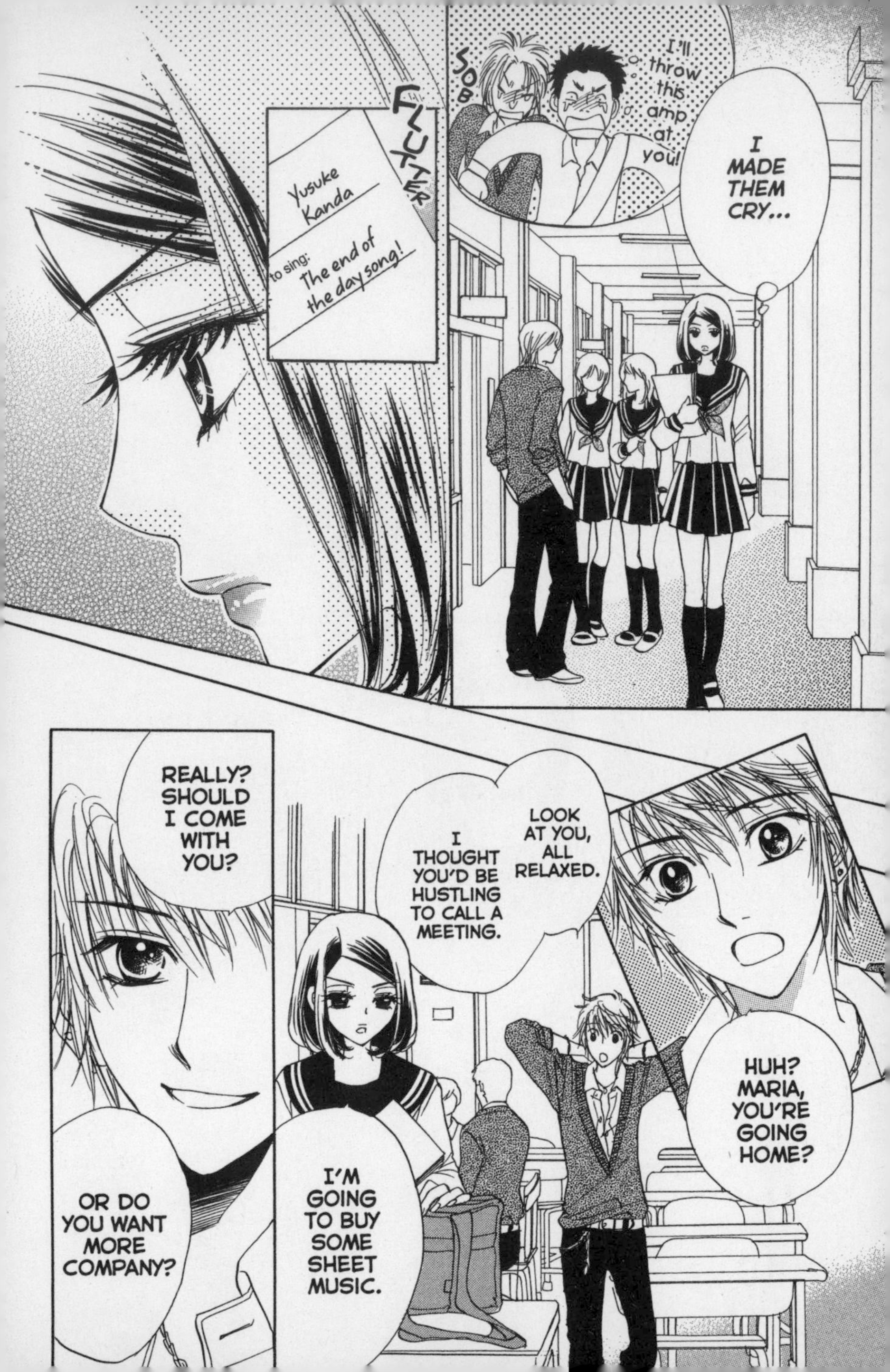
I MADE THEM CRY...
I'll throw this amp at you!
SOB
FLUTTER
Yusuke Kanda
to sing: The end of the day song!
LOOK AT YOU, ALL RELAXED.
I THOUGHT YOU'D BE HUSTLING TO CALL A MEETING.
HUH? MARIA, YOU'RE GOING HOME?
I'M GOING TO BUY SOME SHEET MUSIC.
REALLY? SHOULD I COME WITH YOU?
OR DO YOU WANT MORE COMPANY?

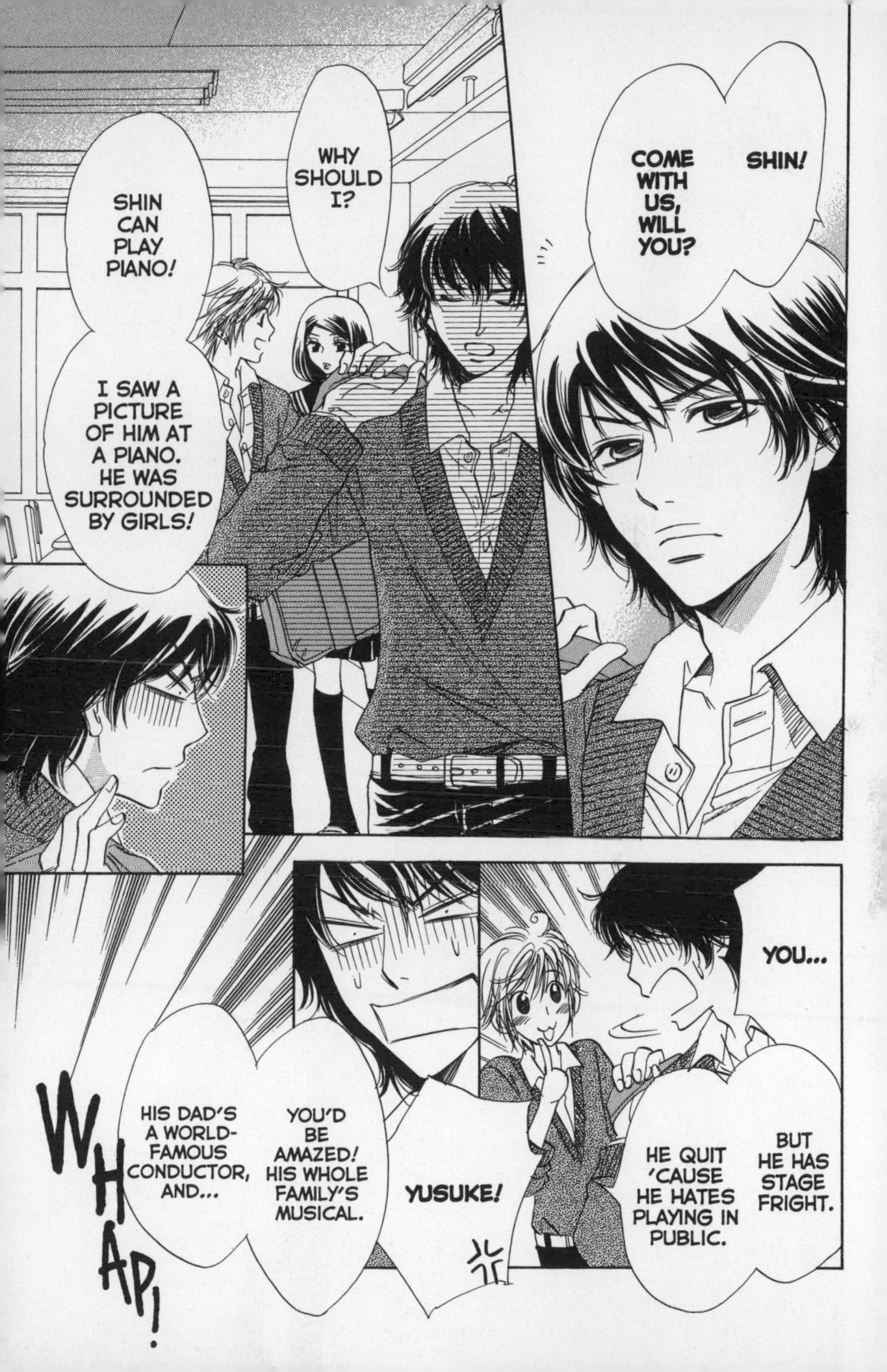
SHIN!
COME WITH US, WILL YOU?
WHY SHOULD I?
SHIN CAN PLAY PIANO!
I SAW A PICTURE OF HIM AT A PIANO. HE WAS SURROUNDED BY GIRLS!
YOU...
BUT HE HAS STAGE FRIGHT.
HE QUIT 'CAUSE HE HATES PLAYING IN PUBLIC.
YUSUKE!
YOU'D BE AMAZED! HIS WHOLE FAMILY'S MUSICAL.
HIS DAD'S A WORLD-FAMOUS CONDUCTOR, AND...
WHAP!

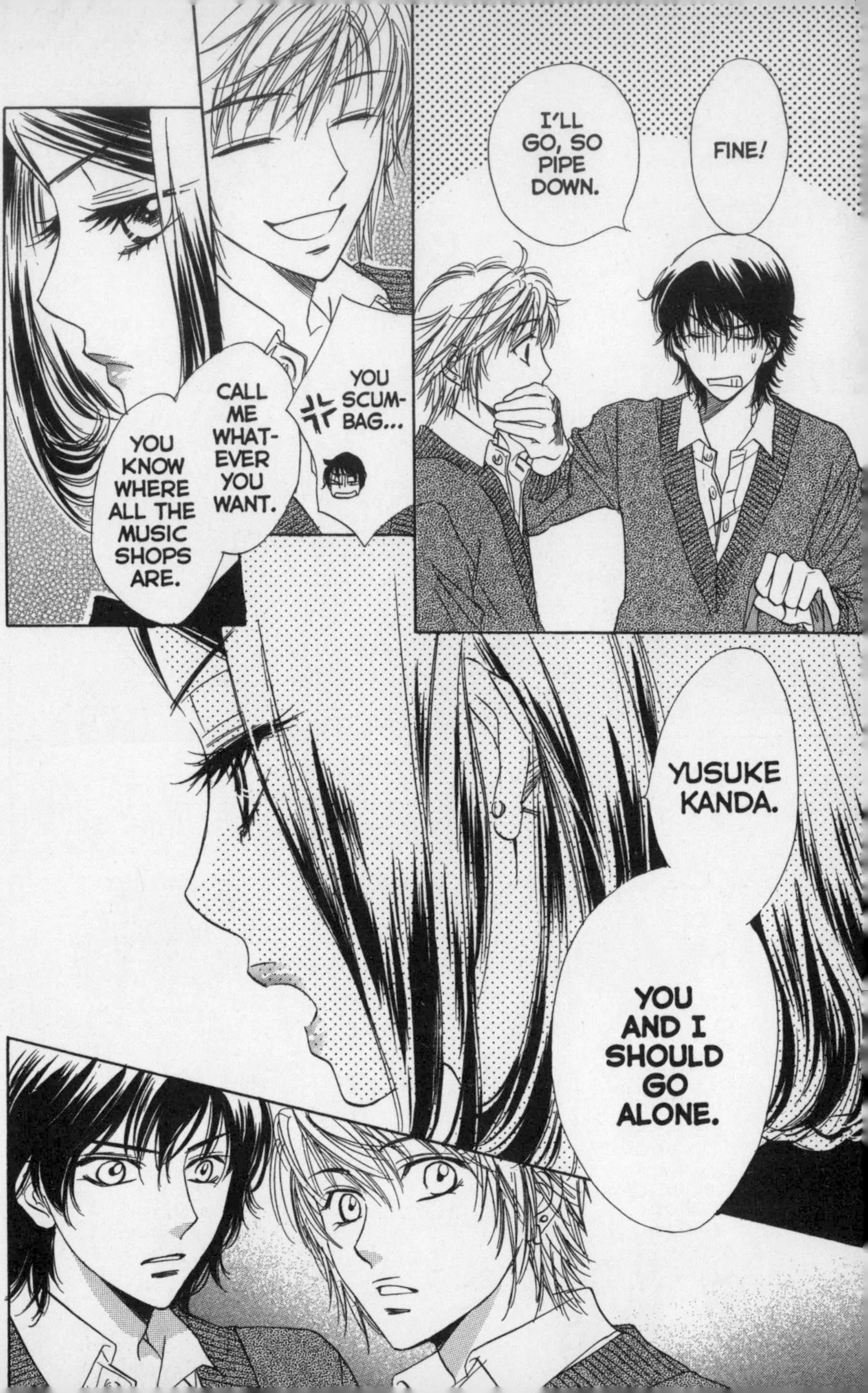
FINE!
I'LL GO, SO PIPE DOWN.
YOU SCUM-BAG...
CALL ME WHAT-EVER YOU WANT.
YOU KNOW WHERE ALL THE MUSIC SHOPS ARE.
YUSUKE KANDA.
YOU AND I SHOULD GO ALONE.

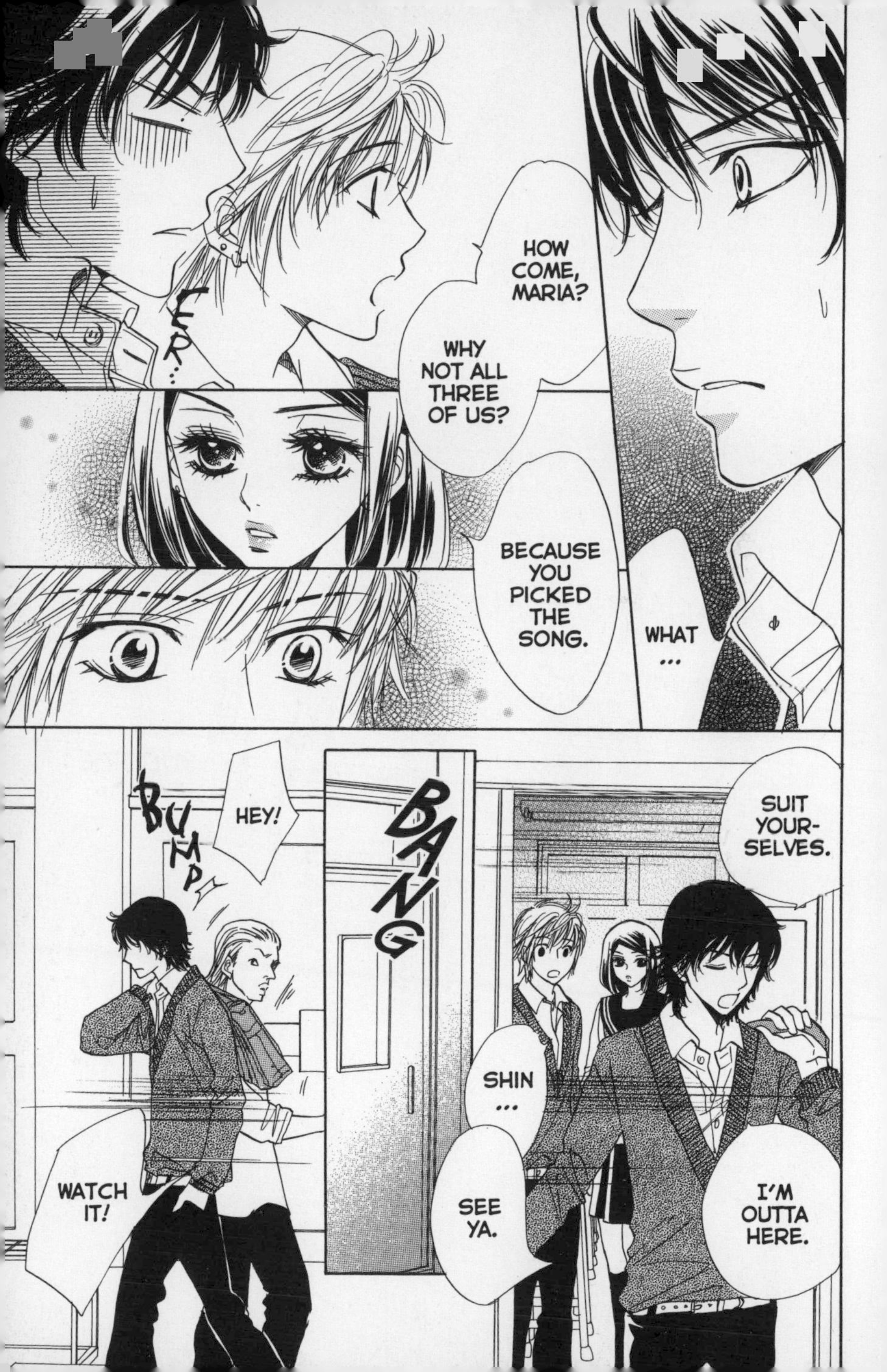
ER...
HOW COME, MARIA?
WHY NOT ALL THREE OF US?
BECAUSE YOU PICKED THE SONG.
WHAT ...
SUIT YOUR-SELVES.
I'M OUTTA HERE.
SHIN ...
SEE YA.
BANG
HEY!
BUMP
WATCH IT!

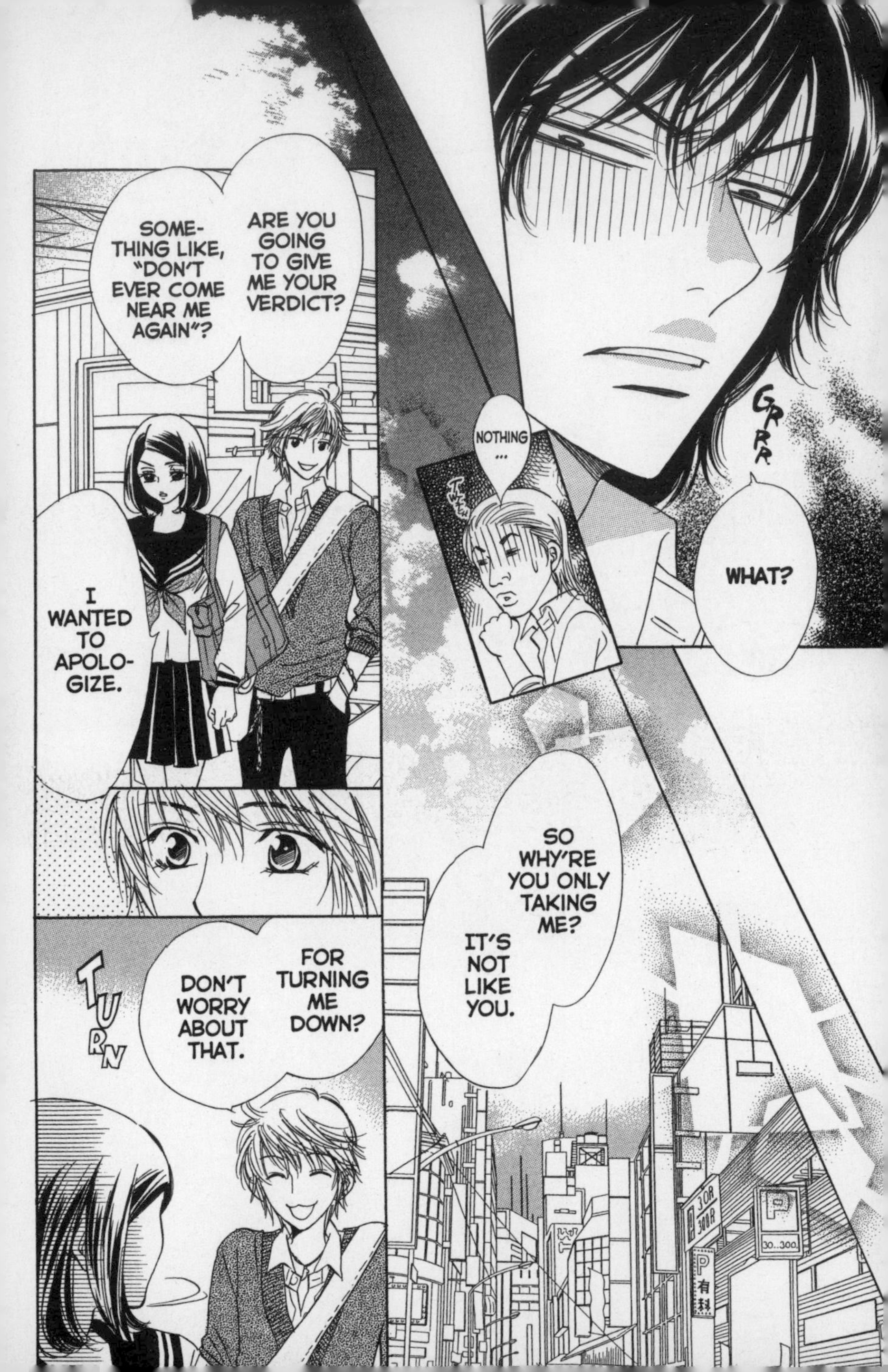
GRRR
WHAT?
NOTHING...
SO WHY'RE YOU ONLY TAKING ME?
IT'S NOT LIKE YOU.
ARE YOU GOING TO GIVE ME YOUR VERDICT?
SOME-THING LIKE, "DON'T EVER COME NEAR ME AGAIN"?
I WANTED TO APOLO-GIZE.
FOR TURNING ME DOWN?
DON'T WORRY ABOUT THAT.
TURN

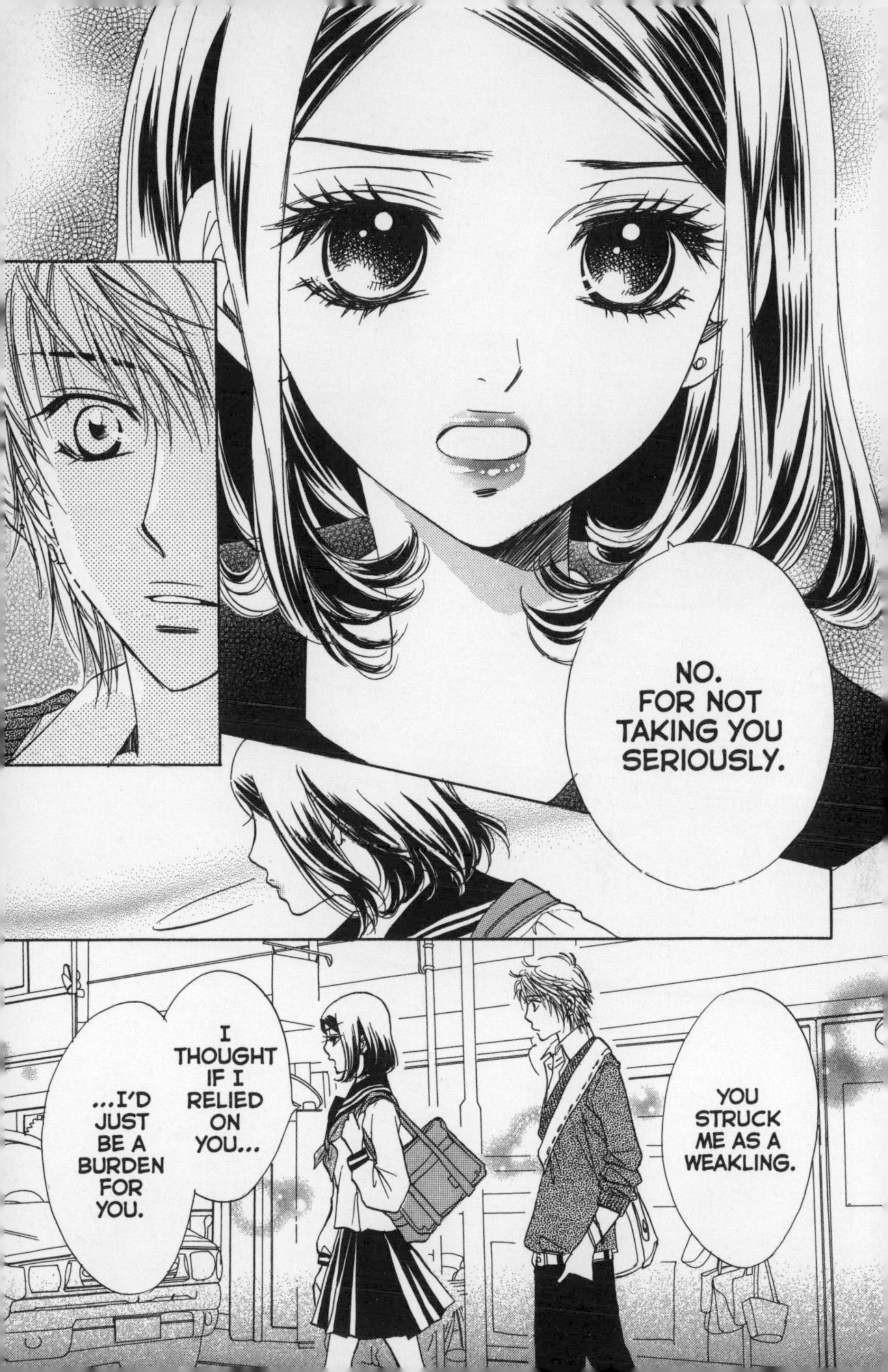
NO. FOR NOT TAKING YOU SERIOUSLY.
YOU STRUCK ME AS A WEAKLING.
I THOUGHT IF I RELIED ON YOU...
...I'D JUST BE A BURDEN FOR YOU.

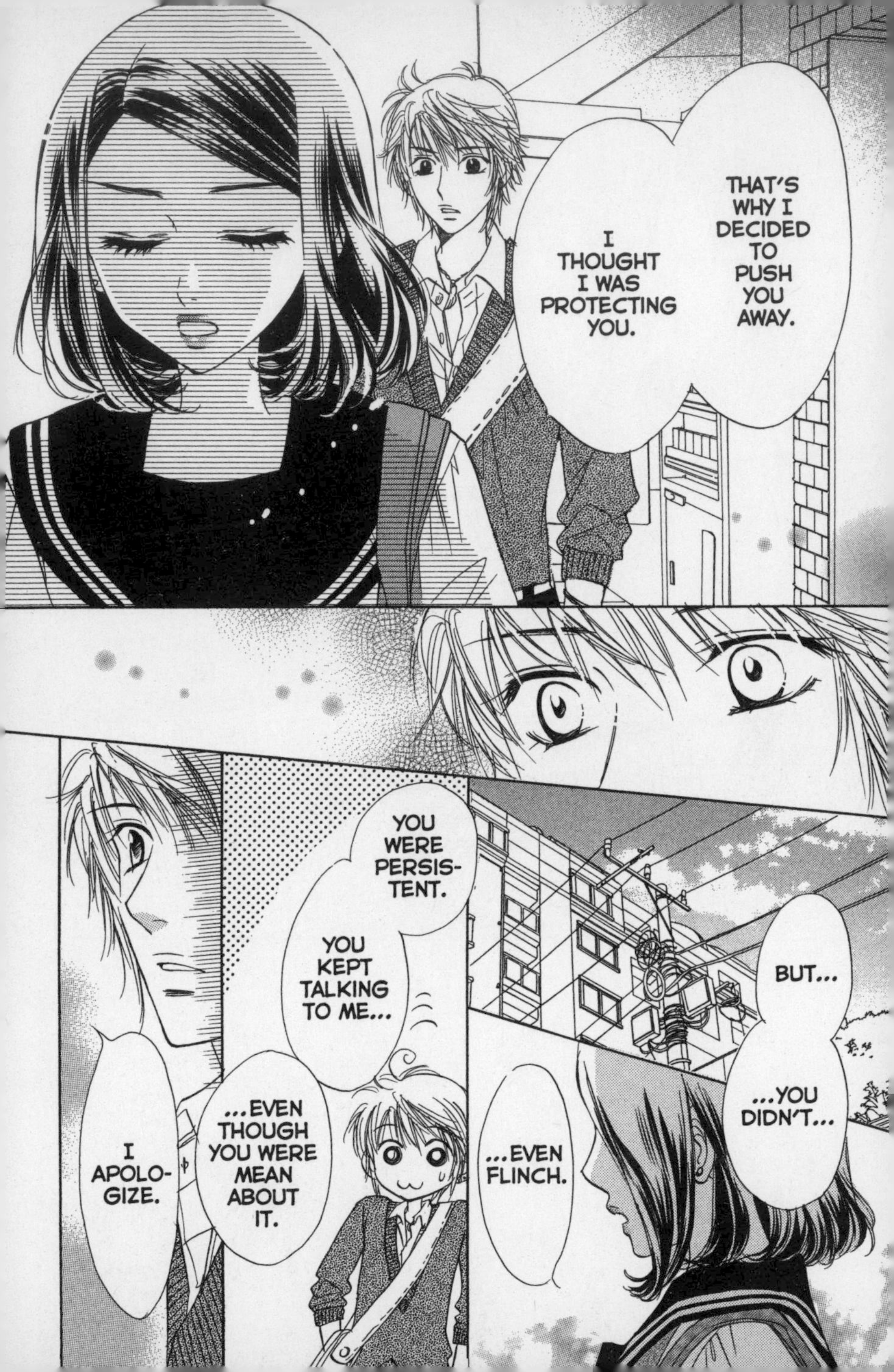
THAT'S WHY I DECIDED TO PUSH YOU AWAY.
I THOUGHT I WAS PROTECTING YOU.
BUT...
...YOU DIDN'T...
...EVEN FLINCH.
YOU WERE PERSIS-TENT.
YOU KEPT TALKING TO ME...
...EVEN THOUGH YOU WERE MEAN ABOUT IT.
I APOLO-GIZE.

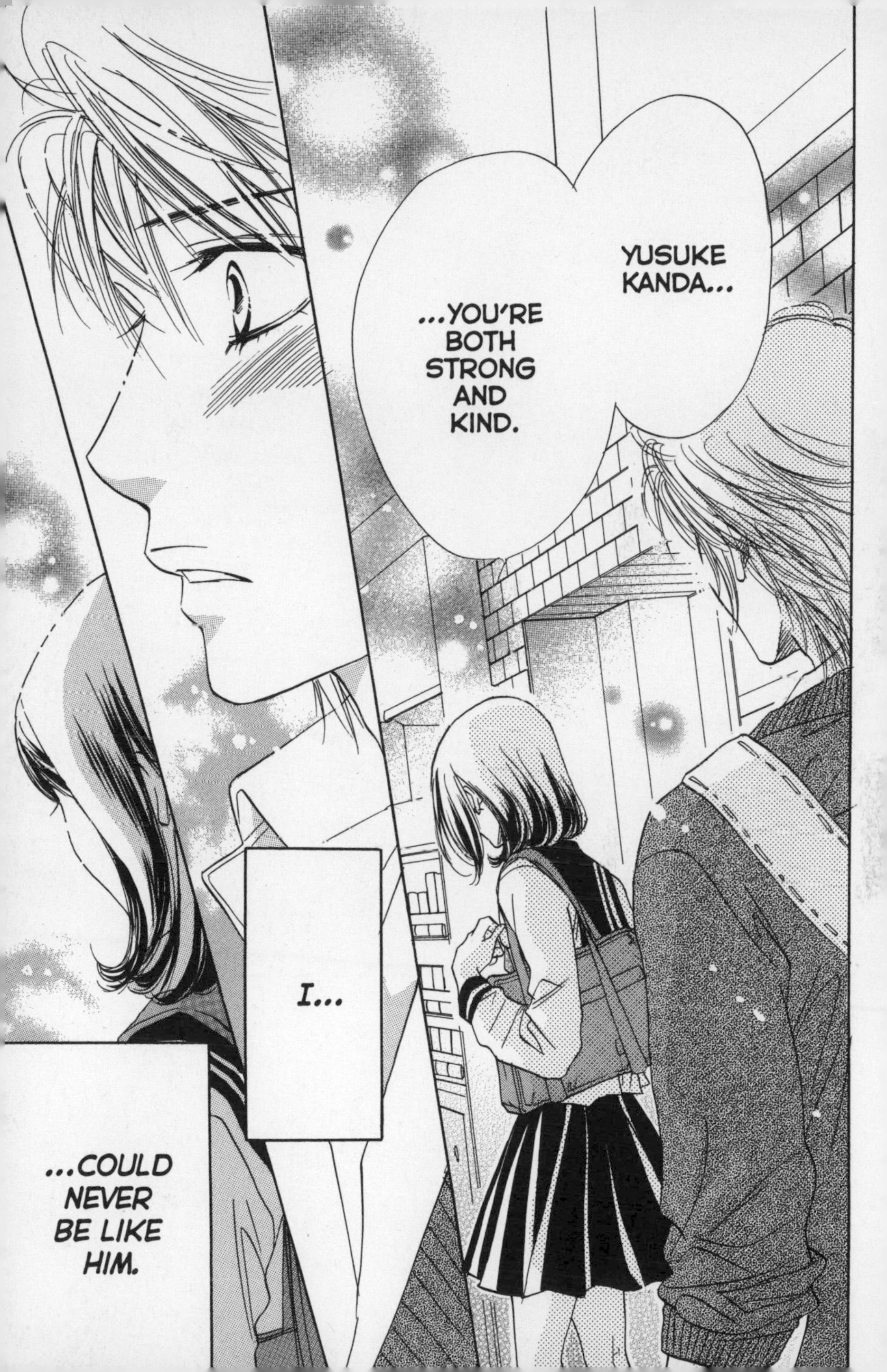
YUSUKE KANDA...
...YOU'RE BOTH STRONG AND KIND.
I...
...COULD NEVER BE LIKE HIM.

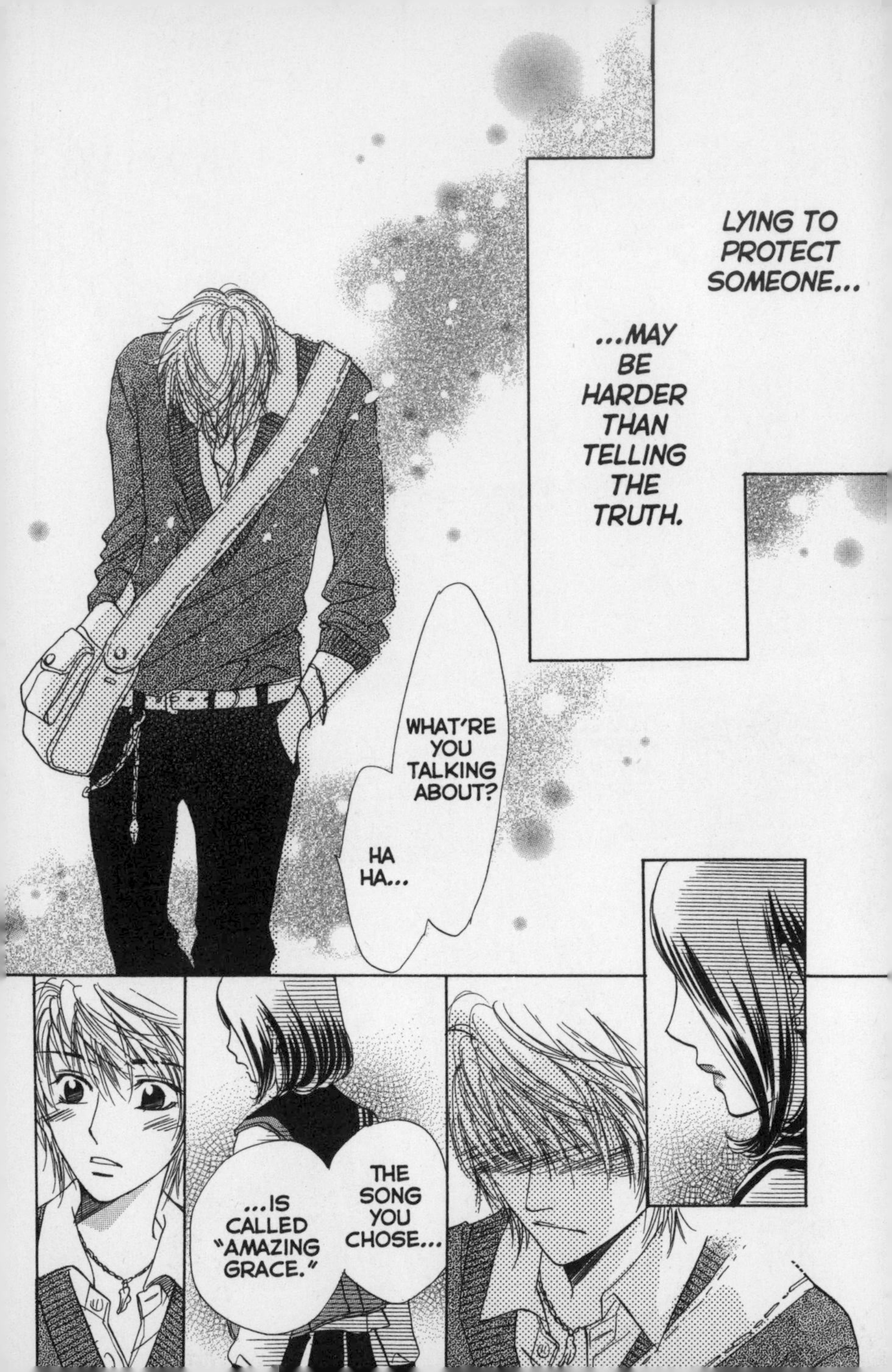
LYING TO PROTECT SOMEONE...
...MAY BE HARDER THAN TELLING THE TRUTH.
WHAT'RE YOU TALKING ABOUT?
HA HA...
THE SONG YOU CHOSE...
...IS CALLED "AMAZING GRACE."

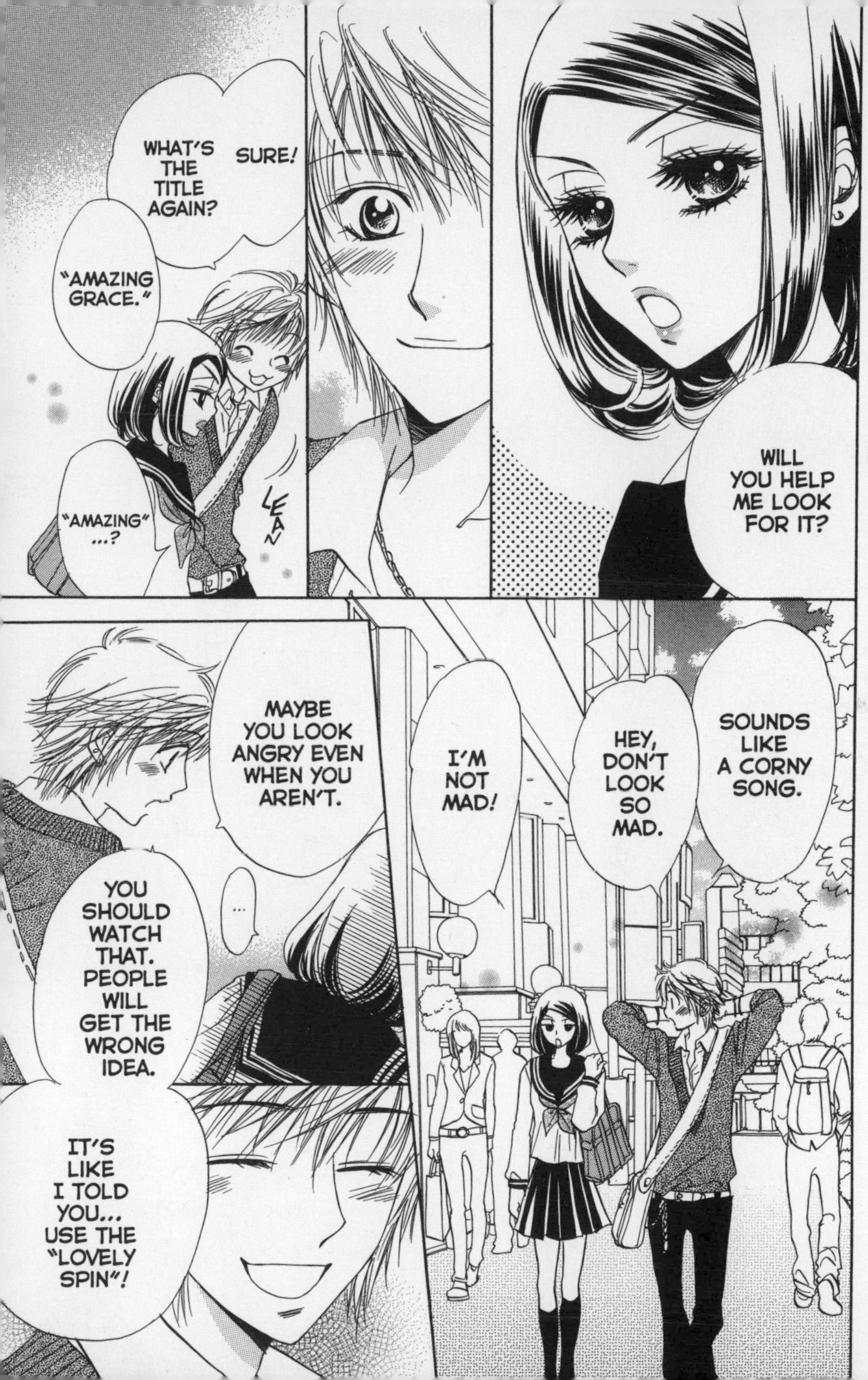
WILL YOU HELP ME LOOK FOR IT?
SURE!
WHAT'S THE TITLE AGAIN?
"AMAZING GRACE."
LEAN
"AMAZING" ...?
SOUNDS LIKE A CORNY SONG.
HEY, DON'T LOOK SO MAD.
I'M NOT MAD!
MAYBE YOU LOOK ANGRY EVEN WHEN YOU AREN'T.
...
YOU SHOULD WATCH THAT. PEOPLE WILL GET THE WRONG IDEA.
IT'S LIKE I TOLD YOU... USE THE "LOVELY SPIN"!

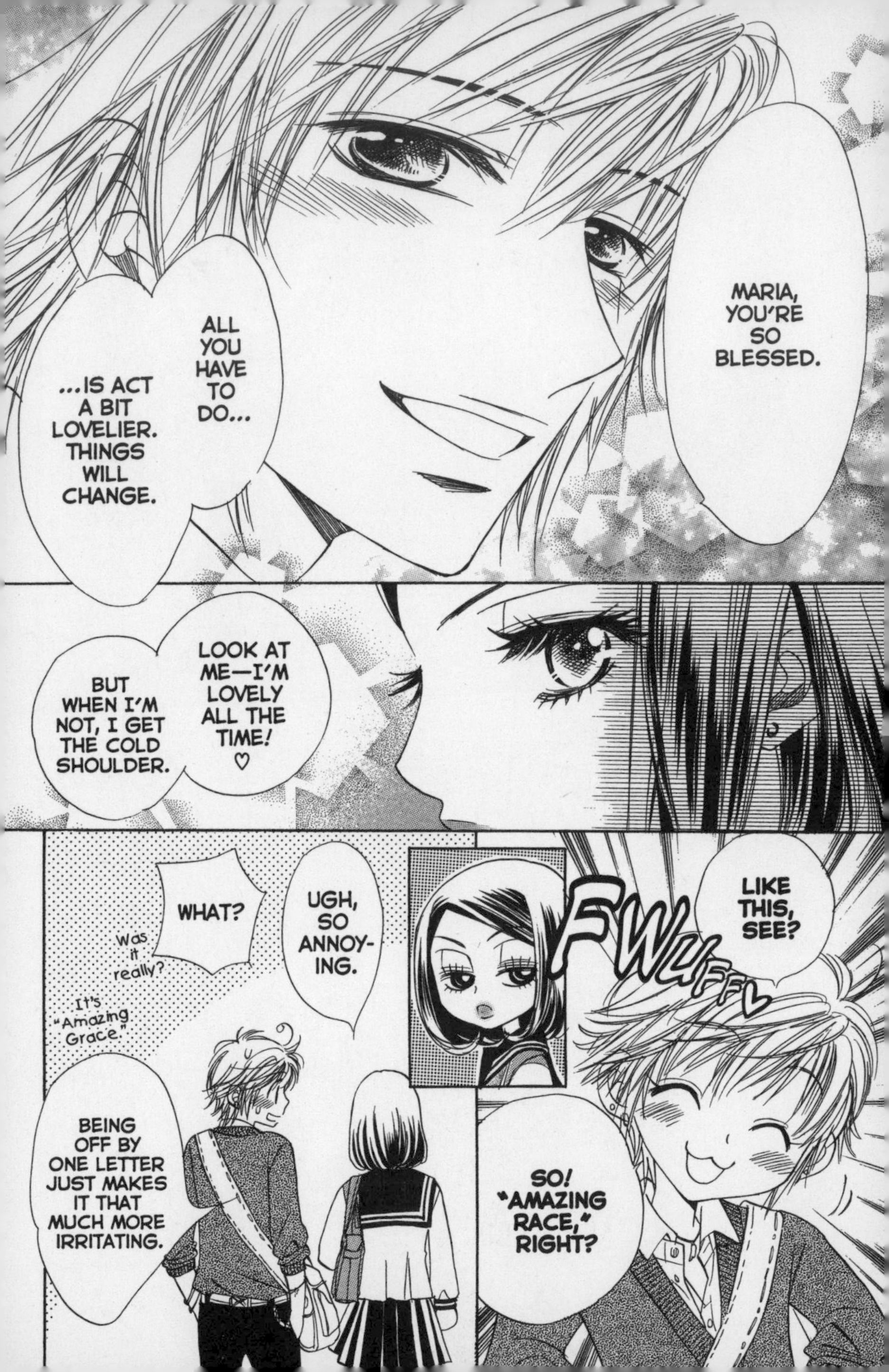
MARIA, YOU'RE SO BLESSED.
ALL YOU HAVE TO DO...
...IS ACT A BIT LOVELIER. THINGS WILL CHANGE.
LOOK AT ME—I'M LOVELY ALL THE TIME! ♡
BUT WHEN I'M NOT, I GET THE COLD SHOULDER.
LIKE THIS, SEE?
FWUFFL♥
SO! "AMAZING RACE," RIGHT?
UGH, SO ANNOY-ING.
WHAT?
Was it really?
It's "Amazing Grace."
BEING OFF BY ONE LETTER JUST MAKES IT THAT MUCH MORE IRRITATING.

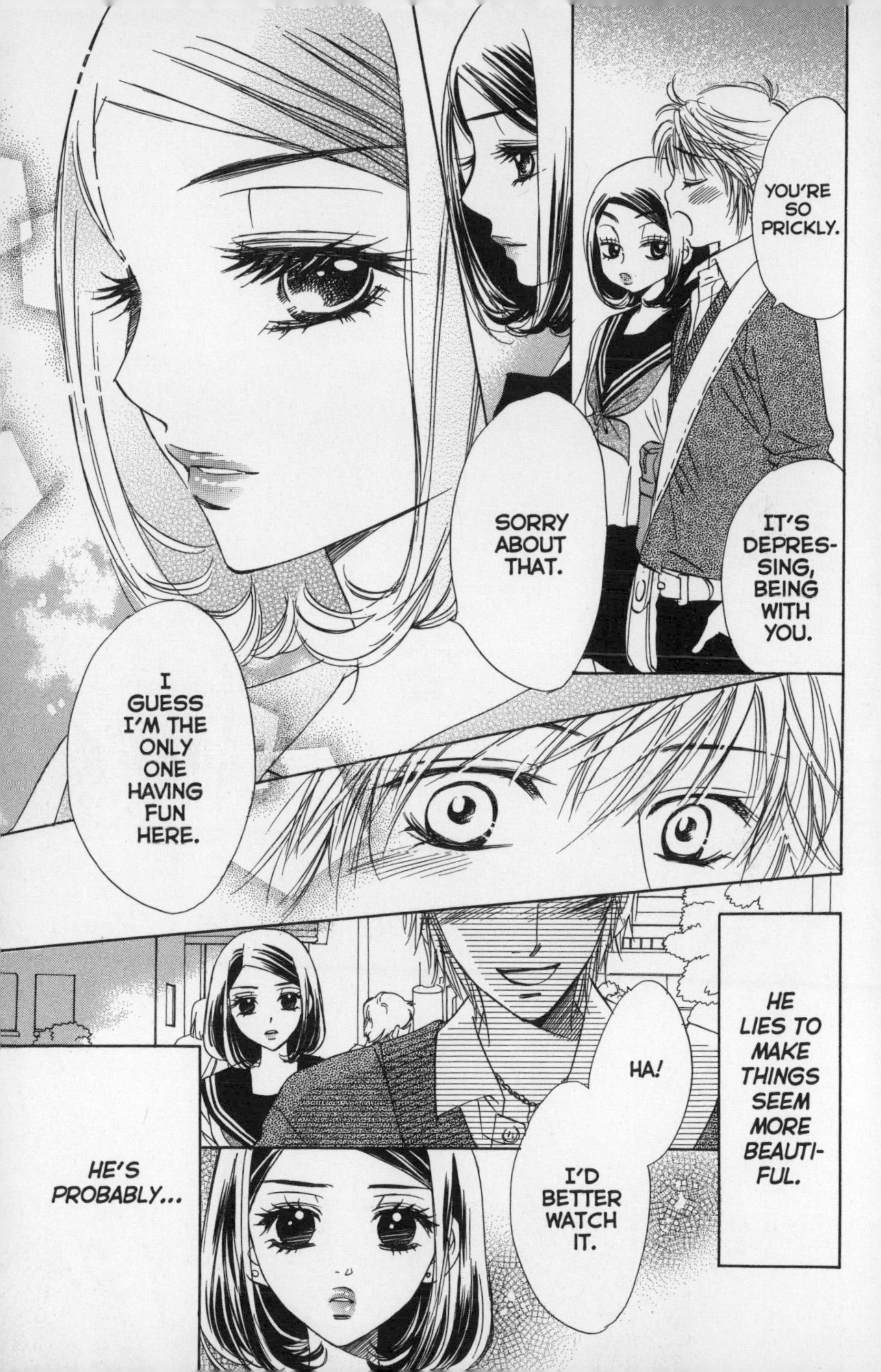
YOU'RE SO PRICKLY.
IT'S DEPRES-SING, BEING WITH YOU.
SORRY ABOUT THAT.
I GUESS I'M THE ONLY ONE HAVING FUN HERE.
HE LIES TO MAKE THINGS SEEM MORE BEAUTI-FUL.
HA!
I'D BETTER WATCH IT.
HE'S PROBABLY...

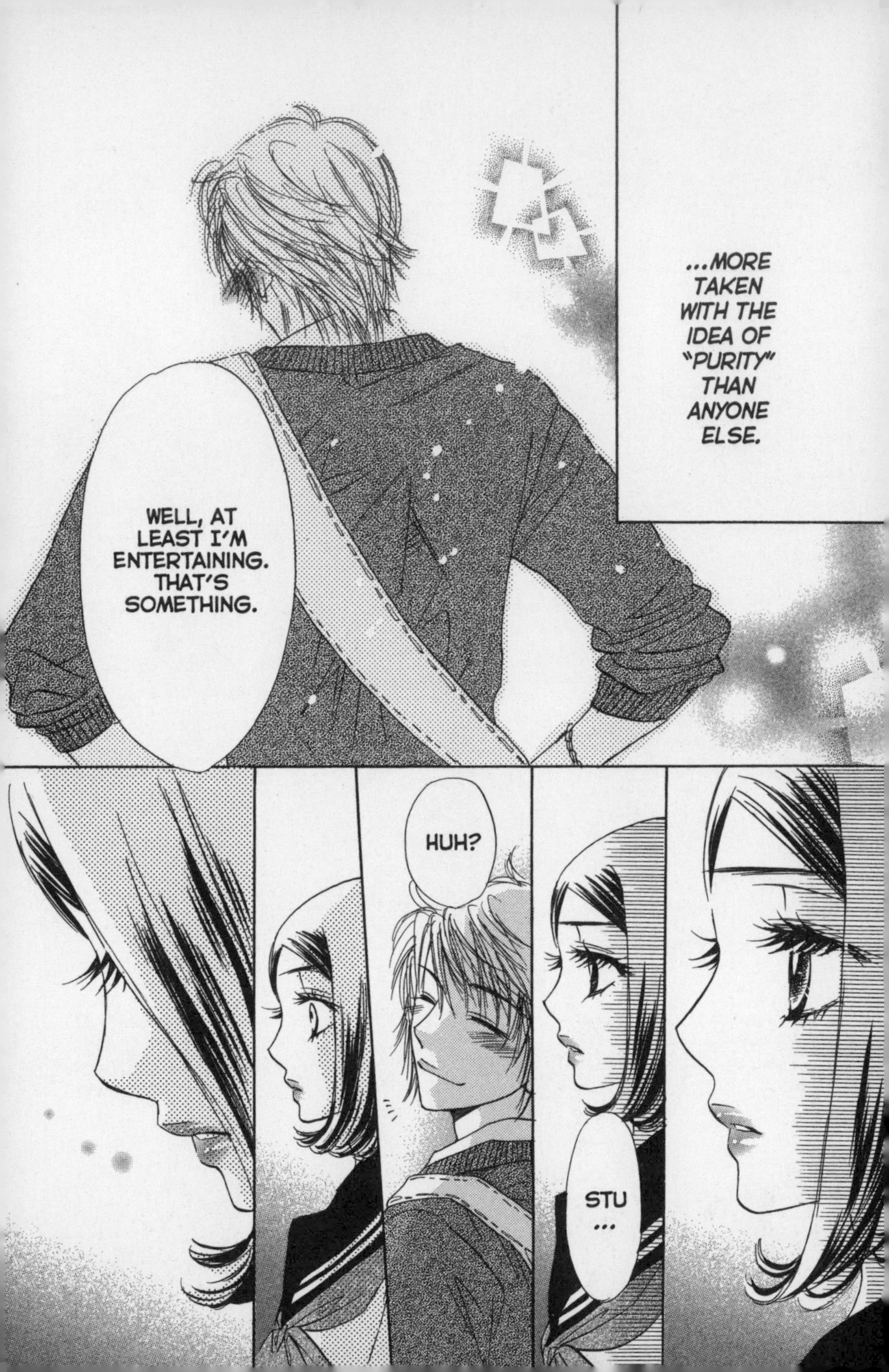
...MORE TAKEN WITH THE IDEA OF "PURITY" THAN ANYONE ELSE.
WELL, AT LEAST I'M ENTERTAINING. THAT'S SOMETHING.
STU ...
HUH?

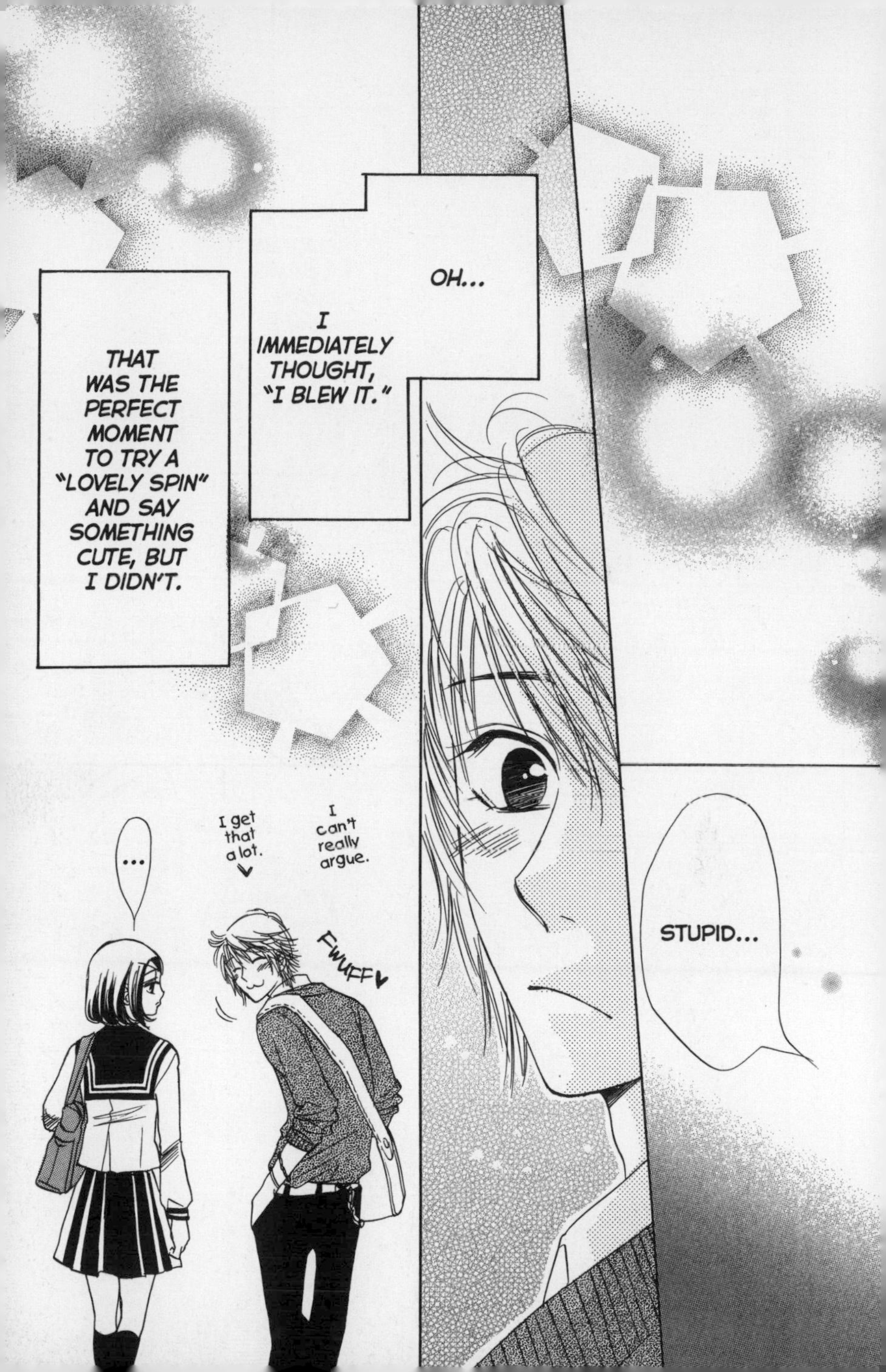
OH...
I IMMEDIATELY THOUGHT, "I BLEW IT."
THAT WAS THE PERFECT MOMENT TO TRY A "LOVELY SPIN" AND SAY SOMETHING CUTE, BUT I DIDN'T.
STUPID...
I can't really argue.
I get that a lot.
FWUFF
...

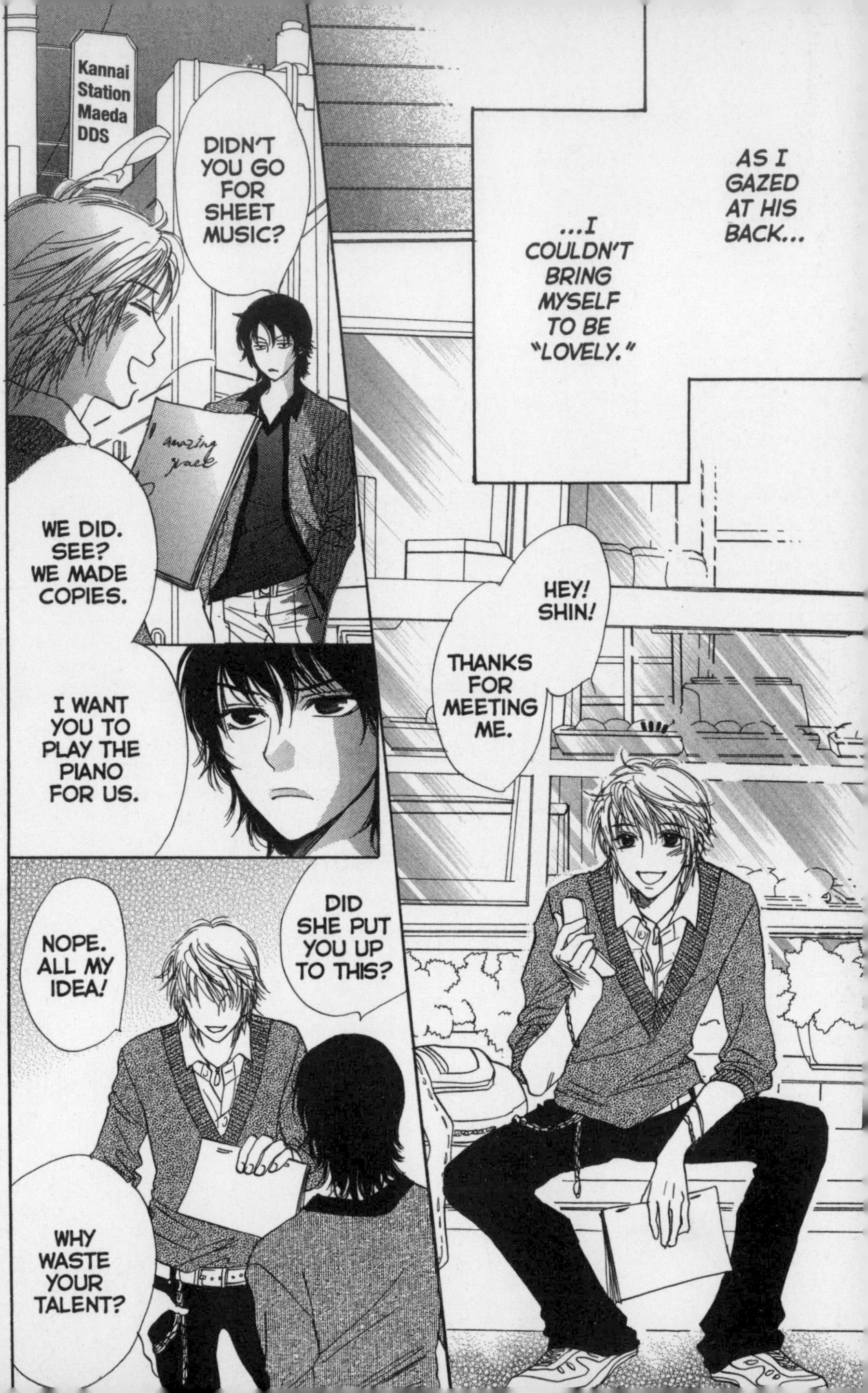

AS I GAZED AT HIS BACK...
...I COULDN'T BRING MYSELF TO BE "LOVELY."
HEY! SHIN!
THANKS FOR MEETING ME.
Kannai Station Maeda DDS
DIDN'T YOU GO FOR SHEET MUSIC?
WE DID. SEE? WE MADE COPIES.
I WANT YOU TO PLAY THE PIANO FOR US.
DID SHE PUT YOU UP TO THIS?
NOPE. ALL MY IDEA!
WHY WASTE YOUR TALENT?

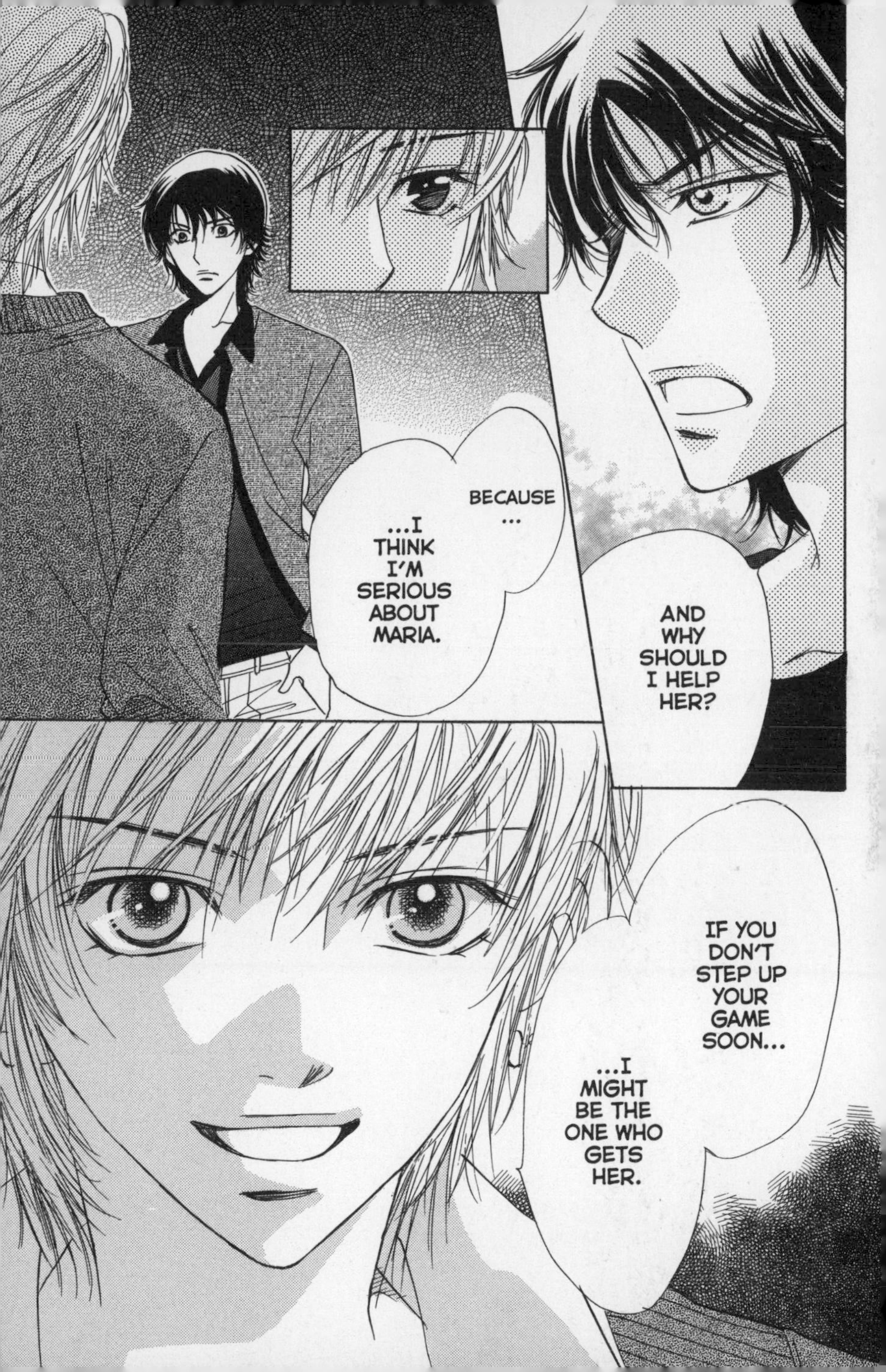
AND WHY SHOULD I HELP HER?
BECAUSE ...
...I THINK I'M SERIOUS ABOUT MARIA.
IF YOU DON'T STEP UP YOUR GAME SOON...
...I MIGHT BE THE ONE WHO GETS HER.

A Devil and
Her Love Song

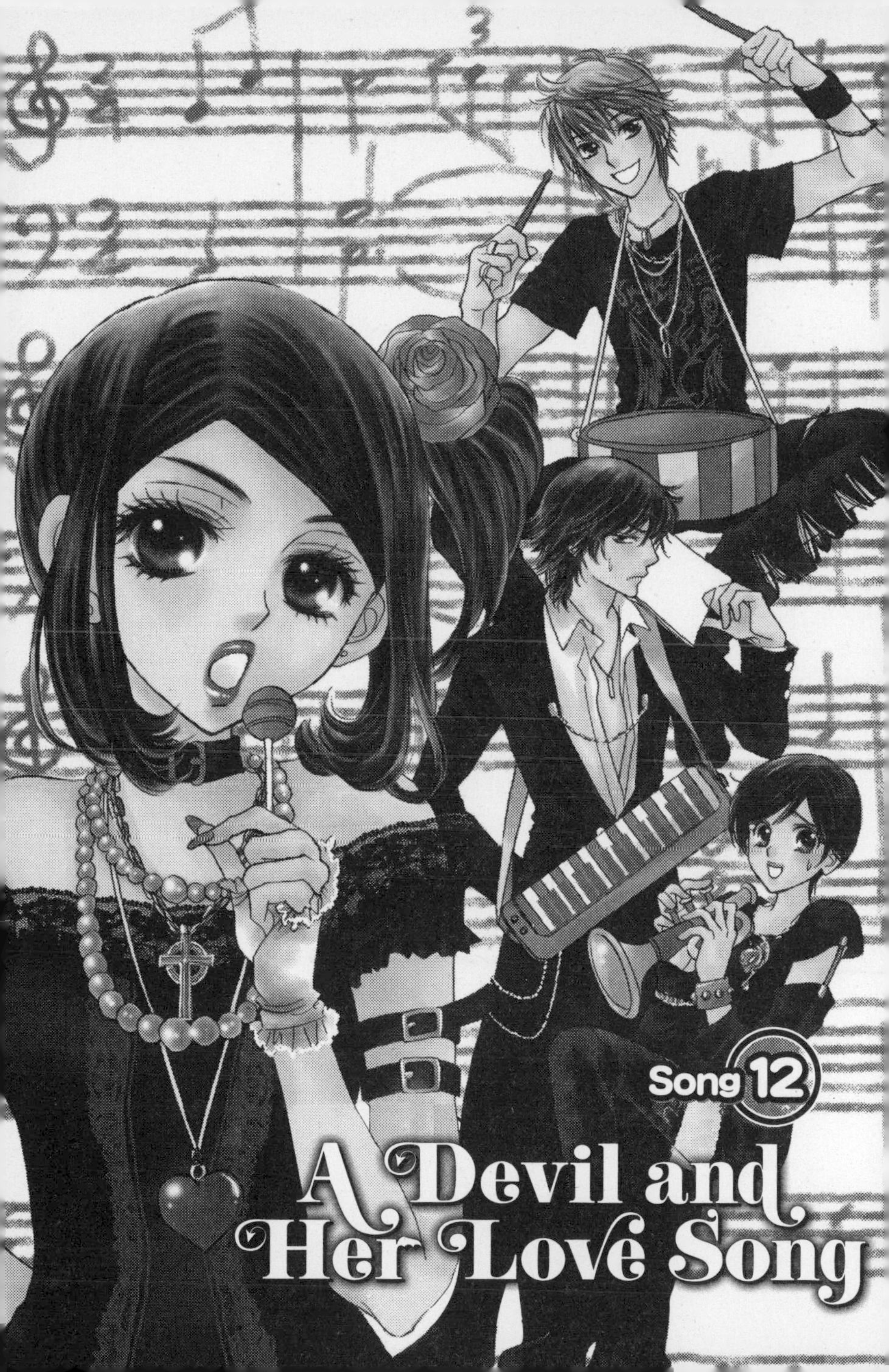
Song 12
A Devil and Her Love Song

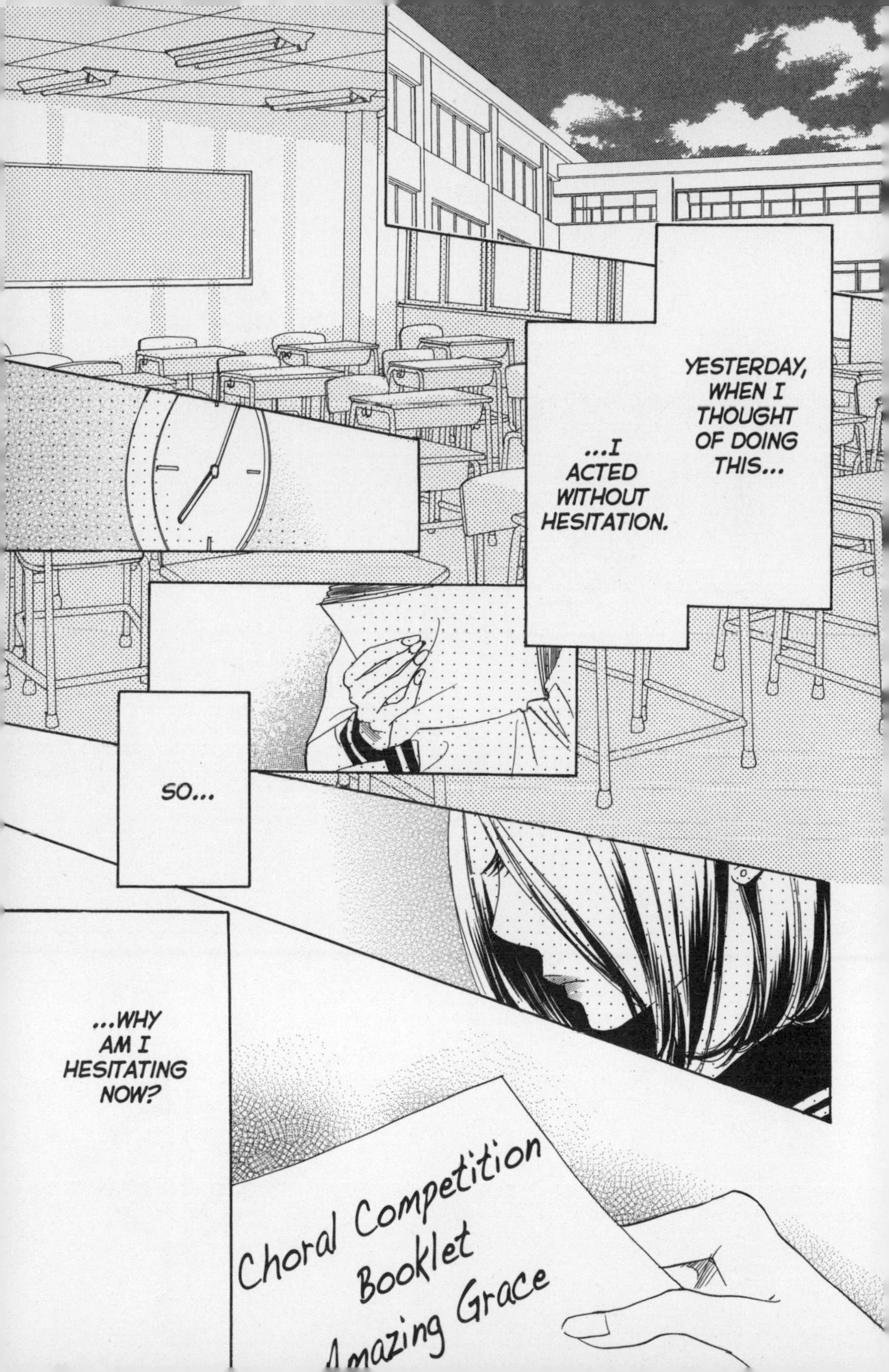
YESTERDAY, WHEN I THOUGHT OF DOING THIS...
...I ACTED WITHOUT HESITATION.
SO...
...WHY AM I HESITATING NOW?
Choral Competition
Booklet
Amazing Grace

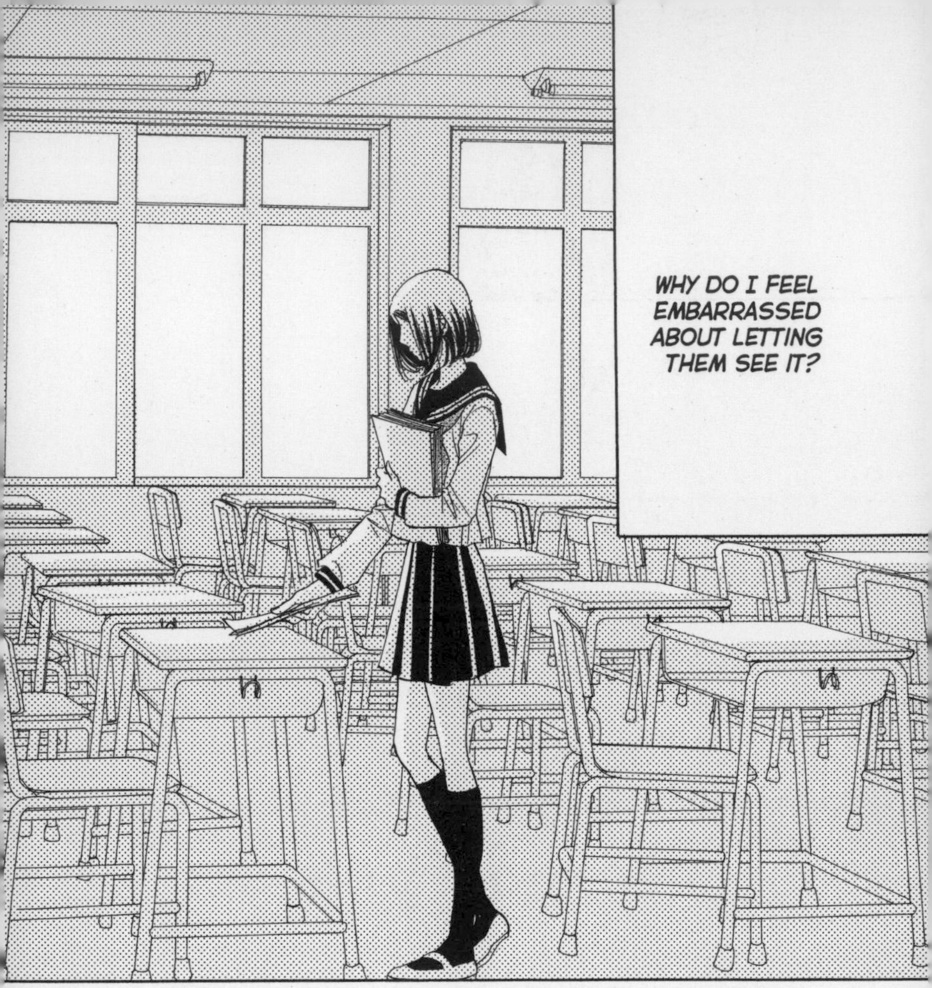
WHY DO I FEEL EMBARRASSED ABOUT LETTING THEM SEE IT?

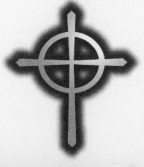

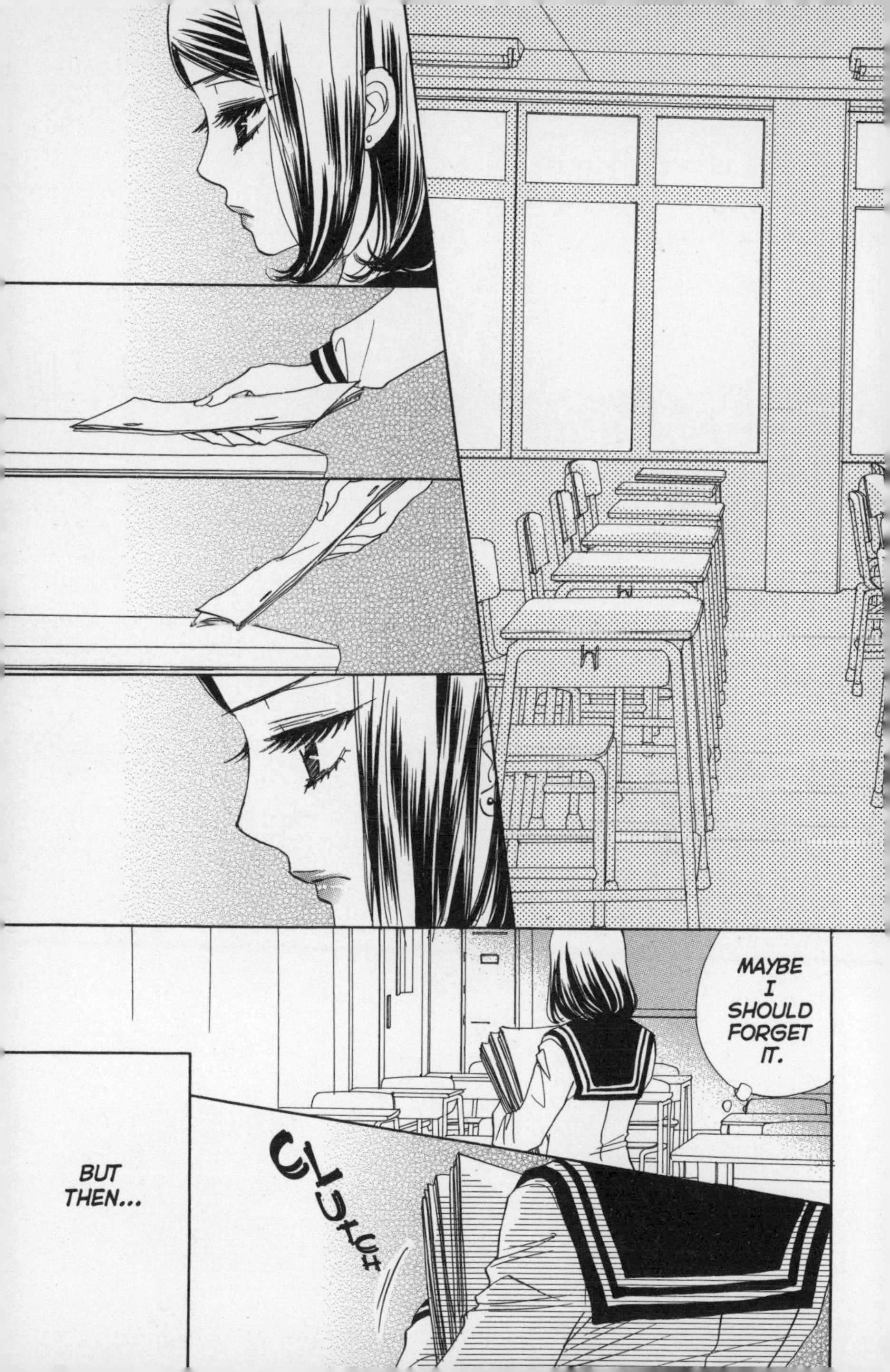
MAYBE I SHOULD FORGET IT.
CLUTCH
BUT THEN...

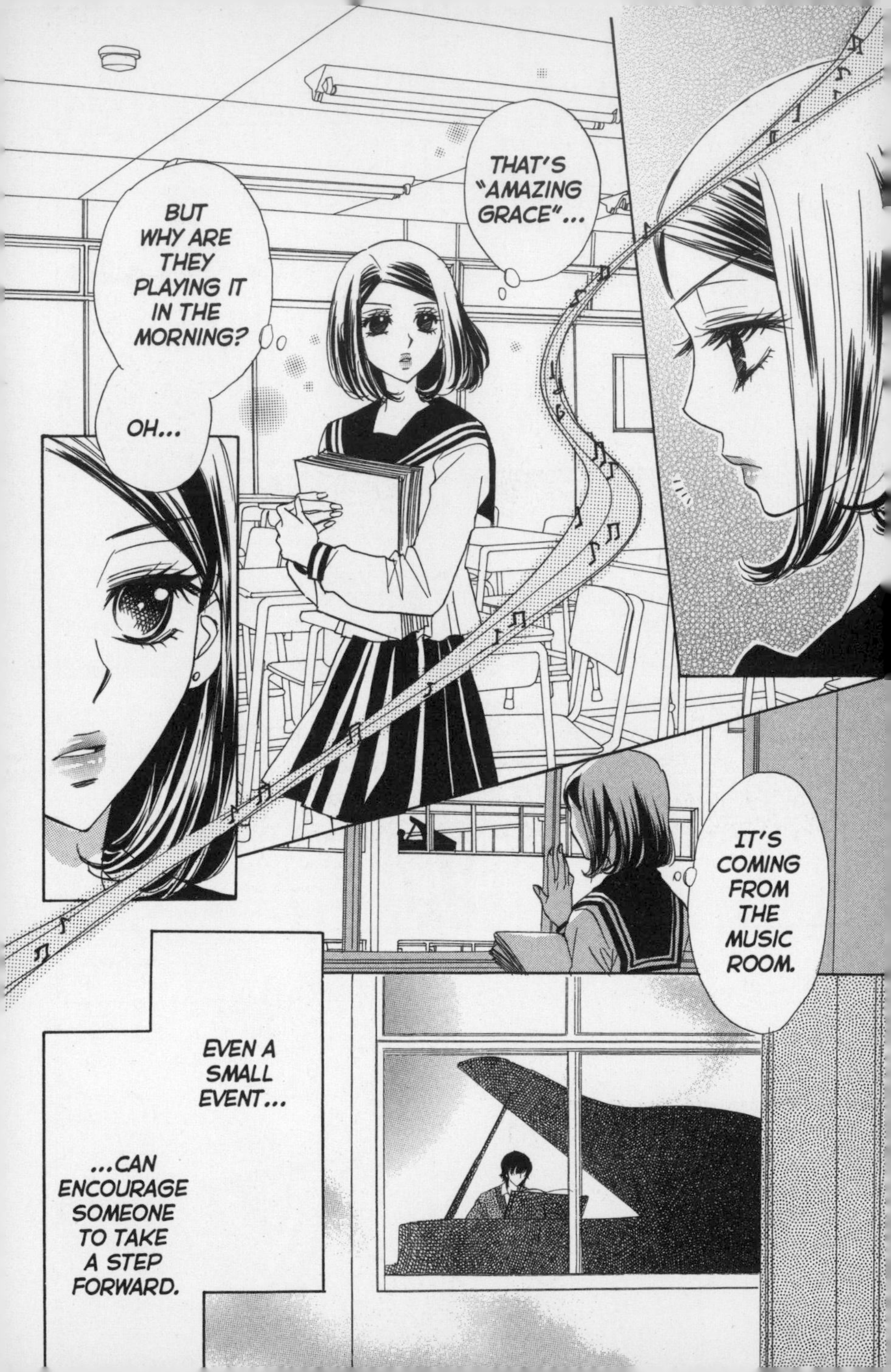
THAT'S "AMAZING GRACE"...
BUT WHY ARE THEY PLAYING IT IN THE MORNING?
OH...
IT'S COMING FROM THE MUSIC ROOM.
EVEN A SMALL EVENT...
...CAN ENCOURAGE SOMEONE TO TAKE A STEP FORWARD.

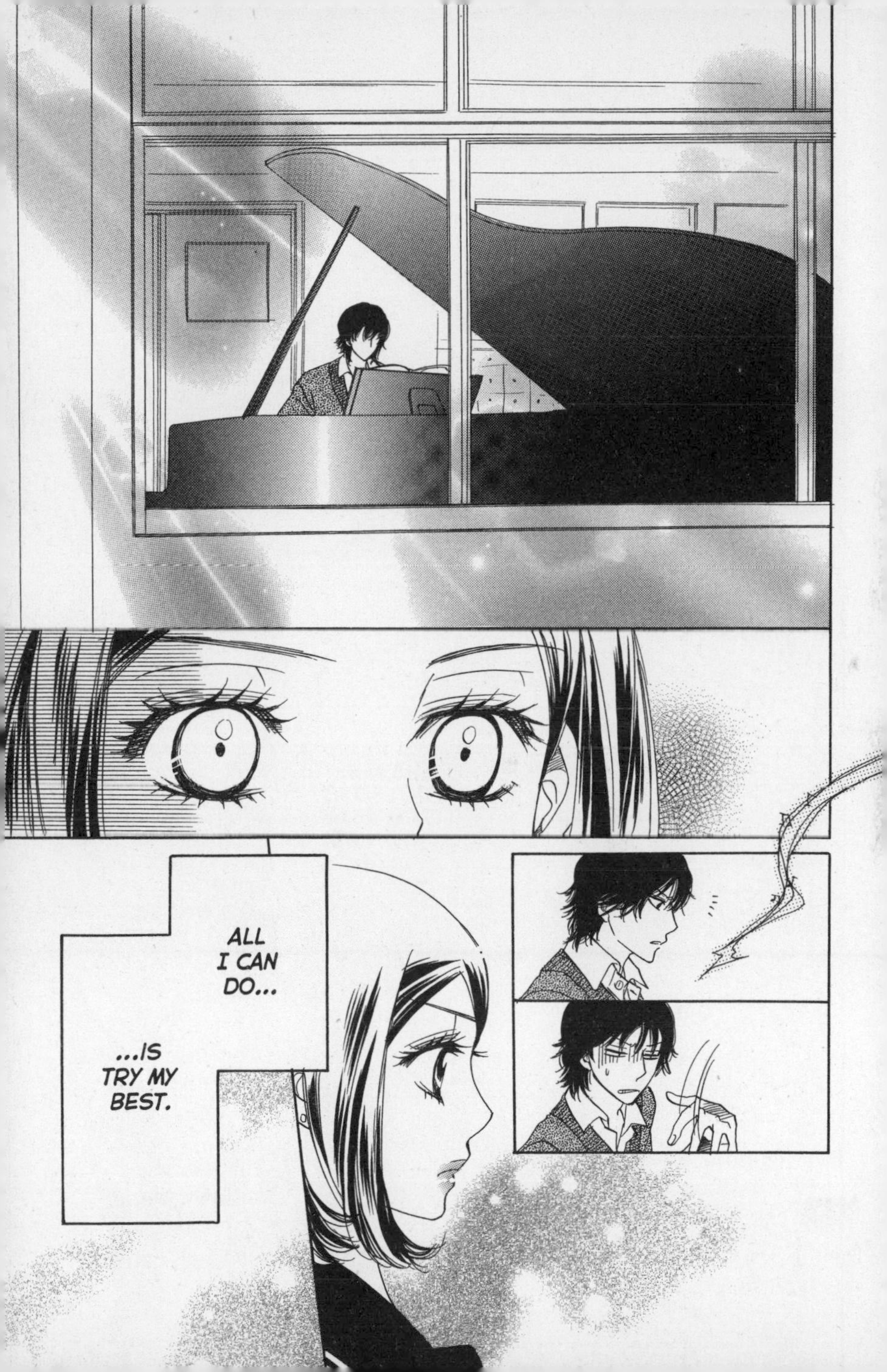
ALL I CAN DO...
...IS TRY MY BEST.

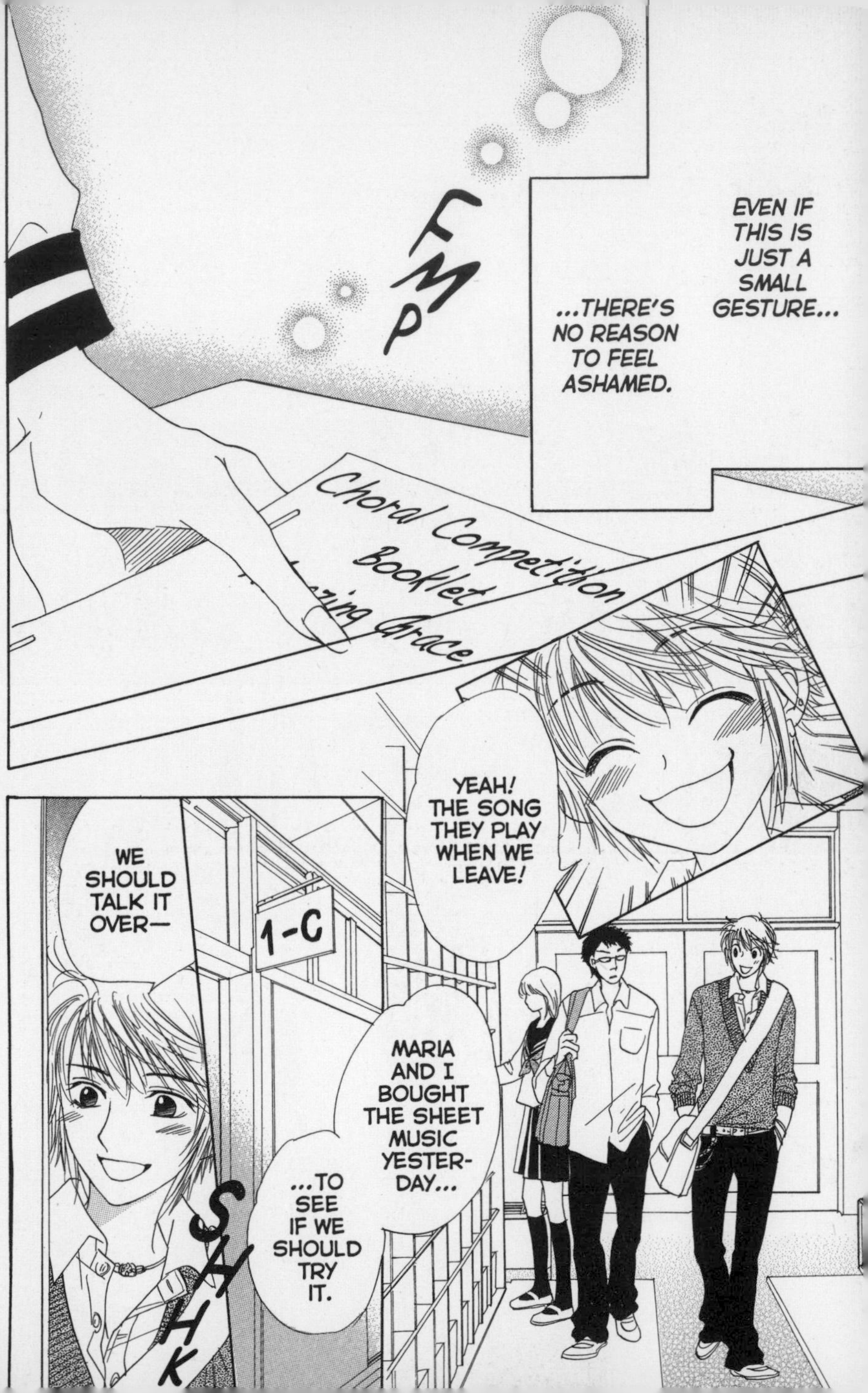
EVEN IF THIS IS JUST A SMALL GESTURE...
...THERE'S NO REASON TO FEEL ASHAMED.
FMP
Choral Competition Booklet
Grace
YEAH! THE SONG THEY PLAY WHEN WE LEAVE!
1-C
MARIA AND I BOUGHT THE SHEET MUSIC YESTER-DAY...
...TO SEE IF WE SHOULD TRY IT.
WE SHOULD TALK IT OVER—
SHHK

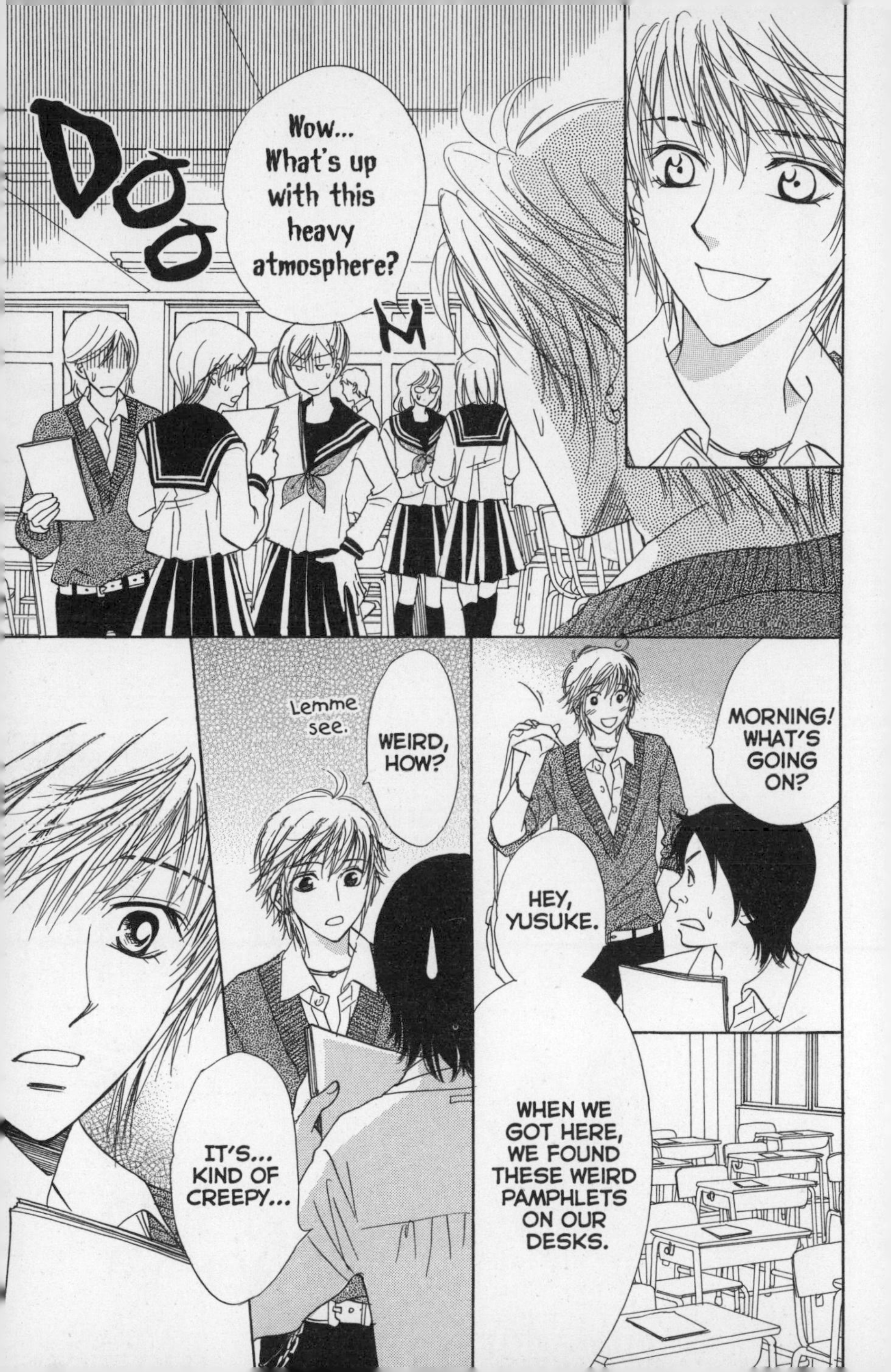
Wow... What's up with this heavy atmosphere?
DOOOM
MORNING! WHAT'S GOING ON?
HEY, YUSUKE.
WHEN WE GOT HERE, WE FOUND THESE WEIRD PAMPHLETS ON OUR DESKS.
WEIRD, HOW?
Lemme see.
IT'S... KIND OF CREEPY...

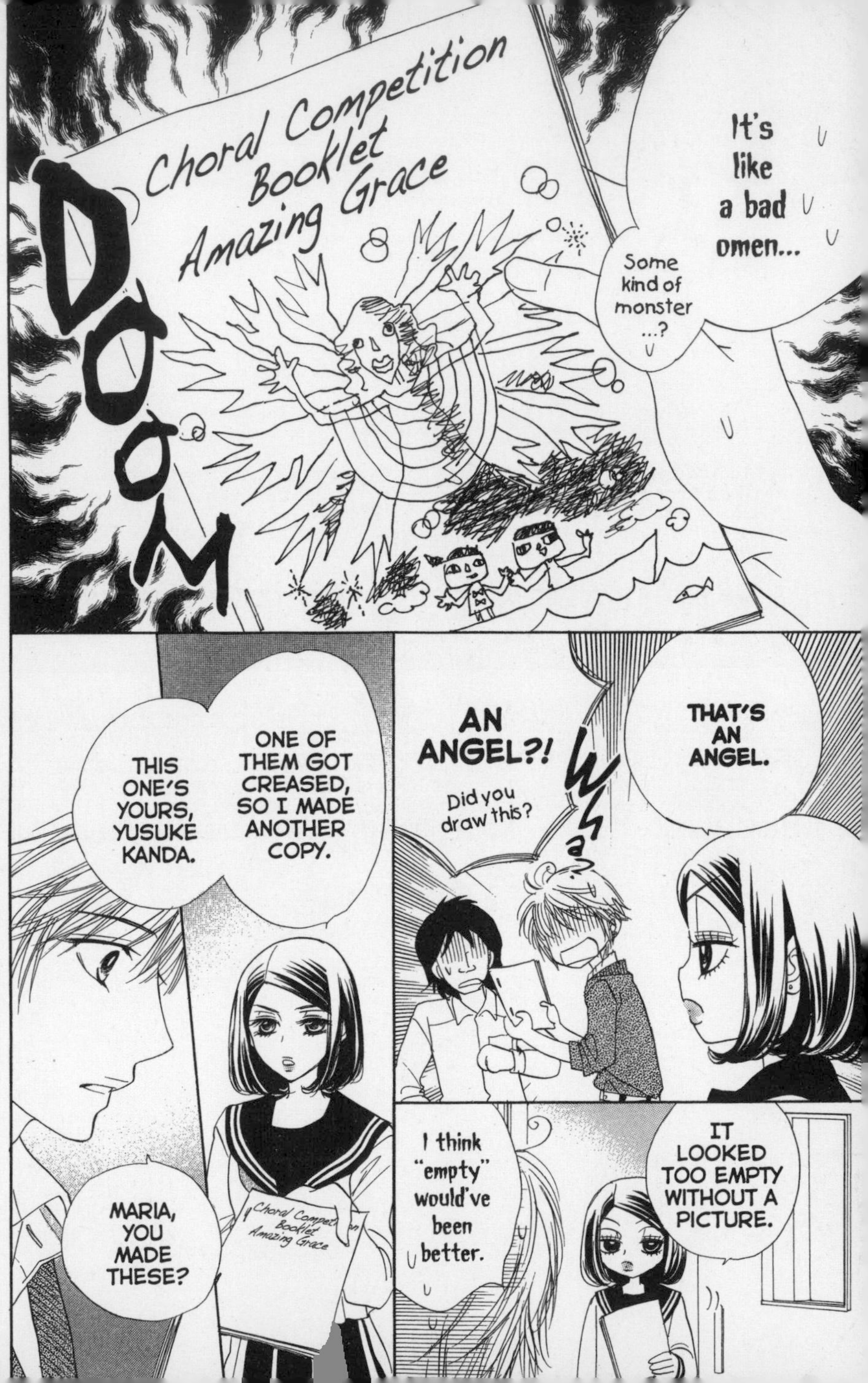
It's like a bad omen...
Some kind of monster ...?
Choral Competition Booklet Amazing Grace
DOOM
THAT'S AN ANGEL.
Wha?
AN ANGEL?!
Did you draw this?
IT LOOKED TOO EMPTY WITHOUT A PICTURE.
I think "empty" would've been better.
ONE OF THEM GOT CREASED, SO I MADE ANOTHER COPY.
THIS ONE'S YOURS, YUSUKE KANDA.
MARIA, YOU MADE THESE?
Choral Competition Booklet Amazing Grace

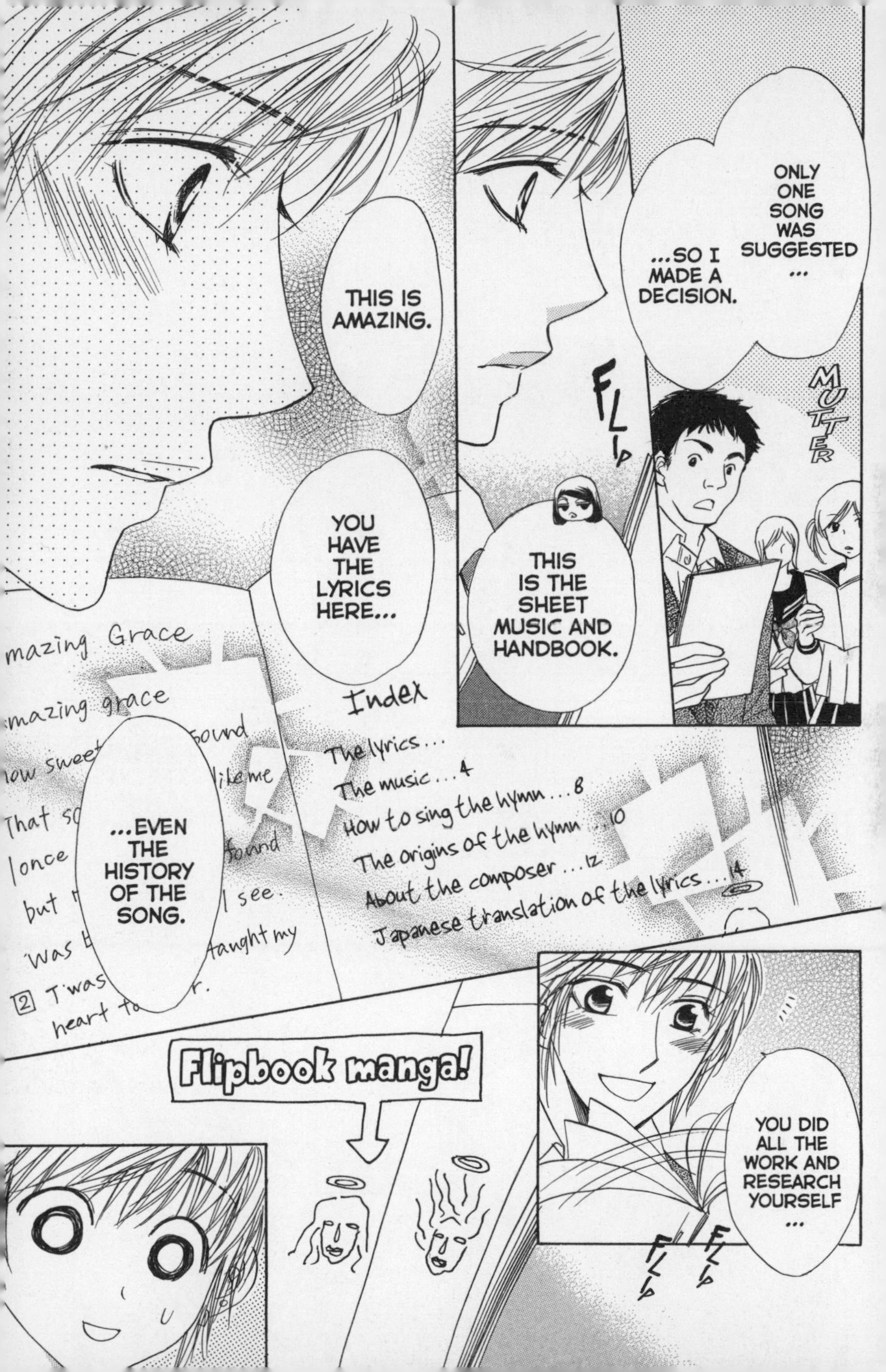
ONLY ONE SONG WAS SUGGESTED...
...SO I MADE A DECISION.
MUTTER
FLIP
THIS IS THE SHEET MUSIC AND HANDBOOK.
THIS IS AMAZING.
YOU HAVE THE LYRICS HERE...
Index
The lyrics...
The music...4
How to sing the hymn...8
The origins of the hymn...10
About the composer...12
Japanese translation of the lyrics...14
...EVEN THE HISTORY OF THE SONG.
YOU DID ALL THE WORK AND RESEARCH YOURSELF...
FLIP
FLIP
Flipbook manga!

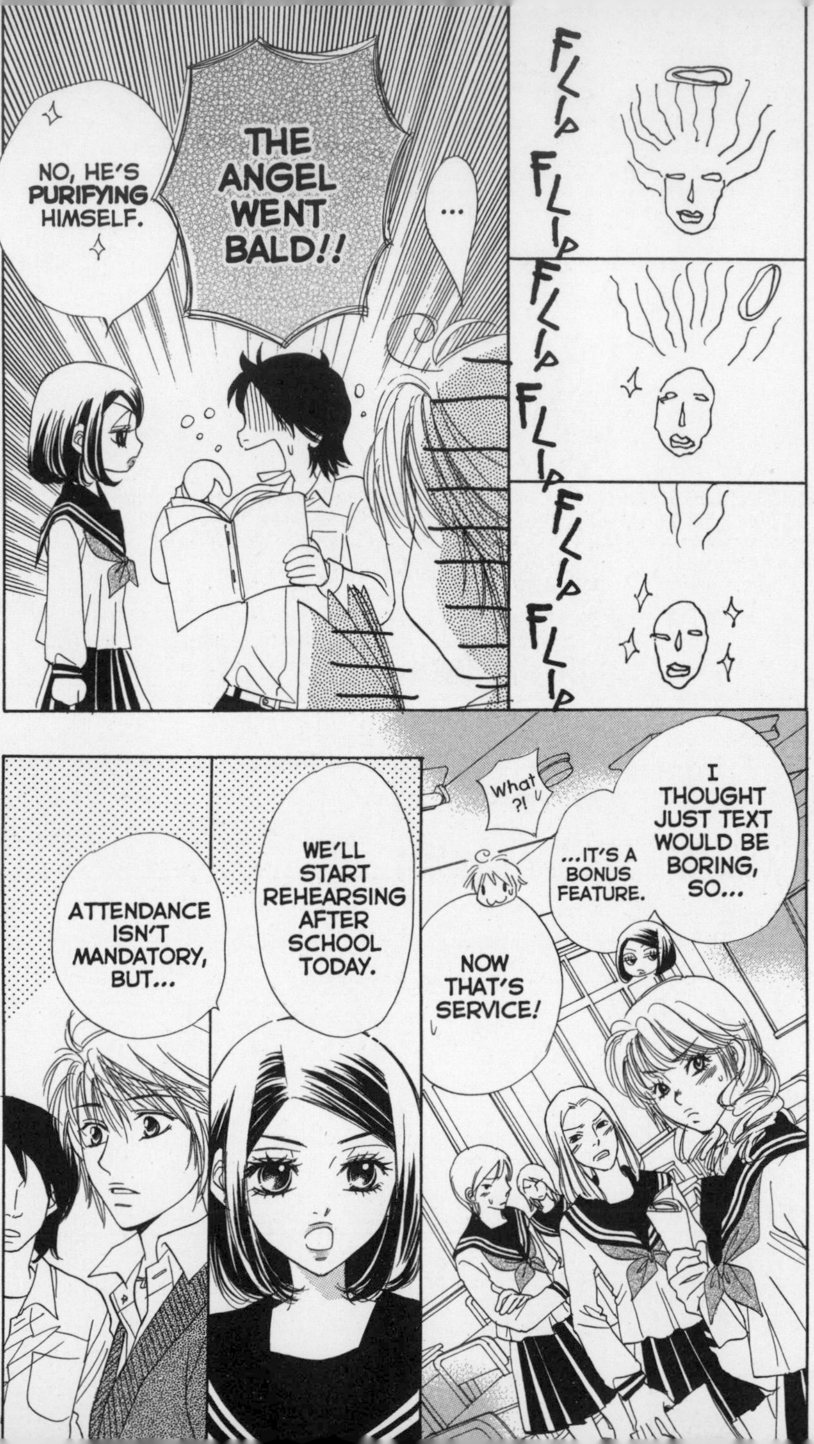
FLIP FLIP FLIP FLIP FLIP FLIP
...
THE ANGEL WENT BALD!!
NO, HE'S PURIFYING HIMSELF.
I THOUGHT JUST TEXT WOULD BE BORING, SO...
What?!
...IT'S A BONUS FEATURE.
NOW THAT'S SERVICE!
WE'LL START REHEARSING AFTER SCHOOL TODAY.
ATTENDANCE ISN'T MANDATORY, BUT...

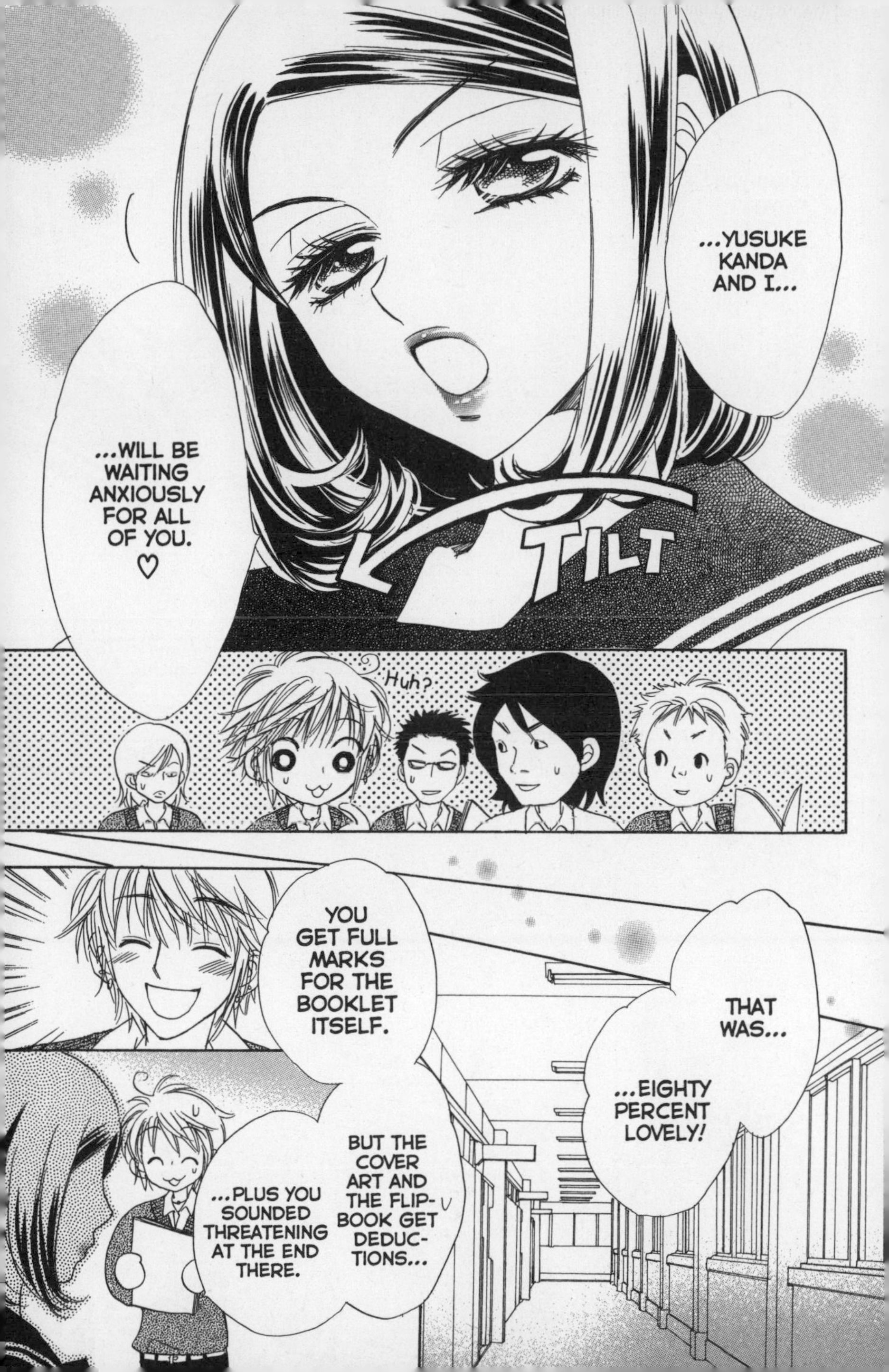
...YUSUKE KANDA AND I...
...WILL BE WAITING ANXIOUSLY FOR ALL OF YOU. ♡
TILT
Huh?
THAT WAS...
...EIGHTY PERCENT LOVELY!
YOU GET FULL MARKS FOR THE BOOKLET ITSELF.
BUT THE COVER ART AND THE FLIP-BOOK GET DEDUCTIONS...
...PLUS YOU SOUNDED THREATENING AT THE END THERE.

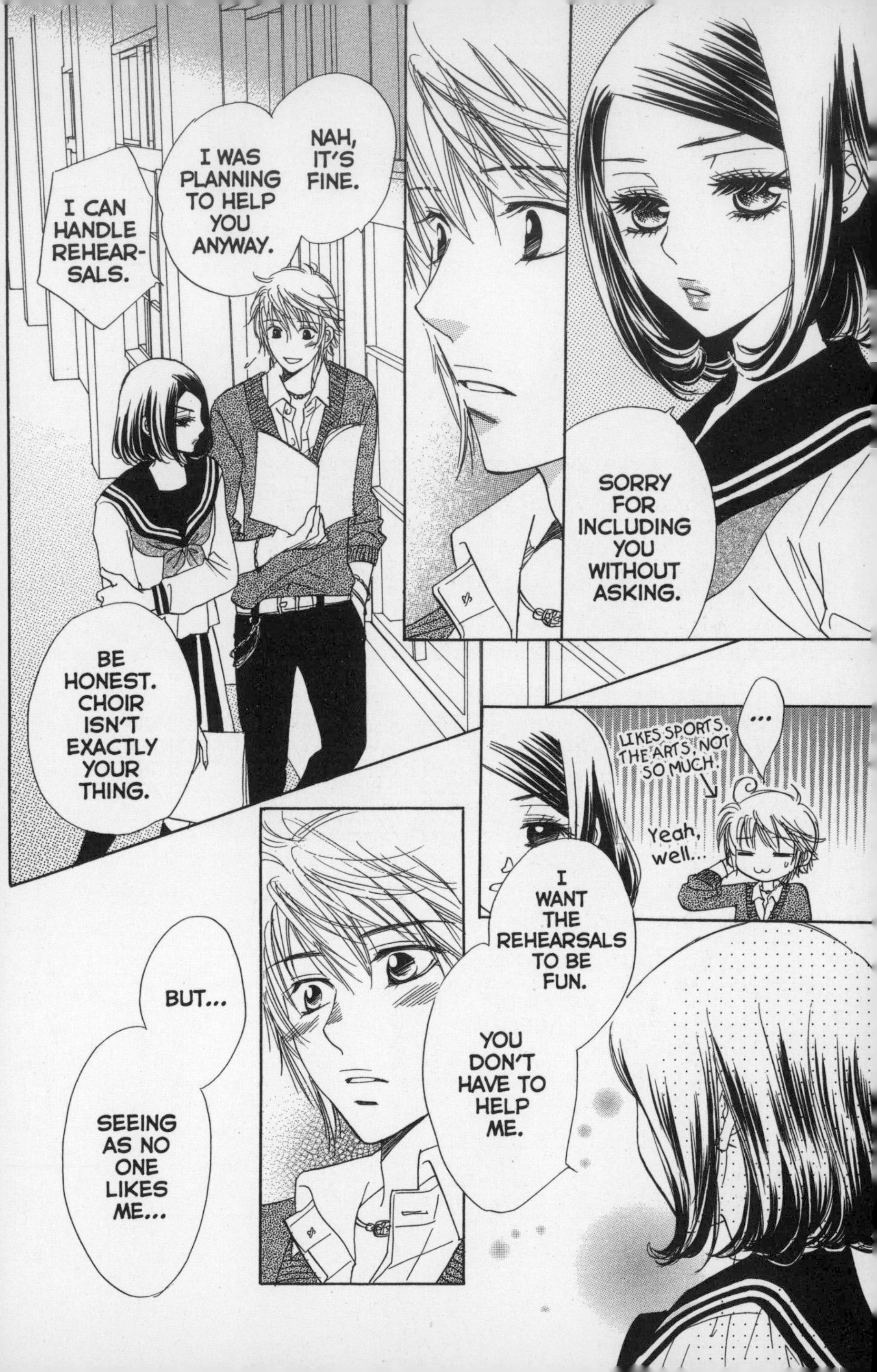
SORRY FOR INCLUDING YOU WITHOUT ASKING.
NAH, IT'S FINE.
I WAS PLANNING TO HELP YOU ANYWAY.
I CAN HANDLE REHEARSALS.
BE HONEST. CHOIR ISN'T EXACTLY YOUR THING.
...
LIKES SPORTS. THE ARTS, NOT SO MUCH.
Yeah, well...
I WANT THE REHEARSALS TO BE FUN.
YOU DON'T HAVE TO HELP ME.
BUT...
SEEING AS NO ONE LIKES ME...

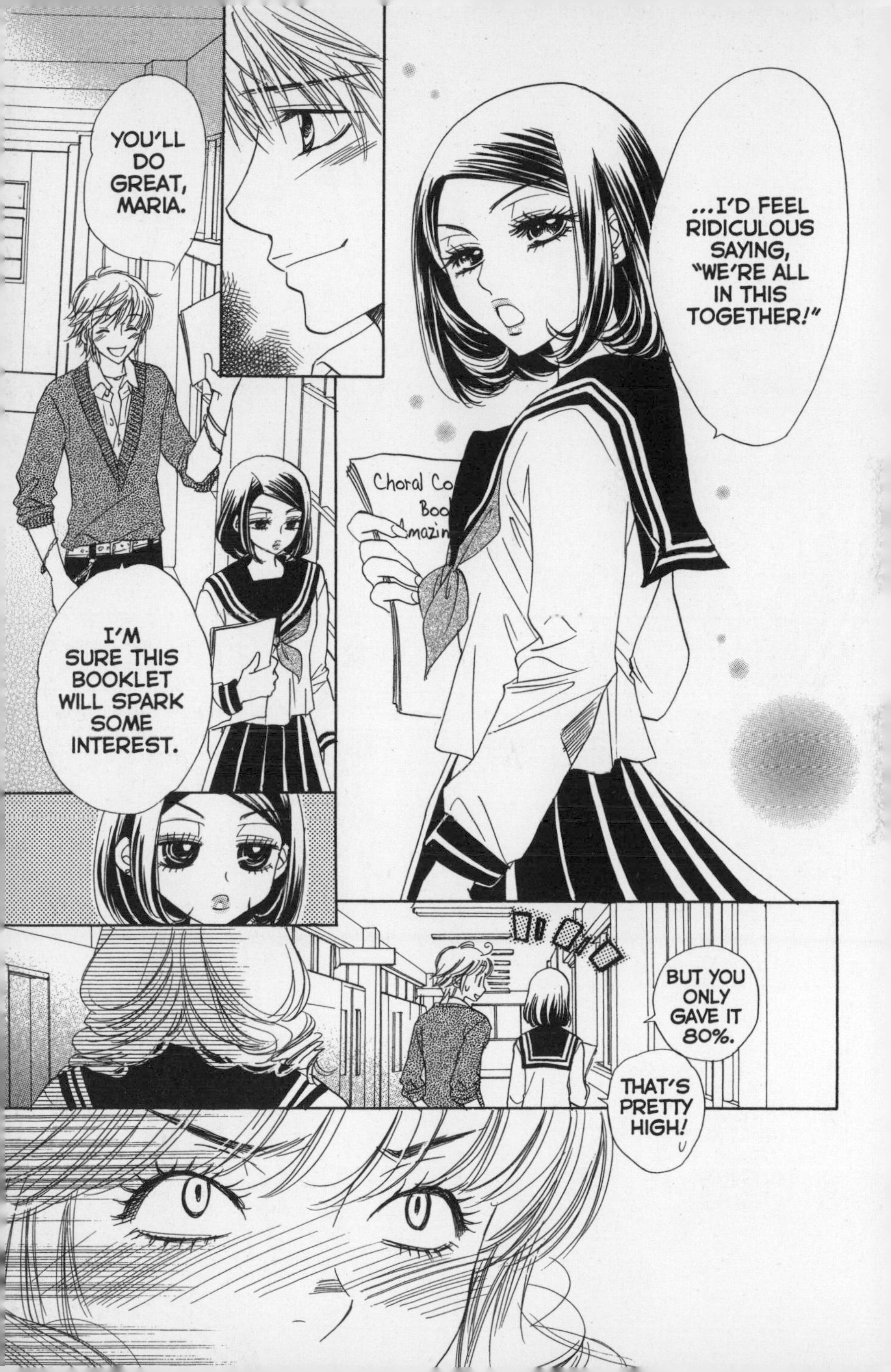
...I'D FEEL RIDICULOUS SAYING, "WE'RE ALL IN THIS TOGETHER!"
YOU'LL DO GREAT, MARIA.
I'M SURE THIS BOOKLET WILL SPARK SOME INTEREST.
BUT YOU ONLY GAVE IT 80%.
THAT'S PRETTY HIGH!

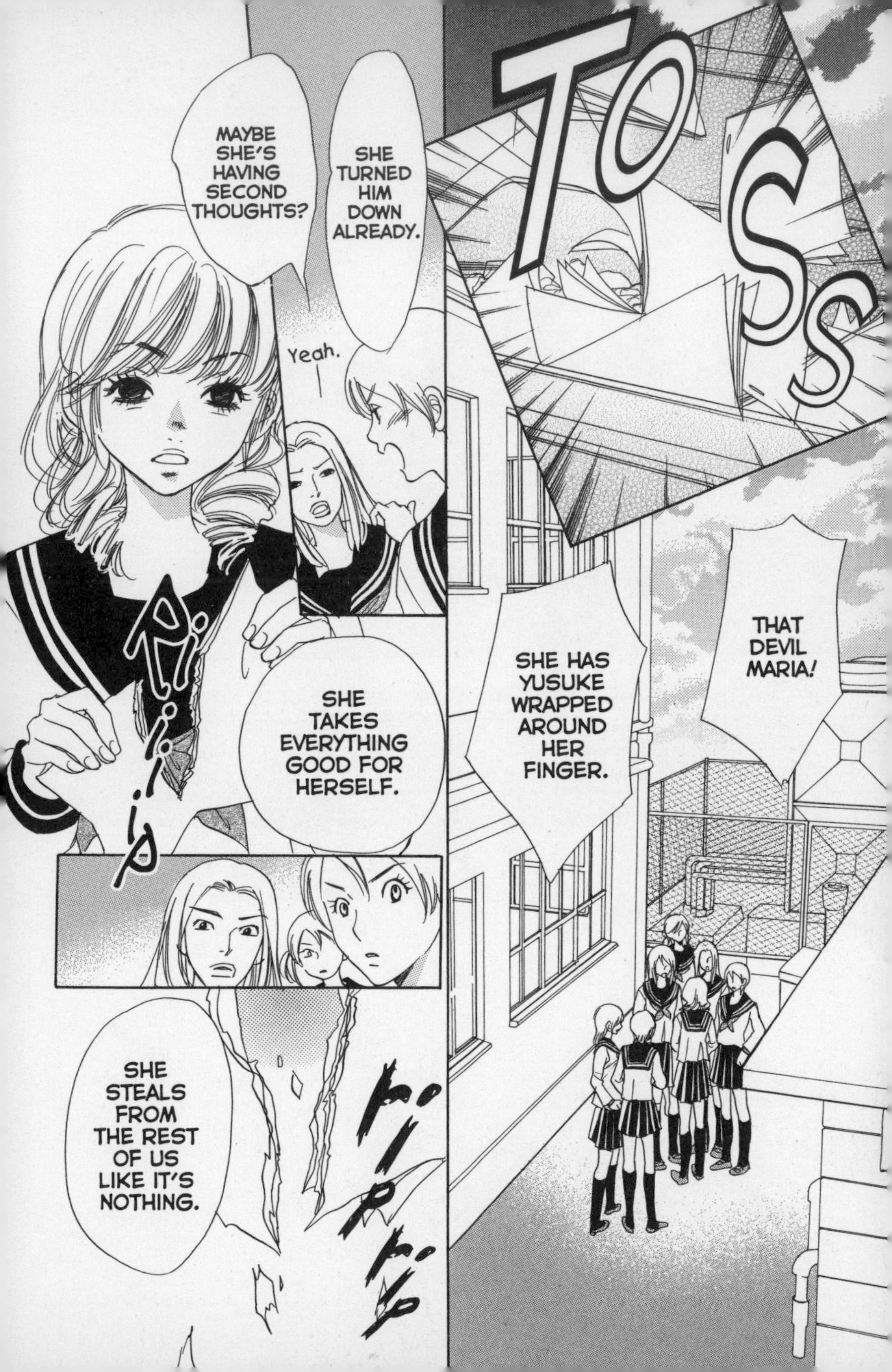
TOSS
THAT DEVIL MARIA!
SHE HAS YUSUKE WRAPPED AROUND HER FINGER.
SHE TURNED HIM DOWN ALREADY.
MAYBE SHE'S HAVING SECOND THOUGHTS?
Yeah.
SHE TAKES EVERYTHING GOOD FOR HERSELF.
SHE STEALS FROM THE REST OF US LIKE IT'S NOTHING.

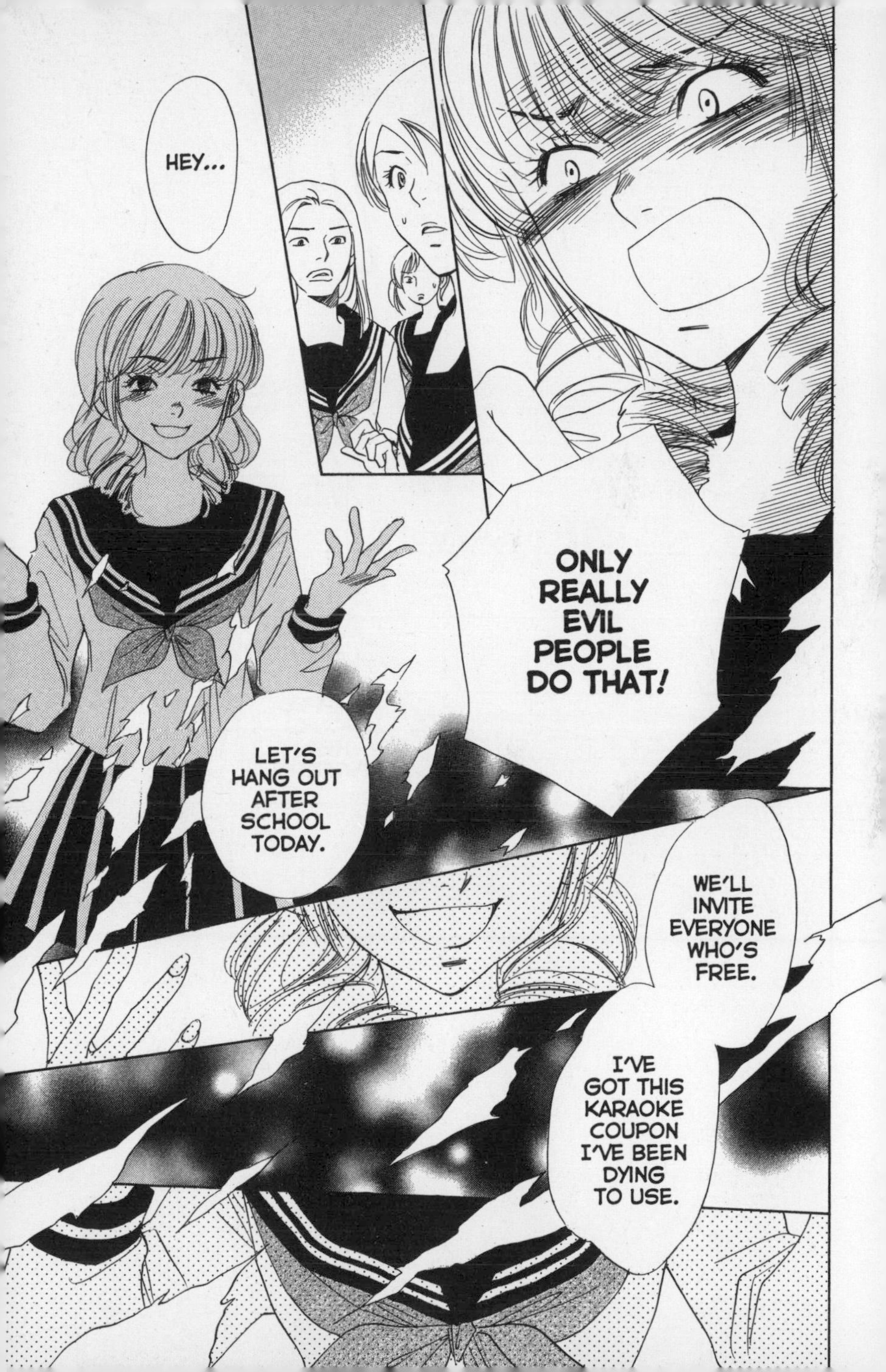
ONLY REALLY EVIL PEOPLE DO THAT!
HEY...
LET'S HANG OUT AFTER SCHOOL TODAY.
WE'LL INVITE EVERYONE WHO'S FREE.
I'VE GOT THIS KARAOKE COUPON I'VE BEEN DYING TO USE.

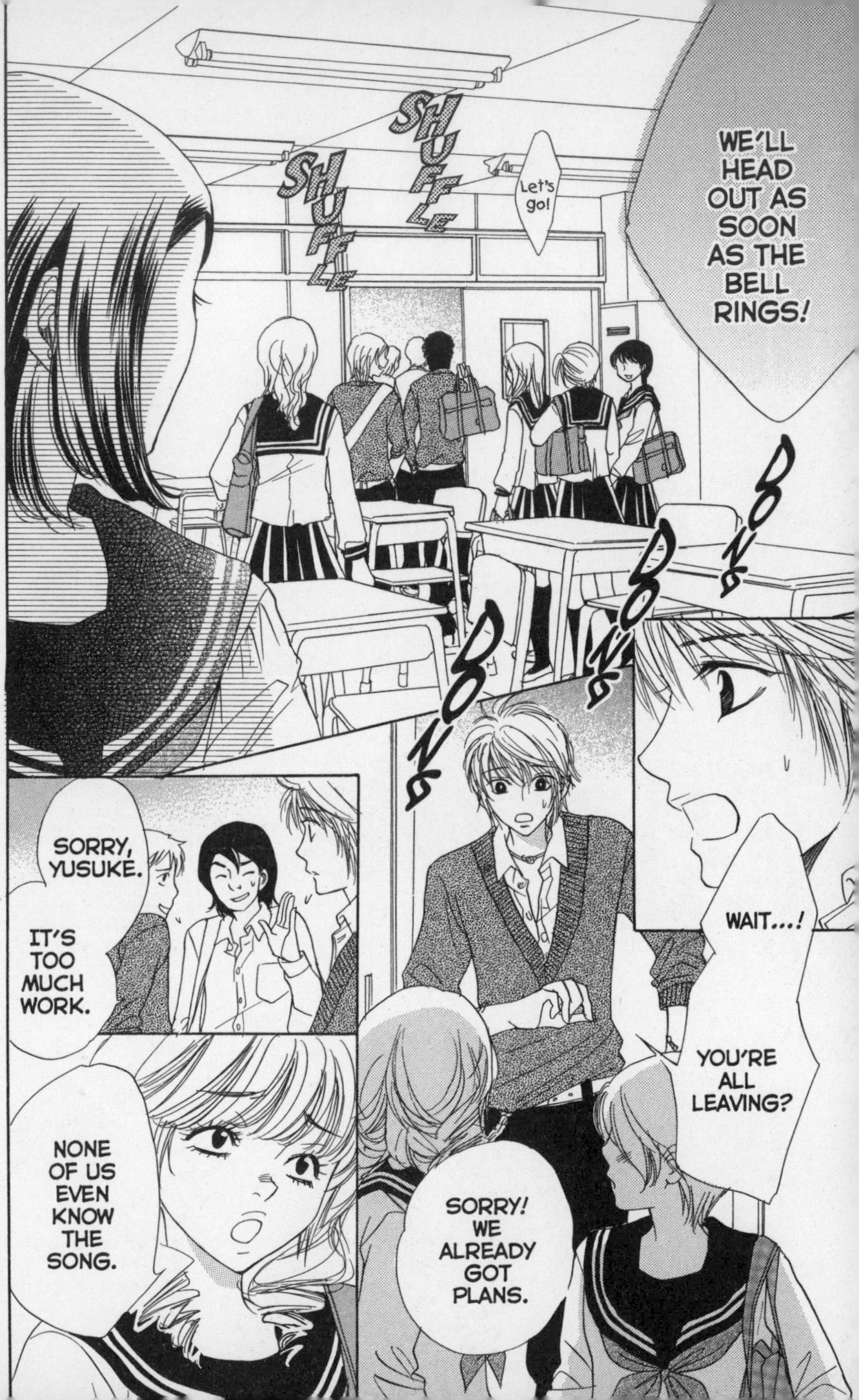
WE'LL HEAD OUT AS SOON AS THE BELL RINGS!
Let's go!
SHUFFLE
SHUFFLE
DONG
DONG
DONG
WAIT...!
YOU'RE ALL LEAVING?
SORRY! WE ALREADY GOT PLANS.
SORRY, YUSUKE.
IT'S TOO MUCH WORK.
NONE OF US EVEN KNOW THE SONG.

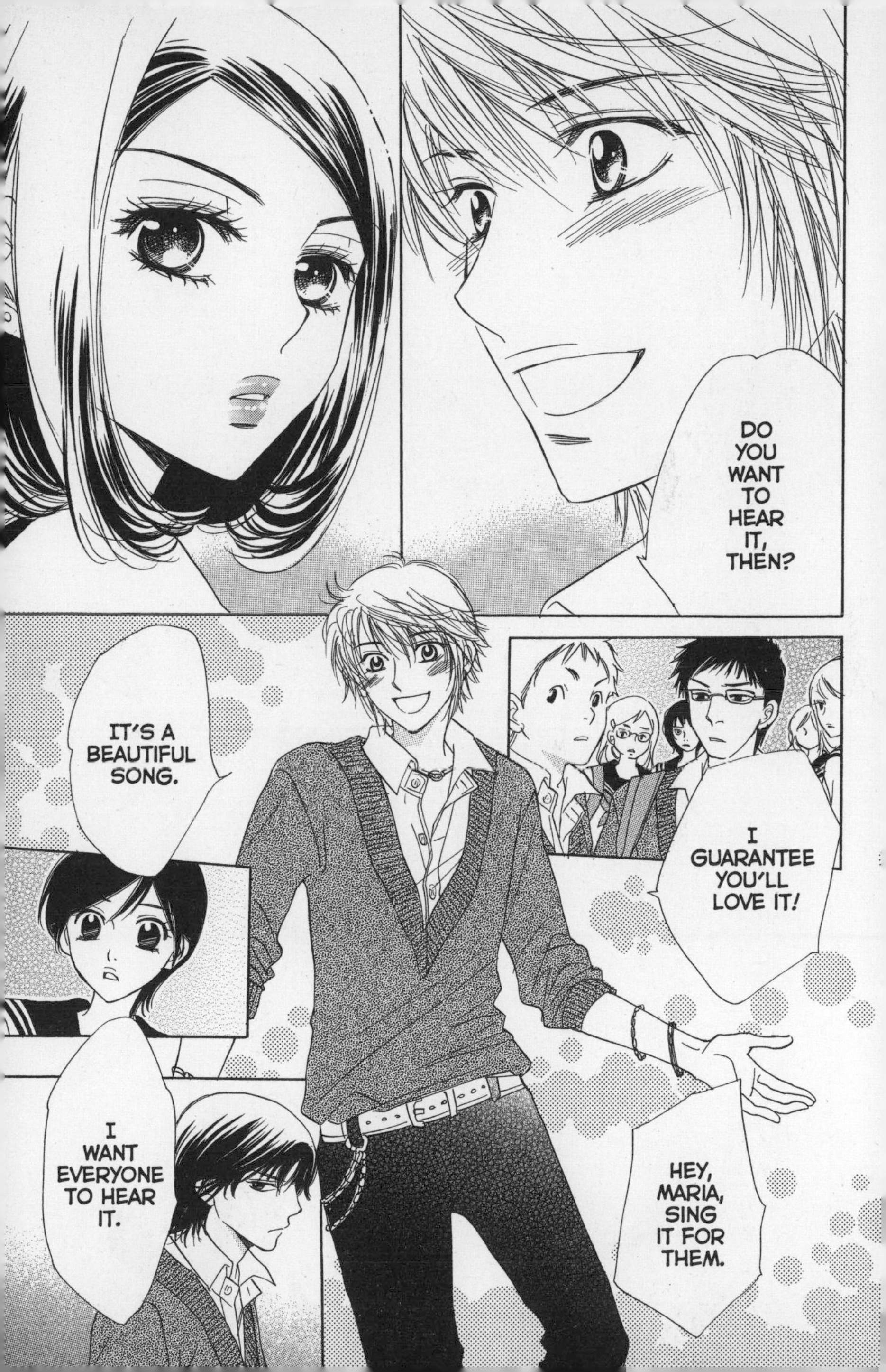
DO YOU WANT TO HEAR IT, THEN?
IT'S A BEAUTIFUL SONG.
I GUARANTEE YOU'LL LOVE IT!
I WANT EVERYONE TO HEAR IT.
HEY, MARIA, SING IT FOR THEM.

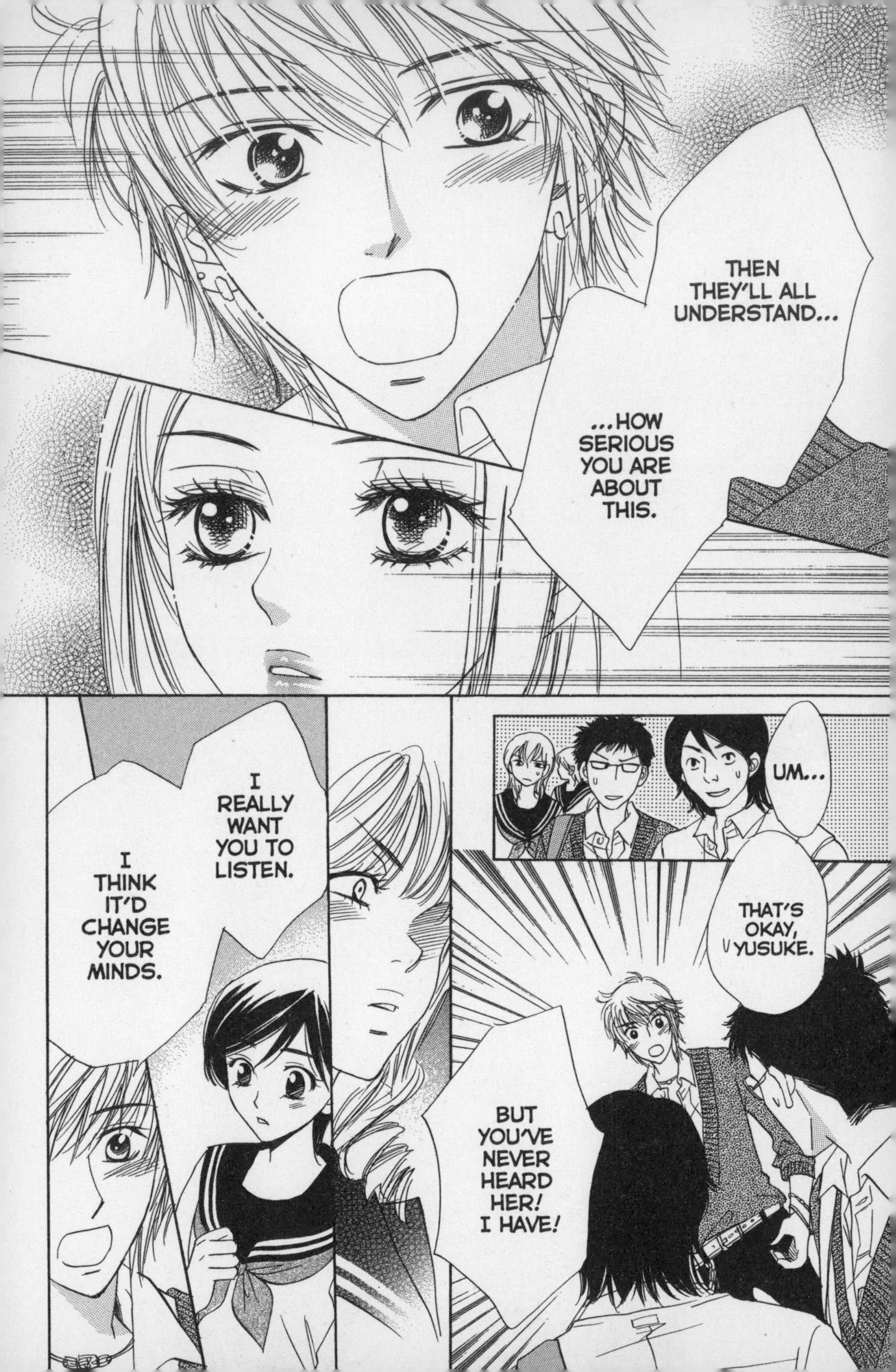
THEN THEY'LL ALL UNDERSTAND...
...HOW SERIOUS YOU ARE ABOUT THIS.
UM...
THAT'S OKAY, YUSUKE.
BUT YOU'VE NEVER HEARD HER! I HAVE!
I REALLY WANT YOU TO LISTEN.
I THINK IT'D CHANGE YOUR MINDS.

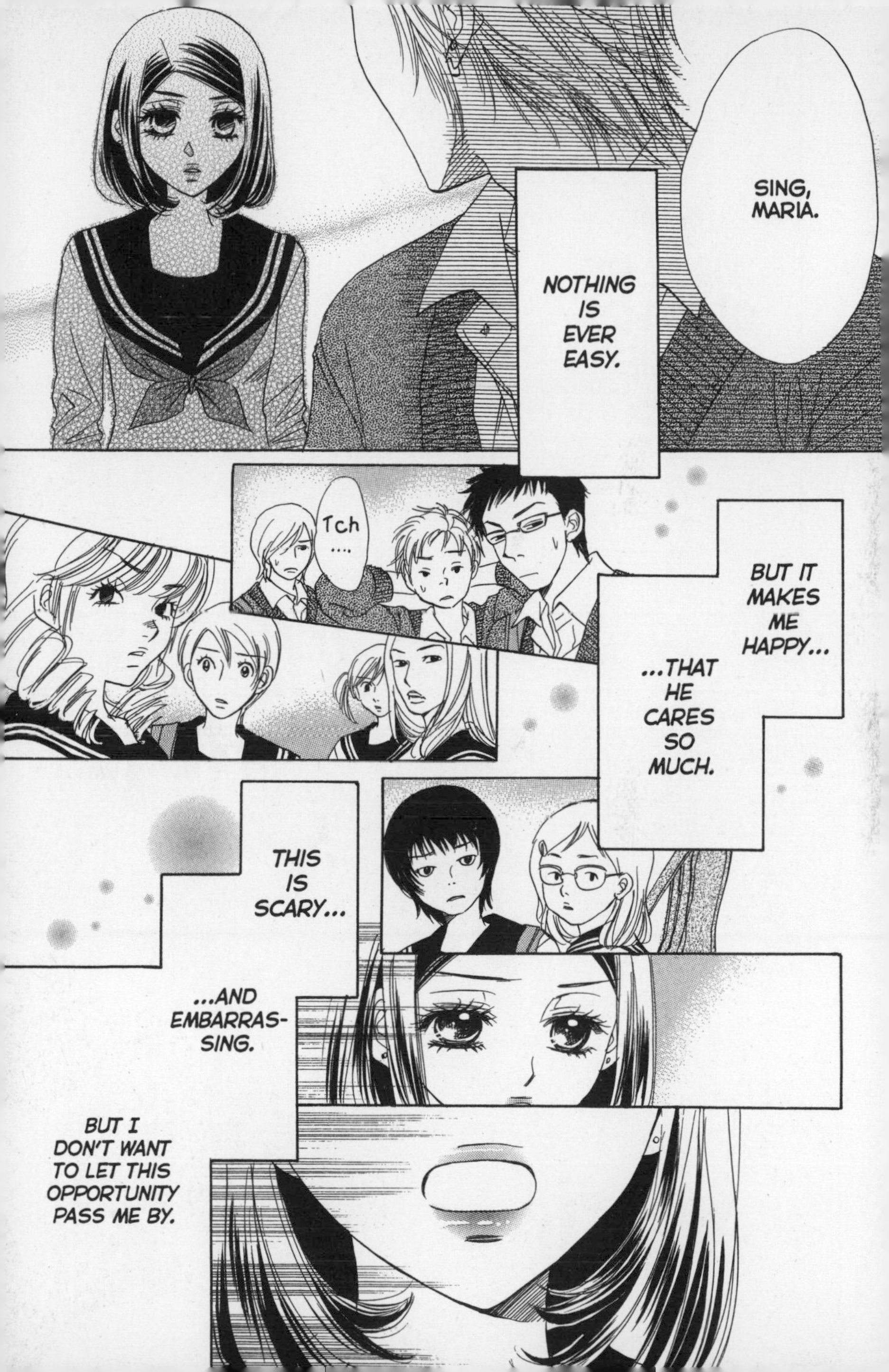
SING, MARIA.
NOTHING IS EVER EASY.
BUT IT MAKES ME HAPPY...
...THAT HE CARES SO MUCH.
Tch ....
THIS IS SCARY...
...AND EMBARRAS-SING.
BUT I DON'T WANT TO LET THIS OPPORTUNITY PASS ME BY.

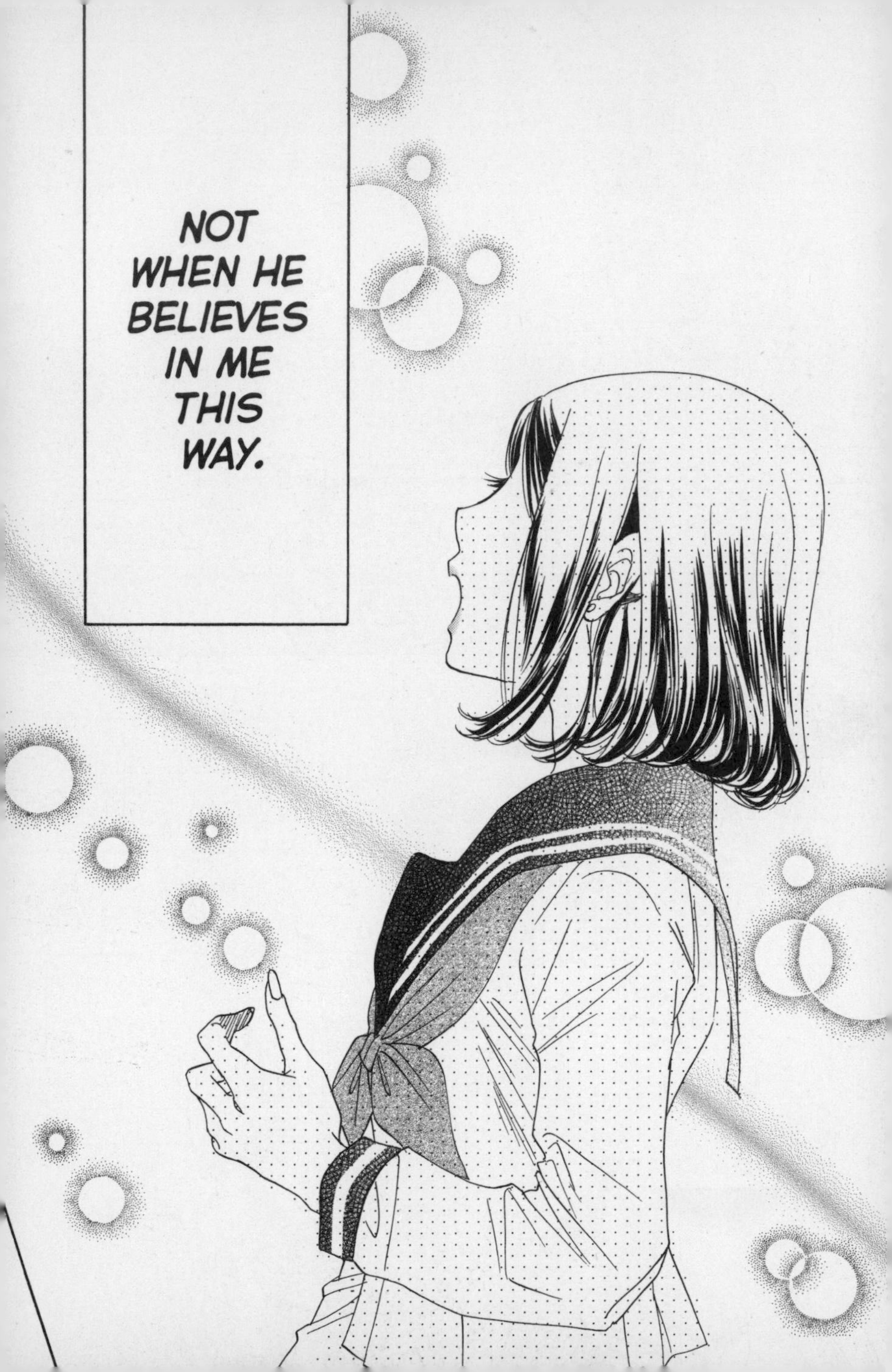
NOT WHEN HE BELIEVES IN ME THIS WAY.

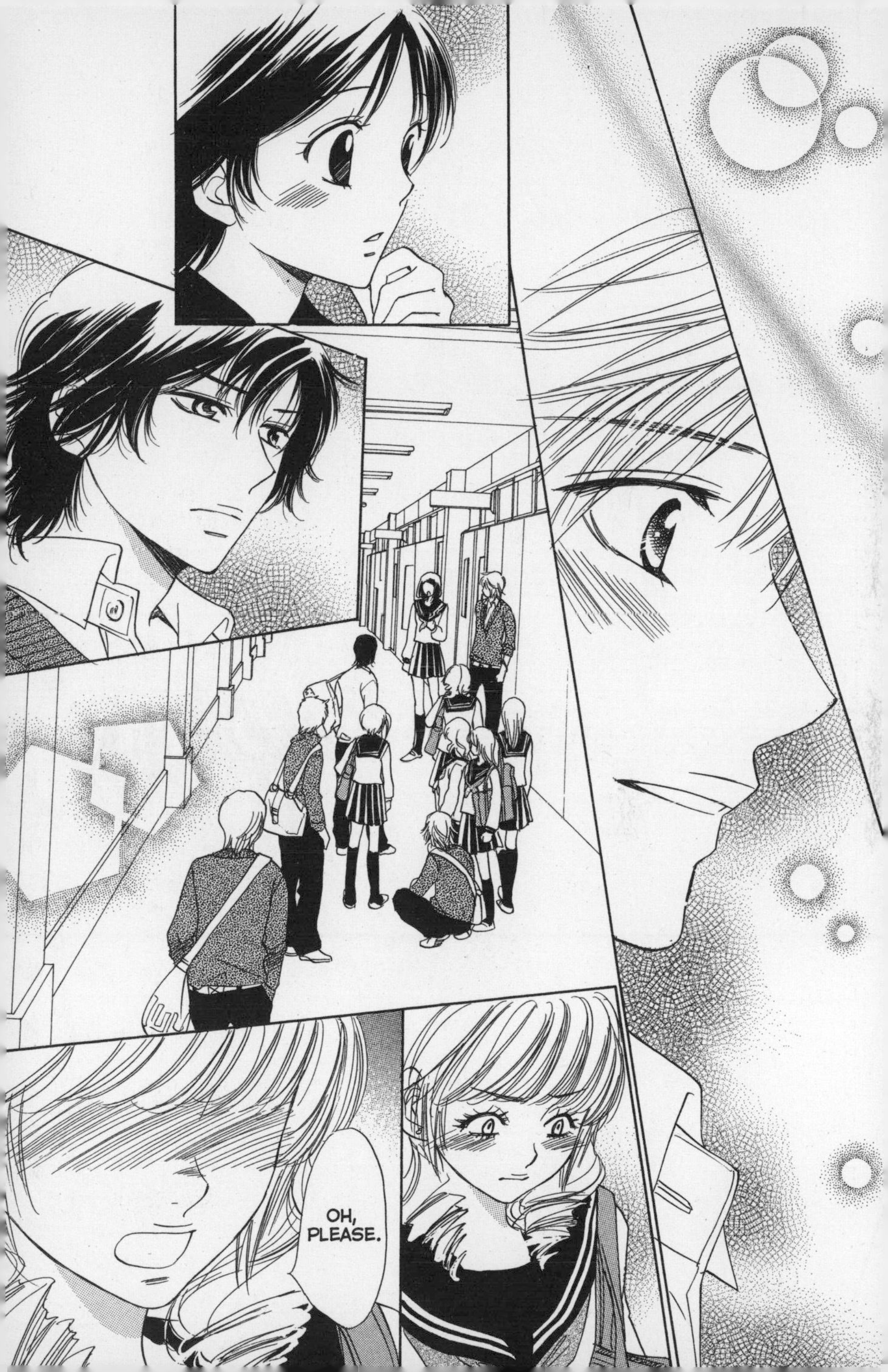
OH, PLEASE.

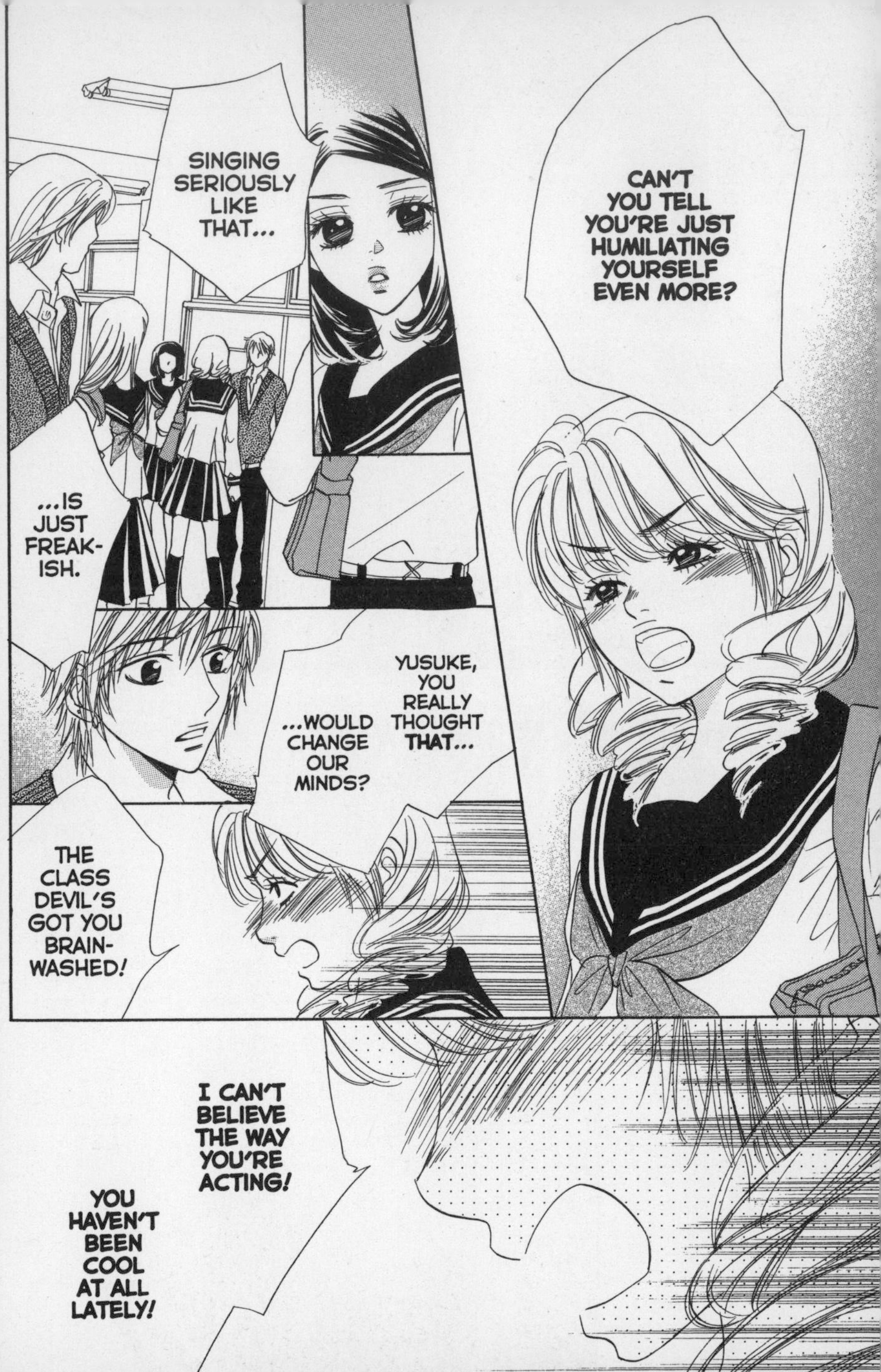
CAN'T YOU TELL YOU'RE JUST HUMILIATING YOURSELF EVEN MORE?
SINGING SERIOUSLY LIKE THAT...
...IS JUST FREAK-ISH.
YUSUKE, YOU REALLY THOUGHT THAT...
...WOULD CHANGE OUR MINDS?
THE CLASS DEVIL'S GOT YOU BRAIN-WASHED!
I CAN'T BELIEVE THE WAY YOU'RE ACTING!
YOU HAVEN'T BEEN COOL AT ALL LATELY!

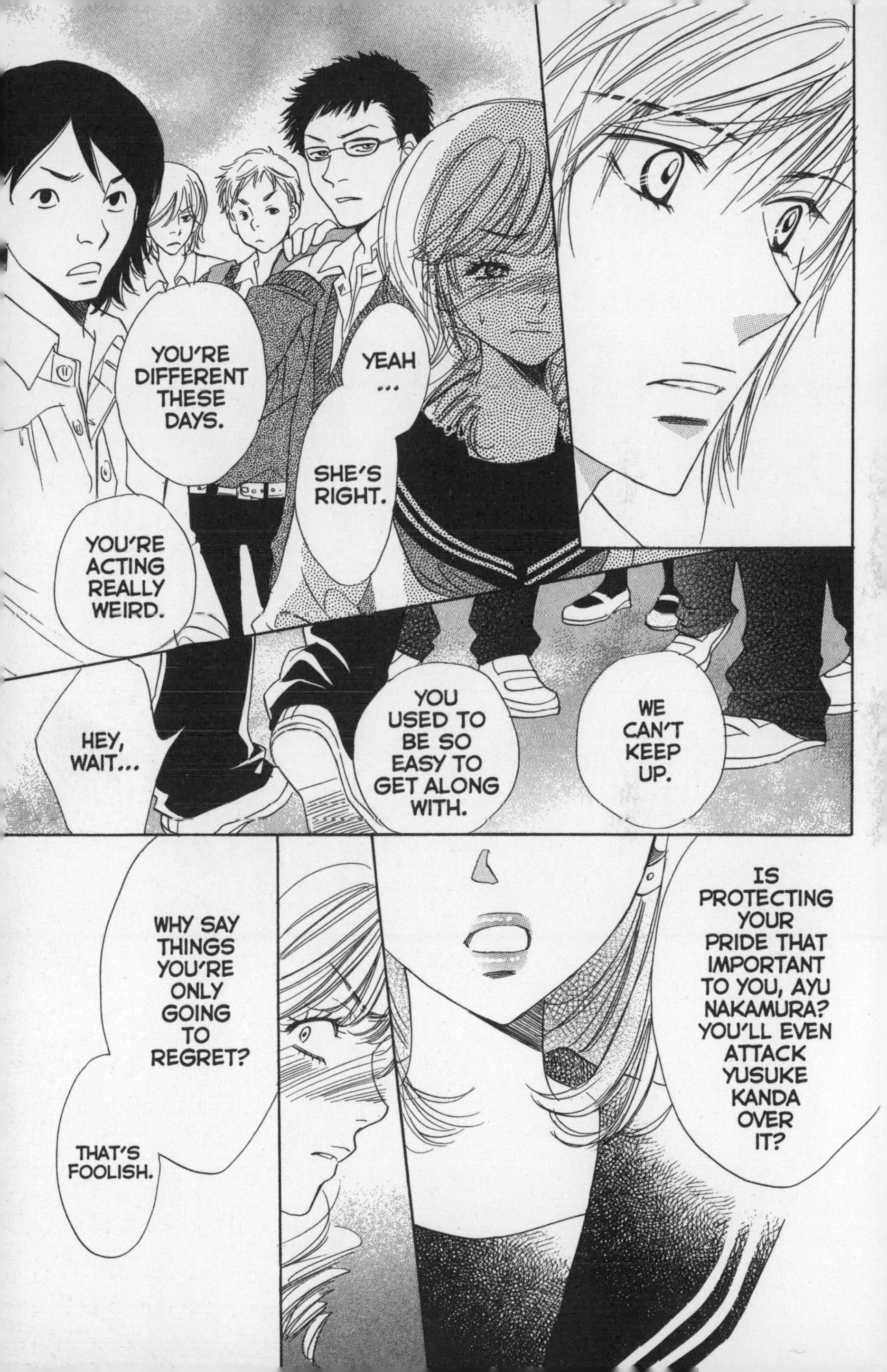
YEAH ...
SHE'S RIGHT.
YOU'RE DIFFERENT THESE DAYS.
YOU'RE ACTING REALLY WEIRD.
WE CAN'T KEEP UP.
YOU USED TO BE SO EASY TO GET ALONG WITH.
HEY, WAIT...
IS PROTECTING YOUR PRIDE THAT IMPORTANT TO YOU, AYU NAKAMURA? YOU'LL EVEN ATTACK YUSUKE KANDA OVER IT?
WHY SAY THINGS YOU'RE ONLY GOING TO REGRET?
THAT'S FOOLISH.

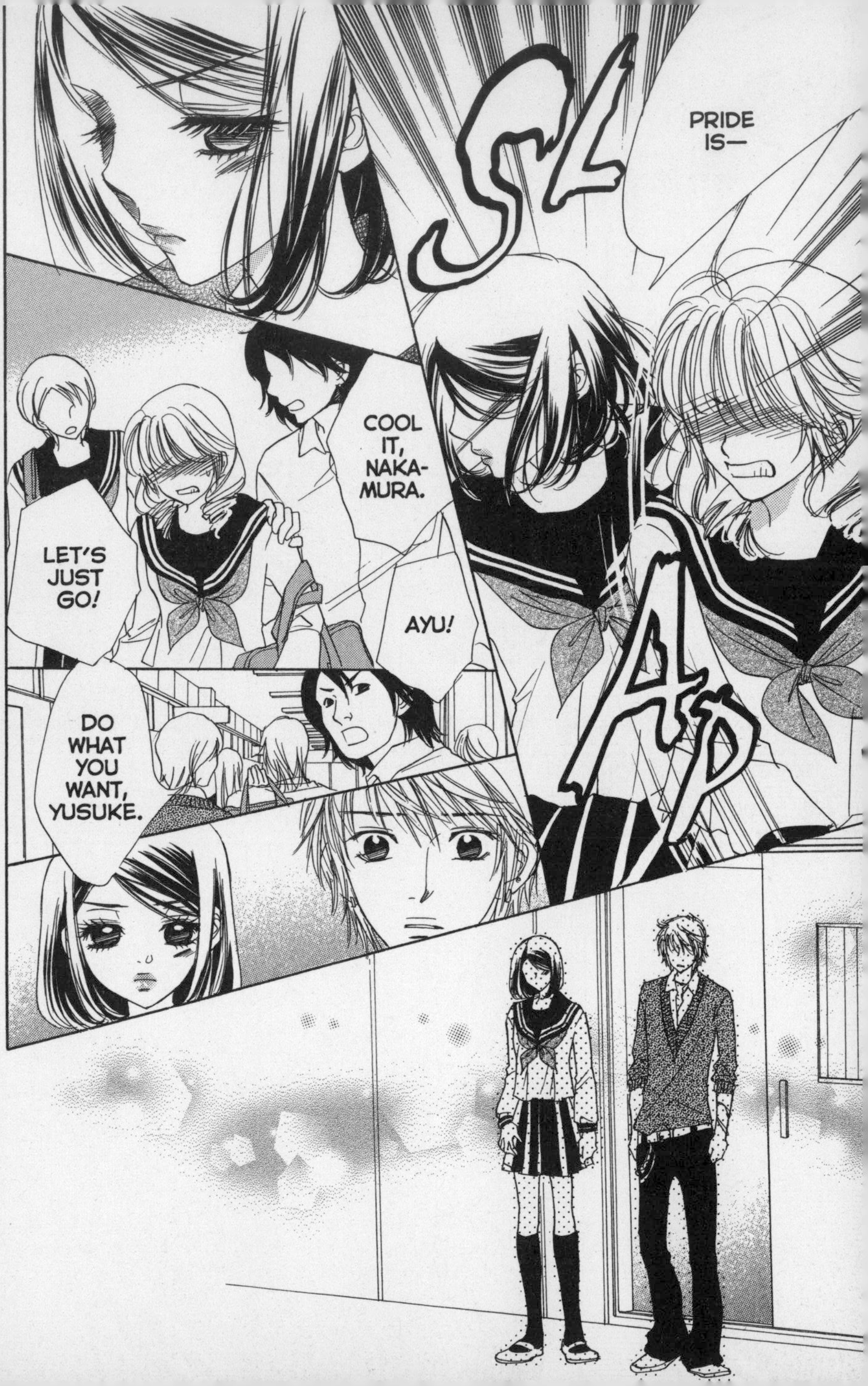
PRIDE IS—
SL
AP
COOL IT, NAKAMURA.
LET'S JUST GO!
AYU!
DO WHAT YOU WANT, YUSUKE.

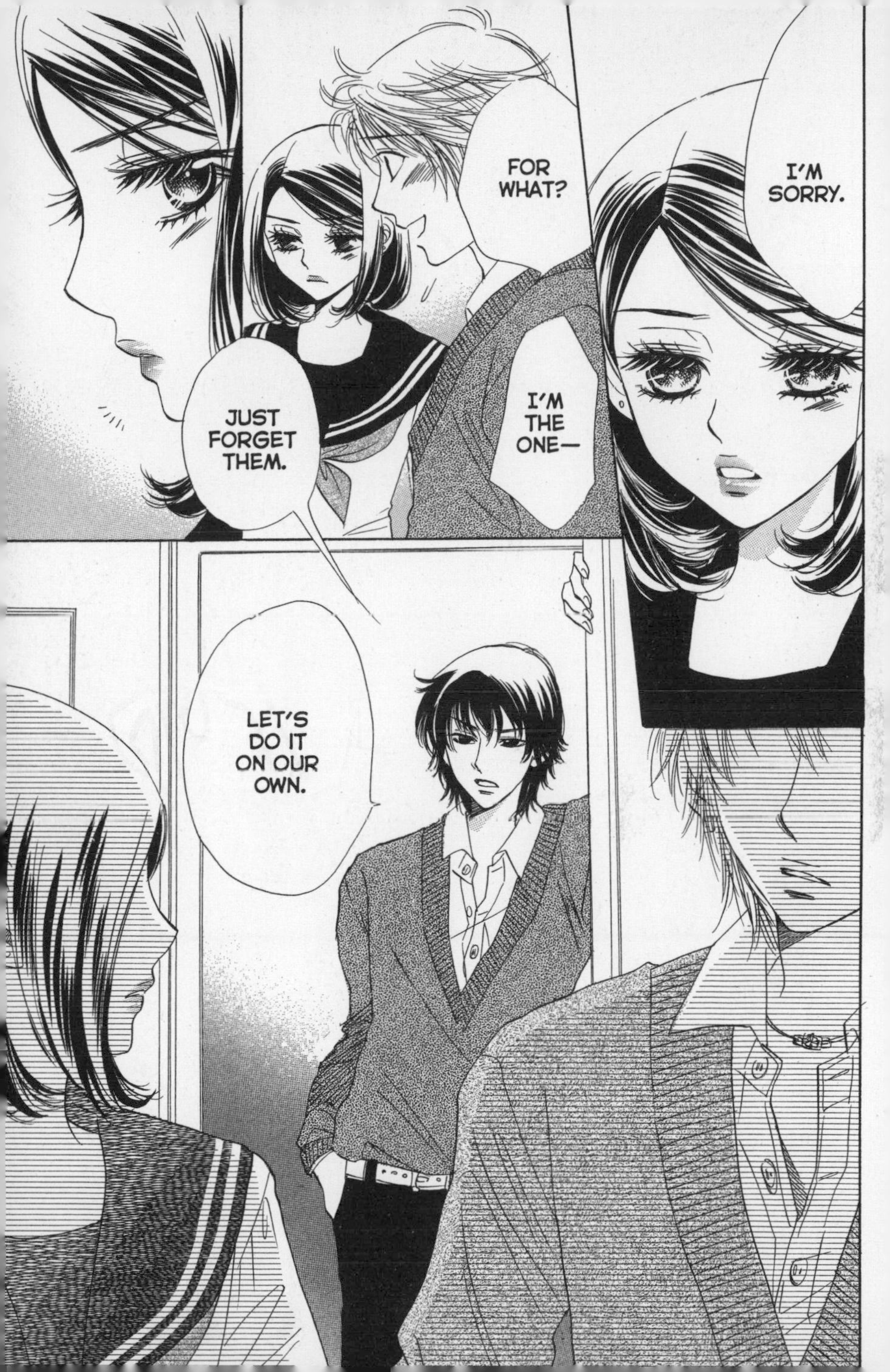
I'M SORRY.
FOR WHAT?
I'M THE ONE—
JUST FORGET THEM.
LET'S DO IT ON OUR OWN.

A Devil and
Her Love Song

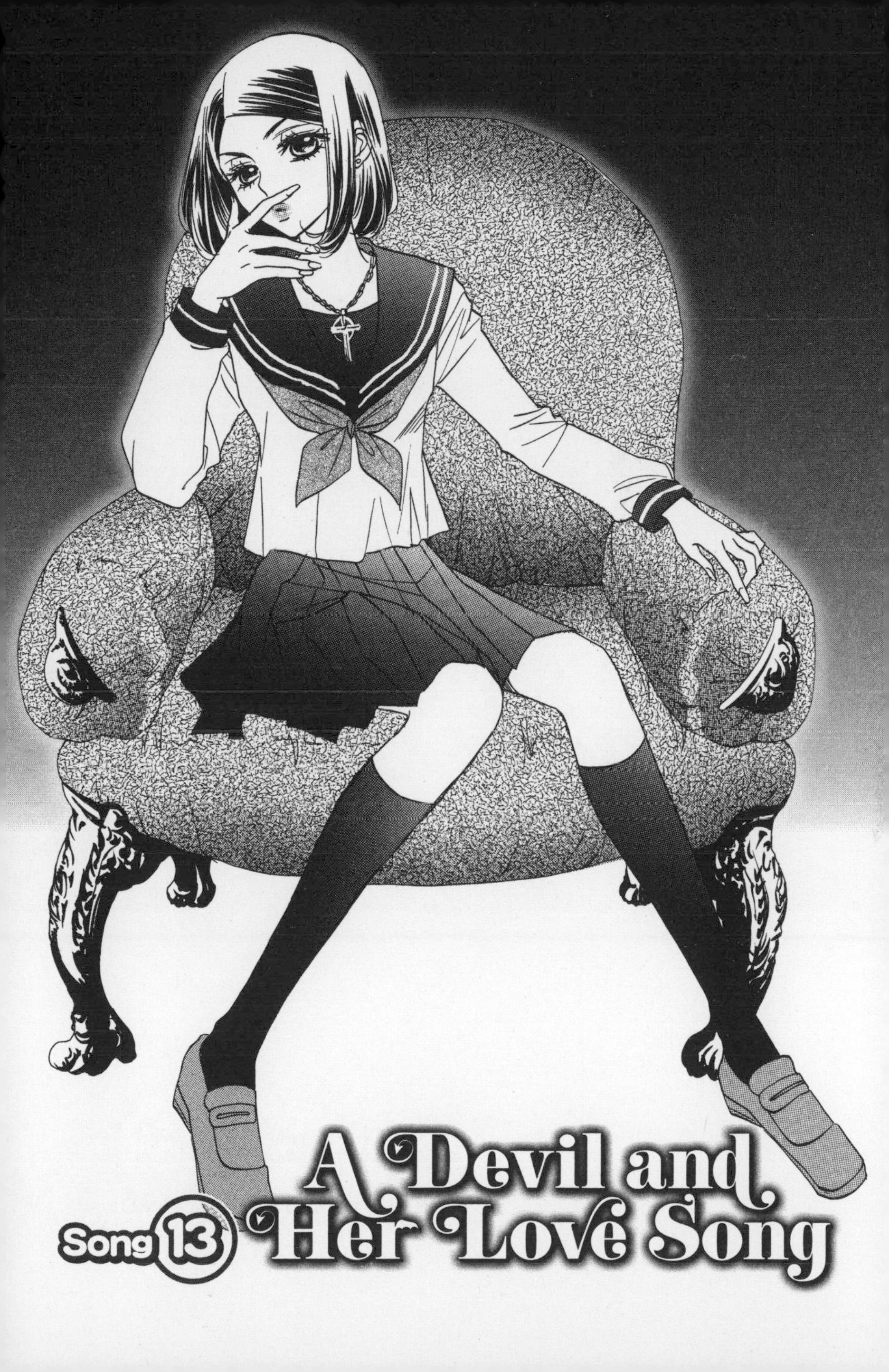
Song 13
A Devil and Her Love Song

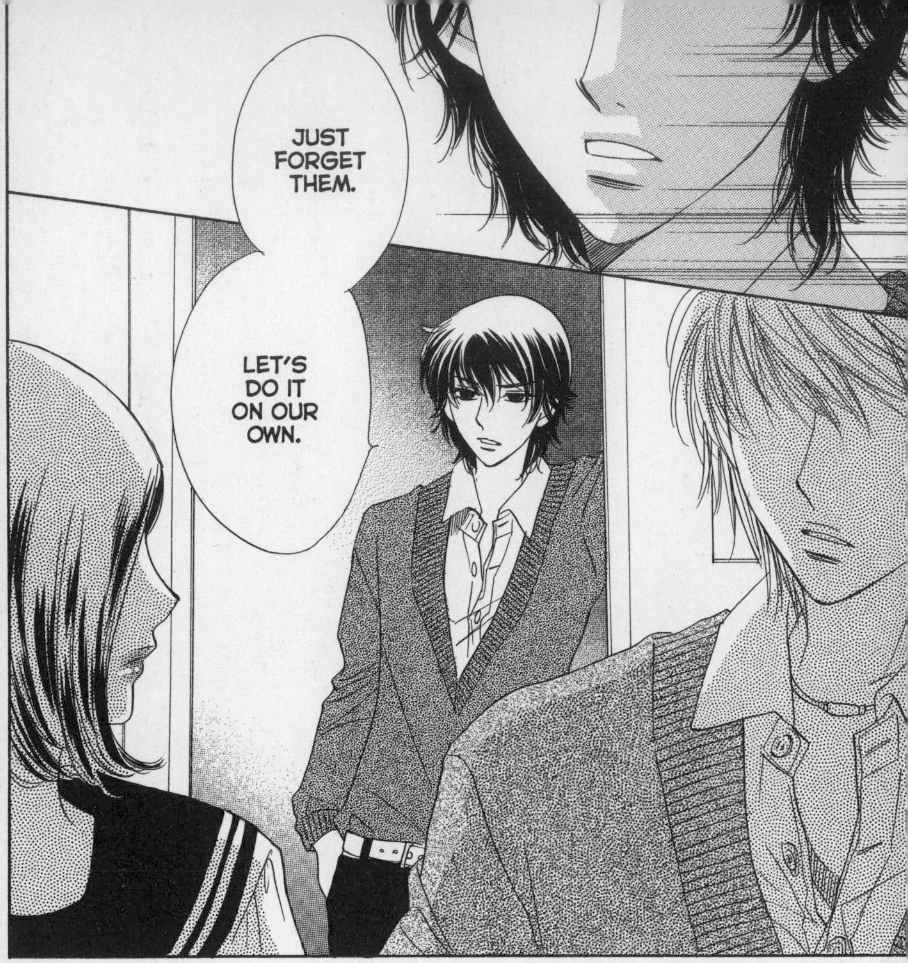
JUST FORGET THEM.
LET'S DO IT ON OUR OWN.

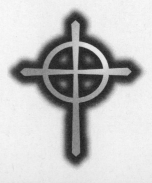

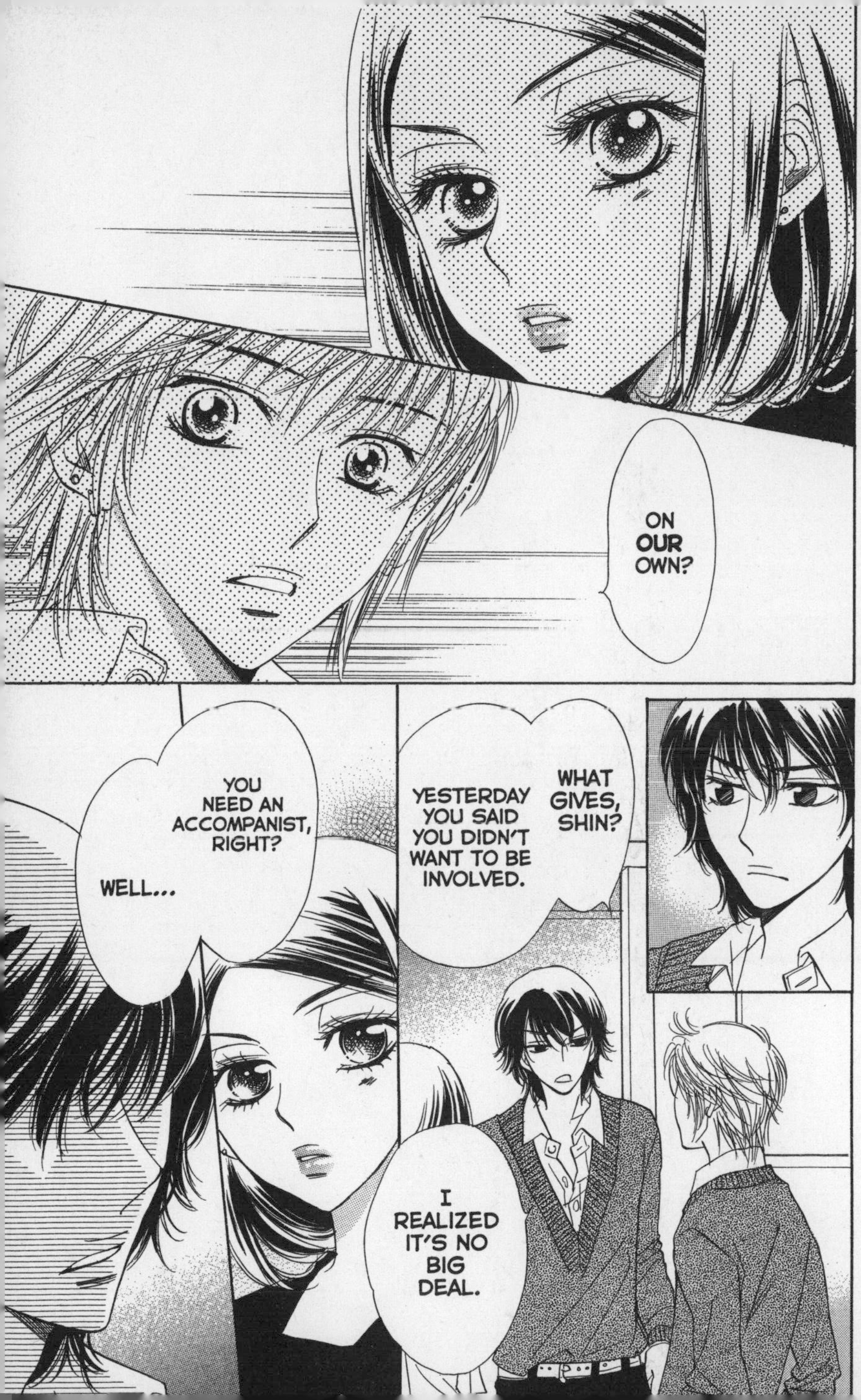
ON OUR OWN?
WHAT GIVES, SHIN?
YESTERDAY YOU SAID YOU DIDN'T WANT TO BE INVOLVED.
I REALIZED IT'S NO BIG DEAL.
YOU NEED AN ACCOMPANIST, RIGHT?
WELL...

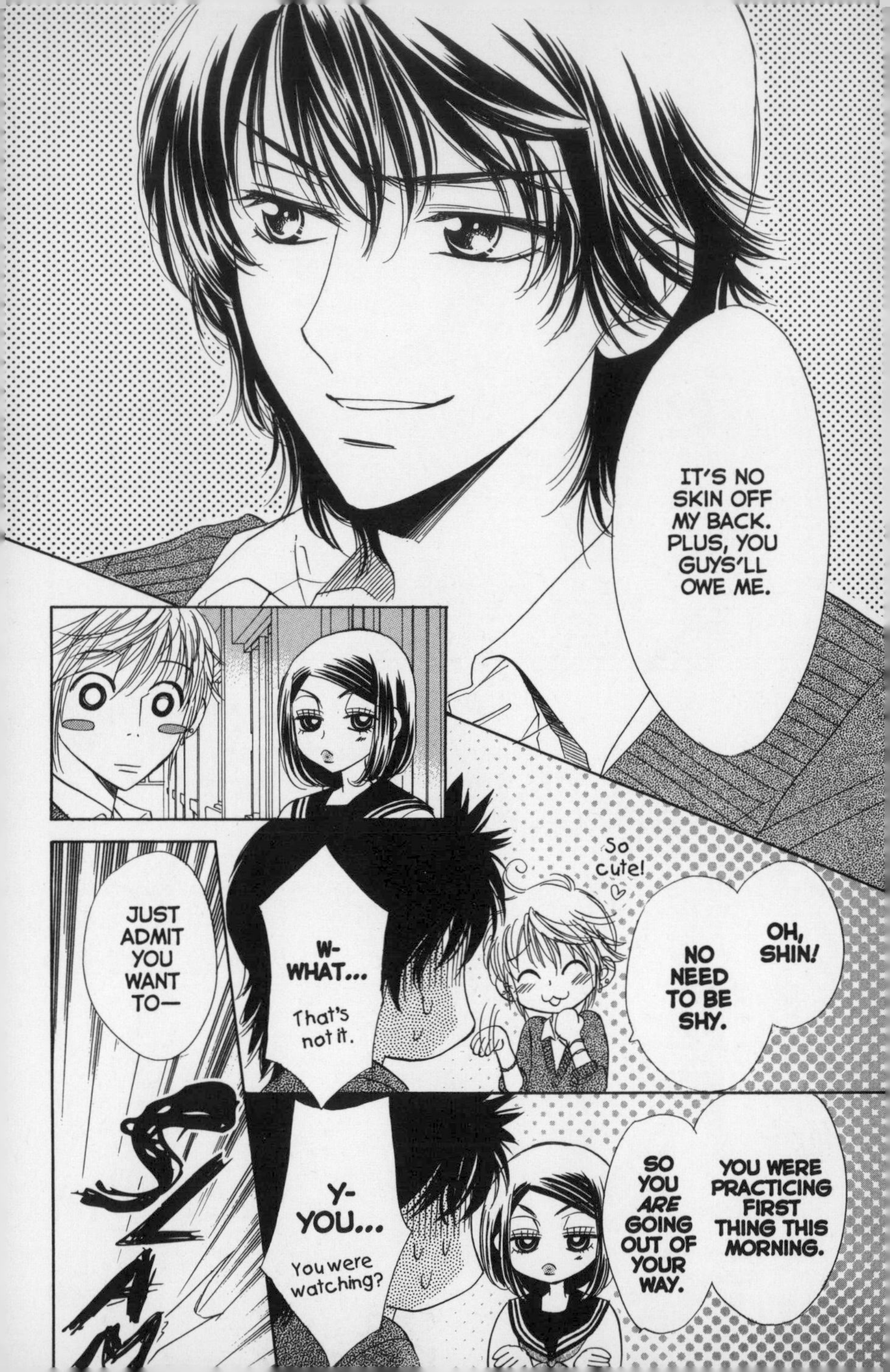
IT'S NO SKIN OFF MY BACK. PLUS, YOU GUYS'LL OWE ME.
OH, SHIN!
NO NEED TO BE SHY.
So cute!
W-WHAT...
That's not it.
JUST ADMIT YOU WANT TO—
YOU WERE PRACTICING FIRST THING THIS MORNING.
SO YOU *ARE* GOING OUT OF YOUR WAY.
Y-YOU...
You were watching?
SLAM

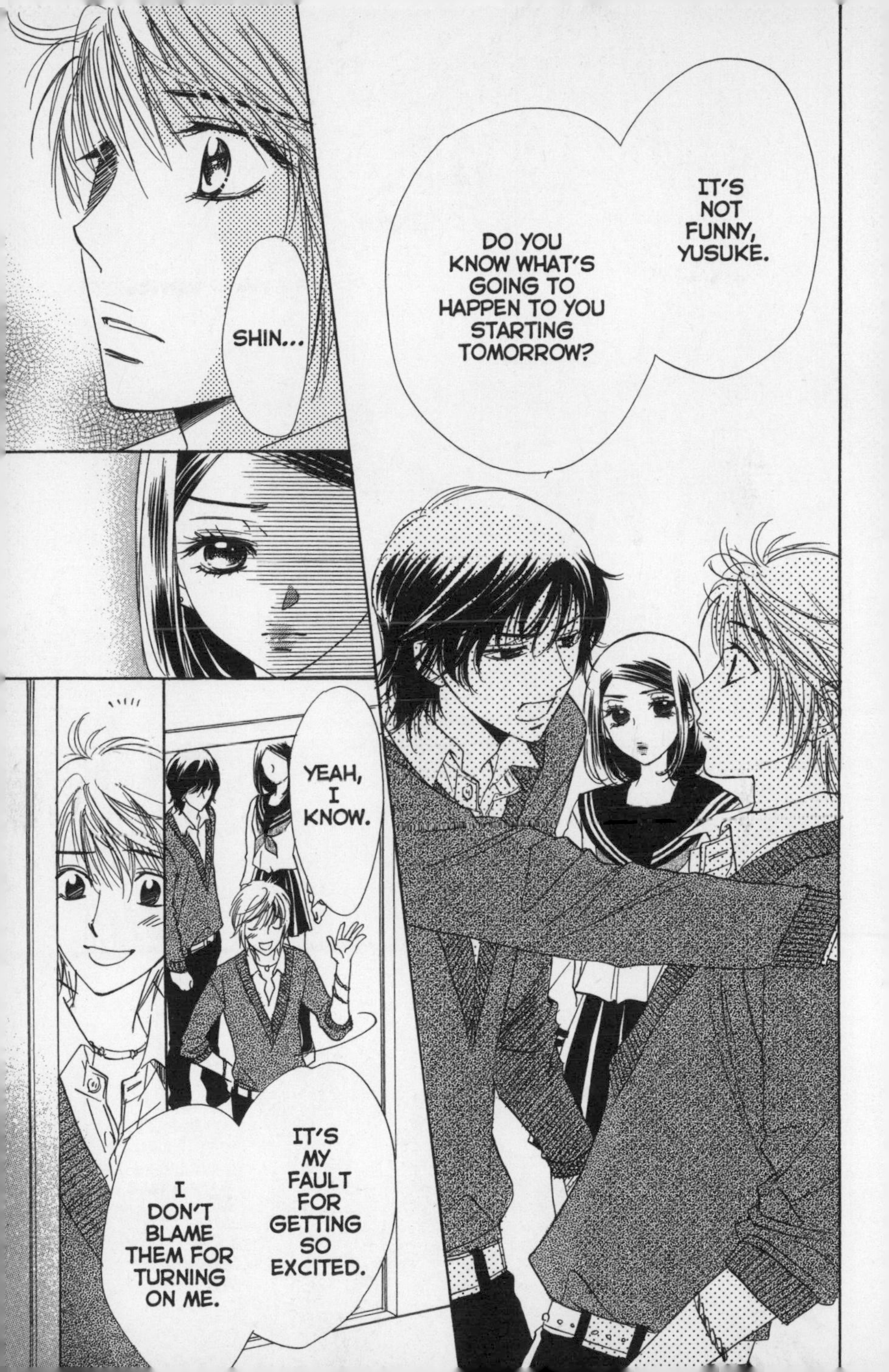
IT'S NOT FUNNY, YUSUKE.
DO YOU KNOW WHAT'S GOING TO HAPPEN TO YOU STARTING TOMORROW?
SHIN...
YEAH, I KNOW.
IT'S MY FAULT FOR GETTING SO EXCITED.
I DON'T BLAME THEM FOR TURNING ON ME.

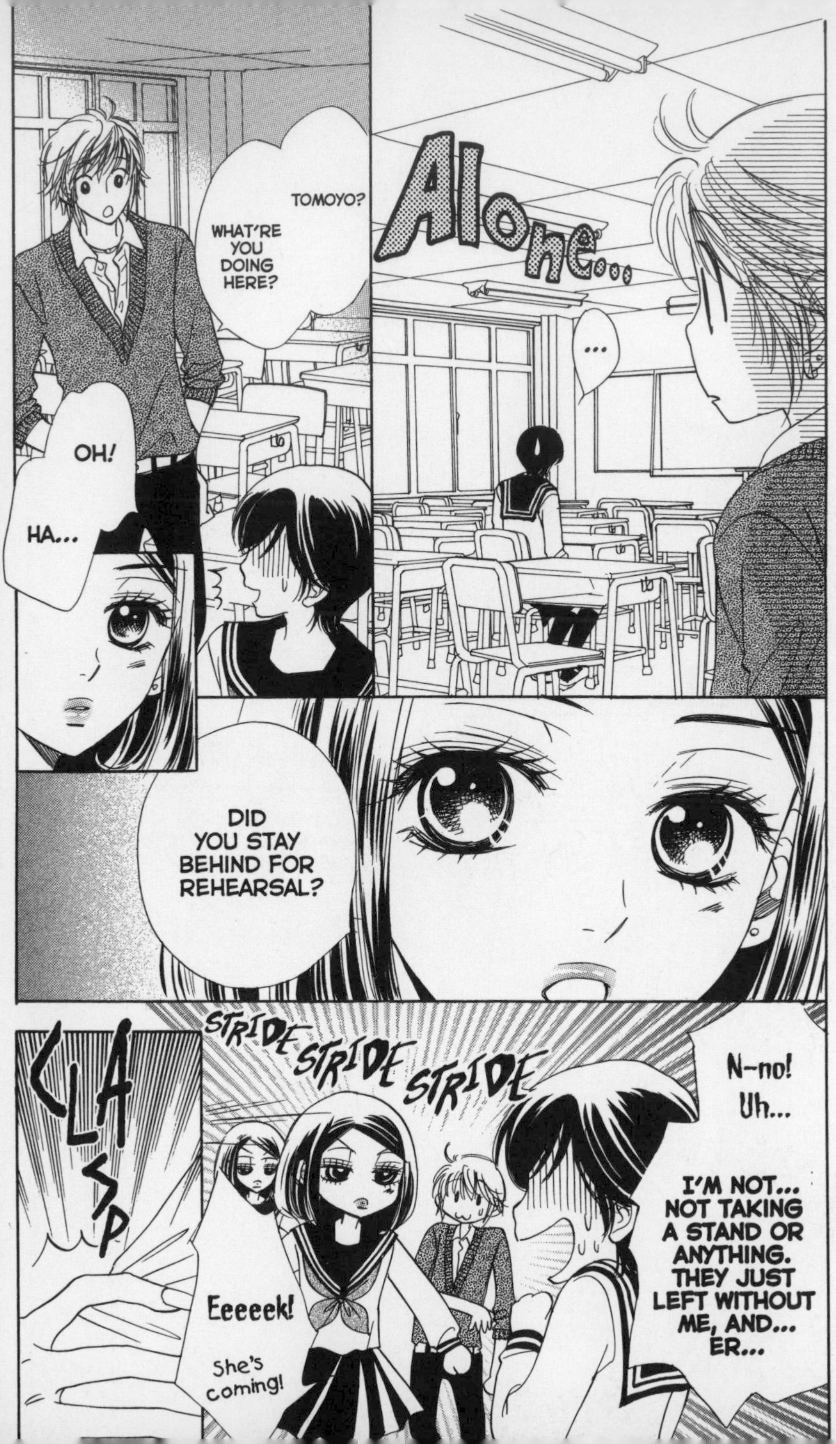
Alone...
...
TOMOYO?
WHAT'RE YOU DOING HERE?
OH!
HA...
DID YOU STAY BEHIND FOR REHEARSAL?
N-no! Uh...
I'M NOT... NOT TAKING A STAND OR ANYTHING. THEY JUST LEFT WITHOUT ME, AND... ER...
STRIDE STRIDE STRIDE
Eeeeek!
She's coming!
CLASP

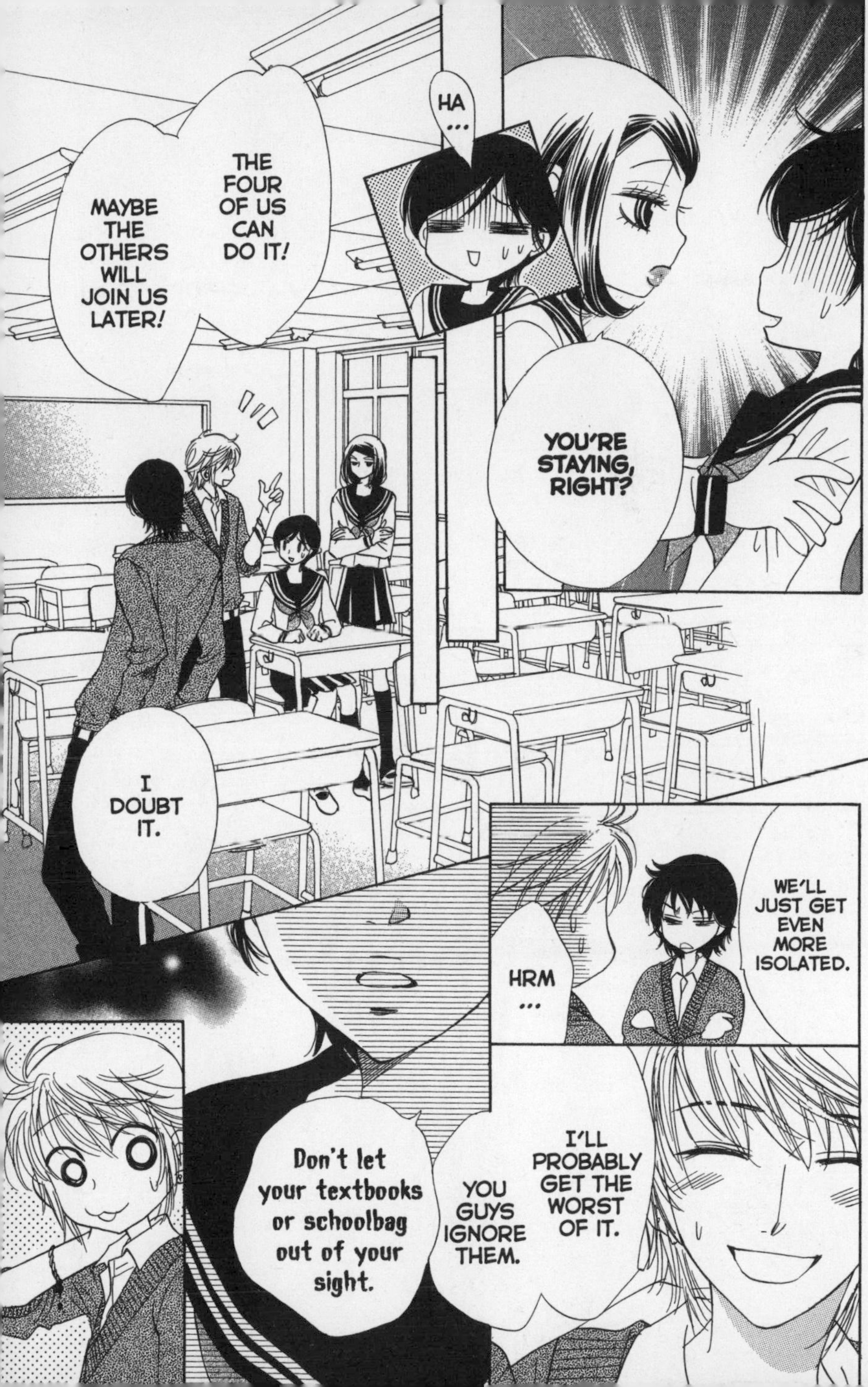
YOU'RE STAYING, RIGHT?
HA...
THE FOUR OF US CAN DO IT!
MAYBE THE OTHERS WILL JOIN US LATER!
I DOUBT IT.
WE'LL JUST GET EVEN MORE ISOLATED.
HRM...
I'LL PROBABLY GET THE WORST OF IT.
YOU GUYS IGNORE THEM.
Don't let your textbooks or schoolbag out of your sight.

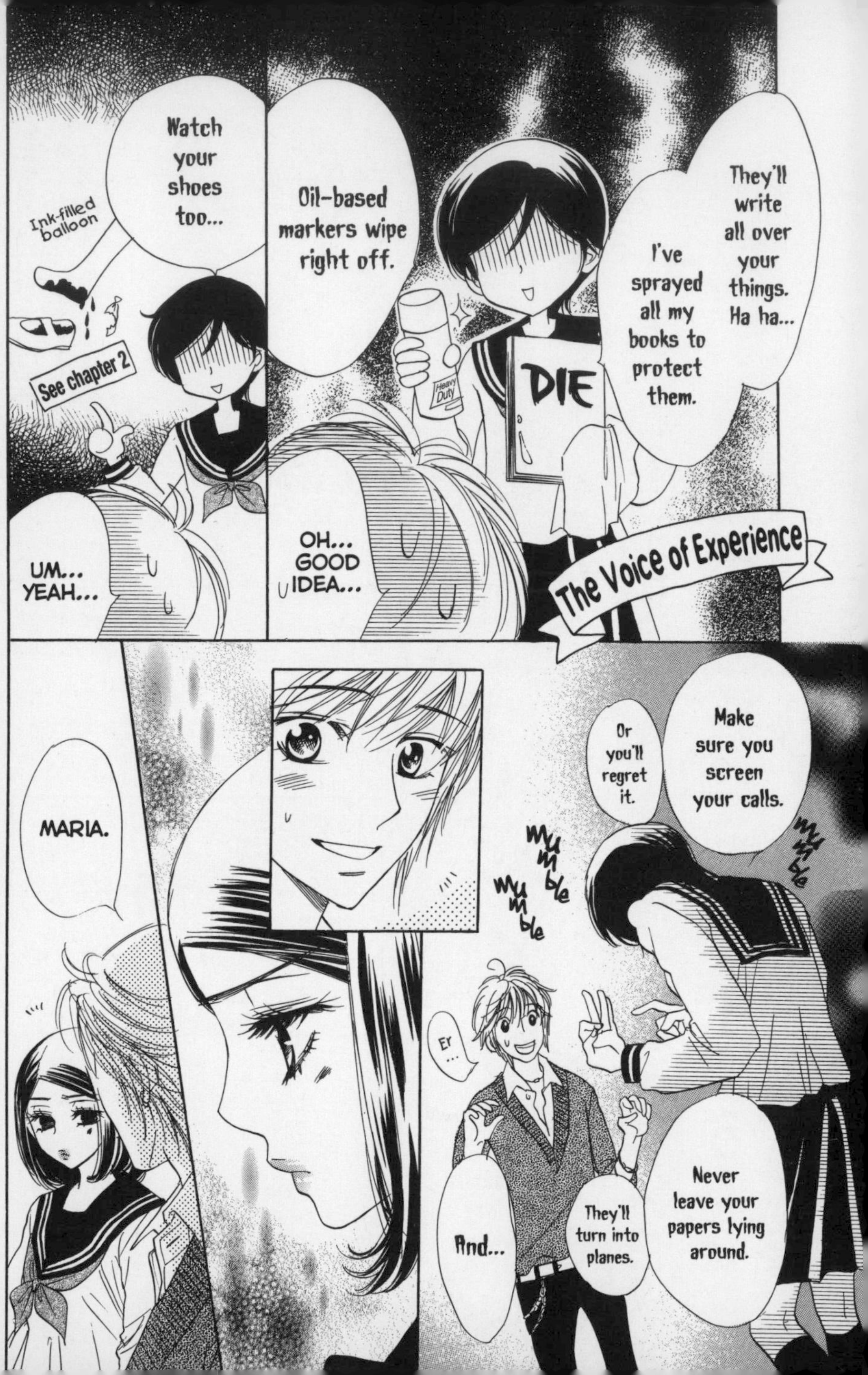
They'll write all over your things. Ha ha...
I've sprayed all my books to protect them.
DIE
Heavy Duty
The Voice of Experience
Oil-based markers wipe right off.
OH... GOOD IDEA...
Watch your shoes too...
Ink-filled balloon
See chapter 2
UM... YEAH...
Make sure you screen your calls.
Or you'll regret it.
mumble
mumble
mumble
Never leave your papers lying around.
They'll turn into planes.
Er...
And...
MARIA.

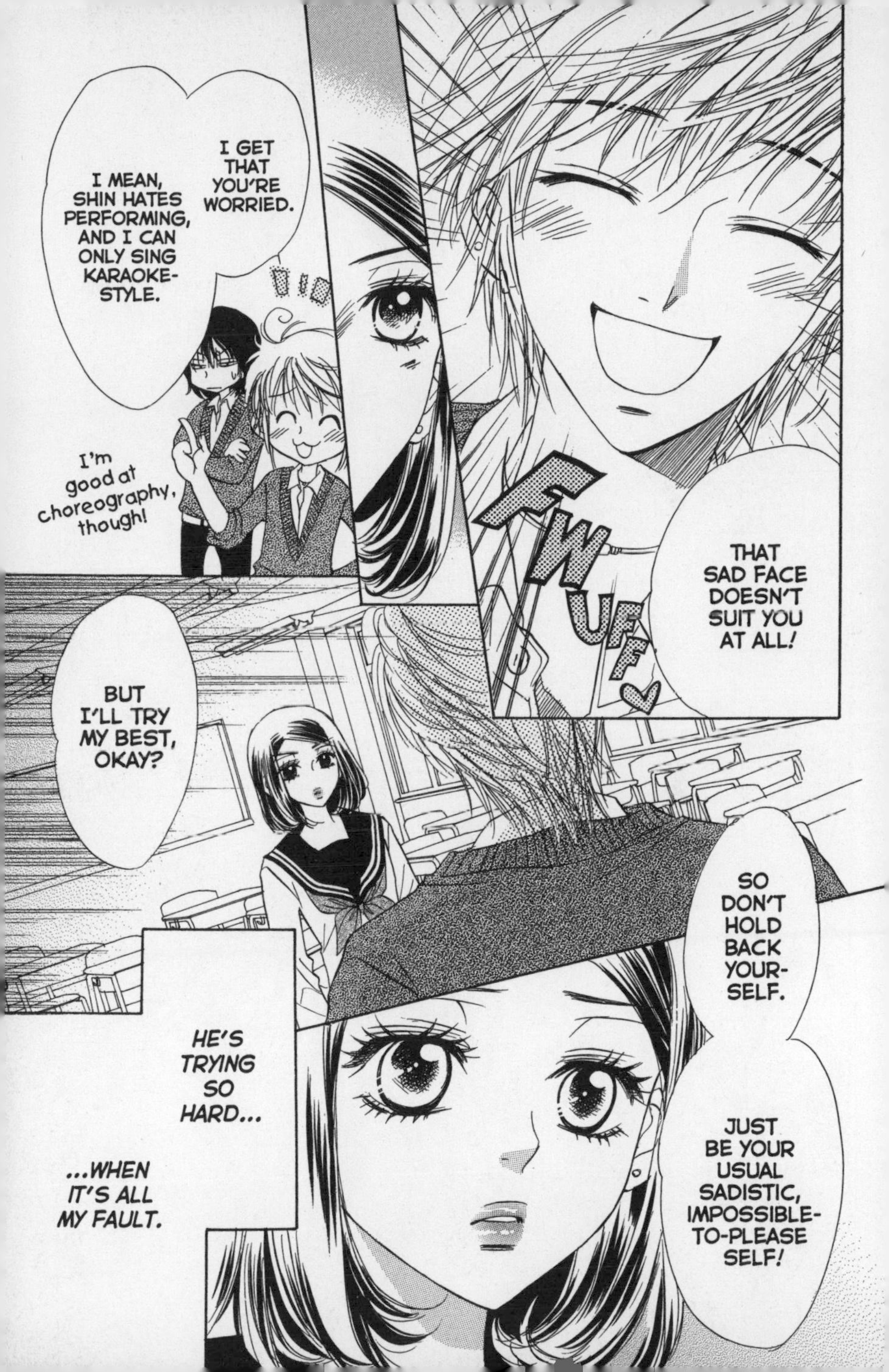
FWUFF
THAT SAD FACE DOESN'T SUIT YOU AT ALL!
I GET THAT YOU'RE WORRIED.
I MEAN, SHIN HATES PERFORMING, AND I CAN ONLY SING KARAOKE-STYLE.
I'm good at choreography, though!
BUT I'LL TRY MY BEST, OKAY?
SO DON'T HOLD BACK YOURSELF.
JUST BE YOUR USUAL SADISTIC, IMPOSSIBLE-TO-PLEASE SELF!
HE'S TRYING SO HARD...
...WHEN IT'S ALL MY FAULT.

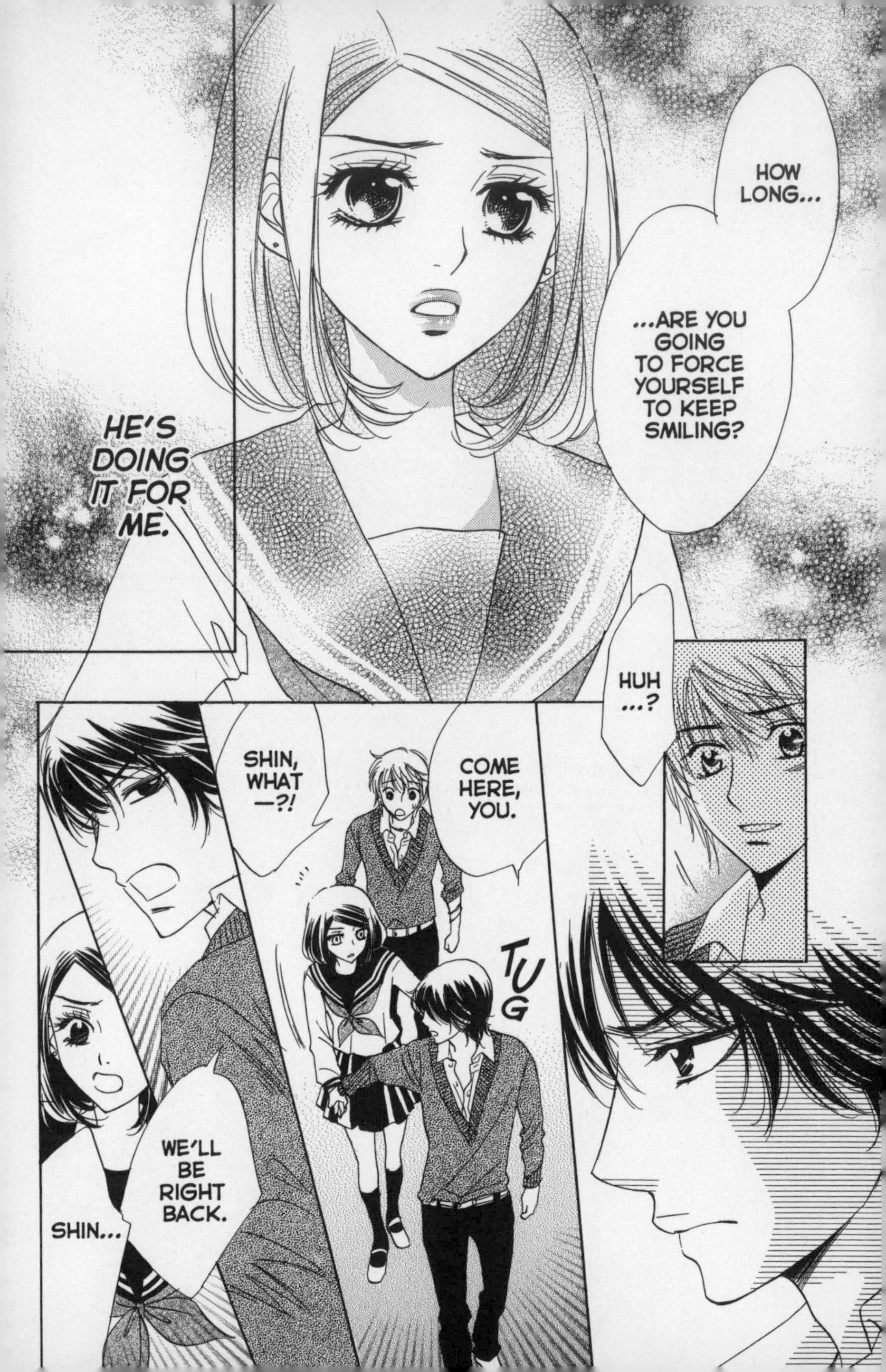
HOW LONG...
...ARE YOU GOING TO FORCE YOURSELF TO KEEP SMILING?
HE'S DOING IT FOR ME.
HUH ...?
COME HERE, YOU.
SHIN, WHAT —?!
TUG
WE'LL BE RIGHT BACK.
SHIN...

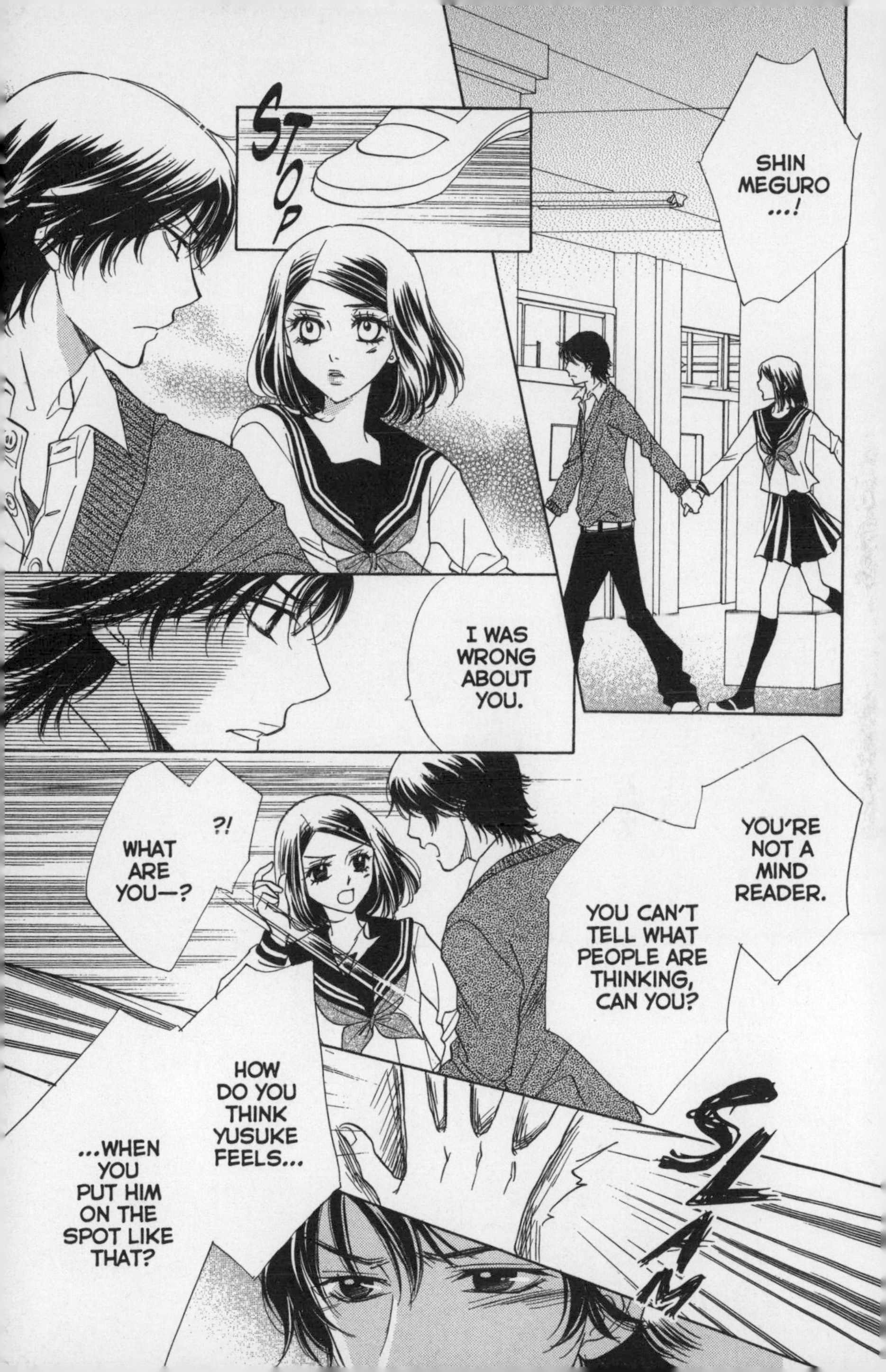
SHIN MEGURO ...!
STOP
I WAS WRONG ABOUT YOU.
YOU'RE NOT A MIND READER.
YOU CAN'T TELL WHAT PEOPLE ARE THINKING, CAN YOU?
?!
WHAT ARE YOU—?
SLAM
HOW DO YOU THINK YUSUKE FEELS...
...WHEN YOU PUT HIM ON THE SPOT LIKE THAT?

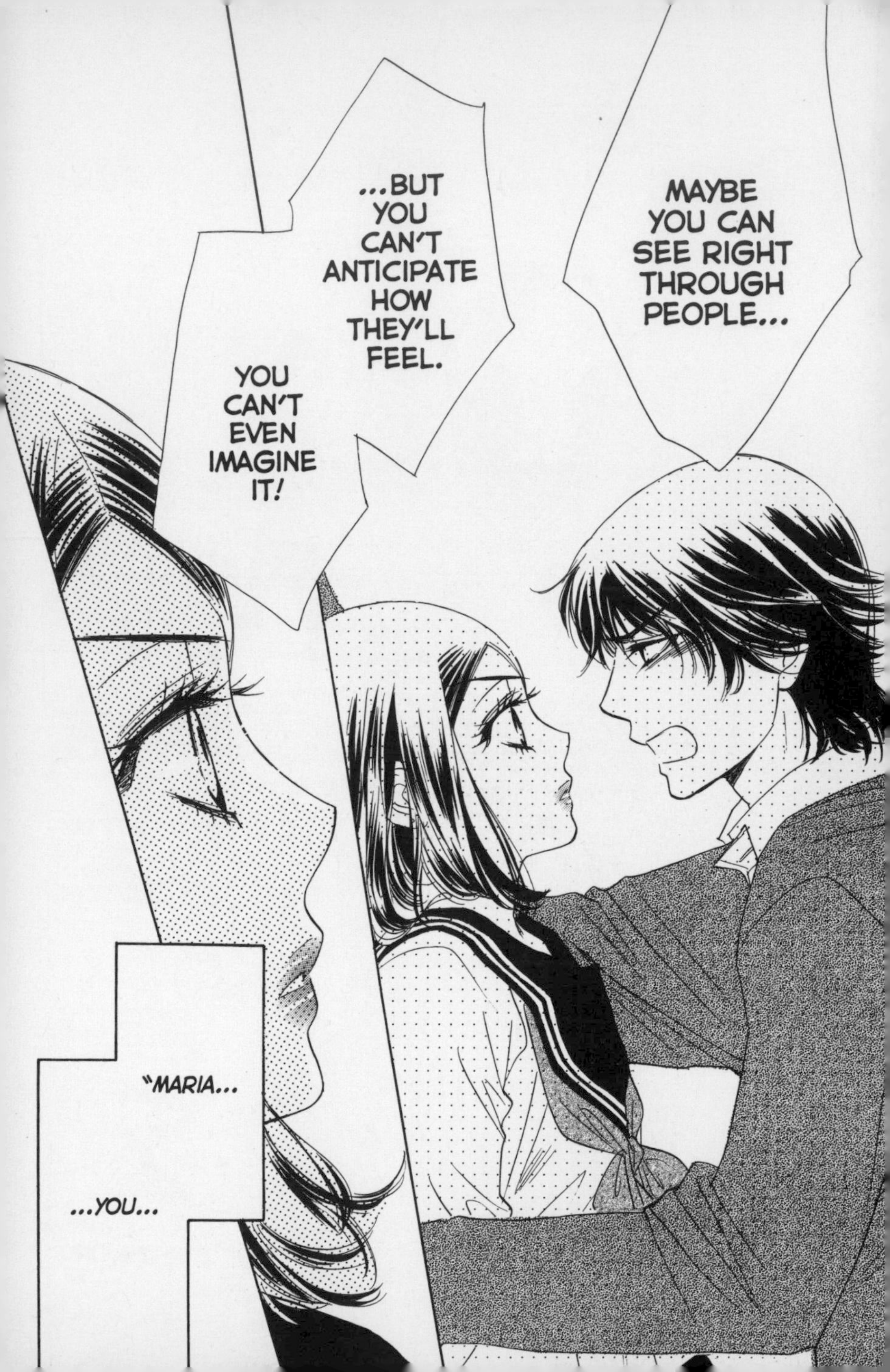
MAYBE YOU CAN SEE RIGHT THROUGH PEOPLE...
...BUT YOU CAN'T ANTICIPATE HOW THEY'LL FEEL.
YOU CAN'T EVEN IMAGINE IT!
"MARIA...
...YOU...

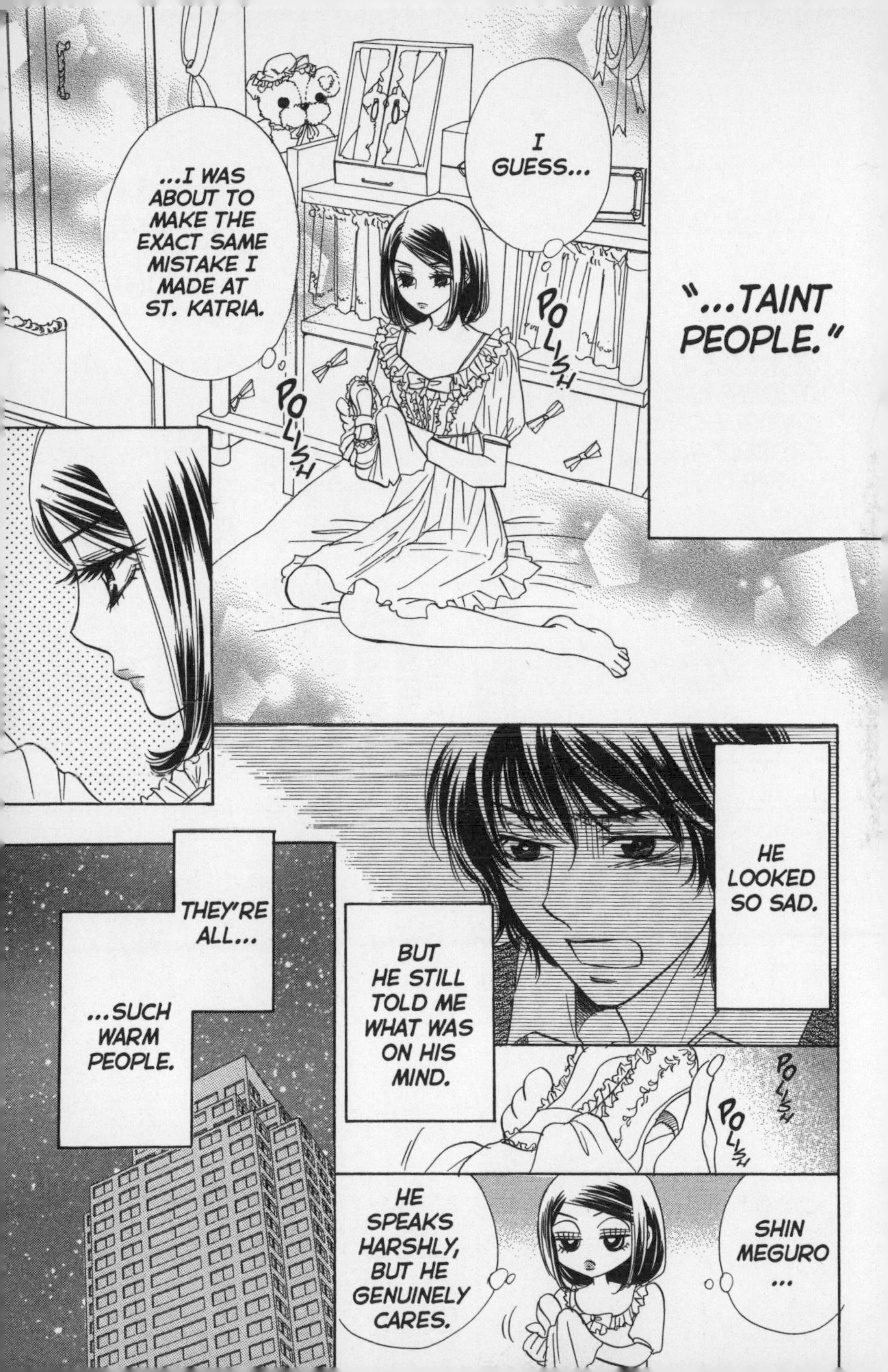
"...TAINT PEOPLE."
I GUESS...
...I WAS ABOUT TO MAKE THE EXACT SAME MISTAKE I MADE AT ST. KATRIA.
POLISH
POLISH
HE LOOKED SO SAD.
BUT HE STILL TOLD ME WHAT WAS ON HIS MIND.
POLISH
POLISH
SHIN MEGURO ...
HE SPEAKS HARSHLY, BUT HE GENUINELY CARES.
THEY'RE ALL...
...SUCH WARM PEOPLE.

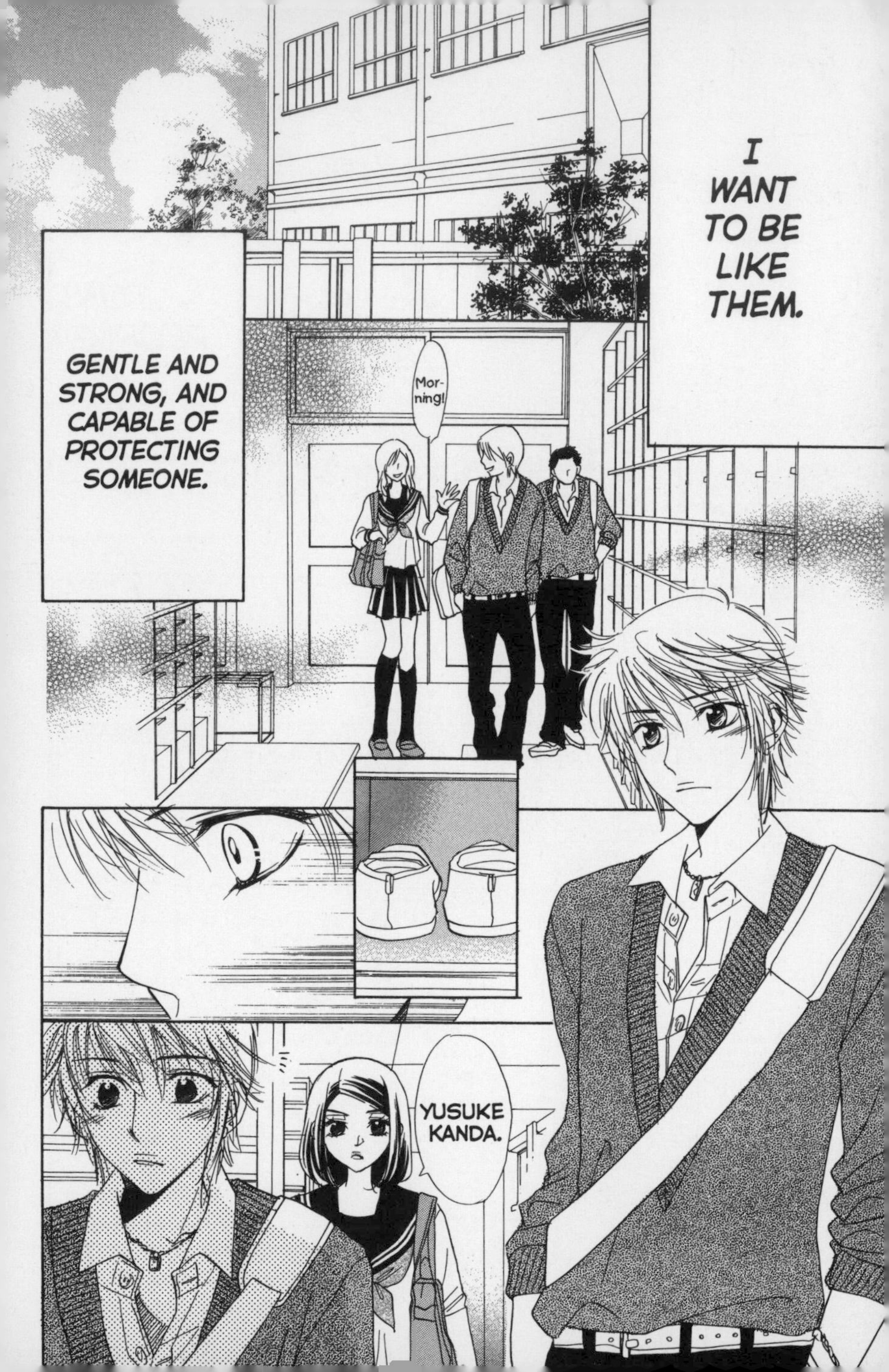
I WANT TO BE LIKE THEM.
Mor-ning!
GENTLE AND STRONG, AND CAPABLE OF PROTECTING SOMEONE.
YUSUKE KANDA.

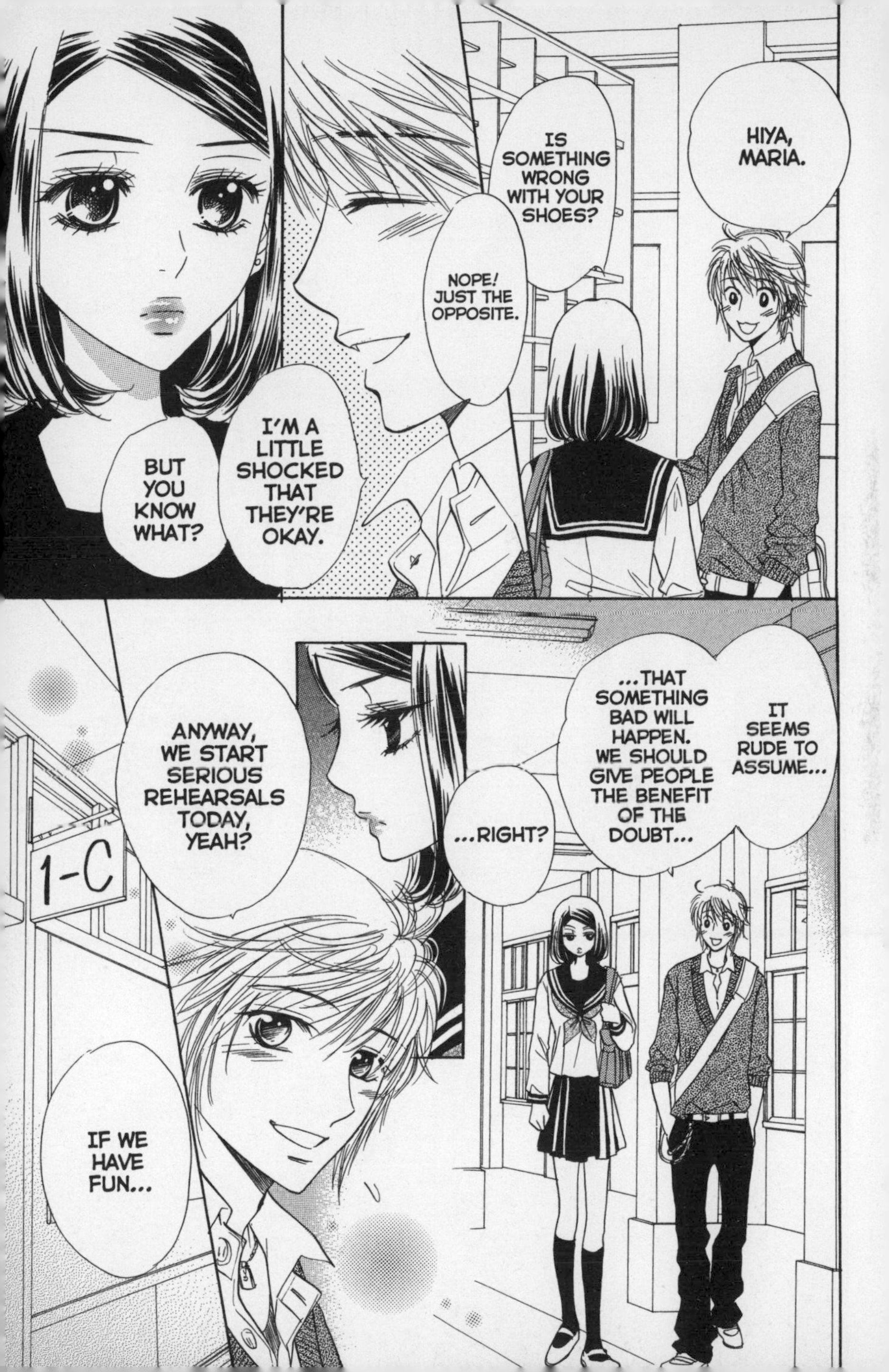
HIYA, MARIA.
IS SOMETHING WRONG WITH YOUR SHOES?
NOPE! JUST THE OPPOSITE.
I'M A LITTLE SHOCKED THAT THEY'RE OKAY.
BUT YOU KNOW WHAT?
IT SEEMS RUDE TO ASSUME...
...THAT SOMETHING BAD WILL HAPPEN. WE SHOULD GIVE PEOPLE THE BENEFIT OF THE DOUBT...
...RIGHT?
ANYWAY, WE START SERIOUS REHEARSALS TODAY, YEAH?
1-C
IF WE HAVE FUN...

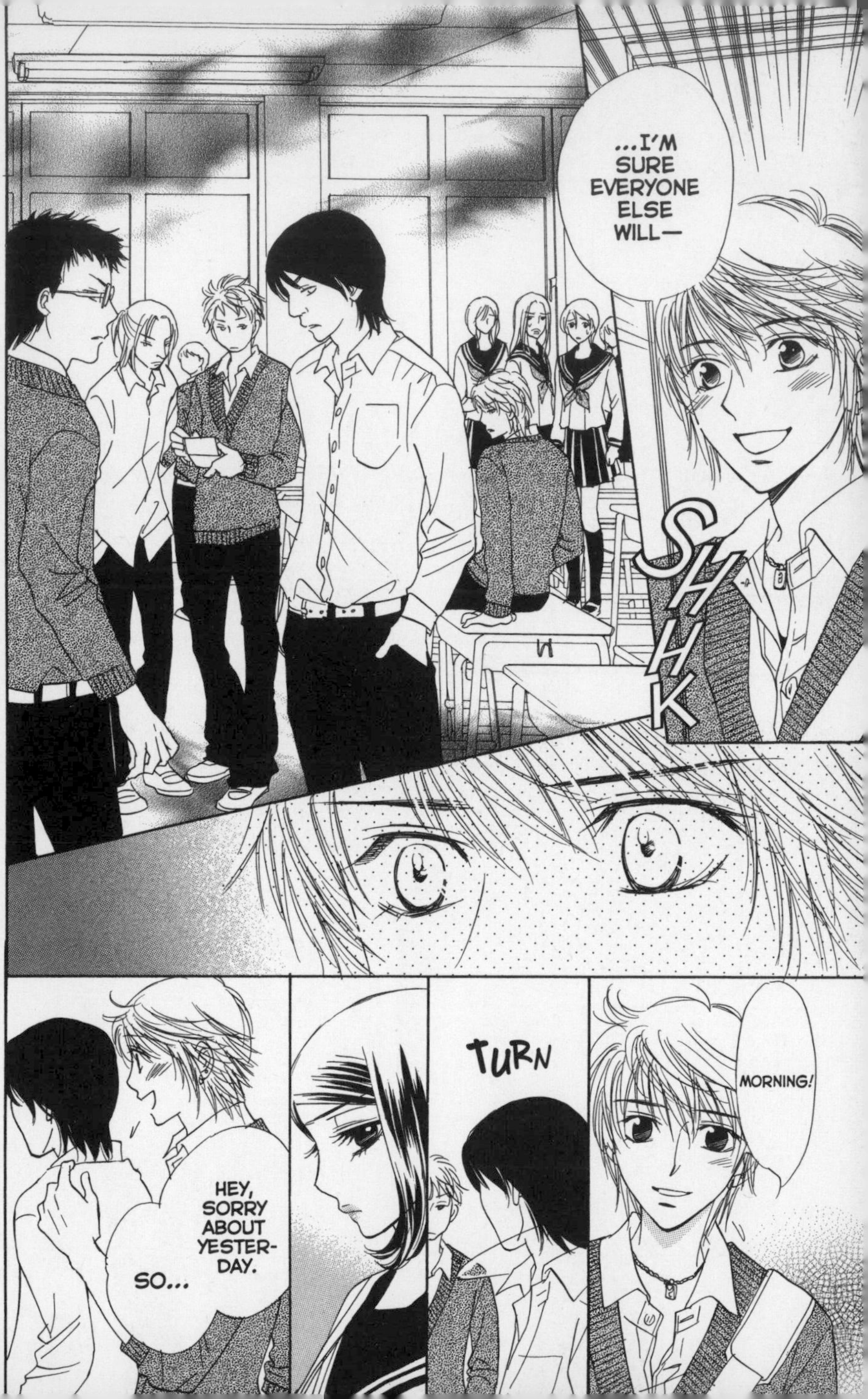
...I'M SURE EVERYONE ELSE WILL—
SHHK
MORNING!
TURN
HEY, SORRY ABOUT YESTER-DAY.
SO...

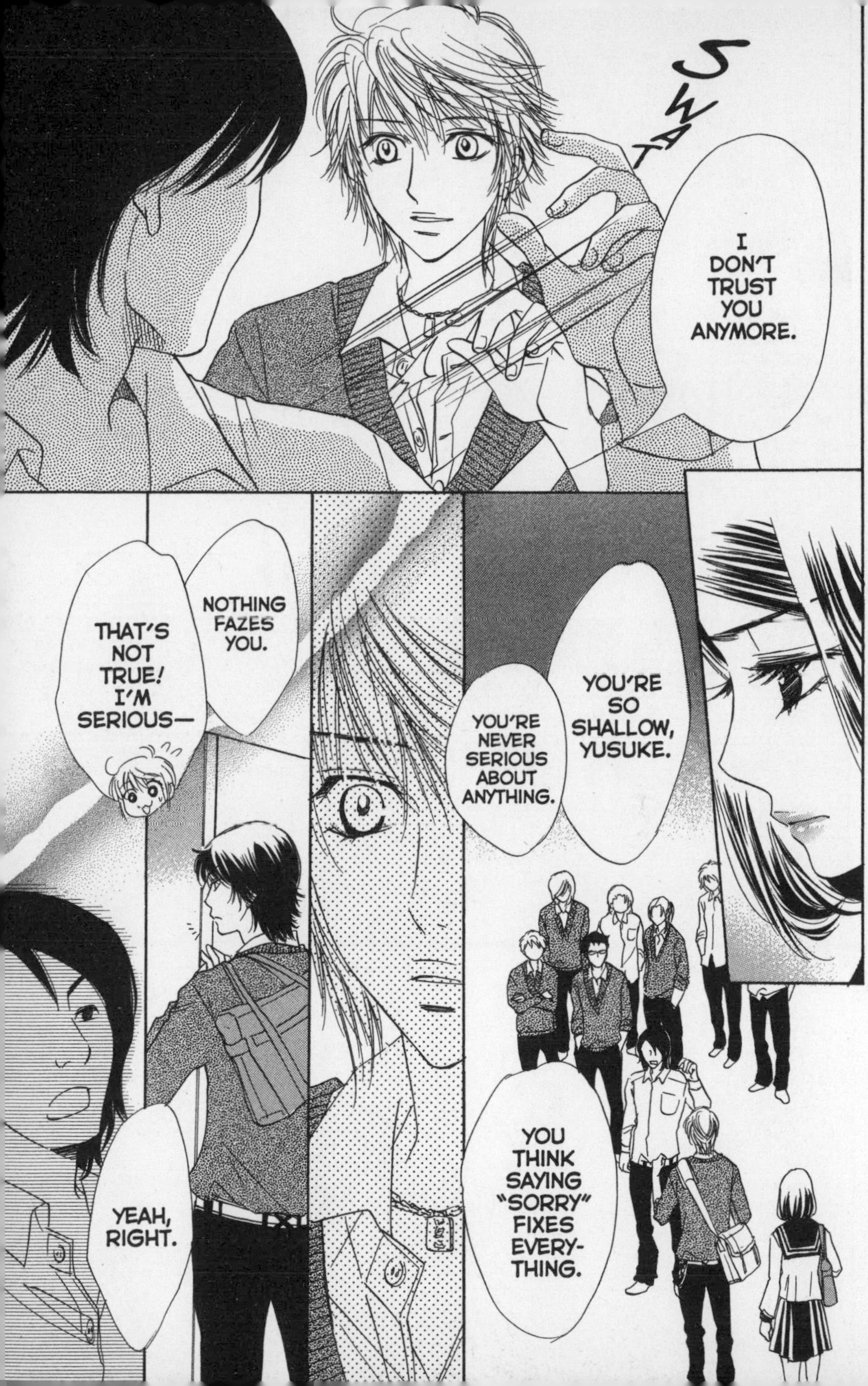
SWAT
I DON'T TRUST YOU ANYMORE.
YOU'RE SO SHALLOW, YUSUKE.
YOU'RE NEVER SERIOUS ABOUT ANYTHING.
YOU THINK SAYING "SORRY" FIXES EVERY-THING.
NOTHING FAZES YOU.
THAT'S NOT TRUE! I'M SERIOUS—
YEAH, RIGHT.

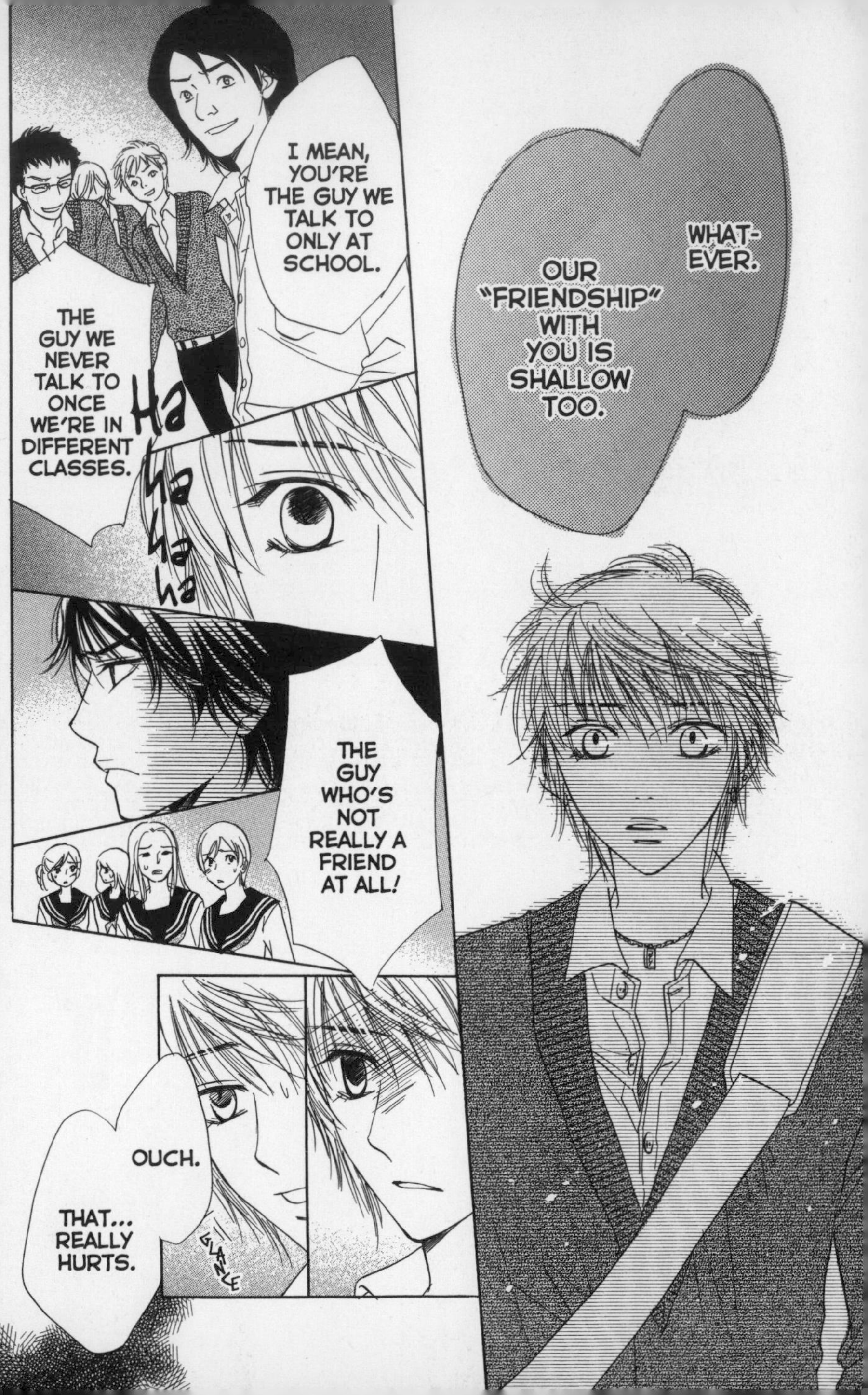
WHAT-EVER.
OUR "FRIENDSHIP" WITH YOU IS SHALLOW TOO.
I MEAN, YOU'RE THE GUY WE TALK TO ONLY AT SCHOOL.
THE GUY WE NEVER TALK TO ONCE WE'RE IN DIFFERENT CLASSES.
Ha ha ha ha ha
THE GUY WHO'S NOT REALLY A FRIEND AT ALL!
GLANCE
OUCH.
THAT... REALLY HURTS.

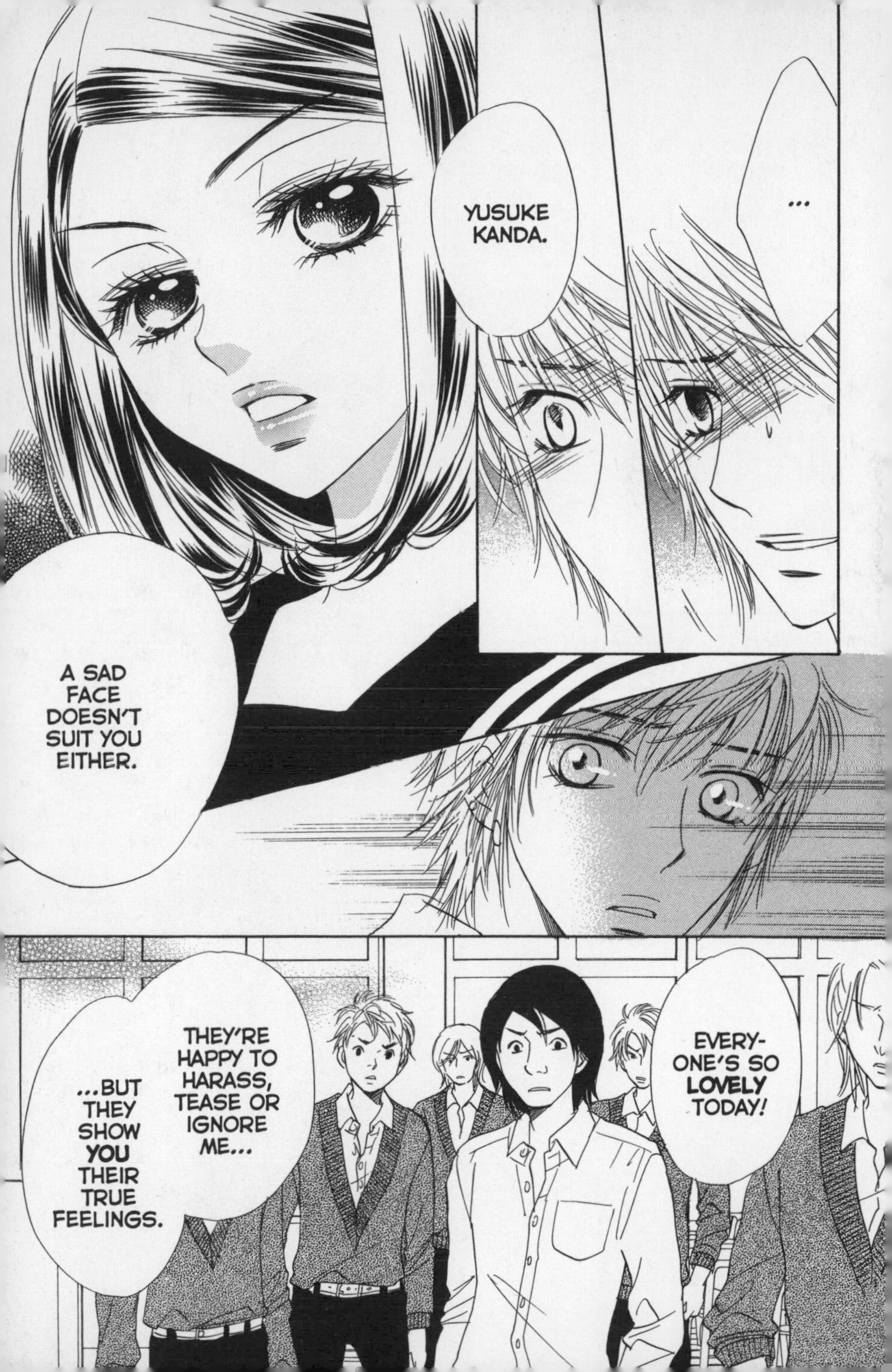
...
YUSUKE KANDA.
A SAD FACE DOESN'T SUIT YOU EITHER.
EVERY-ONE'S SO LOVELY TODAY!
THEY'RE HAPPY TO HARASS, TEASE OR IGNORE ME...
...BUT THEY SHOW YOU THEIR TRUE FEELINGS.

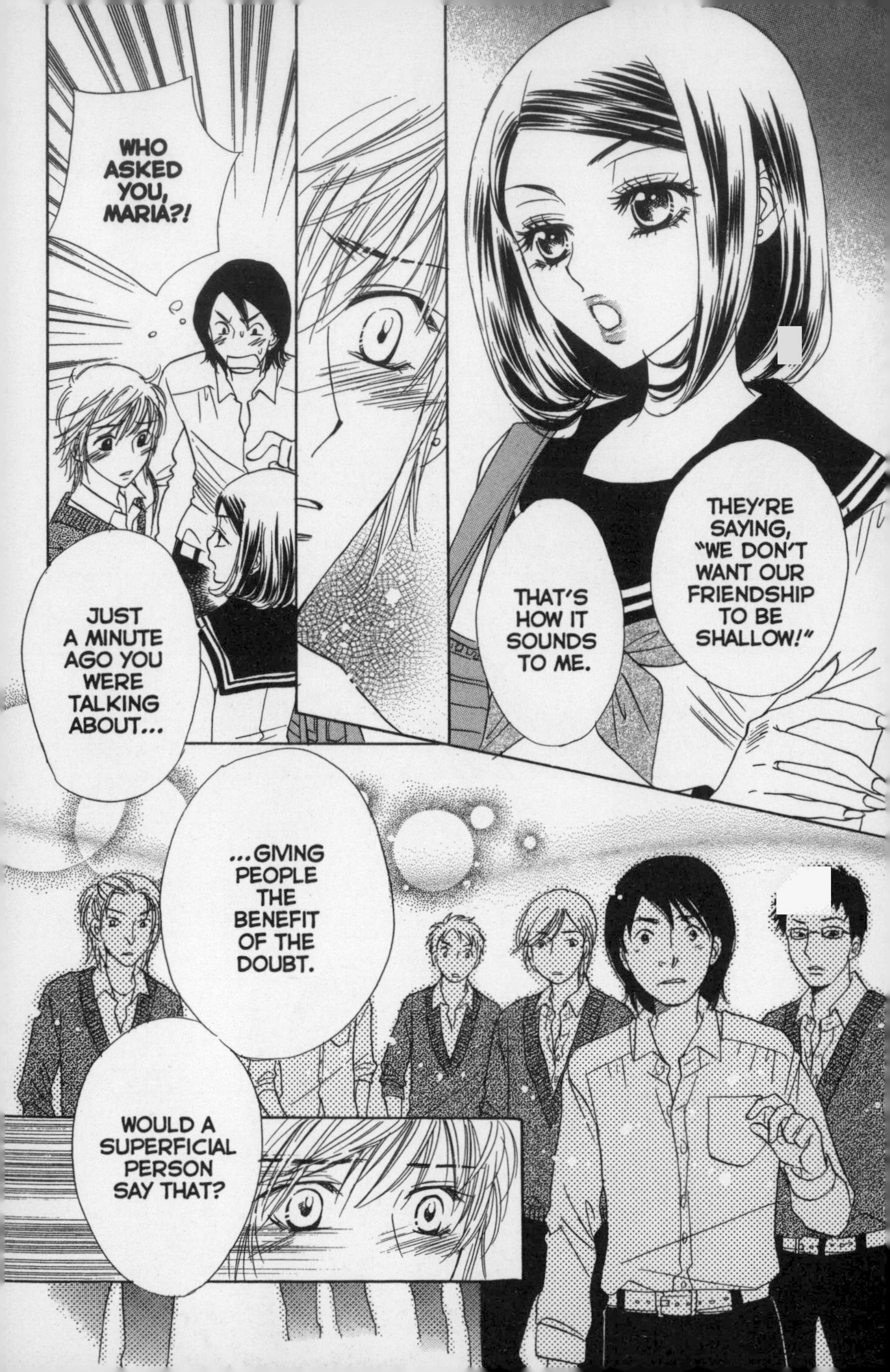
THEY'RE SAYING, "WE DON'T WANT OUR FRIENDSHIP TO BE SHALLOW!"
THAT'S HOW IT SOUNDS TO ME.
WHO ASKED YOU, MARIA?!
JUST A MINUTE AGO YOU WERE TALKING ABOUT...
...GIVING PEOPLE THE BENEFIT OF THE DOUBT.
WOULD A SUPERFICIAL PERSON SAY THAT?

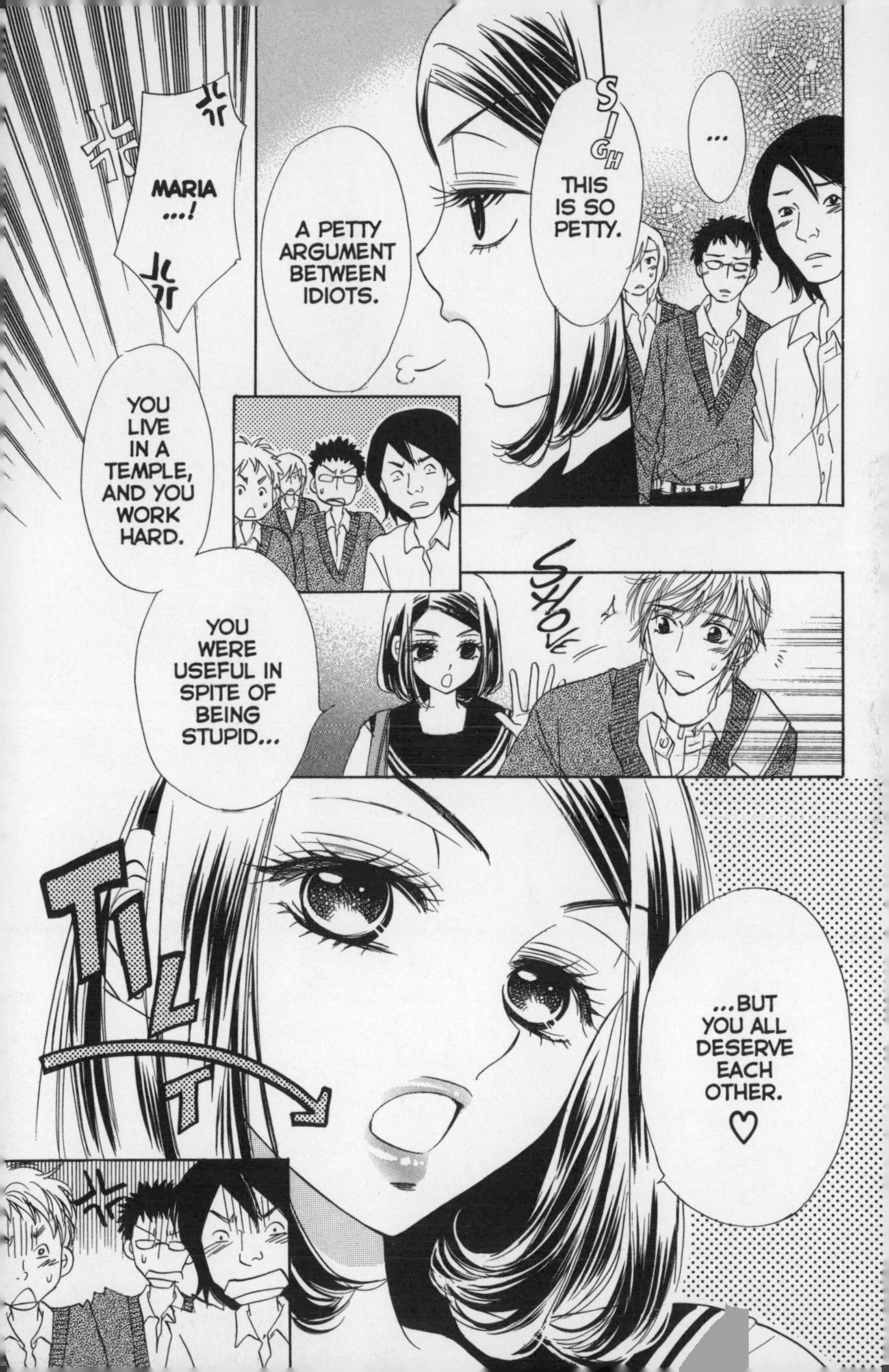
...
SIGH
THIS IS SO PETTY.
A PETTY ARGUMENT BETWEEN IDIOTS.
MARIA ...!
YOU LIVE IN A TEMPLE, AND YOU WORK HARD.
SHOVE
YOU WERE USEFUL IN SPITE OF BEING STUPID...
TILT
...BUT YOU ALL DESERVE EACH OTHER. ♡

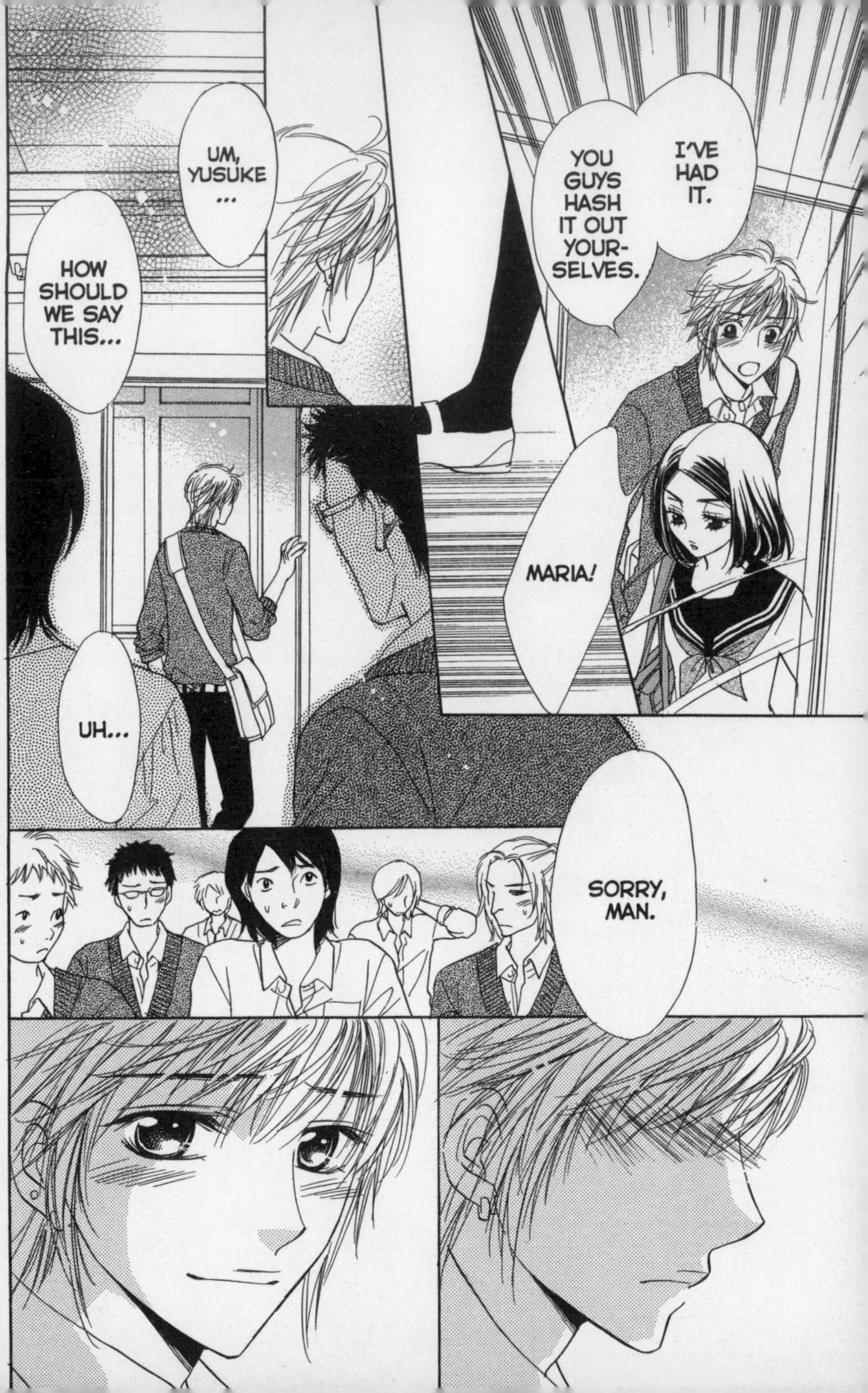
I'VE HAD IT.
YOU GUYS HASH IT OUT YOURSELVES.
MARIA!
UM, YUSUKE...
HOW SHOULD WE SAY THIS...
UH...
SORRY, MAN.

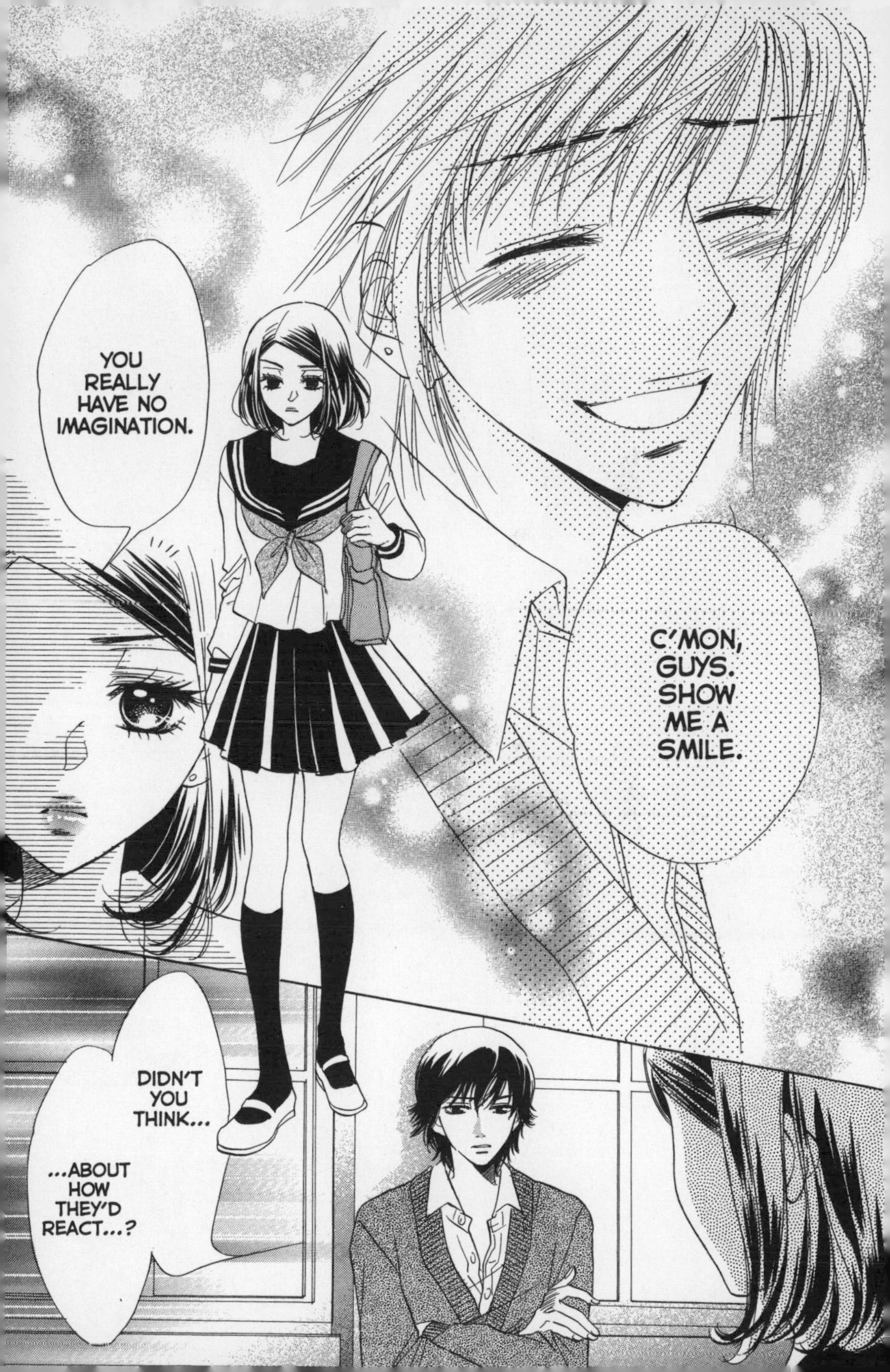
C'MON, GUYS. SHOW ME A SMILE.
YOU REALLY HAVE NO IMAGINATION.
DIDN'T YOU THINK...
...ABOUT HOW THEY'D REACT...?

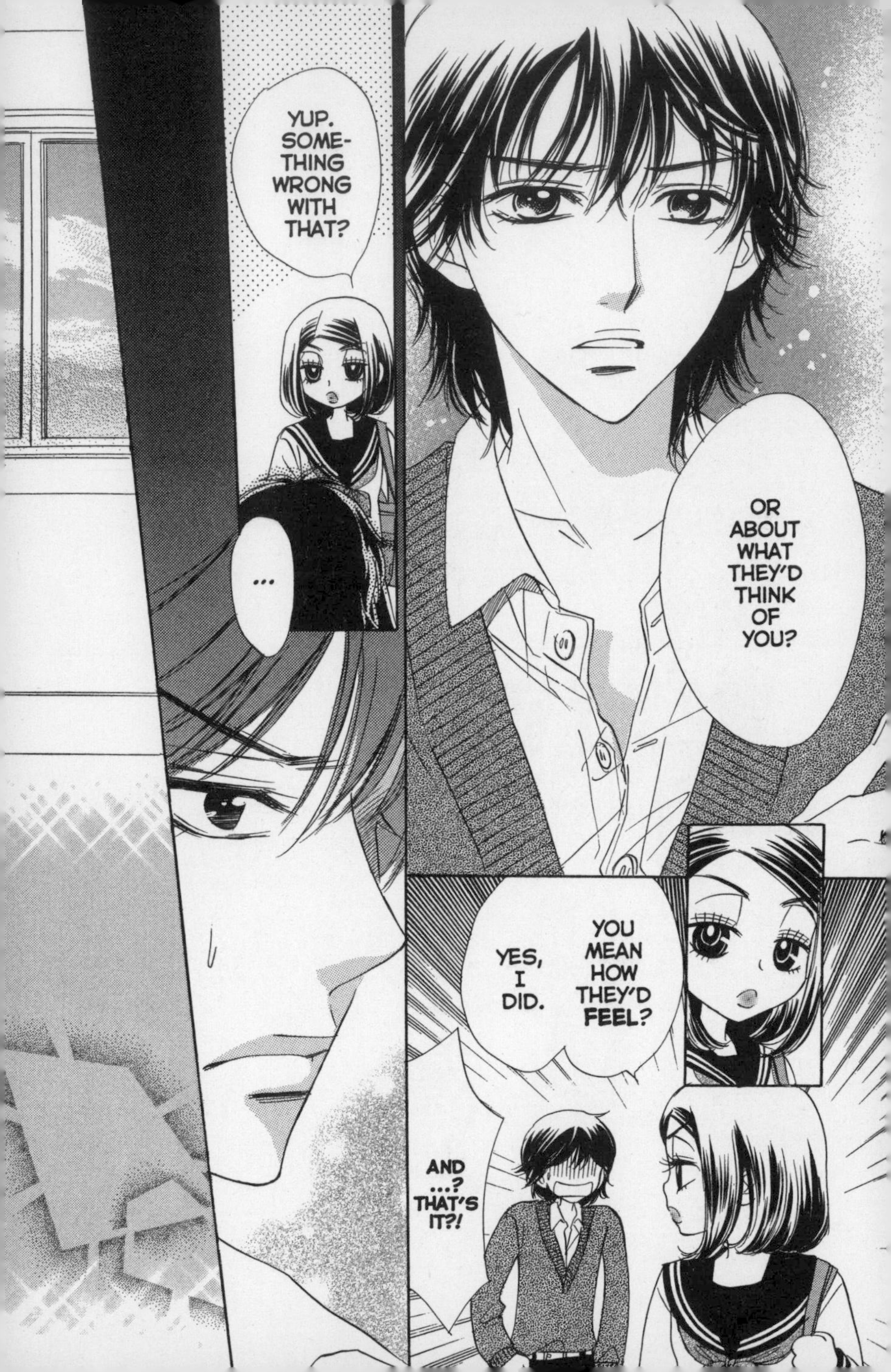
OR ABOUT WHAT THEY'D THINK OF YOU?
YOU MEAN HOW THEY'D FEEL?
YES, I DID.
AND ...? THAT'S IT?!
YUP. SOME-THING WRONG WITH THAT?
...

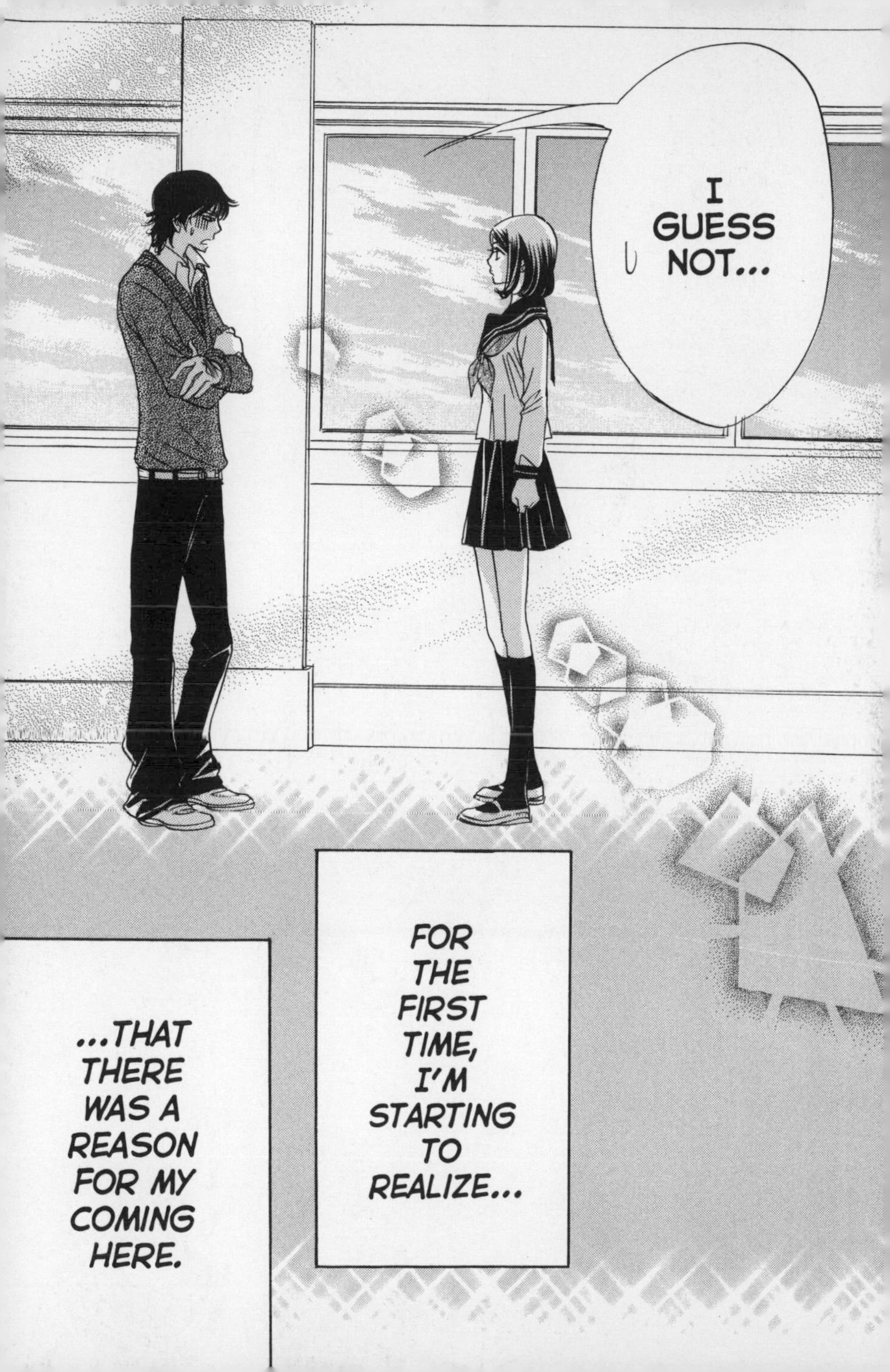
I GUESS NOT...
FOR THE FIRST TIME, I'M STARTING TO REALIZE...
...THAT THERE WAS A REASON FOR MY COMING HERE.

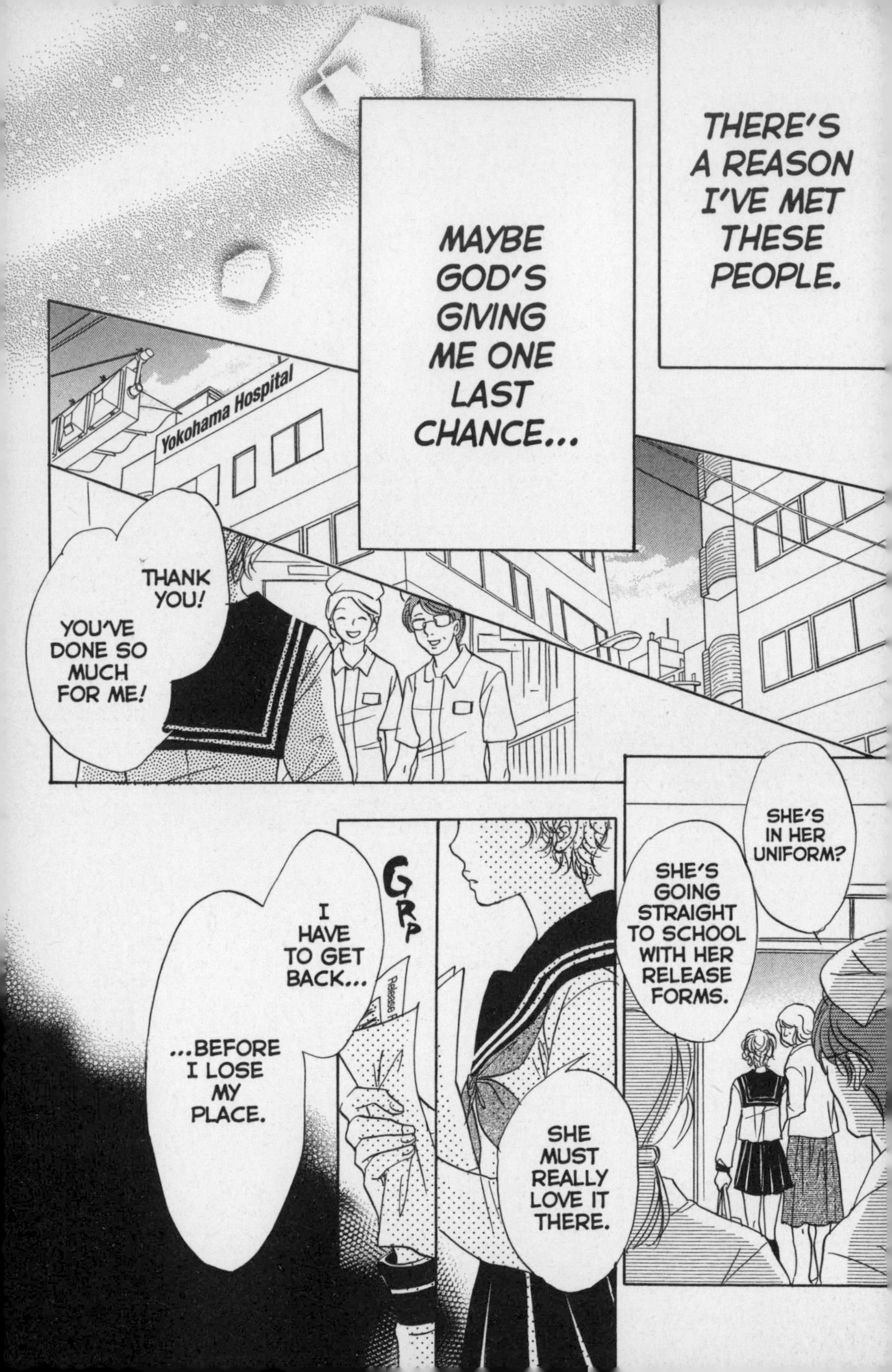
THERE'S A REASON I'VE MET THESE PEOPLE.
MAYBE GOD'S GIVING ME ONE LAST CHANCE...
Yokohama Hospital
THANK YOU!
YOU'VE DONE SO MUCH FOR ME!
SHE'S IN HER UNIFORM?
SHE'S GOING STRAIGHT TO SCHOOL WITH HER RELEASE FORMS.
SHE MUST REALLY LOVE IT THERE.
GRP
I HAVE TO GET BACK...
...BEFORE I LOSE MY PLACE.

Continued
in
volume 3

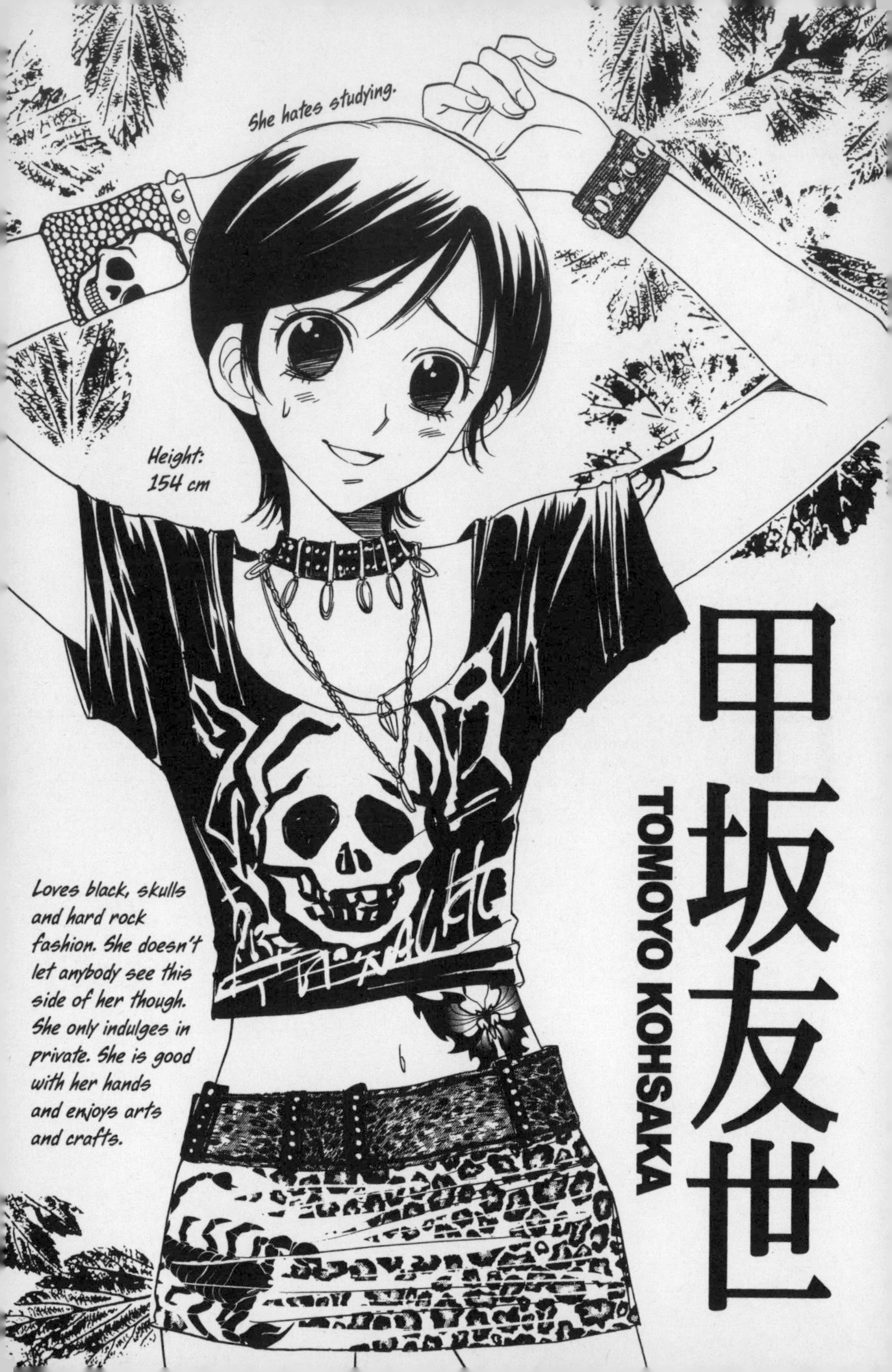
甲坂友世
TOMOYO KOHSAKA
She hates studying.
Height: 154 cm
Loves black, skulls and hard rock fashion. She doesn't let anybody see this side of her though. She only indulges in private. She is good with her hands and enjoys arts and crafts.

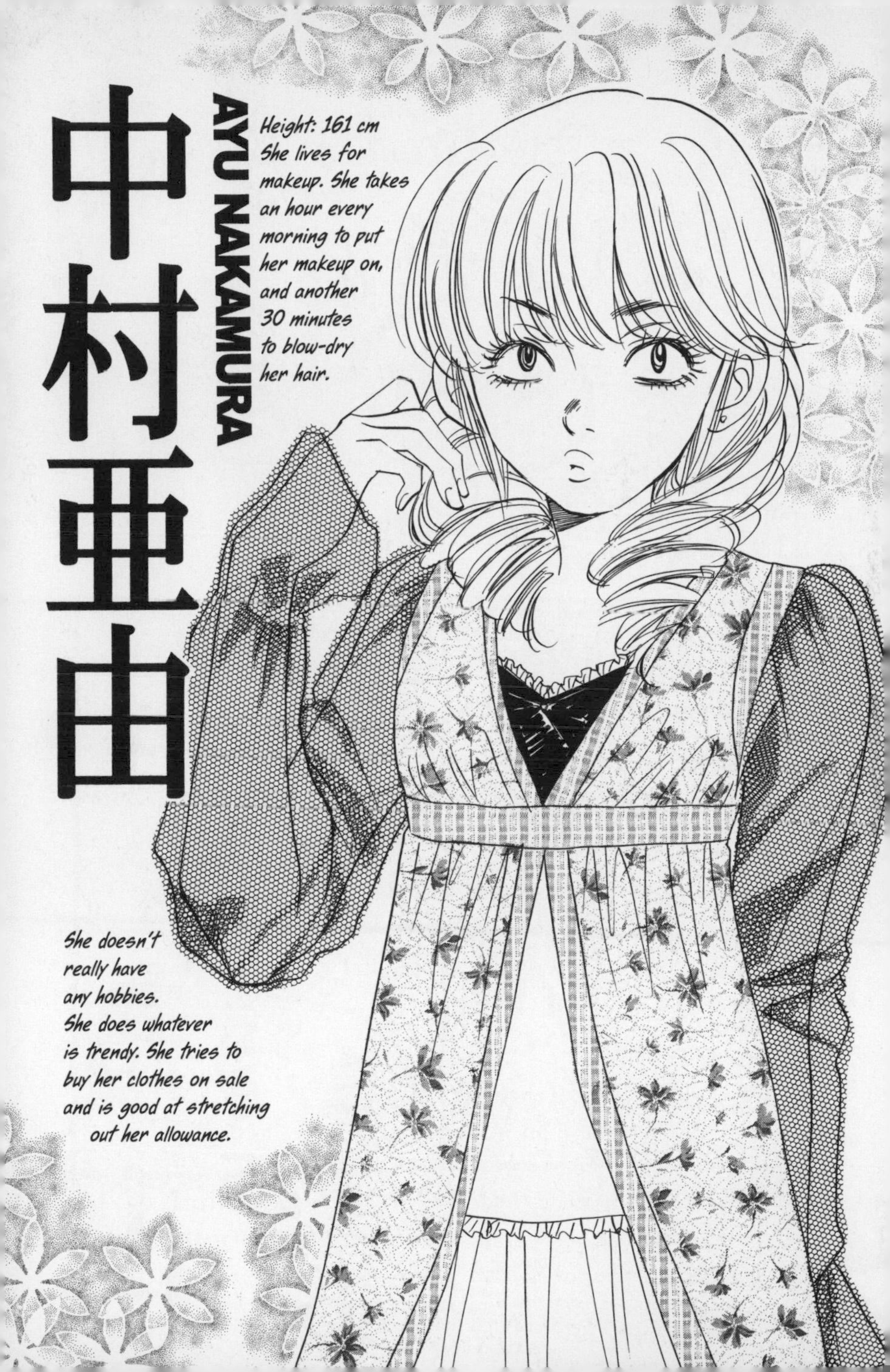
中村亜由
AYU NAKAMURA
Height: 161 cm
She lives for makeup. She takes an hour every morning to put her makeup on, and another 30 minutes to blow-dry her hair.
She doesn't really have any hobbies. She does whatever is trendy. She tries to buy her clothes on sale and is good at stretching out her allowance.

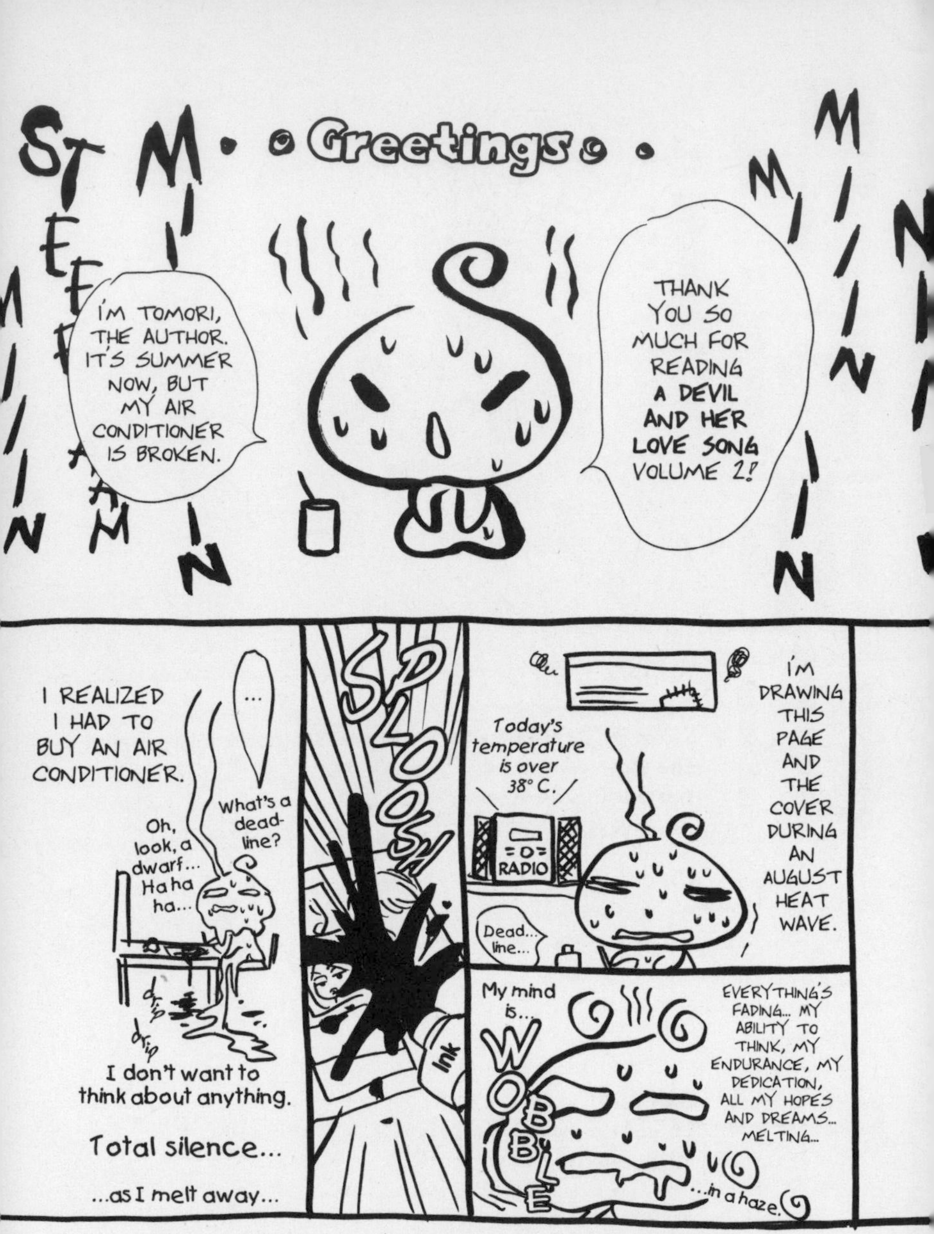
Greetings
MIIIIN
THANK YOU SO MUCH FOR READING A DEVIL AND HER LOVE SONG VOLUME 2!
I'M TOMORI, THE AUTHOR. IT'S SUMMER NOW, BUT MY AIR CONDITIONER IS BROKEN.
MIIIN
I'M DRAWING THIS PAGE AND THE COVER DURING AN AUGUST HEAT WAVE.
Today's temperature is over 38° C.
RADIO
Dead... line...
EVERYTHING'S FADING... MY ABILITY TO THINK, MY ENDURANCE, MY DEDICATION, ALL MY HOPES AND DREAMS... MELTING...
My mind is...
WOBBLE
...in a haze.
SPLOOSH
Ink
I REALIZED I HAD TO BUY AN AIR CONDITIONER.
...
What's a dead-line?
Oh, look, a dwarf... Ha ha ha...
drip
drip
I don't want to think about anything.
Total silence...
...as I melt away...

Please send your thoughts and comments to:
Miyoshi Tomori c/o A Devil and Her Love Song Editor
Viz Media P.O. Box 77010 San Francisco, CA 94107

A DEVIL AND HER LOVE SONG
Volume 2
Shojo Beat Edition

STORY AND ART BY
MIYOSHI TOMORI

English Adaptation/Ysabet MacFarlane
Translation/JN Productions
Touch-up Art & Lettering/Monalisa de Asis
Design/Yukiko Whitley
Editor/Amy Yu

Published by VIZ Media, LLC
P.O. Box 77010
San Francisco, CA 94107

10 9 8 7 6 5 4 3 2 1
First printing, April 2012

www.viz.com   www.shojobeat.com

"I think it's going to rain today."
"Summer's coming to an end."
I can usually predict the weather from
the flow of my pen. When it's humid, it's
hard to draw. When the air is dry, the ink
doesn't last. Right now, there's a rainstorm
with thunder and lightning. Humidity
is 80 percent. When it gets like this, the
weight of a single page changes too. It gets
really damp...

-Miyoshi Tomori

Miyoshi Tomori made her debut as a
manga creator in 2001, and her previous
titles include *Hatsukare* (First Boyfriend),
Tongari Root (Square Root), and *Brass
Love!!* In her spare time she likes listening
to music in the bath and playing musical
instruments.

Own the Complete **Arina Tanemura Collection!**

Mistress ★ Fortune

**Sakura Hime:
The Legend of Princess Sakura**

**The Gentlemen's
Alliance †**

**Short-Tempered
Melancholic and
Other Stories**

**The Gentlemen's Alliance †:
Arina Tanemura Illustrations**

Time Stranger Kyoko

I.O.N.

**The Arina Tanemura Collection:
The Art of Full Moon**

Full Moon